BLACK LIVES, WHITE LAW

BLACK LIVES, WHITE LAW

LOCKED UP AND LOCKED OUT IN AUSTRALIA

RUSSELL MARKS

LA TROBE
UNIVERSITY PRESS

IN CONJUNCTION WITH BLACK INC.

Published by La Trobe University Press in conjunction with Black Inc.
22–24 Northumberland Street
Collingwood VIC 3066, Australia
enquiries@blackincbooks.com
www.blackincbooks.com
www.latrobeuniversitypress.com.au

La Trobe University plays an integral role in Australia's public intellectual life, and is
recognised globally for its research excellence and commitment to ideas and debate.
La Trobe University Press publishes books of high intellectual quality, aimed at general
readers. Titles range across the humanities and sciences, and are written by distinguished
and innovative scholars. La Trobe University Press books are produced in conjunction
with Black Inc., an independent Australian publishing house. The members of the LTUP
Editorial Board are Vice-Chancellor's Fellows Emeritus Professor Robert Manne and
Dr Elizabeth Finkel, and Morry Schwartz and Chris Feik of Black Inc.

9781760642600 (paperback)
9781743822616 (ebook)

A catalogue record for this
book is available from the
NATIONAL
LIBRARY   National Library of Australia
OF AUSTRALIA

Cover and text design by Tristan Main
Typesetting by Typography Studio
Song lyrics reprinted with permission: 'Beautiful Child', written by A. Roach
(Mushroom Music); 'Old Fitzroy', written by D. Sultan/S. Wilson (Mushroom Music).

CONTENTS

You were always to blame
And they put you through hell
Then they locked you away in a dark lonely cell
But you weren't really there, just a little bit wild
Now they'll hound you no more, oh my beautiful child

— 'Beautiful Child', Archie Roach

I hit the road when I was fifteen
When my mother died and my dad got mean
I've been locked up since twenty-one
I was my mother's only son
Forgotten most from early days
But I remember what she used to say
Little boy you're my pride and joy
The only good thing about Old Fitzroy

— 'Old Fitzroy', Dan Sultan

INTRODUCTION

The mass incarceration crisis

'Aaron'

The wire mesh between us makes it difficult for me to see the man sitting opposite – and for him to see me. We're in a small cubicle at the back of the Katherine courthouse in the Northern Territory, and I'm taking instructions from a man who's just signed a retainer to become a client of the North Australian Aboriginal Justice Agency (NAAJA). It's mid-2017, and it's my first day duty lawyering in Katherine, where I'll be based for the next couple of years, but the man opposite me doesn't know that. I'd done a couple of days' duty in the Darwin Local Court, and did plenty in Melbourne, Dandenong and Morwell when I worked for the Victorian Aboriginal Legal Service a few years ago. But the Territory has a fearsome reputation for its use of prison, and I don't really know what to expect.

I glance down at the brief of evidence, collected earlier from the police prosecutor. There's a system in Katherine. Each morning, prosecutors bundle together the briefs for all the Aboriginal people who've been arrested overnight and give them to NAAJA's duty lawyers. Sometimes they're existing clients. Sometimes they're conflicted out – perhaps we're already representing the alleged victim, for instance – in which case they'll go to the Legal Aid Commission, at least at first.

Aaron,[*] the young man opposite me whose features flash briefly into view through the mesh whenever either of us shifts slightly in our seat, isn't new to the criminal justice system. He'd first been sent to Darwin's prison

---

[*] Not his real name, and I've changed many of the details of his offending and his history.

the previous year, before being 'released' to Venndale, an open-air alcohol rehabilitation facility twenty minutes' drive outside Katherine. Venndale is run by the Aboriginal community-controlled Kalano Community Association, but its staff are mostly non-Indigenous and its programs are delivered in English, which is not most of its clients' first language. The remainder of Aaron's prison sentence had been 'suspended', but only if he stayed at Venndale for three months and followed its (very strict) rules, and then stayed entirely alcohol-free for a further nine months. The research says it often takes multiple false starts before addicts are ready to change, and that people living in disadvantaged circumstances tend to have more false starts than others.[1] Aaron did a few weeks at Venndale. But then he hitched a ride back into town and spent the next little while in his community – one of the town camps dotted around Katherine's perimeter – before he was picked up again by police for breaching his suspended sentence (by leaving Venndale). He was re-sentenced to the remaining months of the original sentence he'd received.

Again, the court order released him from prison after a few days. The remaining time on Aaron's original sentence – now just under three months – was suspended once more. He had to stay sober for a year. It's a condition with which very few people who are alcohol-dependent, and whose extended family are also alcohol-dependent, can comply. Add frequent episodes of grief as family members pass away, mix in some childhood trauma and let it all percolate in deep wells of intergenerational trauma, and a year of sobriety for Aaron was about as likely as becoming prime minister; more than once over the subsequent two years I wondered whether many of the judges who ordered a year of sobriety for my clients would be able to do it themselves.

One of the most vicious stereotypes Settler Australia has created is the drunken Aborigine, which functions as way to blame dispossessed people for the decades – centuries – of trauma heaped upon them. With the year-long sobriety conditions they impose on people like Aaron, courts perpetuate this stereotype by setting them up to fail. Judges see a sad parade of people being forced to court for breaching some order by drinking. They form prejudices, and have them confirmed again and again.

By the time I met him, Aaron was on two suspended prison sentences, with a long list of rules he had to obey. Many judges, prosecutors and members of the public believe this is leniency, and consistent with the deaths in custody royal commission's recommendations, but many clients tell me they actually prefer prison to the year-long surveillance of suspended sentences and other community-based orders. The surveillance is both inconstant – which creates confusion – and oppressive. Aaron has now been in the community surveillance hamster wheel for a year and a half.

As well as the assault charge, police had also named Aaron on an alcohol protection order (APO) banning him from drinking, buying or even possessing any alcohol for three months. Any breach of the APO's conditions would also be a crime, itself punishable by up to three months' prison. It was an entirely superfluous order. Both suspended sentences already included conditions banning him from drinking. Controversially introduced by the single-term Country Liberal Party government four years earlier, APOs were modelled on domestic violence orders (DVO): once they were made, breaching their conditions became a crime. But unlike DVOs, which can be made on an interim basis by police but must be confirmed by courts, APOs could be written up by police alone. Experts decried the absurdity of criminalising alcohol dependency. NAAJA predicted – correctly – that APOs would be used primarily against Aboriginal people. The NT Court of Appeal – constituted by three white judges – disagreed that APOs were racist.[2]

Aaron is sitting in the cells today because he'd been arrested overnight. It was now two weeks before his new spot at Venndale was due to open up. A close family member died, so Aaron drank. Why? Asking a person dependent on or addicted to alcohol *why did you drink?* is always a nonsensical question. There will always be reasons. Perhaps it's about numbing the grief, or peer pressure, or habit. None will ever be good enough to satisfy the judge who asks.

While drunk, Aaron was walking along one of Katherine's main streets. He stumbled into a group of white teenagers, who were also drunk. They swore at him. He swore back at them, pushed one of them, yelled loudly, suggested they fight, wobbled onto the road so that a passing car had to stop, and kept walking. So did they. He was breaking the law by being intoxicated, and perhaps also by being 'disorderly'. On another night, in another place, he might have continued home and slept it off. But this was Katherine. One of the first things visitors notice about the town – indeed, anywhere in the Territory – is the sheer number of police patrols. Across the Northern Territory, there are 2.6 times as many police officers per head of population than the national average.[3] Inside the car that stopped in front of Aaron were two (white) police constables. They arrested him, locked him in the cage on the tray of their police utility, and took him to the police station, where he spent the rest of the night in a cell – to 'sober up', in accordance with nineteenth-century practice – before being taken to court the next morning. That's when we meet in the cells.

It takes me a few minutes to do the maths, but eventually I work out that Aaron has just under three months left to serve on the first suspended sentence and just under four months left to serve on the second. The law in the Northern Territory demands that anyone who breaches a suspended prison sentence *must* serve the rest of the sentence in a prison unless a judge believes that 'it would be unjust to do so in view of all the circumstances'.[4] I look again at the new charges. Breach APO; behave disorderly. Minor, in anyone's language. No violence. No property damage. Aaron is young. He obviously has a problem with alcohol. He has a spot at Venndale coming up in a fortnight. Surely, 'in view of all the circumstances', any judge would think it unjust to restore nearly seven months' prison because a young man got drunk and a bit disorderly after his uncle died?

Had I been in Victoria, maybe. But in the Northern Territory, I'm not so sure. Colleagues have warned me that the judge sitting in Katherine today is a harsh sentencer. I explain to Aaron the risks of pleading guilty today. I want time to talk to prosecutors, maybe get them to drop one of the new charges, change some of the more unsavoury parts of the facts they were alleging. I want to find out whether I can get anyone to come to court to say nice things about Aaron. I want to do some research, to make sure I'm able to use existing caselaw to Aaron's best advantage. In a 2013 case, *Bugmy v The Queen*, the High Court confirmed that Aboriginal offenders who grew up in conditions of disadvantage and deprivation were entitled to some mitigation of their sentence, no matter how many times they'd broken the law. I want time to re-read that case. I also want to get Aaron away from this judge. It's a Friday, so I suggest we ask the judge for a short adjournment, perhaps just over the weekend.

Aaron becomes animated for the first time during our interaction. *No adjournment*, he insists. I've told him bail is very unlikely, so to him, an adjournment means a four-hour drive in a prison van to Darwin, a weekend on remand, and a pre-dawn four-hour drive back to Katherine on Monday. *No remand*. He tells me he wants to plead guilty today and 'get it over with'. I spend some time trying to convince him otherwise. He's hungover, but his instructions are clear. I'm bound by them. I leave the cells and check with colleagues who've been in the Territory longer than I have. 'Not ideal, but [the judge] should send him to Venndale,' one tells me as she's rushing back into the cells carrying a stack of files. I try reassuring myself that nobody wants to lock up young Aboriginal people unnecessarily three decades after the royal commission. I skim *Bugmy* on the web, re-enter the courtroom and take a deep breath.

I'm a lamb to the slaughter. The (white) judge bats away my *Bugmy* submissions. He dismisses my observation that Aaron had no previous disorderly or breach APO offences on his record. He shrugs off my submissions about Aaron's difficult childhood and his young age. He says I don't have any evidence that Aaron is addicted to or dependent on alcohol. (Apparently the pages of alcohol-related offending isn't evidence of anything other than a penchant for breaking the law.) He's not impressed by Aaron's early guilty plea – which should attract a 'sentencing discount' by law – or by his recent efforts to engage with an Aboriginal men's program in Katherine while he waited for the Venndale bed.

But it's when I link Aaron's drinking the previous day to his grief and his participation in Sorry Business – a set of cultural practices, including ceremonies, which involve whole communities following a person's death – that the judge takes particular issue with what I'm saying. He wants to know whether I'm suggesting that alcohol is part of traditional Sorry Business. In that moment, I'm not sure. I'm also white, I was raised in a southern capital, and I'm far too ignorant of the cultures I'm now interacting with to be able to competently answer his question. I'm only trying to make the point that Aaron was drinking in the context of his grief, which I naively think is a relatively common experience among many people in Australia, and that he was simultaneously participating in Sorry Business. But I get drawn into a debate on terms that aren't mine. I try to redirect the judge's attention to Aaron's prospects for rehabilitation, which must still be strong because of his youth. The judge points to the multiple pages of priors. Most of them are breaches caused by drinking alcohol when he was prohibited from doing so. To me, the rest look mainly like typical teenage criminality of the kind that generally settles down after the age of twenty-five or so.[5] The judge sees them differently. Aaron's prospects of rehabilitation are practically nil, he declares. He's 'obviously' not interested in Venndale, the judge says, so his spot may as well go to someone else.

His Honour fully restores the suspended prison sentences, and makes them cumulative rather than concurrent – which means Aaron has to serve one *and then* the other, rather than at the same time. For the new charges, he orders three months' prison, equivalent to the maximum penalty for APO breach offences: proportionally, it's the equivalent of getting ten years' prison for stealing a soft drink from a supermarket. All but one month of the new sentence is cumulative on top of the two restored suspensions.

All up, Aaron is going to prison for about eight months and two weeks, because he got noticed by a passing police patrol while he was drunk. In Victoria, where appeals to the County Court were *de novo* until 2021,[6] I would have stood up immediately, applied for appeal bail, and filled out the appeal paperwork almost on the spot. Instead, I stare disbelievingly at the judge, ask to leave the courtroom, and visit Aaron in the cells. He's done prison stretches before, so the result doesn't seem to faze him. But he does instruct me to appeal, mainly on my advice – or more accurately, my urging. I can't believe anyone on the Supreme Court bench could look at these circumstances and agree that eight and a half months' prison is an appropriate sentence for a young Aboriginal man whose main problems are trauma and grog.

I'm wrong again. Our appeal is dismissed four months later. The original sentence stands.

By the time Aaron's appeal is heard, I'm deep in other tragedies. Aaron's isn't the last case that feels like injustice. But I'm finding myself becoming used to the system here, and each injustice feels less unexpected, a little less outrageous.

Numbers

Why does it matter if Aaron goes to prison for a few months? While I've been writing this book, at least thirty-seven Aboriginal people have died in Australia's criminal justice system. Seven relatively young adults were found 'unresponsive in their cells' in the language of prison authorities, as if it's a genuine mystery. Two women and four men – including one young man who had been self-harming for weeks after being frequently locked down because of Covid-19 restrictions – apparently suicided in prisons. Thirty-seven-year-old Veronica Nelson Walker died in January 2020 in the Melbourne's women's prison, the Dame Phyllis Frost Centre, three days after being locked up for shoplifting. Reports suggest that she'd been crying out for help during the night before she was found dead. Less than a year later, another thirty-year-old woman died in hospital after being transferred there from Dame Phyllis. Thirty-seven-year-old Barkindji man Anzac Sullivan was killed during a police pursuit in March 2021. One twenty-seven-year-old man died after being tasered and pepper-sprayed in Gunnedah, and another twenty-seven-year-old man died after what police called a 'violent struggle' in Toowoomba (though police were left only with 'minor injuries'). A sixteen-year-old boy somehow collided with an unmarked police vehicle driving in the opposite direction. (Police now routinely use their vehicles as weapons to 'force' suspects to stop running: the likelihood is that the unmarked car did the colliding.) One twenty-year-old man somehow fell 10 metres to his death as he was being escorted by correctional officers from hospital to prison in Gosford. Three people – a twenty-nine-year-old woman in Geraldton, Stanley Russell in western Sydney and nineteen-year-old Kumanjayi Walker in Yuendumu – were shot dead by police.[7]

Thirty years ago, one of Australia's longest and highest-profile royal commissions – that into Aboriginal deaths in custody – told us that the reason so many Aboriginal and Torres Strait Islander people were dying in prisons, police cells and police vehicles was that they were in those places so often. The five commissioners urged governments to do everything in their power to prevent First Nations people from being locked up. There was a lot of low-hanging fruit. Laws that criminalised public drunkenness in Queensland, Tasmania, Western Australia and Victoria – which authorised police to lock very drunk people in cells instead of ensuring they were properly monitored – had no place in modern Australia. Each state's *Summary Offences Act* – anachronistic laws that mostly protect the virtues of a century-old white middle class – had to go. Imprisonment was to be used only as a last resort.

But it took all of those thirty years for Victoria to decriminalise public drunkenness, which happened when amendments were introduced in December 2020, due in large part to the urging of the family of Aunty Tanya Day (see chapter 12).[8] And during that time, our use of prison has skyrocketed. In 1990, 112 of every 100,000 people in Australia were locked up. As the nation celebrated at the Sydney Olympics and commemorated a centenary of Federation, 148 in every 100,000 were incarcerated.[9] Five years later that figure rose to 163. By 2010 it was 170, and by 2015 we were locking up *nearly 200* people in every 100,000. We reached our carceral peak in 2018, when 221 in every 100,000 were in some form of lawful custody. So much for imprisonment as a last resort. Since the royal commission, Australia's governments, police and courts had worked together to *double* the rate at which we lock people up. Meanwhile, the recommendations made by no fewer than thirteen national inquiries between 2009 and 2020 have been mostly ignored.[10]

The brunt of Australia's carceral thrust has been felt by Aboriginal and Torres Strait Islander men, women, children, families and communities. In 1990, Indigenous people made up just over 14 per cent of Australia's prisoners. That was a very high proportion, given that they constituted just 3 per cent of Australia's general population. The rates of First Nations men being locked up were stratospheric: for every group of 100,000 Indigenous men, 3221 of them were incarcerated. Indigenous people were being locked up at more than *17.5 times* the rate that other people were.[11]

By the end of the century, the proportion of people in Australian prisons who were Indigenous had risen to 19 per cent, or nearly *one in every five* prisoners. The rate of Indigenous incarceration had increased by 13.8 per cent in the decade since the royal commission. And while there had been a steady increase in the rate at which Aboriginal men were being locked up, the bigger story was the sudden and dramatic growth of the Indigenous population in *women's* prisons. During the 1990s, the rate at which Australia was locking up Aboriginal and Torres Strait Islander women shot up by *more than half.*[12]

The disparity continued into the new century. Between 2000 and 2010, almost the entire increase in Australia's rate of imprisonment was among Indigenous people.[13] Between 2011 and 2018, the number of Indigenous people in Australian prisons zoomed up from 7655 to 11,849 – a 55 per cent increase in just seven years. (Over the same period, the number of non-Indigenous prisoners rose by 'only' 45 per cent.) By 2019, an incredible 28 per cent of Australia's prisoners were Aboriginal or Torres Strait Islander, or both.[14]

Then, during the year ending June 2020, for the first time in a decade the number of people in Australian prisons actually decreased. (We'll go into some of the reasons why in chapter 8.) But even though at the end of June 2020 there were nearly 2000 fewer prisoners across Australia, there were also *226 more* Aboriginal and Torres Strait Islander people in prison.

The proportion of Australia's prison population who were Indigenous was now over 29.4 per cent.[15] The over-representation of First Nations people in Australia's prisons had doubled since the royal commission.

If you're an Indigenous man, you are now more than fifteen times more likely to be locked up than a man who isn't Indigenous. If you're an Indigenous woman, you're more than *twenty-one times* more likely to be locked up than non-Indigenous women. Even more glaring are the disparities among children. In Western Australia, for instance, an Indigenous child is *more than fifty times* more likely to be locked up than a non-Indigenous kid. In the Northern Territory, it's now often the case that *every single child* in the Don Dale or Alice Springs Youth Detention Centres is Indigenous. Some of these kids are ten years old.

The over-representation of African American people in United States prisons is widely known in Australia. Well before the #BlackLivesMatter movement surged across the internet and social media, Hollywood and the news had introduced us to many of the ways the American criminal justice system treats, mistreats and ultimately fails black men, women, children and their families. African American people are locked up at five times the rate of white Americans; in some states, that disparity rises to ten times the rate of white incarceration. In eleven states, *one in every twenty* black men is in prison. *One in every three* African American boys born in 2001 can expect to spend at least some time in a prison during his lifetime. In May 2020, #BlackLivesMatter injected a new impetus into an ongoing civil rights struggle following George Floyd's slow death under the knee of police officer Derek Chauvin, who arrested him on suspicion of using a fake $20 note at a nearby convenience store.

But the discrepancies between black and white incarceration in the United States pale against those in Australia. Black Americans are imprisoned at five times the rate of white Americans, but Indigenous people are over *twelve times* more likely to go to prison than non-Indigenous people in Australia. About three years ago, the rate at which Indigenous people are being locked up in Australia *surpassed and overtook* the rate at which African American people are locked up in the United States.[16]

These numbers are extraordinary and, frankly, absurd. But numbers can never tell the human story. 'As an Aboriginal person in this country,' writer and actor Nakkiah Lui told Miranda Tapsell on the *Pretty for an Aboriginal* podcast in 2017, 'I'd been to, like, every jail in New South Wales before the age of eight years old, because every male in my family aside from my dad has been incarcerated.' Among most white people in Australia, that kind of experience is entirely foreign. Most white people in Australia have never even been inside a prison. But it's a common experience in many Aboriginal families. When I visit clients in prison, I watch Aboriginal toddlers already much more familiar, even comfortable, with their securitised routines than I'll ever be. The idea that prison is a normal place to visit Dad or Uncle or, increasingly, Mum is one that's been established through regular weekend visits well before many children even set foot in a school.

○

On 7 November 1968, the anthropologist Bill Stanner told his ABC radio audience that Settler Australia had over the course of the first seven decades of the twentieth century wilfully forgotten Aboriginal and Torres Strait Islander peoples and, pointedly, what it had done to them. 'What may well have begun as a simple forgetting of other possible views', Stanner said in a now-famous Boyer Lecture, 'turned under habit and over time into something like a cult of forgetfulness practised on a national scale.' Anthropology had been the one discipline of the social sciences in Australia which had not simply gone on as if Indigenous people had ceased to exist, and Stanner was keen for other disciplines – history, sociology – to catch up. He observed that there had emerged a 'great Australian silence' about Indigenous experiences and about Australia's colonial history.[17]

But even as Stanner was delivering his lecture, he knew the silence was about to end. A new Indigenous politics, which built on existing activism and which was modelled in part on the radicalism of the American civil rights and global anti-colonial movements, had emerged in the wake of the 'protection' era. Indigenous-run organisations and institutions were being set up by firebrand activists like Gary Foley, Paul Coe and Sam Watson, who found new ways to speak to urban Settler Australia. Settler historians like Henry Reynolds were beginning to re-write Indigenous experiences into the whitewashed record. And as more and more First Nations people forged paths into Australian universities, a newer, middle-class activism has emerged. This book is in large part based on, and indebted to, the groundbreaking work of Marcia Langton, Jackie Huggins, Larissa Behrendt, Aileen Moreton-Robinson, Megan Davis, Maggie Walter, Chelsea Watego and many other activist-intellectuals who are now challenging and changing

Settler Australia from *within* its institutions. The Great Australian Silence, as Arrernte/Kalkadoon filmmaker Rachel Perkins declared in her own Boyer Lectures in 2019, has well and truly ended.

What remains, however, is a 'Great Australian Incarceration'.

This is a book about Australia's extraordinary record of locking up First Nations people. But it's not primarily a book *about* Indigenous peoples and communities. My subject is Australia's system of criminal justice: the system of laws and courts and police and prisons that we use to control behaviour we proscribe as 'criminal'. I'm interested in the ways in which that system interacts with First Nations people and communities. How and why does it lock up so many? Has it always been this way? Why have incarceration rates increased since the Royal Commission into Aboriginal Deaths in Custody? Can – and should – anything be done about it?

We like to imagine Australia as the place of the 'fair go', a classless land of egalitarian virtue. The criminal justice system also presents itself as fair, often to a fault. Defendants are entitled to a fair trial, and judges sometimes need to move mountains to make sure it happens. Witnesses must be treated fairly. Sentences must be fair and proportionate to the crime.

To test these claims of fairness that the system makes for itself, this book looks at how the system responds to Aboriginal and Torres Strait Islander people and communities. Why? Because Aboriginal and Torres Strait Islander people account for *nearly 30 per cent* of all adults locked away in Australian jails, 36 per cent of all adult *women* in prisons, and, astoundingly, *half* of all teenagers in detention centres.[18] Outside prison, Indigenous people are only about 3.3 per cent of the general Australian population. I focus mostly on the situation in the Northern Territory, for two reasons – that's where I've been practising law for the last few years, and that's where the problems I'm describing are among the starkest.

Is this situation fair? Almost everyone agrees that it's not. And yet it keeps getting worse. Nobody, at least since criminologists and sociologists began noticing First Nations people and Aboriginal prisoners in the late 1960s, can say they couldn't see it coming.

Telling stories

There are different stories settler Australians tell themselves to explain why so many Aboriginal and Torres Strait Islander people are in Australia's prisons.

The simplest and most prevalent is one that we can call the carceral three-act narrative. We like the three-act structure in stories. Set-up, confrontation, resolution. In *Star Wars*, the three-act structure of the first film – Luke Skywalker on Tatooine, his quest with Han Solo and Chewbacca, and finally their destruction of the Death Star – is repeated in a trilogy of trilogies. Beginning, middle, end. In the carceral narrative, the three acts are always the same: crime; arrest and court; punishment and prison.

This carceral story is one that looks no further than the person who commits the crime and does the time. The criminal law applies to everyone equally. Each of us has a responsibility to know the law, and to obey it. Offences and their penalties are clearly outlined in codified statutes, most of which reflect prohibitions as old as civilisation. Nobody is allowed to murder or assault anyone else, or steal or damage anyone else's property. A person who intentionally or recklessly breaks the law deserves to be punished. Imprisonment is how the most serious or recidivist offenders are punished. People can avoid going to prison simply by not committing crimes.

This is the story you'll hear over and over again if you sit in magistrates' courts, or read the opinion pages in tabloid newspapers, or scroll through online comments feeds, or even just strike up a chat with a friend or a family member or a complete stranger. I heard this story over and over even during Aaron's plea hearing: the judge repeatedly emphasised that it was Aaron's 'choices' that had led to his presence in that Katherine courtroom, and to his prison sentence. It's the most prevalent story in criminal justice, in part because it's true. Disregarding for a moment issues of wrongful arrest and conviction, the best way of ensuring that you'll never go to prison is to ensure that you don't break the law.

So, the simplest explanation for the over-representation of Aboriginal and Torres Strait Islander people in Australian police and prison cells is that Aboriginal and Torres Strait Islander people commit more serious crimes, more often. Nearly 34 per cent of Indigenous prisoners are in prison because they've been charged with 'an act intended to cause injury'. Another 14 per cent are there because of burglary, 9 per cent because of robbery, another 9 per cent because of sexual assault, and just over 5 per cent because of homicide.[19] More than seven in every ten Aboriginal prisoners, then, are in prison because of some act of serious violence or home invasion. If they'd never done the crime, they wouldn't be doing the time. That maxim applies equally to other offences, from drug crimes to breaches of bail.

To stop the inquiry at this point is to accept two propositions: first, that there is no better, or more effective, or more humane way of responding to the criminal behaviour of individuals than to lock them up; and second, that the devastation wrought by prison on those individuals' families and communities is a kind of sad but inevitable by-product of imprisonment – a form of excusable collateral damage. But does it really make sense to respond to individuals' violence by, for instance, locking people in cages stained with blood and vomit? Depriving people not only of their liberty but also adequate healthcare, sanitation and education? Perpetuating practices which are known to hasten and even cause early death? Most people who accept these propositions have never been confronted by the life-and-death realities of imprisonment and over-policing, and with the opaque promises of Australia's justice and coronial systems.

What's also true is that social scientists can predict, with an astonishing degree of accuracy, how likely it is that people will break the law. These predictions don't work at the level of the individual, so nobody can predict for sure whether a *particular* person will commit a crime. *Minority Report* is still fiction. But at what statisticians call a 'population-wide' or merely 'population' level, it becomes apparent that certain characteristics and experiences either increase or decrease the risk that a person will break the law in a serious way. Not completing high school, using drugs, suffering abuse or neglect by parents and being unemployed – these are the four main factors that make it more likely that people will commit crime. There are many other factors, too, but pretty much all of them – including having spent time in prison, or being involved (as a perpetrator *or* a victim, or both) in family violence – can ultimately be explained by the four 'main' factors. Plus being male makes it more likely – *much* more likely – that a person will commit a crime of serious violence. This knowledge doesn't square well with the simple story we tell about crime. If offending or not was purely a matter of choice, we would expect statistics to confirm that offending patterns are consistent across the entire population regardless of background and circumstance. In other words, we'd expect to see the daughters of Vaucluse offending just as much as the sons of Darwin's town camps. Obviously they don't, so something else is going on.

As to just what that 'something else' is, and how it explains the extraordinary rates of Indigenous incarceration in particular, is the subject of ongoing debate among researchers and policymakers. Part of this debate is set out in a report of the most recent large-scale national investigation into 'Aboriginal incarceration': that undertaken by Matthew Myers – the Federal Court's first Aboriginal judge – and the Australian Law Reform Commission (ALRC) beginning in October 2016. When Myers reported at the end of 2017, he found what similar inquiries had found going back to the Royal Commission into Aboriginal Deaths in Custody in 1991. Between 1910 and 1972, Aboriginal families were shattered by child removal policies, which at their nadir were aimed at 'breeding out the colour', compounding the continuing harm wrought by invasion, colonisation and dispossession. Formal discrimination against Aboriginal people ended in 1972, but only after nearly two centuries of terror that left many First Nations people, families and communities dealing with the legacies of what Jiman/Bundjalung woman and trauma researcher Judy Atkinson calls 'transgenerational' trauma.[20] As a result, Aboriginal people were and remain massively over-represented among the various statistical 'markers of disadvantage' – school dropouts, unemployment, substandard housing, overcrowding, homelessness, poor health, mental illness, cognitive impairment, alcohol and other drug dependency, child abuse and neglect, and children being removed from their parents by child protection authorities[21] – which are also heavily correlated with criminal offending, becoming a victim of crime and going to jail. So, goes this story, it's no surprise that Aboriginal people are spending so much time in prison.

Some researchers stop their analysis here, and claim that if governments and Aboriginal communities alike work hard to address these various deprivations, eventually, fewer Aboriginal people will be locked up. This is the 'deprivation' or 'deficit' story about Aboriginal imprisonment, and it's a true story too. It sees incarceration as an inevitable by-product of disadvantage. The deficits in Aboriginal people and communities are the cause of their higher offending rates, and therefore their higher rates of imprisonment. Provide better support to Aboriginal parents, teach them better parenting skills, keep Aboriginal children at school for as long as other kids, fix their housing problems, improve their diets and lifestyles, stop them drinking alcohol when they're pregnant, make sure they stay healthy, support them to better participate and compete in the labour and capital markets, and the incarceration rate will take care of itself. With this view, the criminal justice system and its institutions – governments, police, courts, prisons – can remain basically neutral: they receive disadvantaged people, including many Aboriginal people, and process them as best they can. The justice system can no more stop an Aboriginal person – or anyone – from being locked up than an oncologist can prevent a person from growing a cancer. But to stop here is to accept that imprisonment – and all that goes with it – will remain a reality for a high proportion of First Nations people, families and communities until they can be dragged into the middle class. It's a grimly utilitarian position – and a deeply illiberal one – which ignores people's lived experience in the meantime. 'In the long run', wrote the economist John Maynard Keynes famously, 'we are all dead'.[22]

Myers and the ALRC also acknowledged another body of research that goes back at least to the deaths in custody commission, which crisscrossed the country from 1987 until it reported in 1991. The royal commissioners came to several conclusions about Australia's criminal justice system itself. While many Aboriginal people were committing serious crimes, *most* Aboriginal people were being locked up for very minor offences, such as public drunkenness, offensive behaviour and the non-payment of fines. Police were regularly using their discretion *against* Aboriginal people, and were arresting them and locking them up in situations where they would have simply issued a summons – or even a warning – had the offender been white. Bail laws that required financial sureties effectively discriminated against Aboriginal people, many of whom didn't have the money to pay. As a result, many Aboriginal people remained on remand in situations where they could have been released pending trial. Corrections departments had often failed to create community-based alternatives to imprisonment, especially in regional and remote areas; so many Aboriginal offenders were being sent to prison when they could have stayed in the community on a supervised order had one been available. And Aboriginal legal services weren't adequately funded to deal with the high numbers of people needing in-court representation, which meant that many Aboriginal defendants were still going to court unrepresented.

These observations pointed to what appeared to be a widespread bias against Aboriginal people that permeated the institutions of the criminal justice system. The story of *institutional bias* isn't inconsistent with the *deprivation* story, though subscribers to the bias thesis obviously don't see the system as neutral. Rather, bias works to augment the already high rate at which Aboriginal people are being locked up because of their multiple disadvantages. After the royal commission reported, a dispute arose between those who saw institutional bias as a major contributing factor in Aboriginal people's incarceration, and those who saw it as a kind of red herring. In practical terms, this is a debate about where governments should direct their efforts. To what extent should governments spend scarce resources on retraining police, establishing community-based offender programs in regional areas, reforming bail laws and funding Aboriginal Legal Services (ALS), when doing so would divert resources from addressing Aboriginal disadvantage?

There is also a fourth story, one that maintains that *none* of the existing stories – neither the three-act narrative, the one about deprivation, nor the one about institutional bias – goes anywhere near far enough to explain the sheer extent of the problem. The story with the most truth, some say, is that Aboriginal and Torres Strait Islander people and their communities are locked in a one-sided and ongoing relationship with Settler Australia and its government that commenced in 1788, and has continued substantially on the same terms. The whole system of crime and punishment, this critique suggests, is *designed* to continue to punish Indigenous people unless and until they adopt the cultural norms of the settler middle class.

Does history matter?

Arguments in favour of change now run headlong into one gigantic stumbling block. That block is Indigenous men's violence, especially against Indigenous women. As I was completing this book, *The Australian* published a three-part report detailing the extreme violence inflicted on one twenty-one-year-old woman, 'Ruby', by men, including her father, in Yuendumu. The journalist, Kristin Shorten, had met Ruby while she was there covering the police shooting of Kumanjayi Walker by Constable Zachary Rolfe (see chapter 12). In *The Australian*'s coverage of that shooting, the violence police officers routinely contend with in Aboriginal communities was presented as context for its readers to understand – and to excuse – Rolfe's own actions.[23] In her report, Shorten gave her readers graphic detail of Ruby's repeated rapes at the hands of her biological father, and the horrific punishments she received from other family members when she testified against him in court.[24]

Settler Australia has told this kind of story to itself for four decades. It fulfils a particular function: to shock readers into staying the colonial course. Questions of history and sovereignty are overwhelmed by the violence. As if on cue, *The Australian* then featured an exclusive interview with Judith Kelly, a sitting Supreme Court judge who told journalist Amos Aikman: 'I just want people to know what's happening to Aboriginal women.' 'She praised the Black Lives Matter movement's focus on allegations of excessive force by authorities,' Aikman wrote after interviewing her, 'but questioned whether those ought to be the top priority.' Kelly pointed out to Aikman that while police have shot two Aboriginal men in the Territory since 2000, fifty-two Aboriginal women have been killed during the same period, 'mostly by their partners'. Kelly – who is white – told Aikman that claims of racism in the justice system were 'very unhelpful'. The problems to be solved are unemployment, passive welfare dependency, substance abuse and intergenerational trauma. The 'epidemic' of domestic violence in the Territory isn't caused by racism, she said. 'It's the violence of the men against the women.'[25]

Following Kelly's intervention, Professor Marcia Langton told *The Australian*: 'The safety of women and children must be the overriding and first concern; not fear of increasing incarceration rates for Aboriginal men.'[26] Some reformers and activists do tend to downplay the prevalence and extent of this violence, and to focus almost exclusively on the violence and surveillance deployed by police and prison officers, and the myriad ways courts excuse and endorse them. But this book argues that prison doesn't protect women either.

Like all criminal defence lawyers, I'm regularly asked: *How do you represent men who bash women? How do you defend rapists?* My job, in the end, in this adversarial system inherited from England, is to defend and assert people's right to be assumed innocent until proven guilty. But I do see a lot of horrific violence, or at least its aftermath: photos, videos, terrified victims. For many, that's enough to demand a lifetime of prison and hard labour: *do the crime, do the time*. The big problem is that prison doesn't work. Violent men come out more violent. Children come out hardened. Everyone comes out broken – when they come out at all. One of this book's big asks is a preparedness to distinguish the *criminal act*, committed by the individual, from the *criminal justice system* which responds to it by way of policing and punishment. Whether we accept it or not, each – the act and the system – has a history. Knowing some of that history, I think, lets us ask questions about what's happening now: questions that aren't asked when we're blinded by horror and moral outrage, which are understandable responses following a vicious crime.

I'm not an Aboriginal or Torres Strait Islander person. My ancestors are all from Europe. They arrived from Ireland, London and Germany between the 1830s and 1947 to 'settle' on Kaurna land, by then called Adelaide by settlers. I was raised in a red-brick home in that city's western suburb of Fulham Gardens, its name recalling both the Bulgarian and Chinese market gardens it had been and John White's earlier estate of Fulham, originally purchased from the South Australian Company in 1836. My parents purchased their land from developers in the late 1970s. But the Kaurna people, who had lived on, managed and cultivated – in other words, owned – that same land for tens of thousands of years, have never once agreed to these transactions. They were driven off their land during South Australia's speedy settlement, and for that theft they've never been compensated, despite the requirement to do so in British law. Later I worked for Aboriginal Legal Services, firstly in Melbourne and then in Katherine, in the Northern Territory, representing Aboriginal people charged with criminal offences. Nothing in my own middle-class experience as a 'white' guy – nothing in my childhood, my education, my law degree, the things I'd been taught to believe about our system of criminal justice – had prepared me for what I learned about it when I saw, from close up, how it treated Indigenous people.[27]

I regularly use the term 'Settler Australia' or 'settlers' in this book, especially to refer to Australians who don't identify as Aboriginal or Torres Strait Islander: 'those who've come across the seas', and the institutions and ideas and practices and cultures they brought with them. 'Australia', by itself, seems too vague, too reconciled. 'Non-Indigenous Australians' is too clunky. But if the history of what happened here is taken seriously, then it must be recognised that there are two main groups: the beneficiaries of settlement and the dispossessed. I'm a beneficiary. The more than 12,000 Aboriginal and Torres Strait Islander people presently locked up in Australia's prisons and police cells are not. I'm not talking about 'race' or ethnicity here: people have complicated ethnic histories, and 'race' is literally a social construct: a 'technology of power instituted in precise historical contexts, most significantly colonialism and slavery', as researcher and former public servant Debbie Bargallie, descendant of the Kamilaroi and Wonnarua peoples, explains.[28] I'm talking in part about the worlds we've been raised into, and the structures of power that govern us. White settlers rarely think in these terms, and react with bewilderment and even anger when they're asked to, because settlers are beneficiaries of the colonisation which occurred here. In my experience, the Indigenous people I've represented in courts think in these terms constantly.

Does history matter to the growing problem of the over-incarcerated First Nations? Plenty – they tend to be settlers – claim that it ultimately does not. Those who perform the carceral three-act play – magistrates, judges, police, politicians, tabloid editors – look barely any further than the criminal act itself and the immediate damage or loss it causes. And those who see the problem of Aboriginal incarceration as one that can be explained by Aboriginal deficits – of education, of parenting, of community – may acknowledge the history that has left those deficits as its legacy, but argue that the solution must lie in moving Aboriginal people beyond the bounds history has created.

The secret history of the criminal law

This is not another book about Aboriginal deficits, perceived or otherwise. There are plenty of those. The crimes Aboriginal people commit are only part of the story. To focus on them exclusively is to ignore the possibility that we're *compounding* existing problems with the way we insist on dealing with offenders.

This is a book that turns the gaze back onto Settler Australia's system of criminal justice. It examines the history of how that system came to be in this land, and how it grew from non-existence – before 1788 – into the system as we know it today. Above all, that system is *universalist*. It jealously claims that *its* law is the one true law, and that all others are given by false prophets. Just as they were in the nineteenth century, Aboriginal communities are still prohibited from practising significant aspects of their own distinct cultures, namely, their methods of dispute resolution, which aim to resolve tensions and restore balance in ways that are meaningful to the people involved.

Much of this still has an oddly 'secret history' feel to it. For a very long time, Australian textbooks – drawn from serious histories – repeated the claim that the settlement of the Australian continent was uniquely peaceful, that there were no wars here. Now we know that at least 60,000 Aboriginal men, women and children were deliberately killed in an unrelenting, undeclared and illegal frontier war *in Queensland alone.* The vast majority of the perpetrators – police officers, pastoralists, squatters, settlers – were never charged, let alone convicted and imprisoned, even though what they were doing was clearly prohibited by the law they brought with them from Britain.

Aboriginal communities and nations had distinct cultures and laws before 1788. Many of those cultures and laws continue today in updated form, just as the culture and laws British people arrived with have also changed. So then the claim that settler criminal law makes – that it is the one true law – seems a long way from neutral. If we also acknowledge that the criminal law did nothing to protect the victims of some of the greatest land-thefts in human experience, and some of its bloodiest massacres, then how can it claim fairness and legitimacy? Both the 'deprivation' and even the 'institutional bias' theses downplay or ignore the extent to which the ongoing one-sided relationship between Settler and Indigenous Australia – a relationship whose terms are continually imposed by the one on the other – governs Aboriginal lives and dictates their opportunities, including their opportunities to recover from generations of trauma perpetrated by the settler state, to heal and to thrive.

I must also state at the outset what this book is not: it isn't an argument in favour of reversing the tides of history so that Aboriginal and Torres Strait Islander people can finally be afforded the separate and uncolonised existence they should have had from the beginning. Nor is this a history of the two centuries of First Nations activism aimed at reforming or replacing the settler justice system. This book makes an argument specifically against the enduring practice of *imposing laws and solutions* onto colonised nations and communities, especially where there is ample evidence that those 'solutions' – especially where they involve imprisonment – barely work in settler culture, let alone for colonised First Nations.

This book is about the stories that Settler Australia has told *itself* about Indigenous crime and how to control it. Many of those stories serve settler-colonial interests. They emphasise violence perpetrated by individual Indigenous people, and routinely ignore, downplay or excuse both the historical and social context within which that violence takes place, and the violence perpetrated by the settler state and its agents and institutions, most notably police and prisons. Because this book draws from the historical record *created by* settler courts and governments, many contemporary readers will observe that my focus is often very one-sided. *Where is the truth about the frontier violence?* the reader is entitled to ask. *Where are the contemporary accounts of police violence?* The most straightforward answer – and the most shocking one – is that the court records are overwhelmingly silent about these acts of state-sanctioned (or wilfully blind) violence. That in itself creates, at the very least, a legitimacy problem for the settler system of justice. Police get away with what they do because of courts' complicity. More recent court records do show occasional prosecutions of police officers for killing Indigenous people, but all of them – *all* of them – are stamped with acquittals.

Other readers, meanwhile, are likely to reject the entire premise of this book. *How can there be anything but a single justice system?* these readers may ask. *Do the crime, do the time.* This points to one of the reasons this book exists. The conversations occurring about crime, justice and sovereignty at exclusive academic conferences and in pricey academic texts are taking place in a moral universe which seems entirely remote from that within which, say, the *Daily Telegraph* or a typical commercial TV news bulletin exists. The approach this book takes is to attempt to bridge this gap: to draw from the best of the contemporary research and, guided by interpretations and perspectives provided by an expanding group of Indigenous and settler researchers and writers, talk to a general Australian audience. Many of this book's readers are likely to be white: ultimately I'm talking to Settler Australia about *its* need to change.

Some caveats and explainers. I recount some of the cases I've been involved in as a lawyer. As a way of protecting my clients' identities, and those of any victims, I've used pseudonyms and altered some of the facts of the offending. I've also given pseudonyms to most of the people likely to still be alive whose real names appear in published court documents. Court records contain findings of 'fact', and often include facts to which defendants have agreed to plead guilty. This doesn't mean they're accurate. As a practising lawyer, I've been privy to enough of the distorting processes of the criminal law to know that at least sometimes, and probably often, the 'facts' courts hear – even on guilty pleas – bear little relationship to what actually happened. Readers should be aware of this as they're reading the 'facts' in the cases discussed in this book, some of which record brutal violence. Sometimes the truth is even worse than what the court hears. And sometimes the court hears a version that's much more serious than the real-life incident. In most cases I write about in this book, the identities of individual people caught up within the settler justice system don't need to be known in order to talk about that system. So I mostly conceal individuals' identities. In all cases the system creates its *own* stories.

If we can see how these stories have changed over nearly 235 years, we may be able to see more clearly how the way Settler Australia talks and thinks about Indigenous crime might change again. It may then be possible to see that Settler Australia can't 'reform' its own system – its police forces, its criminal courts, its correctional agencies – without first dropping its jealously guarded universality and sheen of neutrality, and entering into, at long last, a relationship of genuine respect and mutuality with Aboriginal and Torres Strait Islander communities and nations. Indigenous people have been asking for that kind of relationship for more than two centuries. Now, as prisons continue to fill with more and more Indigenous men, women and children, it's well past the time Settler Australia began to properly listen.

SETTLERS

How the criminal law came to Australia

When they arrived on the Australian continent in January of 1788, Arthur Phillip and the 1500 mostly pale-faced convicts and officers of the First Fleet brought guns, chains, shackles and lashes. And they brought their own law, perhaps the most powerful weapon of all in what would become, eventually and inevitably, a decades-long undeclared war for control of the continent whose frontline would inch ever inland and northward. It was a war that many of its beneficiaries never even knew was being waged.

The people experiencing the invasion, however, knew they were at war. It was difficult not to know. They were being murdered, and massacred, and driven off their lands so that the invaders could begin using it for their own, foreign purposes. Many groups fought back. Direct confrontation mostly didn't work. Wooden spears were no match for muskets. So the Australian nations chose indirect methods, which might today be called guerrilla tactics. They raided farms, killed animals, stole weapons and, occasionally, attacked individual settlers and small groups in retaliation for earlier 'dispersals' committed on them by the invaders.

And when they did perpetrate these acts of resistance, they would often be punished, 'summarily' or by being 'dispersed': both were euphemisms for murder. Sometimes, when settlers didn't know for sure which particular Aboriginal person committed the 'crime', they'd kill a person who looked like the offender. Or they'd kill the first person they found. Or they'd go looking for a handful of Aboriginal people, or a dozen, or more, and massacre them as a vengeful 'example' to their countrymen and women: *This land is now ours. Stay away.* There was nothing in the law the settlers brought with them from Britain that allowed anything like this.

And sometimes, just sometimes, Aboriginal 'offenders' would be arrested, charged, tried and punished according to a set of imported rules known as the criminal law of New South Wales.

The invasion of the British

When James Cook, botanist Joseph Banks and more than forty others approached the shore at Kurnell in small boats on 28 April 1770,[1] two Dharawal men – including the warrior Cooman – came to meet them, yelling and brandishing spears and, Cook's party thought, waving them away. More recently, Dharawal researchers have suggested that what the two men were shouting – recorded as 'warra warra wai' by Cook's artist Sydney Parkinson[2] – might have been *warrawarrawa*: literally, 'they're all dead' or 'they are ghosts' or 'they are white', as they were astonished at the newcomers' pale skin.[3]

Alarmed, Cook fired a musket between the two men. One of them threw a stone back at Cook, who fired at Cooman's leg. Cooman ran to one of the huts on the beach, retrieved a shield and returned. When Cook's group landed on the rocks, the Dharawal men threw spears in their direction and Cook fired more shots. The men retreated to beyond the tree line, to where others had run at the first sign of Cook's approach. Cook and Banks approached the huts, observed children inside them, threw some beads and other gifts inside, and went around the camp stealing all the spears and shields they could find. The next day the camp was deserted. The Dharawal had left behind every gift the British men had 'given' them.[4] Thus began relations between British people and the people of the Australian continent – with an assault, a theft and a 'home invasion' by the visitors.

Cook, Banks and the *Endeavour* eventually left Botany Bay, sailed up the continent's east coast and returned to England via Java and the Cape of Good Hope. The whole voyage had come about because of a successful petition to King George III by the Royal Society to study the transit of Venus in 1769 so as to measure the distance between the Earth and the sun; the Royal Navy thought the scientific nature of the expedition a suitable pretext to also search for the much-theorised Terra Australis Incognita. In case he found it, Cook had his secret instructions, now well known:

You are also with the consent of the Natives to take Possession of Convenient Situations in the Country, in the Name of the King of Great

Britain; or, if you find the Country uninhabited, take Possession for His Majesty by setting up Proper Marks and Inscription, as first discoverers and possessors.

Cook duly claimed possession of Australia's east coast, called it New South Wales, and returned to London to commend Botany Bay as a site for a new colony.

There was interest, given the race between European states to colonise the world, but New South Wales' distance from Britain meant the government couldn't justify the idea. Then came the thirteen American colonies' declaration of independence in July 1776. Its need to divert military resources to the defence of the colonies led Britain to 'temporarily' suspend the transportation of its convicts across the Atlantic. Thousands of petty criminals were now piling up inside rotting hulks on the Thames, awaiting transportation but with nowhere to go. Politicians began casting about for strategic solutions.[5]

Joseph Banks, now famous, was happy to provide them. He told a parliamentary select committee in March 1779 that in Botany Bay there was grass ('long and luxuriant'), fresh water, 'an abundance of timber and fuel' and plenty of fish. Cook had met his grisly end in Hawaii the previous month but, Banks advised the select committee, the probability of any opposition from the natives of New South Wales was low. During the full week he had been there a mere nine years earlier, he'd estimated there were fewer than fifty locals 'in the entire neighbourhood', and while those he did see were 'treacherous and armed with lances', they were also naked and 'extremely cowardly'. Botany Bay was the perfect place to send convicts, said Banks: not only would escape be impossible, but in the future one could imagine that 'a tract of land such as New Holland, which was larger than the whole of Europe, would furnish matter of advantageous return' to the Mother Country.[6] In December 1785 the government issued orders to establish a penal colony in New South Wales.

It was an extraordinary undertaking that was built on not much more than the recollections of a botanist based on a single week's visit a decade and a half earlier. Banks' description of the Dharawal people was highly influential: it was echoed in nearly everything written about them before the First Fleet sailed.[7] It was also extraordinarily ignorant. Banks had never been inland, and simply assumed nobody lived there. He had no knowledge of Dharawal language, culture or law, let alone that of any other Aboriginal nation.

Plans for the First Fleet proceeded on the assumption that the people Banks had briefly encountered were at such an 'early stage' of human development that they were incapable of occupying land or of holding property rights. 'I do not remember to have read of any inland nation who did not cultivate the ground more or less,' Banks wrote in his *Endeavour* journal.

> Even the North Americans who were so well versed in hunting sowd their Maize. But should a people live inland who supported themselves by cultivation these inhabitants of the sea coast must certainly have learn'd to imitate them in some degree at least, otherwise their reason must be suppos'd to hold a rank little superior to that of monkies.[8]

This was the impression of Aboriginal people that the first English colonists brought with them in 1788. It was less a 'legal' view than it was a 'racial' one. This is important because it explains so much of what happened afterwards. There would be no need to obtain the natives' informed consent, which was the usual way European nations secured the possession of necessary locations in the New World, because it was widely assumed the natives didn't have capacity to provide it. After their false start at Botany Bay, which wasn't the paradise Banks had promised, Phillip set up around 30 kilometres north at Port Jackson (in Sydney Harbour). Well over a thousand convicts, marines and crew lived in hot tents while they set about securing their stores of food and establishing a penal colony under martial law. With few farmers, builders and craftsmen among the petty thieves and naval officers, this was no simple exercise.

Phillip had arrived, famously, with instructions to 'endeavour by every possible means to open an intercourse with the natives, and to conciliate their affections, enjoining all our subjects to live in amity and kindness with them'. After 'taking measures for securing' the settlers 'from any attacks or interruptions of the natives', he was to punish colonists who killed or hurt them, or gave them 'unnecessary interruption in the exercise of their several occupations'. At the same time, Phillip was to 'proceed to the cultivation of the land' and the expansion of the settlement, granting at least 30 acres to each emancipated convict.[9] This brief was obviously contradictory. Cultivating the land would, by definition, interrupt the natives' occupations.

As they established themselves, Watkin Tench recorded that some 'unprincipled individuals among us' committed 'unprovoked outrages' upon the locals. This violence wasn't sanctioned by Phillip or by his original instructions. Phillip was faithful to the spirit of these orders, at least initially, though conciliating the affections of people while simultaneously taking over their land and 'liaising' with women – often by force – was always going to pose challenges. When the locals responded by wounding and killing 'unarmed stragglers', Phillip's men claimed to not know why.

The first man detained

The first winter was difficult, and by the end of the year relations between the British occupiers and what they called the Eora people had descended into what Tench described as 'unabated animosity' and 'petty warfare'. Facing mounting pressure to respond to the locals' 'mysterious conduct', Phillip made a decision. He wanted to capture some of them to force an explanation out of them. He sent two boats into the harbour, the crews of which found some locals on a beach, lured them with 'courteous conversation and a few presents', and then seized two men. There was a struggle and one of them escaped, so only a man the settlers called 'Manly' – after the name Phillips had given to the cove he was captured from, due to what he saw as the locals' 'confidence and manly behaviour' – was brought back to the settlement and shackled there for two months, primarily to act as a kind of enslaved guide for his kidnappers. They eventually discovered what they believed to be his real name, and recorded it as Arabanoo.[10] When the shackle restraining him was removed in February 1789, he mostly remained with his captors until he died of smallpox a few months later. Oddly, Arabanoo's incarceration didn't improve the occupiers' relations with the locals.

As far as we can tell, Arabanoo was the first Aboriginal person to be detained by the British occupiers – and it's something of a harbinger of things to come that his detention bore no relationship to anything he was accused of having done. He may have been the first Australian Aboriginal person detained in the history of the world. Incarceration seems to have been unknown to Aboriginal cultures, which had other techniques of punishment and regulation. And while incarceration had been a part of British,

European and 'Western' cultures for centuries, dating at least to ancient Rome, by the time the First Fleet arrived, the mere deprivation of liberty had become an end in itself in British penal culture only recently. In their squalor, most prisons still resembled their precursors of the Middle Ages, and were often mere holding pens before the main game: the public hanging, the firing squad, the stocks or the lash. Arabanoo was, Tench tells us, disgusted at seeing convicts flogged, even after those convicts had attacked Aboriginal people.[11]

But transportation (though less so by the late eighteenth century) and the modern prison were part of a reform movement, guided by humane and Enlightenment thought and supported by the emerging industrial economy.[12] This movement pushed back against the rapid proliferation of hanging offences during the seventeenth and eighteenth centuries as Whig parliaments, especially, had made laws protecting property against workers and paupers. The *Black Act* of 1723, for instance, had made hanging offences out of such activities as burning haystacks, fishing without permission and appearing in any commons where game is usually kept while having a blackened face and carrying a weapon. Anyone merely suspected of these crimes and who didn't surrender themselves within forty days could be judged guilty *in absentia* and sentenced to death. Collectively, these laws became known as the Bloody Code.

Incarceration and transportation may have been considered an improvement on the Bloody Code, but they were wholly unknown to Aboriginal peoples on the Australian continent. So were guns, though they became familiar with them rather quickly.

The lawless frontier

Phillip and his settlers arrived with assumptions that had tumbled down from the militaristic Christianity of the anti-Islamic Crusades through nearly three centuries of staggeringly hubristic thought among Western Europeans about their claims to the world. In 1608 Edward Coke, then chief justice of the Common Pleas, thought all 'infidels' were 'perpetual enemies' whose laws became invalid after they were conquered.[13] (Lord Mansfield would scuttle this notion in a case decided thirteen years before the First Fleet sailed.[14]) Between 1680 and 1690 John Locke, then secretary of the Board of Trade and Plantations, dreamed up the convenient – and uninformed – notion that the

First Nations of North America were 'natural' beings incapable of owning property or exercising sovereignty, because property required an ability to 'improve' the land – which of course they were doing, but Locke and those who wanted to agree with him overlooked that troublesome fact.[15]

These ideas and more would have been swirling about in the minds of Phillip's commissioners, but they weren't actually explicit about which theory they expected him to apply in New South Wales. In his influential *Commentaries on the Laws of England*, the judge William Blackstone – who had died in 1780 – observed that unpeopled lands (his famous phrase was 'desart and uncultivated') could be 'claimed by right of occupancy only', and that 'already cultivated' lands could either be 'gained by conquest, or ceded to us by treaties'.[16] We tend to assume, now, that the British planners intended Phillip to 'settle' Australia on their assumption that it was *terra nullius*, but that term only began to be used by courts much later. What had taken place before 1776 in many parts of what is now the United States of America might lead us to assume that Phillip was expected to create a similar settlement: to negotiate treaties with Aboriginal nations and, if necessary, declare wars against them and conquer their territories. Settlers in northern America had occasionally appealed to First Nations' systems of laws (or at least their own understandings of such laws) to justify retaliatory punishments for perceived crimes committed against the settlers. Just how would Phillips' settlers engage with the Australian First Nations?

The truth was that Phillip's expedition hadn't really considered Indigenous peoples much at all beyond a brief mention towards the end of a sparse set of instructions. Those instructions amounted to 'leave them alone', and implicitly assumed Indigenous people would also largely leave the settlers alone. Given Banks's descriptions of them, perhaps that was not surprising. The colonists were thinking much more about their potential economic bounty than about the rights of the continent's 'natives'. 'The colony of a civilized nation which takes possession either of a waste country, or of one so thinly inhabited that the natives easily give place to the new settlers,' Adam Smith had observed in his *Wealth of Nations* (1776), 'advances more rapidly to wealth and greatness than any other human society.' But what happened when Phillips and the settlers worked out that Banks was wrong? What happened when the settlers began to understand that Aboriginal nations had systems of laws and were prepared to fight back against land theft?

Unsurprisingly, the situation descended inexorably into what we now know as the Frontier Wars of colonial invasion. The reality of frontier warfare meant that acts of Aboriginal resistance were initially met with negotiation and/or violence more often than with, say, criminal trial and punishment.[17] After the resistance leader, Pemulwuy, speared Phillip's gamekeeper in 1790, an incensed Phillip ordered Tench to lead a retaliatory expedition against the Bidjigal and execute ten people. Tench apparently talked him down, and set out instead to *capture* six Bidjigal and kill none of them.[18] In the end he didn't find anyone to capture *or* kill. But Pemulwuy's act of resistance was the match to the tinderbox, the spark that lit the settlers' fury. Pemulwuy convinced the Dharug and Dharawal peoples to join a war of resistance against the settlers. From 1792 he led raids throughout the settlement, burning crops and killing livestock, until the colony's third governor, Philip King, issued a 'dead or alive' order for Pemulwuy's capture in 1801. Just over six months later, Henry Hacking, a sailor who had very likely been the first colonist to shoot and kill an Aboriginal person (when he fired on a group of about forty people at Middle Head in September 1789), shot Pemulwuy dead.[19]

The Colonial Office's original instructions to Phillip were blatantly ignored as, again and again, posses of soldiers and settlers were dispatched to murder and to terrorise. In his diary entry on 26 September 1794, judge advocate Richard Atkins recorded, almost in passing, that 'The Settlers at the Hawkesbury have kill'd 6 of the Natives'. Those settlers were never charged; apparently they were never even investigated. 'How far this is justifiable I cannot say' was the only thing Atkins could say about it.[20] In response to the (alleged) killings of two settlers in mid-1795, Captain William Paterson of the New South Wales Corps sent a military party of sixty-eight officers and soldiers 'with instructions to destroy' as many Bidjigal people as they could find and 'in the hope of striking terror, to erect gibbets in different places, whereon the bodies of all they might kill were to be hung'.[21] All of this was highly illegal under British law unless war had been declared, which it hadn't. They eventually boasted of killing 'seven or eight' Bidjigal. Neither Paterson nor any other colonist was ever investigated, arrested, charged or tried.

An Aboriginal man, recorded only as 'John Randall', was accused in 1799 of trying to steal plates and glasses from John Hunter's house. (Hunter had been Phillip's second-in-command and had succeeded him as governor.) Hunter's servant and a constable gave evidence before the Bench of Magistrates, which decided to leave any punishment up to Hunter himself to administer.[22] (In the event, Hunter set Randall free after the accused apologised.)

The court's continued refusal of jurisdiction would become one rationale for summary 'justice'. Sometime before September 1799, an Aboriginal man known as 'Charley' was arrested by a corporal in the NSW Corps following the death, apparently by spearing, of a marine settler. When Charley was brought to Hunter, the governor said he 'could not take upon himself to punish the Native in cold blood' – but then added that he should instead have been punished 'on the spot where he was taken'.[23]

As relations between the invaders and the invaded deteriorated – inevitably, one is tempted to conclude now, given that what the invaders wanted was land, and they weren't trying to negotiate treaties – the record shows the rather extraordinary delusions under which the colonists were operating. Pemulwuy's son, known to the settlers as 'Tedbury', carried on Pemulwuy's resistance, and was among those who successfully – if temporarily – repelled attempts to settle the Hawkesbury until 1804.[24] When he was captured in May 1805 following a series of raids on settlers at Windsor (which King had initially interpreted as responses to starvation), Tedbury was brought before the notorious magistrate Samuel Marsden, known as the 'flogging parson'. The fledgling colonial legal system – which was still essentially a military court – hadn't yet claimed jurisdiction over the 'crimes' of Aboriginal people, although this was how their acts of resistance were being described in the *Sydney Gazette*, essentially a government propaganda sheet. Marsden convinced Tedbury to lead a party of settlers to where he and other resistance fighters had hidden property they'd 'stolen'. They came across another resistance leader, the young Gai-Mariagal man 'Musquito', who 'saluted them in good English' and declared 'a determination to continue [his] rapacities', before making off.[25] Tedbury was then brought back to Sydney and locked up, without trial. In mid-June, Musquito set fire to a farmer's barn and stacks. Other detained Dharug men offered to search for Musquito in exchange for Tedbury's release, and were themselves freed at the beginning of July. The *Gazette* obtusely interpreted this offer as gratitude for King's fair treatment of them, and King himself saw it hubristically as surrender.

Five days later, on 6 July, the Dharug delivered both Musquito and another warrior, 'Bull Dog', to King in Sydney, convincing him that Musquito was the main aggressor. King immediately declared both victory and an end to hostilities, and released Tedbury a month later. The *Sydney Gazette* hoped the 'leniency' the authorities had shown to the Dharug despite their 'spirit of destruction' would convince them of 'how much they are indebted to the liberal clemency' of King's government.[26] King's was a unilateral declaration. In his cell inside the Parramatta Gaol, Musquito threatened to destroy the prison and kill every white man inside it. He attempted escape by loosening the mortar between the stones, and almost succeeded.[27]

King thought he had more than enough evidence to secure a murder conviction or two against Musquito in court, based on Musquito's resistance activities up and down the Hawkesbury. But Aboriginal people had never been tried in New South Wales. In 1805 King asked his judge advocate, Richard Atkins, whether Musquito could be tried according to English law. That in itself was a fraught exercise. Atkins may have been the colony's principal legal officer, but it was rare to catch him sober. And he was not actually a lawyer.[28] But apparently he dutifully read a range of materials and came up with a brief opinion: 'the evidence of Persons not bound by any moral or religious [tie] can never be considered or construed as legal evidence'. Aboriginal people were, of course, under the protection of the Crown, though exactly what this meant was very unclear. It was absurd, Atkins concluded, to think they could be brought to trial, to 'plead Guilty or not Guilty to an Indictment, the meaning and tendency of which they must be totally ignorant of'. Instead, there was no choice but to allow settlers to continue to 'pursue and inflict such punishment as they may merit', including shooting them dead.[29] King summarily banished Musquito and Bull Dog to Norfolk Island.

The unwillingness of settler authorities to legally try Aboriginal people occasionally led to outcomes that seemed to favour them. It was common for highwaymen and bushrangers to be hanged after trial, but in mid-1815 when an Aboriginal man purloined a jacket with some bills of exchange in the pockets – after its owner had taken it off in order to chop wood along the Parramatta Road – a magistrate simply ordered his solitary confinement, without trial, as a way of inducing him to return the stolen property.[30] When this measure failed, due to the fact that the accused had apparently already spent the bills, the police superintendent simply let him go on a promise not to reoffend.[31]

But very often the courts' lack of jurisdiction – especially on the frontier – had terrible consequences. In April 1816, Macquarie sent a British army regiment to capture as many Aboriginal men, women and children as it could in the Nepean, Hawkesbury and Grose River valleys. He authorised the soldiers to shoot at any Aboriginal man who refused to surrender. Anyone they killed was to be 'hanged up on trees in conspicuous situations, to strike the survivors with the greater terror'.[32] Just after midnight on 17 April, soldiers under the command of Captain James Wallis massacred at least fourteen Gundungurra men, women and children – seven by shooting, and seven by driving them off the cliff – at the gorge of the Cataract River in northern New South Wales.[33] Macquarie later recorded that the regiment had 'executed the several parts of their instructions entirely to my satisfaction' and rewarded its leaders with extra supplies of alcohol.[34] A survivor, Duall, had taken refuge on the property of a sympathetic settler. He was captured and locked in the Liverpool Gaol for three months before Macquarie summarily banished him to Van Diemen's Land for seven years.[35] Without trial, Macquarie himself had determined Duall's guilt ('having excited and encouraged, and been himself actually concerned with several of his Tribe in committing various atrocious Acts of Robbery, Depredation, and Barbarity, on the Property and Persons of His Majesty's loyal Subjects') and his sentence ('I do hereby remit the Punishment of Death, which his repeated Crimes and Offences had justly merited and incurred').[36]

Trying the un-triable

In the settled areas,[37] the courts' insistence on principles of British fairness – which meant that Aboriginal people who didn't speak English couldn't be tried – produced unhappy results for the settlers. Convinced that they were the peaceful and rightful occupiers, even owners, settlers increasingly demanded that something be done in response to what they perceived as more and more frequent Aboriginal 'attacks'. So, in May 1816, Macquarie issued a Proclamation:

> The Aborigines, or Black Natives of this Colony, have for the last three Years manifested a strong and sanguinary Spirit of ANIMOSITY and HOSTILITY towards the British Inhabitants residing in the Interior and remote Parts of the Territory, and been recently guilty of most atrocious and wanton Barbarities, in indiscriminately murdering Men, Women and Children, from whom they had received no Offence or Provocation.

Aimed at settlers in the grip of a kind of existential panic, its rhetoric was the most preposterous inversion of truth. Macquarie assured his audience that the colonial government 'has heretofore acted with the utmost Lenity and Humanity towards these Natives, in forbearing to punish such wanton Cruelties and Depredations with their merited Severity, thereby hoping to reclaim them from their barbarous Practices, and to conciliate them to the British Government, by affording them Protection, Assistance, and Indulgence ...' In fact, governors had launched no less than seven military offensives against Aboriginal nations, *each* of which had led to the apparently indiscriminate massacre of between seven and thirty Aboriginal people.[38] And yet, because Aboriginal people had 'persevered to the present Day in committing every species of sanguinary Outrage and Depredation on the Lives and Properties of the British Inhabitants, after having been repeatedly cautioned to beware of the Consequences', something had to be seen to be done. Any Aboriginal person found 'armed' within one mile of any town, village or farm, Macquarie declared, would be considered an 'enemy' of the colony and 'treated accordingly'. So would any group of more than six *unarmed* Aboriginal people who came to 'lurk or loiter about' any farm.

Aboriginal people caught committing these 'crimes' couldn't be tried if they didn't speak English, so 'treated accordingly' meant 'shot summarily': Macquarie was adding a sheen of legality to the practices governors had endorsed only tacitly for the first three decades of occupation. The Proclamation also formalised the practice of military aid being provided to settlers to defend them from Aboriginal 'attacks': its legality is questionable, but this seemed to be as close to a declaration of war that a colonial governor ever made.[39] Macquarie also took the first major step toward claiming the jurisdictional dominance of the British criminal law by declaring that the Aboriginal practice 'of fighting and attacking each other on the Plea of inflicting Punishments on Transgressors of their own Customs and Manners, at or near Sydney, and other principal Towns and Settlements in the Colony, shall be henceforth wholly abolished, as a barbarous Custom repugnant to the British Laws ...'[40]

It was amid the general climate of settler fear, which had led to Macquarie's Proclamation, that, at about midday on Tuesday, 6 August 1816, Hannah Russell set off on foot from Paramatta in the direction of her home, about 5 miles away. Hannah was the fifteen-year-old daughter of an emancipated convict, and accompanying her were two settler women.

Shortly after she passed the gate of John Macarthur's farm, she later told the court, a naked ('tribal') Aboriginal man appeared in front of her. She didn't recognise him. 'Where are you going?' he was said to have asked the girl. 'Home,' she replied. 'No, you are not,' he apparently said, before dragging her by the neck into the adjacent bush, beating her head against a tree and raping her. He released her, only to follow her and subject her to further beatings against the stump of a tree. Hannah said another Aboriginal man was urging her assailant to 'kill her, kill her', before Macarthur's stockman approached and the two Aboriginal men fled. The stockman helped her to Macarthur's farm, made sure she wasn't seriously injured, then sent a workman to accompany her home.[41]

This crime – the rape of a white virgin by a 'tribal Aborigine' – triggered outrage in the colony. Two days later, a Dharug man in his mid-twenties known as Daniel Moowattin, or Mow-watty, was arrested, protesting his innocence. Moowattin had achieved fame as the third Aboriginal person – following Bennelong and Yemmerrawanne – to visit England. He was not considered a 'tribal Aborigine'. He'd been raised culturally 'white' in the family of Richard Partridge, a convict who'd 'adopted' him as a young child, and he now worked as a farm labourer. (Partridge would later be known as 'Rice', the colony's notorious hangman.) Moowattin spoke and understood English. Various white witnesses testified as to his acquaintance with British culture and manners, his 'intelligence', his capacity to distinguish right and wrong. While this made it unlikely that Moowattin was the naked man Hannah described, it also meant that, unlike other Indigenous people, he could be tried. The settlers could achieve their justice.

In court, the stockman corroborated Hannah's evidence that she cried for help during the assault, and said he observed bruising on her throat. Hannah, the only eyewitness to her naked assailant's identity, testified that several marks on Moowattin's arm were the same as her assailant's. But the Parramatta constable, James Oldgate, told the court he'd known Moowattin for over a decade, during which time Moowattin had told him that 'he could not live in the bush now, from his being habituated to the white people's mode of living'. But Samuel Marsden said he *had* seen Moowattin 'naked in the woods' since his return from England. In keeping with the English law of the first half of the nineteenth century, Moowattin was prohibited from testifying in his own defence (on the grounds that a defendant's obvious interest in his acquittal created too high a risk of perjury).[42] But he was allowed to be tried, convicted and sentenced by a legal system that prided itself on its fairness. Notwithstanding the obvious deficiencies in the identification evidence, the court found Moowattin guilty and sentenced him to death.[43] He was executed, by hanging, on 1 November 1816.[44]

But most Aboriginal people were 'tribal', and remained practically un-triable. 'Dulmike' was locked up in 1817 after allegedly killing another Eora man, apparently for his own protection. He wasn't tried.[45] Two men – 'Hatherly' and 'Jackie', most likely of the Awabakal nation – became in 1822 the first Aboriginal people to be charged with murder. Their alleged victim was a settler. They both admitted their involvement, though each accused the other of being the instigator. There was no other hard evidence of their participation. The court still couldn't rely on the testimony of Aboriginal witnesses, even when it was self-incriminatory, and found them both not guilty. This had been the outcome Deputy Judge Advocate John Wylde had foreseen when he'd asked the new governor, Thomas Brisbane, whether the trial should have simply been abandoned.[46]

Forgotten laws

Confronted again and again with empirical realities, settler courts found them increasingly difficult to ignore, especially after New South Wales ceased to be a martial state when, in 1823–24, it was granted its first Legislative Council, its first proper Supreme Court, its first attorney-general and, as a consequence of all that, trial by jury. The last was in fact a right to be tried 'by one's peers'. In the early nineteenth century, British common law had long recognised that 'aliens under the protection of the Crown' had a right to expect that six of their *actual* peers – as long as they weren't women, who didn't get full jury rights until well into the twentieth century – would be part of any twelve-person jury empanelled to decide their fate at a criminal trial.[47] Invoking the British Constitution, Dowling, in an 1828 case, asked the attorney-general, Alexander Baxter, how 'Binghi Multi' – a man from Moreton Bay who was accused of spearing a settler – could possibly be tried for murder in a British court with an all-settler jury. To proceed in the absence of six Aboriginal jurors would indeed depart from 'the spirit of the British Constitution', Baxter conceded. But 'in the present untutored and savage state of the natives', he argued, that requirement was 'next to impossibility to effect'. Dowling apparently agreed. He dispensed with the otherwise fundamental trial-by-peers requirement, and adjourned the case so that an interpreter could be arranged.[48]

Many Aboriginal people spoke little or no English, so in the absence of interpreters, British courts committed to the principle of a fair trial were still unable to try them. William Charles Wentworth and Dr Robert Wardell, *The Australian*'s brash and brilliant publishers, attempted to extend the problem of the 'un-tryable Aborigine' to those rare situations in which settlers were charged with crimes against them. Representing a NSW Corps lieutenant charged with murder after he'd executed an Aboriginal man known as 'Jacky' without trial, Wentworth and Wardell told Chief Justice Forbes in 1826 that Aboriginal people were not subjects of the King: they hadn't been conquered, and there had been no treaty. Therefore, they couldn't be tried by settler courts, and settlers couldn't be tried for killing them. Forbes had parried that challenge away, though it was the earliest articulation of an argument that would later pose a real problem for the colonial project.[49]

When Aboriginal people began appearing in courts charged with acts of violence against other Aboriginal people, courts were initially prepared to extend Wentworth and Wardell's reasoning to take account of Aboriginal communities' own systems of dispute resolution. When Robert Barrett (or Ballard) was indicted in 1829 for the murder of Borrondire (known as 'Dirty Dick'),[50] Chief Justice Forbes, with Dowling concurring, discharged Barrett 'for want of jurisdiction':

> The prisoner is accused of the murder of one of his own tribe – one of the original natives of this Country, in the same state as himself – wandering about the country, and living in the uncontrolled freedom of nature. In some way or other he has caused the death of another wild savage … I believe it has been the practice of the Courts of this country, since the Colony was settled, never to interfere with or enter into the quarrels that have taken place between or amongst the natives themselves … [T]he savage is governed by the laws of his tribe – & with these he is content. In point of practice, how could the laws of England be applied to this state of society? By the law of England the party accused is entitled to his full defence. Then how could this beneficent principle be acted upon, where the parties are wholly unacquainted with our language, laws & customs?

Leaving aside the language of noble savagery, this is as good an articulation of the principle of a fair trial in British law that we're likely to come across, in early nineteenth century New South Wales or anywhere. Forbes had been born in Bermuda, where legal pluralism was a fact of life and law, and raised as the grandson of a loyalist in the American south. His particular reasoning was a mixture of pluralism, ignorance and a kind of benevolent racism:

> There is one most important distinction between the savage & civilized state of man, namely that amongst savages there are no magistrates. The savages decide their differences upon a principle of retaliation. They give up no natural rights. This is not merely matter of theory but practice. In the civilized state, man gives up certain natural rights, in exchange for the advantage of social security, & other benefit arising from the institutions of civilized life. It may be a question admitting of doubt, whether any advantages could be gained, without previous preparation, by ingrafting the institutions of our country, upon the natural system which savages have adopted for their own government.

But the conclusion he arrived at was closer to the reality of what was known and observed than any decision of any Australian court since:

> It is known as matter of experience that the savages of this part of the globe, have a mode of dressing wrongs committed amongst themselves, which is perfectly agreeable to their own natures & dispositions, and is productive, amongst themselves, of as much good, as any novel or strange institution which might be imparted to them.[51]

Had these fundamental tenets of British law prevailed, the colonisation of Australia may have looked very different. Instead, courts began looking for – and often found – ways around them so that First Nations 'criminals' *could* be tried and punished, especially for crimes against settlers. The so-called interpreters arranged for 'Tommy, alias Jackey Jackey' – brought to court on charge of murdering a 'quiet, harmless just-keeper' at Bathurst in late 1827 – were Bungaree (who was so enamoured among the settlers that they anointed him 'King of the Blacks') and the circus performer-turned-missionary Lancelot Threlkeld.[52] They seem to have done more cross-examining than interpreting. There were no eyewitnesses, but there was evidence that Tommy had run away as soon as he saw white men on horseback approach him some time after the murder. Even if Tommy wasn't specifically aware of the prohibition against murder in British law, Chief Justice Forbes concluded that he obviously knew he'd offended against some kind of law – 'or why scream out and fly at the approach of a pursuer?' That's not evidence of anything other than fear of the pursuer, but Forbes told the jury to return a guilty verdict. Five minutes later, it did. Two days after that, Tommy hanged.[53]

On the other hand, where a principle of British justice could be invoked *against* Aboriginal people, Forbes invoked it. He refused to allow an Aboriginal person to interpret in the 1834 murder trial of a man known variously as 'Wong-ko-bi-kan' and 'Jackey', because the would-be interpreter, 'being of no religion at all, could not be sworn'. When Jackey asked for a jury of 'black-fellows', Forbes said he didn't have the power to grant it.[54]

The determination of courts to step outside the longstanding limitations imposed by the British Constitution to find ways of convicting Aboriginal defendants wasn't a simple function of judicial bias. After he'd been 'interpreting' in criminal trials for about a decade, Lancelot Threlkeld was able to clearly see the link between British justice and settler violence. In November 1837, Threlkeld had – with the assistance of two Aboriginal people – painstakingly pieced together the defence of a man called Wombarty, who was from the remote Port Macquarie region and spoke a language with which the settlers were entirely unfamiliar. But when it came to his trial on charges of murdering four white men as they slept, James Dowling, by then chief justice, refused to allow the Aboriginal interpreters to be sworn. As a result, Wombarty was discharged.[55] The record isn't clear about Wombarty's fate after that, but we can surmise it from a report Threlkeld wrote the next month. For many settlers, Threlkeld observed, summary 'justice' – or revenge – was the only practical solution to the problem of the 'un-triable Aborigine': a solution that 'will surely, secretly and speedily annihilate the Aborigines from the face of this land'. 'Thus that just and equitable principle which declares that "The Aborigines are subject to and under the protection of British Law,"' a frustrated Threlkeld concluded, 'becomes a mere Legal Fiction ... and the strictness of the administration of the Law becomes the height of injustice to all.'[56]

British subjects and settler crimes

The Colonial Office in London wanted the theory of peaceful settlement based on respectful relations with the 'natives' to hold, and repeatedly sent orders to the effect that all British subjects – including Aboriginal people – were to be treated equally and fairly. But there were practical difficulties in the colonies that London preferred to ignore. Despite the theory of Crown sovereignty preferred by parliaments and courts, Aboriginal people did *in fact* answer to their own laws and customs. Empirical reality belied the colonists' fantasies. When Aboriginal people acted in ways that weren't sanctioned by their own laws, their own societies arranged consequences, including punishment. In practice, colonists often left internecine disputes to Aboriginal societies to sort out, and only tended to intervene when the colonists' lives and interests were threatened. But this reality increasingly did not marry with London's theory of 'settlement'.

Even on the internal logic of the colonists' justice system it made little sense, in most cases, to involve criminal courts: barriers of language, comprehension, culture and different legal systems meant that it was very difficult for judges and magistrates (assuming they wished to remain within the constraints of their law) to satisfy themselves that Aboriginal defendants had both the *capacity* to participate in British court proceedings and the requisite *intention* to commit crimes against British law. Unless a person has internalised a law and the system within which it sits, 'law' is little more than its enforcers' coercive power.[57]

Each trial – aborted, purported or actual – of an Aboriginal defendant during this period took place within a broader social context that was systematically and methodically ignored by the judge who presided over it. That context was the often-brutal frontier violence perpetrated by agents of the settler state, or by settlers acting privately. Most of this violence was illegal by the standards of settler law, though few colonists were ever charged.

There were exceptions. The first settlers to be charged and tried for murdering Aboriginal people were Edward Powell – a constable – and a posse of local farmers. In 1799, in the notorious Hawkesbury region, Powell and posse killed two Aboriginal boys. The boys had possibly slept in the company of another farmer, Hodgkinson, the night before he himself was killed, apparently by Aboriginal assailants. The boys denied any involvement, but the settlers wanted revenge. They led the boys into the bush, tied their hands behind their backs, stabbed both with a cutlass and shot one.[58]

On one view, this was simply 'summary justice' in action. But Hunter accurately described the murders as 'shocking' and 'barbarous', and convened a court in accordance with Phillip's original instructions.[59] Powell and his posse admitted to killing the boys, but claimed their actions were justified on the grounds of self-defence, which was patently preposterous. The deputy judge advocate, Richard Dore, and the six Corps officers, who collectively constituted the bench, unanimously found them guilty of murder. It was an unpopular finding. They wanted express permission from London before sentencing them to death. While waiting for the Colonial Office to respond, Governor Hunter let them go home to their farms. When the response eventually came, in the form of a letter from Lord Hobart dated January 1802, Hunter had been replaced by King. Hobart directed King to make it clearly understood that 'on future occasions, any instance of injustice or wanton cruelty towards the natives will be punished with the utmost severity of the law.' Powell and posse, though, were 'proper objects of His Majesty's mercy'. So they were pardoned.[60]

The way in which settler justice dealt with Edward Powell became a template. Far from being 'punished with the utmost severity', settlers – in the rare instances they appeared in courts for killing Aboriginal people – found institutions willing to sanction or forgive them. This was a peculiarly Australian practice, officially unsanctioned by the Colonial Office or by the law. The *Sydney Gazette* regularly reported on Aboriginal deaths at the hands of settlers, often adding only the thinnest veneer of justification. In the moral universe the settlers inhabited, they were compelled to shoot Aboriginal people if they so much as touched a spear, or ran away.

But the institutions of settler law always insisted they were fair. John Wylde, the colony's last deputy judge advocate before Forbes's arrival as chief justice, 'wished it to be properly and lastingly impressed in the minds of all', the *Sydney Gazette* recorded following the 1822 trial of Seth Hawker, 'that the aboriginal natives have as much right to expect justice at the hand of the British law, as Europeans; and that such ever would be the case ...' Hawker was overseer at the Illawarra estate of a NSW Corps captain. Awoken one night by barking dogs, he'd seen what looked like a person running away near a corn field. He fired, and didn't investigate until the next morning, when he discovered the figure he'd shot was an Aboriginal woman who'd been carrying two nets full of shelled maize. Her body had by then been mauled by dogs. Hawker was charged, but Wylde wouldn't have a bar of it. He led much of the testimony from witnesses in court, asking them to agree that the local 'natives' had been 'troublesome', that they'd been warned about the consequences of stealing food, and that Hawker had only fired into the night because he'd been in fear of his life. It was a sham trial. Hawker was merely protecting the captain's property. Not guilty.[61]

Settlers, soldiers, police and judges knew what British law said about self-defence: it provided a lawful excuse for homicide where the killer was in genuine fear of life or limb, but only where the killer's act was proportionate to the threat they perceived. They also knew about other justifiable homicides, such as to prevent a prisoner's escape (though only where the imprisonment itself was lawful). Invariably, then, settler participants – including juries – in trials would make sure the evidence fit the defence. Aboriginal people generally weren't allowed to testify, and when they were they weren't believed, so conspiracy was rather easy to effect – especially where nobody seemed to have a problem with the idea that guns were a proportionate response to spears. When a posse of five settlers pled 'not guilty' to manslaughter after killing three Aboriginal women in 1824, their lawyer argued self-defence and lawful justification (on the basis of Macquarie's 1816 Proclamation). Chief Justice Forbes told the jury the evidence didn't support these arguments, but the all-settler jury acquitted the posse anyway.[62] Settlers continued to use and abuse the notion of self-defence well after the Supreme Court added a facade of independence to criminal proceedings after 1824.

Efforts by the institutions of settler justice to simultaneously protect settler interests *and* convince themselves they were just and fair reached farcical levels. When his watchman went missing, settler John Jamieson became convinced that an Aboriginal man known as 'Hole-in-the-Book' had killed and eaten him. Jamieson shot and killed Hole-in-the-Book and was charged with murder. When the watchman showed up in court, very much alive and uneaten, Justice John Stephen asked the jury to consider whether it was reasonable for Jamieson to have suspected Hole-in-the-Book to be Preston's murderer, notwithstanding the fact that Preston was not dead. Of course it was reasonable, the jury said, and found Jamieson not guilty. 'It should never be understood for a moment,' Justice Stephen then pontificated in the common refrain, 'that the natives are not equally under the protection of the laws with any of His Majesty's subjects in the Colony.'[63]

This pattern – of settler courts contorting the evidence to ensure settlers escaped punishment for what were clearly very serious crimes against their own law – continued throughout the century. Largely, for the most terrible crimes, nobody was ever charged. The University of Newcastle's *Colonial Frontier Massacres in Australia, 1788–1930* project shows an Australian map dotted with dozens and dozens of massacres, with particularly thick groupings in the Kimberley and the Top End, the Cairns coast, and especially western Victoria, northern New South Wales and southern Queensland. But there is practically no reference to these massacres in the court records of this period. If this scale is too large to comprehend, consider the teenage girl, found naked and crucified to an iron bar at Albert River in 1890. Nobody was ever charged.[64]

And in the few cases where charges *were* actually laid against white people, they were either withdrawn by prosecutors before trial or resulted in 'not guilty' verdicts by (all-white) juries. Even in the rare cases of conviction, there were twists in the tale. When an Irish-born settler, Lockier Burges, was sentenced to five years' prison in 1872 for murdering Aboriginal man Muekellwellyer, by shooting him in the back, there was outrage on the frontier.[65] Seven years earlier, Burges had participated in the La Grange massacre of up to twenty Yawuru and Karajarri people, for which nobody was charged.[66] Maitland Brown, who had led the La Grange massacre and was a local justice of the peace at the time of Burges' sentencing, wrote to a Perth newspaper in defence of Burges, arguing that settlers on the frontier had the right to act as judge, jury and executioner for 'savages' on the basis that the government could not protect them. A petition to the Colonial Secretary was successful in reducing Burges's prison sentence to one year.[67]

The handful of exceptions to the general rule include the 1820 trial, conviction and execution of the convict John Kirby, and that of seven colonists found to be responsible for the massacre at Myall Creek in June 1838.[68] There's no obvious difference between that massacre, which killed at least twenty-eight unarmed people, and the many before it and after it. Just six months before Myall Creek, for instance, a group of police troops opened fire on a large number of trapped Aboriginal people at Waterloo Creek in New South Wales and hacked with their swords those who tried to flee. The police then pursued survivors into other camps, and perpetrated massacres there too. They admitted to killing forty Aboriginal 'warriors', though the actual death toll is conceivably much higher. Despite concern from the

Colonial Office and an official inquiry the following year, no charges were ever laid.[69] The Waterloo Creek massacre occurred exactly fifty years to the day after Phillip's arrival at Port Jackson, and is one of the many reasons 26 January is a wildly inappropriate date for national celebration.[70] And if the Myall Creek trials resulted in a kind of justice – with the executions of seven colonists – historian Bruce Elder observes its legacy: that 'nearly all further massacres in New South Wales went unrecorded' by the press, and settlers increasingly turned to poison instead of pistols to ensure that government authorities never found out about frontier murders.[71]

Cunning justice

Despite, and often regardless of, what the institutional agents of colonisation told themselves about the niceties of British justice, colonialisation meant the claiming of sovereignty over land. *How* that was done mattered less than *that* it was done. The result was a confused legal culture that prevaricated between maintaining both the theory of peaceful British settlement and the 'rights' of settlers engaged in undeclared frontier warfare. The practical difficulties of bringing Aboriginal 'criminals' in from the frontier for trial meant that pastoralists were given effective carte blanche to enact swift and certain summary justice – often in the form of executions and, as we've seen, massacres. Obviously this can't be called 'equal treatment' of 'British subjects' under the common law.

Until the 1830s, there was a practical reason why Aboriginal people outside the settled areas were rarely brought to court: policing was practically impossible outside the settled districts. But Britain's rapid industrialisation during the 1820s drove population growth in the colonies, and its growing demand for Australian wool drove enterprising pastoralists out beyond what had hitherto been the boundaries of settlement. Governor Darling in 1826 and again in 1829 declared the 'limits of settlement' – beyond which settlers could not rely on the state and its police for their protection – but he was sandbagging a flood.[72] But from the 1830s, policing was increasingly deployed at the frontier, and was often integral to the colonial land-grabs.[73] And it was of a qualitatively different order to the 'bobby' style police who kept order in the settled districts. Indigenous men were recruited into the Native Police Corps that 'policed' the Port Phillip region and throughout Victoria after 1837, often by conducting punitive raids against Aboriginal people and murdering large numbers.[74]

Native Police units were created in Western Australia (in 1840), what became Queensland (in 1848) and in the Northern Territory (in 1884) which did much the same thing. The Queensland unit is perhaps the most notorious.[75] Not only was there no prosecution of these paramilitary frontier-enforcement units. They were often celebrated by settlers, at least on the frontier.

I'll recount just one story here, but there are dozens of others. In February 1872, survivors of a shipwrecked brig, the *Maria*, washed ashore near the mouth of a river on Queensland's Cassowary Coast. By then, the notorious paramilitary force, Queensland's Native Police, had been raining terror on Aboriginal people on behalf of European occupiers for the better part of three decades. When Mamu men found the shipwrecked white men they killed ten of them. A punitive Native Police expedition murdered eight Aboriginal people in retaliation, but the local police magistrate didn't think that number was high enough. He despatched a second expedition. This one was led by Robert Johnstone, newly restored to his earlier post of acting sub-inspector after a stint as manager of a sugar plantation.

Johnstone's reputation since joining the Native Police in about 1867 was brutal, but the terror he inflicted up and down the Cassowary Coast in March of 1872 – from Cardwell to Cooper Point – was of another order. He and his troopers, along with armed sailors and other volunteers, stalked the coast for any sign of Aboriginal camps and murdered everyone they found – including women and children. Contemporary reports make it difficult not to imagine Johnstone as a kind of state-sanctioned nineteenth-century Anders Breivik, zealously hunting down anything that moved. This extreme violence wasn't hidden. Newspapers reported that Johnstone's expedition killed ninety-three people; the actual number could be lower – or much higher. The sheer savagery of Johnstone's serial killing reached colonial authorities in London, who ordered an investigation. The Queensland government duly performed one, but found Johnstone's psychotic rampage justified on the basis that it was actually the locals who were 'savage and treacherous'. Needless to say, Johnstone wasn't charged.

The following year, Johnstone returned to head a further revenge attack following another episode of frontier violence. It was during this campaign that Johnstone wrote the words which lured Innisfail's founders: 'A most glorious view appeared – noble reach of fresh water, studded with blacks with their canoes and catamarans, others on the sandy beaches; deep blue fresh water expanding to an imposing breadth.' An Irishman, Thomas Fitzgerald, arrived in 1880 with a coffle of blackbirded South Sea Islanders to begin a sugar planta-tion, and the town was born. Originally called Johnstone River, it was renamed Geraldton (after Fitzgerald) in 1883 and then Innisfail (the name Fitzgerald gave to his property) in 1910. Johnstone became a magistrate and spent his twilight years writing his memoirs, *Spinifex and Wattle*, which was serialised in *The Queenslander* newspaper between 1903 and 1905. Occasionally he defended his reputation against the accusations that had dogged his career since it began.[76] The river which runs through Innisfail still bears Johnstone's name, as did Innisfail's local council until it was merged in 2008.

In the experience of Aboriginal people, the colonists' law must have seemed particularly cunning: it was able to deny their own laws and sov-ereignty on the basis that they were not 'advanced' or 'developed' enough as a race *and*, at the same time, to punish individual members of that race on the basis that they were 'advanced' enough to be imputed to have auto-matic knowledge of the laws that had been imposed on them.[77] Tricky. The practical realities were evident to any settlers willing to observe them, as did William Charles Wentworth's *The Australian*, which argued in February 1834 that it was 'unreasonable, oppressive and impolitic' – indeed, 'absurd' – for the New South Wales authorities to consider trying two Aboriginal men, Quart Pot and Numbo, who had been remanded in custody for weeks for the alleged murder of another of their own tribe. 'They do not ask our interference,' the editorial continued. 'They have their various modes of pun-ishment.'[78] In the same vein, Wiwar (or We-war), an Aboriginal man who was convicted of murder after he killed another Aboriginal man in accor-dance with Aboriginal law, told public servant and future Congregationalist minister Henry Trigg in 1842:

> If a white man kills a white man, we never interfere. Some time back, the white men killed many of the natives and the Governor took no notice. Now, why should the Governor take any notice of me, if I kill a fellow native, that steals my wife, or kills my brother, when it is accord-ing to our law?[79]

Wiwar was sentenced to life imprisonment. By at least the 1830s, judges knew that to recognise Aboriginal laws and punishments would be effec-tively to recognise Aboriginal sovereignty – and this would pose too great a problem for the colonial project.

'British justice', then, meant remarkably different things to a Supreme Court judge in a capital city, a farmer on the colonial frontier and an Indigenous person who had survived a massacre of their family and community. The same pattern was evident all around the country: Europeans would arrive and commence an occupation, often kidnapping local children for labour and girls and women for sex, or simply shooting people to 'disperse' them from the land; the locals would resist or retaliate, which the colonists would use as a pretext for what were often genocidal reprisals. While most colonists subscribed to a doctrine of 'forward defence', they nearly always saw actual self-defence by Aboriginal people as an outrage.[80]

For a long time, the sheer brutality of the frontier violence inflicted by the invading British was difficult to believe, for those colonists who never witnessed it, their institutions and their descendants. Significant remnants of this disbelief persist today. That's largely because the frontier violence is inconsistent with the internal rules, practices and ideologies of British, then 'British-Australian' and ultimately 'Australian' society. British culture and law was fair and based in reason; the culture of 'natives' was savage and brutish. All kinds of justifications were trotted out to rationalise or excuse settler atrocities. Queensland's 'protection' commissioners concluded in 1875 that the colony's Native Mounted Police was a civil force deployed 'in what were really military operations'. But without an armed force, the commissioners reasoned, 'the frontier settlement could not be maintained'.[81]

SOVEREIGNTY

How Aboriginal law disappeared as if by magic

A lawyer is standing at the bar table in the Katherine Local Court. It's early 2018. He's lived mainly in southern capitals, and arrived in Katherine some weeks ago to work for NAAJA. He's my newest colleague. On the bench is Elisabeth Armitage, who was appointed judge in 2013 after two decades working as a prosecutor and as counsel assisting the Territory's coroner. A police prosecutor sits to the lawyer's right. I'm sitting in one of the plastic bucket chairs behind them, waiting for my own cases to be called on.

My colleague's client isn't sitting behind him. He's in Darwin, on remand at the new Berrimah 'super-prison'. It's a three-hour drive to Katherine on a really good run, and much longer in a prison van, so prisoners and remandees who have to physically appear in Katherine are typically woken up well before 4 a.m. It's also expensive for the justice department to transport people down and back up again. So if it's at all possible for a person to appear in court via video link, that's what happens. Nobody's quite sure whether judges find it easier to sentence defendants to prison when they appear in two dimensions rather than three, but it seems likely.[1]

After introducing the man on the screen, the lawyer explains to Armitage that his client would be entering a plea of guilty. The police prosecutor withdraws one of the charges, reads out the remaining ones, and Armitage asks the defendant what his plea is. 'Guilty,' he confirms in the Aboriginal-accented English common in the continent's northern regions. It's the only word the defendant will say for the entire proceeding. The lawyer sits down, and the prosecutor stands and reads the summary of the offending circumstances onto the record. 'Any priors?' Armitage asks. 'Yes, your Honour.' The prosecutor flicks to the back of his brief, pulls the last few pages from the stapled bundle and hands them to the court officer, who in turn gives them to Armitage. She studies them for a few moments before looking up at my colleague, signalling that it's his turn now.

The lawyer begins his plea in mitigation. As he explains the circumstances of the offence he hits the usual notes. His client is young. He's remorseful. He's pleading guilty early. Then, almost in passing, he says something about one of the charges – a driving disqualified charge – that he doesn't expect to be controversial. 'My client was under a strict obligation to ensure he was at Ceremony, so even though he knew he shouldn't be driving under whitefella law —'

Armitage interrupts him. She knows this lawyer is new to the Territory, and it's her responsibility as much as anyone's to ensure that he gets a few things straight from the beginning. 'There is no "whitefella" law. The law that operates in the Northern Territory, and in this courtroom, is law that applies equally to everybody. Is that understood?' Like most judges and magistrates, Armitage slips easily into the role of teacher or parent to naughty children, who are – variously – defendants, their lawyers, and sometimes prosecutors. My colleague responds in the only way he can. 'Yes, your Honour.' There's no gain in debating the point. His job is simply to get the best sentencing outcome for his client, and arguing with a judge on a point of history or philosophy isn't the best way of achieving that end.

The concept Armitage is drawing on is *sovereignty*: the power to govern, to make laws, to set the rules about who's in and who's out and what happens here. A sovereign power asserts a monopoly over the question of who is and isn't allowed to use violence. There's only one criminal law of universal application, because there's only one source of law-making power: the Crown. (The Crown is physically in England, though since 1953 we've also called it 'Australian'.[2])

I scan the room. None of the people in any position of authority – Armitage, the police prosecutor, my colleague, the other lawyers waiting their turn, the police officers moonlighting as court security – is Indigenous, though the vast majority of the defendants who are brought before the court for judgement and 'justice' are. There are equal opportunity programs trying (and succeeding, at a glacial pace) to increase the numbers of Aboriginal court staff, police officers, lawyers and judges. But would this make an iota of actual difference to the law that's being applied?

Probably not. James Forman Jr is a former public defender in Washington DC, the US's equivalent to a Legal Aid lawyer in Australia. The son of parents who met in the Student Nonviolent Coordinating Committee, one of the main civil rights organisations in the 1960s, Forman became a public defender because, he writes in his book *Locking Up Our Own*, it was 'the unfinished work of the civil rights movement'. He begins the book by recalling an appearance he made on behalf of a fifteen-year-old client, Brandon. Both he and Brandon were black. So was the judge, Curtis Walker. After Walker sentenced Brandon to six months' prison, he was escorted to the court's cells. 'It wasn't only Brandon and the other young men in the cell block who were black,' Forman writes. 'So was everybody in the courtroom – not just the judge, but the court reporter, the bailiff and the juvenile prosecutor. So was the police officer who had arrested Brandon, not to mention the police chief and the mayor. Even the building we were in – the H. Carl Moultrie I Courthouse, named after the city's first black chief judge – was a reminder of the African American influence on DC's legal system.'[3]

Locking Up Our Own is a searching examination of why, even in jurisdictions where practically everyone involved in the criminal justice system is black, prisons and court cells are full of young African Americans. In Australia, it's highly unlikely that police forces and courthouses will ever employ a majority of Aboriginal people, who constitute between 3 and 4 per cent of Australia's total population, and 30 per cent of the Northern Territory's population. But even if they did, it's very likely that Aboriginal judges would also be 'locking up their own'. When NAAJA's principal lawyer, David Woodroffe, descendant of the Jingili Modburra clan group, was appointed the Northern Territory's first Indigenous judge in July 2022, NAAJA's chair, Colleen Rosas, expressed understandable pride. 'We've got it, we've got this black judge up there,' she told the ABC. 'It's just a wonderful thing to be happening.'[4] But after a decade of trying to keep Aboriginal people out of prison, now he'll be ordering them in. Woodroffe will still be applying the system of crime and punishment that was introduced here, along with rabbits and cane toads.

I glance up at the man on the screen. The quizzical expression on his face suggests he may not even be hearing much of what's happening to him down in Katherine, through the tinny speakers throwing whatever is being picked up by courtroom microphones into the echoey environs of his cell. He grew up mainly in Ngukurr, formerly the Roper River Mission, about five hours' drive along mostly dirt roads east of Katherine. Despite the actions of the Church Missionary Society and the Eastern and African Cold Storage

Company, which drove people off their traditional lands, Ngukurr continues to be substantially governed by traditional arrangements, with laws, rules and norms enforced (where not prohibited by police, Darwin or Canberra) by families, communities and Elders. In his world, making sure he's meeting the obligations of the community he lives in tends to trump the more abstract obligations he has to the driving laws of the Territory, which were made in remote Darwin without any input from him or his community.

That there is no such thing as 'whitefella' law – that there's only the one law which applies to everyone equally – is a fiction that all judges and magistrates must perpetuate. It's a fiction that's backed by the overwhelming power of the settler state, but it's a fiction nonetheless.[5] It's possible that Armitage, before she was appointed to the bench, didn't subscribe to it herself. In 2005, when she was working as a prosecutor, Armitage contributed a brief article to *Balance*, the NT Law Society's magazine, describing her role in the Supreme Court's first-ever sitting in Yarralin, 380 kilometres southwest of Katherine. 'I found it a little challenging to appear in that small community,' Armitage wrote then. My emphases: 'Imagine the effect *our* Supreme Court must have on Indigenous persons arriving from communities to face *our* justice.'[6]

The King v Jack Congo Murrell

Just before Christmas in 1835, altercations between two pairs of Aboriginal men occurred on the highway between Richmond and Windsor, in the Hawkesbury region. Jack Congo Murrell (allegedly) hit Jabinguy on the head with a 'tomahawk' in a drunken assault and killed him; and George Bummaree killed Pat Cleary as a payback killing in (apparent) accordance with Aboriginal law. There was an inquest, and both Murrell and Bummaree were committed for trial, in part because white witnesses saw what happened and were shocked and appalled.

It seemed that everyone wanted Murrell and Bummaree tried, including Bungaree's son Bowen, a young man already 'well absorbed' into colonial society and who described the dead men as his 'brothers-in-law'.[7] But when Murrell was brought before the Supreme Court in early February and indicted for murder, the lawyer appointed to represent him – Sidney Stephen – reminded Chief Justice Forbes of the general position colonial courts had taken on violence committed between Aboriginal people.

Stephen had grown up in the law, and his uncle and cousin had been prominent in the movement against slavery.[8]

The scene was set in the Supreme Court for a definitive statement of settler law concerning Aboriginal 'crimes', and whether they could be lawfully tried in British courts. Stephen urged that, like the case against Robert Barrett in 1829, Murrell's should be thrown out. Before it was occupied in the name of King George III, Stephen said, the territory called New South Wales 'was inhabited by tribes of native blacks, who were regulated and governed by usages and customs of their own from time immemorial'. Moreover, they 'have continued to be, and still are regulated and governed by such usages and customs, and not by the laws of Great Britain'. Stephen said that Murrell simply was not a subject of the King, and nor was he answerable to any of the King's laws. Rather, he 'can and may be made to stand punishment' for his crime according to the practices and customs of his own people.

'It is an ingenious plea,' Forbes acknowledged, perhaps because it applied his own reasoning from seven years earlier. But memories were short, and the pace of colonial settlement fast. As Sydney developed, consciousness of its frontier origins receded. Forbes's decision in Barrett's case had scandalised many settlers, and those who agreed with it lamented its consequences, which amounted to settlers taking the law into their own hands. Echoing Forbes, the *Sydney Herald* described Stephen's plea as 'ingenious and puzzling',[9] though it was really just a variation on an assumption that had been common only a few years earlier. When he returned to the bench the next day – a Saturday – Forbes said he wasn't prepared to dismiss the charge, but thought the Legislative Council should consider the problems raised by Stephen's plea. Still wanting the charge thrown out, Stephen asked Forbes to have his two judicial colleagues, James Dowling and William Burton, join him on the bench.[10]

When they did, Stephen took his argument to its logical conclusion, and indeed came closer to the true history of what had taken place on the continent than Australian law has ever come, before or since. Referring to Blackstone's famous distinction between 'conquest' and 'settlement', Stephen said the Hawkesbury region was neither 'desert' nor 'uncultivated'.[11] So it couldn't have been legally 'settled' under British law. Nor could it be lawfully described as 'conquered' because Britain had never declared war. And Aboriginal people had never ceded the land. Rather, it was a country 'which had a population having manners and customs of their own, and we had come to reside among them'.

Stephen's next sentence is still breathtaking in its implications: 'Therefore, in point of strictness and analogy to our law, we were bound to obey their laws, not they to obey ours.'

If the prevailing theory of settlement meant anything, Stephen went on, Aboriginal people 'would have a right to come into the courts, and sue for any property they might possess'. Yet they had no such right. 'The natives were not protected by [British] laws; they were not admitted witnesses in courts of justice; they could not claim any civil rights; they could not obtain recovery of, or compensation for, those lands which had been torn from them, and which they had held probably for centuries.'[12] The settlers' story had to be false.

Unlike Forbes, Dowling, Burton and John Kinchela – the attorney-general who was prosecuting Murrell and Bummaree – Sidney Stephen has (at the time of writing) no entry in either the *Australian Dictionary of Biography* or Wikipedia.[13] Stephen's plea to the Supreme Court is in no collected anthology of great Australian speeches. It has been practically forgotten.

Kinchela responded with the same circular logic that the Supreme Court had been using since 1824. Murrell was charged with a murder allegedly committed 'within the jurisdiction of the court'. Stephen's argument – that Murrell was not subject to British laws – 'could not be admitted', because 'the laws of Great Britain did not recognise any independent power to exist in a British territory'.[14] For Kinchela, New South Wales belonged to Britain because Britain's government and parliament said so.

Had justices Forbes, Dowling and Burton agreed with Sidney Stephen, it's likely the case would have gone to the Privy Council, where arguments based on the old ideas of Locke and Joseph Banks and the supreme right of the Crown under God may yet have conspired to reassert Britain's sovereignty over New South Wales. But they did not agree with him. William Burton, trained in London and fresh from a judicial stint in the Cape Colony, preferred the old ideas to the observable realities. 'The various tribes had not attained at the first settlement of the English people [to such] numbers and civilisation, and to such a form of government and laws, as to be entitled to be recognised as so many sovereign states governed by laws of their own.' Also, the British parliament had designated the land as British. And anyway, the Supreme Court had already been trying and even executing Aboriginal people for twelve years.[15] If Stephen was right, these actions were unlawful and barbaric. And since Britain wasn't barbaric, Stephen had to be wrong.

In the seven years since Forbes had thrown out Barrett's murder charge, ideas about the kind of jurisdiction that 'British' colonies ought to claim over colonial territories had dramatically shifted. In 1836, Forbes put his position even more starkly than Burton had. At the time Cook 'took possession' of the colony in 1770, the people already living here just weren't advanced enough to be considered 'free and independent tribes'. 'They had no sovereignty,' he declared.[16] Murrell was ordered to stand trial.

For its part, the jury failed to convict Murrell. We can't know why, but eight days before the trial in May, an anonymous correspondent – was it Sidney Stephen himself? – wrote a long letter to the *Sydney Herald* pointing out the various and obvious flaws in Forbes and Burton's reasoning. The main argument in favour of the decision to try Murrell 'is that the act was committed in a territory possessed by the English', the letter said. 'But how was the possession of this territory obtained by them?' The writer wondered whether the judges' reasoning was not perhaps a rationalisation of the maxim 'that might may overcome right'. The writer pointed out that none of the judges had made any effort to quantify the level of 'strength and government' a people should reach before their rights as a nation could be recognised in British law; nor had they explained just how and why the Aboriginal nations failed to meet this standard. Moreover: 'How can he have a fair trial?' Would there be Aboriginal witnesses? Aboriginal jurors? 'Suppose a black nation were to invade England and they were to put to death one of us for an act done to one of our fellow-countrymen, which would not have been capital with us,' the writer asked rhetorically. 'Should we not think it barbarous?'[17] Perhaps the unassailable logic of the letter had some effect on the jurors. Murrell was acquitted and walked free, and Kinchela dropped the associated charge against Bummaree.

Aftermath

In notes he made during Murrell's case, Justice William Burton contrasted the self-evident fairness and reason of British laws with the 'practices' of Murrell's community, which were 'consistent with a state of the grossest darkness and irrational superstition' and 'founded entirely upon principles ... of vindication for personal wrongs' and 'the wildest most indiscriminatory notions of revenge'.[18] Again, it's difficult to imagine a more glaring inversion of the truth. Just three months later, Thomas Mitchell and his party of 'Australia Felix' explorers – that was the name he famously gave to lush country in western Victoria – would shoot dead perhaps twenty Kureinji or Dadi – maybe more – as they fled in terror across the Murray River, Mitchell's men 'pursuing and shooting as many as they could'.[19]

Despite his popularity, Mitchell was hauled before a Legislative Council committee after the massacre. Initially, though, not even Wentworth's *Australian* newspaper, with its liberal/reformist editorial line, was prepared to condemn him: the 'expenditure of life' was simply 'an every-day occurrence in the annals of colonisation', and may have been 'a necessary consequence of his journey'.[20] Predictably, Mitchell claimed the kind of pre-emptive self-defence frequently pled by those who led massacres on the frontier. The committee wasn't satisfied with Mitchell's justification, but it ultimately recommended no punishment. Mitchell was later excoriated by the *Sydney Gazette* after Whig governor Richard Bourke, more liberal and humane than most of those in positions of NSW authority at the time, published the committee's proceedings.[21] But this hardly damaged Mitchell, even when he retreated to London, where the Whigs' select committee – established in 1837 at the request of the recently formed Aboriginal Protection Society – was investigating allegations of maltreatment of Aboriginal people in Australia.[22] Untroubled, Mitchell published his Australia Felix journals and returned as Australia's most famous explorer.

Bad law

It was the Supreme Court's 1836 rationale, therefore, rather than Murrell's acquittal, that prevailed.[23] But was the law expounded by justices Forbes, Dowling and Burton even good law at the time?

The first maxim they relied on was that Cook had taken 'possession', on behalf of the King of Britain, of Port Jackson and much of the east coast in 1770. This is still what most history books and legal texts teach. If it's true, then there is no question of whether Britain has sovereignty over Australia, either in 1836 or in 2022. In his books *The Law of the Land* (1987), *Aboriginal Sovereignty* (1996) and *Truth-Telling* (2021), Henry Reynolds examines what it meant, in eighteenth-century English and international law, to 'take possession' of a land. One component was discovery. But Cook

and Banks could clearly see that the Australian coastline had people living on it. In 1625, the Dutch lawyer Hugo Grotius wrote that land already
peopled could not again be 'discovered', even where 'the Possessor should
be a Wicked Man, or have false Notions of GOD, or be of a stupid mind'.
There are limits to a word's meaning. Fundamental to the right of discovery was that it applied, fairly obviously, 'to those Places only which are not
[already] appropriated'.[24]

There were only two ways in which Cook's secret instructions of
1768 authorised him to take possession of any land he came across. One
depended upon him finding that land 'uninhabited'. Clearly that did not
apply to Port Jackson or to the rest of the Australian coast. British and
international law, like their Roman progenitor, had long recognised that
even hunter-gatherers and nomads had rights in the land they lived on.
'They are the natural, and in the strictest sense of the word, the legal possessors of the several Regions they inhabit,' Lord Morton had informed
Cook before the *Endeavour* set sail.[25] Cook's only other authorised option
to take possession was 'with the consent of the Natives'. No consent was
given. Did Cook, therefore, take possession?

If he did, it could only have been to assert a right against other European
nations, and *not* against Australia's First Nations. Australian courts consistently got this important nuance wrong. Four years before the NSW
Supreme Court decided *Murrell*, the United States Supreme Court had
considered the very question of how a land claim based on the doctrine
of 'discovery' related to Indigenous nations. Samuel Worcester, missionary to the Cherokee, was among eleven settlers charged under an 1830
Georgian law prohibiting white men from living on First Nations land without a license. Worcester argued that the law, while purporting to protect the
Cherokee Nation, in fact encroached upon its sovereignty: surely, he said, it
was for the Cherokee to decide what happened on their land. The Supreme
Court's chief justice, John Marshall, agreed. The United States had inherited
all the rights of the British Crown. But the Crown's rights did not extend
to the right to take possession of First Nations land without consent, or to
overwhelm their laws. Therefore, the state of Georgia had no right to make
a law that sought to exert control over what happened on Cherokee land.
Worcester v Georgia (1832) was one of the earliest cases recognising what
became known in the United States as the doctrine of 'tribal sovereignty',
which became the basis of self-rule in the latter part of twentieth century.[26]

No such doctrine was ever recognised by Australian courts. Yet, the idea that Cook had taken 'possession' of anything at all was highly questionable, given that he'd simply bunny-hopped up the eastern coast for a few weeks before leaving for good. For discovery to amount to the acquisition of sovereignty, wrote Grotius, it had to be accompanied by *actual* possession. On an island he called 'Possession' – actually Bedanug in the Torres Strait – Cook stuck a pole in the ground and hoisted a British flag. He told his journal that, as a result, 'the whole Eastern Coast ... together with all the Bays, Harbours[,] Rivers and Islands' along it were now possessions of King George III under the name 'New South Wales'. But if sticking a flag in the ground meant legally claiming the land around it, then apparently the Dutch had 'owned' Tasmania since 1642 (after Abel Tasman hoisted a flag at what is now the Prince of Wales Bay) and France had taken the whole western half of the Australian continent in 1772, when François de Saint-Alouarn unveiled the tricolour at Turtle Bay, on the north end of Dirk Hartog Island. These claims were merely par for the course in the European age of arrogant expansion. The Treaty of Tordesillas, signed by Spain and Portugal in 1494, had ludicrously purported to assign the whole of the Australian continent's eastern coast to Spain.[27]

'The whole Eastern Coast'? It was a preposterous idea, even in 1770. 'What the discoverer's state gained,' explained the scholar Mark Lindley later in *The Acquisition and Government of Backward Territory in International Law* (1926), was merely 'the right, as against other European powers, to *take steps* which were appropriate to the [later] acquisition of the territory in question.'[28] This is what is known as the assertion of 'external' sovereignty. But 'internal' sovereignty – the authority to make binding laws on inhabitants *inside* the claimed territory – is another matter entirely.

This leads to the next of the NSW Supreme Court's 1836 propositions: that steps *were* taken, just eighteen years later, when Arthur Phillip and his First Fleet arrived to take actual possession. But Lindley's next sentence provides a qualifier: 'What those steps were,' he continued, 'would depend on whether there was already a native population in possession of the territory ... ' Getting the informed consent of a native population was crucial, even in the British law of the late eighteenth century. Reynolds points out that instructions to this effect were standard. Cook's own 1776 instructions for his third and final voyage – which brought him to his grim fate in Hawaii – also included the need to gain 'the consent of the natives'.

The House of Commons Committee on Transportation wrote explicitly in 1785 of the hope that land could be rented from existing occupiers on the West African coast. And the British actually used an argument based on natives' consent in a dispute they were having with Spain in 1790.[29]

Neither Phillip nor any subsequent governor obtained any consent from the Aboriginal 'natives'. Why? Because they were too backward. Joseph Banks said so. They weren't developed enough. 'They had no sovereignty.' Banks was shown to be wrong within months of Phillip's arrival. 'The natives are far more numerous than they were supposed to be,' the governor wrote in mid-1788. The interior was clearly inhabited, which was another thing Banks got wrong. And what's more, the locals appeared to be living off the land – and apparently even cultivating it – in accordance with their own cultures, customs and laws. They had clear tribal boundaries, which the various tribes appeared to respect. They managed the land with fire, and they spoke numerous languages. And they resisted the settlers' invasion wherever it extended. William Darling recorded that the Tasmanian First Nations 'considered themselves as engaged in a justifiable war against the invaders of their country'.[30] There was no consent. As these empirical realities became clearer, any right the settlers believed they had to take possession without consent or war faded away. How legal, exactly, was the British 'settlement'?

When a group of investors successfully lobbied the new Whig government in London to establish the colony of South Australia, there were plenty who saw problems with it. The Whigs had returned to the ministerial benches in 1830 for the first time in a generation, on a platform of parliamentary and humanitarian reform. Under the Earl Grey and then the Viscount Melbourne, William Lamb, the Whigs abolished slavery,[31] promoted treaties with original owners, and established the Select Committee on Aborigines, which reported in 1837. But the *South Australia Act* of 1834 assumed there were large tracts of 'waste and unoccupied lands' to sell in small parcels. Some, like Charles Napier, saw it for what it was: 'an act to seize, by force, a territory ... as large as France and Spain; and calls this territory "*uninhabited*", when it is well known to be *inhabited!*'[32] When James Stephen – Sidney's cousin, and under-secretary in the Colonial Office – considered the Act, he couldn't imagine 'how it can be done at all with any due regard to the rights of the present Proprietors of the Soil or rulers of the country.'[33]

Australian jurisprudence has repeatedly reached back to *R v Murrell* (1836) to satisfy itself that the question of sovereignty has been settled. But as we've seen, just seven years earlier, Chief Justice Forbes and Justice Dowling had decided the Supreme Court had no jurisdiction over 'the original natives', who were governed by 'the laws of [their] tribe'. And in 1841, another judge reached similar conclusions when he presided over the trial of one Aboriginal man, 'Bon Jon', for killing another, Yammowing, in accordance with tribal law near Geelong. 'Can I legally exercise any jurisdiction,' asked Justice John Willis, 'with reference to any crimes committed by Aborigines against each other?' Willis made enemies easily among the establishment. He'd been a judge in Upper Canada, where he'd questioned the legal foundations of its court and got himself removed back to England for his troubles. He'd also been a judge in British Guiana, where he made himself unpopular by refusing to acquit former slave owners who continued to whip their former slaves, which was common practice.[34]

In his decision about Bon Jon's trial, Willis quoted extensively from the select committee's report: 'Europeans have entered their borders uninvited, and when there, have not only acted as if they were the undoubted lords of the soil, but have punished the natives as aggressors if they have evinced a disposition to live in their own country.'[35] Willis recognised, and documented, the errors made by Joseph Banks and by Phillip's commissioners. New South Wales had not been 'discovered' by Cook. The Aboriginal tribes had never been conquered, and had never agreed to allow the British to settle on their lands. Willis disagreed with Forbes and Dowling's decision in *Murrell*, and Bon Jon was discharged. Colonial authorities from Sydney to London rained fire on Willis, as did the colonial press. By 1841, settler authorities had convinced themselves that any questions about Britain's sovereignty over the Australian continent had been resolved by Dowling and Forbes in the *Murrell* case. Willis didn't think so, and wanted the sovereignty question referred to the British solicitor-general. Dowling, by now chief justice, wrote to George Gipps, governor, about Willis's 'very strange opinion'. Willis's recommendation was refused, and Gipps arranged his removal.[36]

Willis's decision in *R v Bon Jon* was referred to at least once again, three months later, when five Tasmanians – two men, Tunnerminnerwait and Maulboyheenner, and three women, one of whom was Truganini – were tried for the murder of two white whalers. The five were among sixteen people, all survivors of the (undeclared) 'Black Wars', brought by George Augustus

Robinson to the Port Phillip district in 1839. They'd endured unimaginable terror on Van Diemen's Land. One of the women, Planobeena, had been kidnapped by sealers and held in sexual servitude before Robinson rescued her. Tunnerminnerwait probably learned of the Convincing Ground massacre – which had occurred less than a decade earlier – when he accompanied Robinson on a tour of Gunditjmara Country in mid-1841.[37] Beginning in early October, he and the four other Tasmanians began their own campaign of resistance near Dandenong, where they burgled food and guns from isolated settler stations. Nobody saw how the two whalers were shot, but the Tasmanians remained at large for six weeks afterwards, during which time they became the district's greatest talking point. Newspaper reports feigned complete ignorance about their motivations.[38] They were eventually arrested. At their trial, Redmond Barry – recently appointed standing Defence Counsel for Aborigines – made submissions based on Willis's decision three months earlier, and reminded the jury of the horrific wrongs done to them in Van Diemen's Land. 'Could it be thought that, in consequence of a short abode with Mr Robinson, the savage had forgot his wrongs, buried in oblivion the injuries he had suffered ... ?' he asked rhetorically.[39] Yet this time, most likely because the Tasmanians were notorious and their (alleged) victims were white, Willis took a different view, despite the deficiencies in the evidence against them. 'Permitting the blacks to remain on the [settlers'] runs was a spurious humanity,' Willis told the jury in summing up.[40] The jury found the men (though not the women) guilty but recommended mercy. Willis wasn't interested, and Tunnerminnerwait and Maulboyheenner became the first people hanged in Melbourne/Naarm, in front of a crowd of five thousand settlers.[41]

Willis's decision in *R v Bon Jon* was never referred to again, while the *Murrell* judgement echoes noisily through Australian jurisprudence right down to the present: a Queensland District Court judge cited it in 2021.[42]

Along with *Murrell*, Australian jurisprudence has tended to prefer another line of thought, which was expressed most clearly by John Locke: that communities had to be making *particular* use of land they lived on – such as 'tilling' its soil – before they could legally qualify as its possessors or sovereigns. Henry Reynolds, in *Truth-Telling*, cites a range of 1970s legal textbooks that make variations on that claim, which led to an equally common conclusion: as the future judge Elizabeth Evatt told an international conference in 1968, 'Australia is in fact one of the rare examples of a large tract of inhabited territory acquired peaceably by occupation without any consent being sought from the native population.'[43] But there was little in British or international law of the late eighteenth or early nineteenth centuries that required 'tilling'. To the contrary, most legal commentators emphasised that actual possession, coupled with a will to maintain it, was more than enough to establish lawful possession, regardless of the particular use being made of the land.[44] That was also the view of courts in the United States, Canada and New Zealand.[45] But not in Australia. If the conclusions reached by the twentieth century's smartest legal minds – like Evatt's – are puzzling to us now, we should remember that lawyers who are appointed judges are rarely known for challenging prevailing common sense.

Clearly, Aboriginal and Torres Strait Islander peoples were governed by 'laws of their own', though Australian courts avoided acknowledging that reality until 1971.[46] The Australian continent was obviously never *terra nullius*, though it took until 1992 for an Australian court to recognise that fact in law.[47] So, if First Nations peoples never consented to the takeover of their lands, their dispossession can only be described – in settler law – as theft. Unless of course they were 'conquered'. The right and law of conquest was indeed used by many European states to gain control of territory on other continents. Until it was outlawed after World War II, conquest was a means by which the conqueror vanquished the sovereign leader. Subjects changed their allegiance as a result, but their property remained untouched and their laws generally unchanged, until the conqueror takes some further sovereign act. This is clearly not what happened in Australia.

But by the 1840s, the legal story of British 'settlement' was set, at least in the minds of settler authorities. Where New South Wales had no law before 1788, now it had British law. Anyone who happened to be here already – not occupying it, obviously, but merely running around nomadically on top of it – was now automatically subject to British law, and to any subsequent changes made by local authorities. Any acts of resistance must, logically, be merely 'criminal' and not 'resistance' or 'defence'. Aboriginal people who stole or killed cattle, or burned farmhouses, or damaged property, or assaulted or killed Europeans – or each other, even in accordance with their own law – could be brought before the colonisers' courts, tried and punished as 'criminals'. Aboriginal law had no standing here. There was nothing for the British to conquer. They merely 'settled'.

Illusions of law

Faced with undeniable empirical evidence that the Australian continent was in fact populated, owned and used, how did English and settler courts, parliaments and governments respond?

They doubled down.[48]

'[I]t is not to be asserted that Great Britain has any disposition to sanction unfair dealing,' the select committee reported in 1837. It observed that 'to require from the ignorant hordes of savages living in Eastern or Western Australia the observance of our laws would be absurd, and to punish their non-observance of them by severe penalties would be palpably unjust'. On the other hand, 'the duty of introducing into our relations with uncivilised nations the righteous and the profitable laws of [our] justice is incontrovertible'.

What, then, to do? Apply the righteous laws of British justice, of course, but 'it seems right that the utmost indulgence compatible with a due regard for the lives and properties of others should be shown for their ignorance and prejudices'.[49] In other words: punish Aboriginal criminals according to British law, but exercise leniency. George Grey, an explorer who owed his life to a Whadjuk man, 'Kaiber', from whom Grey then learned the Whadjuk language, agreed. In a report he wrote to the colonial secretary in mid-1840 on 'the best means of promoting the civilisation of the Aboriginal inhabitants of Australia', Grey recommended that colonial authorities do three things: ban Aboriginal people from practising their own 'barbarous' punishments; apply the criminal law of Britain to them; and exercise leniency when punishing them. As we'll see, this is precisely how Australian courts would approach their task well into the late twentieth century. Lord Russell was so impressed by Grey's report that he appointed him the third governor of South Australia the following year.[50]

But the question of whether and how to subject Aboriginal people to settler law was still sufficiently unresolved by the 1880s that the Privy Council's Judicial Committee, then the British Empire's court of last resort, decided to weigh in.

The two William Coopers

In May 1823, Thomas Brisbane, having replaced Lachlan Macquarie to become New South Wales' sixth governor, gave a sizeable parcel of land to a man called William Hutchinson. Hutchinson was lucky to be alive.

Convicted at the Old Bailey in mid-1796 of stealing items worth more than £168 – more than $33,000 in today's money – his death sentence was commuted to transportation for seven years, and he arrived in Sydney in 1799. He was promptly convicted of another theft and sent to Norfolk Island, where, contrary to expectations, he flourished. By 1814 he was back in Sydney and in Macquarie's employ as principal superintendent of convicts, on a good public service salary. Hutchinson became one of Macquarie's closest confidants. This is not to say he'd entirely left his old ways behind. His role meant that he received cash owned by convicts when they arrived. He occasionally invested this cash and kept the interest for himself. This, perhaps, explains his active role in the establishment of, and on the board of, the Bank of New South Wales. By 1825, with Brisbane's help, he was also a significant landowner.[51]

Brisbane's grant of 1400 hectares of land south of Botany Bay had been to Hutchinson and 'his heirs and assigns'. The grant was subject to some caveats. Brisbane made it clear that the government retained a right to any timber from trees growing on the land that could be used for building boats. He also made sure that the government could build roads through the land if required in the future, and could reclaim up to 10 acres 'as may be required for public purposes'. All well and good. Hutchinson died a wealthy man in 1846, and his assets did indeed pass to his heirs and assigns. Then, nearly four decades later, the government at last claimed its 10 acres for a public park, around which it immediately built a fence.

By the late 1880s, those acres were owned by one William Cooper, who also owned a lot of other acres in and around Sydney. In response to the government's claim, he sued, arguing that the original caveat was invalid because it contradicted a two-centuries-old principle of English property law.[52] Cooper's appeal eventually made its way to the Privy Council (which would remain the final court of appeal for Australian litigants for another century). On behalf of five judges from all four nations of the United Kingdom, Lord Watson – a Scottish lawyer and former Tory MP – thought that Brisbane's original grant probably didn't offend the centuries-old rule, so long as the laws of England did *in fact* operate in New South Wales in 1823.

So, Watson took it upon himself to enquire into the status of British law in the colonies. He started, as was fashionable, with Blackstone's *Commentaries on the Laws of England*, and the 'great difference' between a colony 'acquired by conquest or cession, in which there is an established system of law', and one which was essentially 'a tract of territory practically unoccupied, *without settled inhabitants or settled law*, at the time when it was peacefully annexed to the British dominions'. (The emphasis is mine.) Rather staggeringly, though, that's where Watson's enquiry stopped. He'd never been to the Australian colonies, so he couldn't fall back on personal knowledge. Rather, he made a simple assumption, on the basis of what appears to be little more than received wisdom: 'The Colony of New South Wales belongs to the latter class.'[53]

It was an assumption that spelt doom for Cooper's appeal, and Watson ordered him to pay costs. But Watson's assumption also spelt doom for Aboriginal people hoping to lodge future challenges to the right of settler parliaments and governments to control their bodies and their destinies with laws they never wanted. As Henry Reynolds wrote in *The Law of the Land*, Lord Watson's view 'would have been difficult to sustain in 1789, let alone in 1889'. It didn't matter that *Cooper v Stuart* was bad law, based on a 'factual' finding that was blatantly false. *Cooper v Stuart* was a decision of the Privy Council, and so became a precedent that not even the High Court would be comfortable overturning without an extraordinarily good reason and a shot of colonial courage.

Coincidentally, another William Cooper made an appeal at about the same time. Born on Yorta Yorta Country in December 1860, Cooper had been forced to work for white pastoralists as a child before he and other family members went to the Maloga Aboriginal Mission when he was thirteen. In his twenties, he read widely of movements for indigenous rights in North America and New Zealand. And in 1887 – two years before the Privy Council's decision in *Cooper v Stuart* – he was one of eleven signatories to the second Maloga Petition. Addressed to the governor, Lord Carrington, the petition read:

> The following of the Aborigines and half-castes on the Maloga Aboriginal Mission Station, and the neighbourhood thereof, hereby showeth that while grateful for the benefits conferred upon on them by the liberality of our Government, in aiding the Aborigines Protection Association to provide a home for them and their families, and also recognising their debt of gratitude to that association, they would suggest that on the recommendation of that society those among us, who so desires, should be granted sections of land of not less than 100 acres per family in fee simple or else at a small nominal rental annually, with the option of purchase at such prices as shall be deemed reasonable for

them under the circumstances, always bearing in mind that the Aborigines were the former occupiers of the land.[54]

Most of the text betrays the power relationship between author and addressee, but the final pointed phrase – *'always bearing in mind'* – was clearly designed to appeal to the settlers' strong sense of their own fairness. It didn't work. In November the same year, Cooper also wrote a personal letter to his local member of parliament, 'respectfully begging' for a grant of land for his family. Both petition and letter amounted to nothing. Unlike his namesake's challenge to the government's desire to claim 10 acres of 'his' land, Cooper's appeals were never heard by any court, let alone the Privy Council. He made a further (unsuccessful) petition to Henry Parkes, premier, in 1890. Cooper didn't give up. In his seventies, Cooper became perhaps the most identifiable campaigner for Aboriginal land and legal rights, and was instrumental in establishing the Australian Aborigines' League and organising the Day of Mourning in 1938, the first national protest by Aboriginal people.[55]

Subjects or aliens?

There were three fundamental problems for the British criminal law when it was brought by the settlers to the Australian continent. The first was how to prosecute Aboriginal 'criminals' when they knew neither the law nor the English language, and especially when they were acting in accordance with their own laws and customs. The second was how to account for the non-prosecution of settlers for the massacres piling up the bodies on the frontier. The third, and in some ways the most troubling, was the question of the land thefts.

Property had an exalted place, above even human life, in British law. Nothing in that law entitled one person to usurp the property of another without permission or compensation. 'By the laws of England,' declared Lord Camden in 1765, 'every invasion of private property, be it ever so minute, is a trespass.'[56] Even more famous was William Pitt's earlier affirmation of the rights of the individual – including to private property – against government intrusion:

The poorest man may in his cottage bid defence to all the forces of the Crown. It may be frail; its roof may shake; the wind may blow through it; the storm may enter; the rain may enter; but the King of England cannot enter – all his force dares not cross the threshold of the ruined tenement![57]

And yet, British settlers were trampling all over Aboriginal land, pushing off – and killing – its owners in a determination to make it their own. The first theft was probably Cook's, when he and his *Endeavour* crew stole thirteen green turtles from the reefs off Gangaar, now Cooktown, in July 1770. The explorers were stranded and in danger of starving. Had they simply asked the Guugu Yimithirr people for food, it may have been given. The thirteen turtles they took would no doubt have fed the Guugu Yimithirr for some time. When ten Guugu Yimithirr warriors saw the turtles on the *Endeavour*'s deck and demanded one, Cook refused. The warriors retaliated by setting fire to some long grass next to the explorers' fishing net, which was drying onshore. Cook shot one of them, wounding him.[58] Within decades, Aboriginal people were *themselves* being charged with theft, as were the men known as 'Boatman' and 'Billy Bulli', in 1832, when they allegedly made off with sheep owned by a Hunter River farmer, John Palmer. Their lawyer, Roger Therry, objected to the court's jurisdiction on the ground that Aboriginal people were not subject to British laws of property crime. Dowling allowed the trials. As long as an Aboriginal defendant appeared 'a reasonable and responsible being', he was answerable to British law.[59]

On 18 January 1835, a Sunday, Patrick Sheridan – a settler – was travelling along the Kings Highway near Brisbane Water when he became the victim of highway robbery at the hands of a 'party of blacks'. That is, he was relieved of a pipe and a knife by an Aboriginal man, 'Lego'me' (or 'Leggamy'), who then stuck his spear into the ground at Sheridan's feet. Lego'me was likely of the Walkeloa people, who had been actively resisting white settlement in the area. When he was captured and brought to trial for highway robbery, a capital offence, his lawyer (Therry again) asked Sheridan whether he was aware that he – Sheridan – had been squatting on Lego'me's land for some time, and had 'frequently committed great depredations on his kangaroos'. Bewildered, Sheridan fumbled for an answer. 'I believe the land belongs to Government,' he said. 'As for kangaroos, I have something else to do than look for them.' Forbes approved jurisdiction, the jury found Lego'me guilty, and the chief justice sentenced him to transportation – possibly to Norfolk or Cockatoo Island – for seven years.[60]

○

The question of how Britain came to be the only sovereign power over the entire Australian continent has never been conclusively or satisfactorily answered. In his 1889 judgement in *Cooper v Stuart*, Lord Watson left the door to a future challenge slightly ajar. 'There was no land law or tenure existing in the Colony at the time of its annexation to the Crown,' he observed. This is clearly inaccurate. But two other observations in the same paragraph are more interesting to us now. The first is that Watson and his judicial colleagues had 'not been referred to any Act or Ordinance declaring that the laws of England, or any portion of them, are applicable to New South Wales'. The second was that 'as soon as colonial land became the subject of settlement and commerce, all transactions in relation to it were governed by English law, *in so far as that law could be justly and conveniently applied to them*'.[61] Watson was specifically thinking about land law, but the same logic had to apply to criminal law. It was one thing for colonial authorities to claim the right to try and to punish their own people. It was entirely another to claim that everything that happened on the continent was now subject to their laws, and not to the laws of the First Nations peoples.

Watson's door has since – apparently at least – been slammed shut. First came the British parliament's *Commonwealth of Australia Constitution Act* of 1900, and the subsequent Acts which transferred more and more sovereign authority to Australian parliaments and courts. Then, in their decision in the *Mabo* case in 1992, High Court justices William Deane and Mary Gaudron declared that the door didn't even exist. 'Under British law in 1788, it lay within the prerogative power of the Crown to extend its sovereignty and jurisdiction' to new territory, they observed. When the Crown said it acquired New South Wales by 'settlement', they went on, that 'was an act of State whose primary operation lay ... in international politics or law'. The validity of an act of State 'could not be challenged in British [or Australian] courts'. 'It must be accepted by this court,' concluded Deane and Gaudron, 'that the whole of the territory designated in Phillip's commissions was, by 7 February 1788, validly established as a "settled" British colony.' The British government may not have had the lawful power to 'settle' places that were already occupied. But no court can hear that argument. What Australian courts can do, of course, is to punish Indigenous crimes against settler law.

SOLUTIONS

How settlers 'solved' their First Nations problem in different ways at different times

Although Aboriginal and Torres Strait Islander peoples had been subject to the British criminal justice system – including its sanction of imprisonment – since the early nineteenth century, it was only after colonial governments committed to new policies of 'protection' late in the century that they really began to apply the full weight of the criminal justice system to Indigenous offenders. Western Australia was the trailblazer. There, Aboriginal people made up a third of all prisoners by 1905 (and 42 per cent by 1909), largely as a consequence of decades of imprisoning Aboriginal 'offenders' – including on Rottnest Island, which was a designated Aboriginal prison between 1838 and 1902 – for frontier 'crimes' like cattle-killing, instead of executing them summarily or massacring their families and communities, which tended to be the practice on the east coast.[1]

By the twentieth century, judges – all white – were confident that settler law applied to Aboriginal and Torres Strait Islander peoples: as British subjects, Aboriginal people were entitled to the law's protection and subject to its sanctions. The judges' view may not have been representative of broader settler opinion, however. By the late nineteenth century, a schism had opened up in settler opinion between the settled districts, which were more likely to condemn the massacres and 'summary justice' of the frontier, and remote areas such as cattle stations and stock routes, where settlers were much more likely to justify taking the law into their own hands.[2] Settler opinion was also divided over how to respond to 'crimes' committed between and among Aboriginal people. In April 1933, sixty white jurors petitioned the NSW Supreme Court, asking that when Aboriginal people were charged with crimes in circumstances where they'd been 'merely meting out justice to delinquents according to their customs', any trial should occur in accordance with those customs instead of the criminal code.[3]

A survey of Northern Territory judges' written reasons for their decisions – of jurisprudence – during the twentieth century shows a consistent and firm commitment to the theory of Crown sovereignty, but differences over time in the precise ways in which settler law should apply to Aboriginal people, especially over the question of punishment. Although we like to think judges are independent of governments and their policies, it shouldn't be surprising to learn that judges' views substantially mirror those of the government of the day. Judges are, of course, appointed by governments, but this 'mirroring' perhaps owes more to the dominance of prevailing ideas. Ideas of segregation, protection, assimilation and self-determination each find expression in twentieth-century Northern Territory jurisprudence.[4]

Dashwood's compromise

Charles Dashwood was a politician in South Australia when the Privy Council decided *Cooper v Stuart*. The son of a naval officer, Dashwood had careers as a farmer and a lawyer before he entered parliament. In February 1892 he became Darwin's first Australian-born resident judge. This was at a time when the pseudoscience of 'race' was becoming particularly prevalent in mainstream thought, especially among 'white' people, who found in it convenient justifications for their belief in their own superiority. It was also a time when the Northern Territory coast was perhaps more multicultural than anywhere else on the continent, as people from China and other parts of Asia and the South Pacific participated in the various industries. Dashwood saw how important non-white labour was to the Territory's development and was highly critical of the White Australia policy, which kept much of it out. But Dashwood's liberalism did not initially extend to Aboriginal people. In his first sitting in February 1893, Dashwood presided over the trial of eight Yolngu people who were charged with murdering six fishermen – probably from Timor – at Malay Bay, at the very top of Arnhem Land.[5]

The case had caused a scandal in what was then called Palmerston (now Darwin). A group of Aboriginal people, likely Iwaidja, came across a proa (a kind of outrigger canoe) that was wrecked on the beach, and soon encountered its crew. The Iwaidja offered to guide the crew to where the Timorese settler Tingha de Hans lived near the ruins of the old Port Essington.

The crew followed. After travelling some distance through Bowen Strait, the Iwaidja went ashore again. The crew followed once more, but found themselves surrounded by the Iwaidja, who were now armed with wad-dies (wooden clubs). All six fishermen were killed. When the case came to Dashwood's court, he and the (all-white) jury were told that the Iwaidja attack was entirely unprovoked and even unresisted. Afterwards, the attack-ers had returned to the proa, which they looted and burned, before returning to bury the bodies of their victims. This, at least, was the version that the jury heard. No evidence was led in the Iwaidja's defence. The whole 'trial' was wrapped up in a single day. After five minutes' deliberation, the jury returned verdicts of guilty against all eight prisoners.[6]

It was only then that one of them, 'Wandy Wandy', said anything at all. This man had apparently already served a sentence for murder, and was named as the 'ringleader' in the earliest newspaper reports. In 'clear and fluent broken English', Wandy Wandy said that the fishermen had been ini-tially hostile, threatened to chop off the Iwaidja people's hands, and fired two shots at them from a rifle.[7] And it wasn't until 1991, when Peter and Jay Read published their collected accounts of Aboriginal versions of Territory history, *Long Time, Olden Time*, that settlers had any sense of what might have motivated Wandy Wandy and the Iwaidja. The fishermen had appar-ently used ceremonial string to make nets, then a capital offence in Iwaidja law. But neither the jury nor Dashwood understood this in 1893. Nor would it have mattered if they had, because Iwaidja law was irrelevant to settler law. Dashwood sentenced all eight Iwaidja to death.

The *Northern Territory Times and Gazette*'s reporter observed that, apart from Wandy Wandy, the Iwaidja 'did not have a very clear conception of the punishment allotted to them'. Perhaps for this reason the others were eventually reprieved.[8] But Wandy Wandy, the alleged ringleader, was taken back to Malay Bay, where a gallows was built and he was hanged. He was only the second person to be lawfully executed in the Territory. The first was Charlie Flannigan, two days earlier – another Aboriginal man who'd been tried and convicted of murder during Dashwood's same February sitting.[9]

Eventually, Charles Dashwood came to realise something was amiss in the administration of settler 'justice' to Aboriginal people who spoke little or no English and who could hardly be expected to know in any-where near enough detail what was happening in settler courts. In 1894, Dashwood publicly expressed concern about the apparent fact that many

Aboriginal defendants in his court were 'utterly ignorant of what is going on'.[10] Dashwood's dawning realisation became a repeated theme among future judges and lawyers. For Dashwood, this necessitated at least some form of retreat from the principle in *Cooper v Stuart*, and greater measures to protect Aboriginal people from exploitation by settlers. From 1896 he began throwing out murder charges against Aboriginal defendants which relied entirely on evidence of a defendant's confession.[11] He sought to codify that proposition in a bill he drafted for South Australia's parliament in 1899, based on Queensland legislation. It was strenuously opposed by pastoral interests, and ultimately defeated.[12]

In early 1900, a man named Jimmy approached an Aboriginal camp near Pine Creek. Four years earlier, Jimmy's son had accidentally speared an old woman in the same camp, killing her. Jimmy had come to make amends. He made sure those present knew what he was there for, and then invited anyone who 'bore a grudge' (in the language of the *Northern Territory Times and Gazette* report) to do what they wanted. Two of the woman's sons threw several spears at Jimmy, to little effect. Then her brother, an old man known as 'Long Peter', had a go. His first spear missed. But his second struck Jimmy just under a cheekbone and pierced his brain. Jimmy died, and Long Peter was charged with murder. When he was brought into Dashwood's court for trial, Long Peter's lawyer argued that his client had killed Jimmy in accordance with 'tribal custom'.

In summing up for the (all-white) jury, Dashwood did something interesting. While *Cooper v Stuart* had made it clear, by implication, that tribal custom could not *excuse* an offence against British law, Dashwood thought that it might be relevant for the jury in deciding whether the degree of 'malice' in Long Peter's mind constituted murder or the lesser crime of manslaughter. The jury took its cue, found Long Peter guilty of manslaughter and 'strongly recommended him for mercy on the ground that the evidence goes to show that the prisoner's act was the outcome of tribal custom'. Dashwood sentenced Long Peter to three months' hard labour, which was extraordinarily lenient. On the same day, Dashwood sentenced a white man to three *years'* hard labour for assaulting a police officer.[13]

To the problem of the obvious contradiction between the *theory* of British 'settlement' and the empirical reality of Aboriginal law and culture, Dashwood arrived at a heavily compromised 'solution': he would maintain the principle that settler law was supreme, but he would order 'lenient' punishments for Aboriginal people convicted of crimes that weren't crimes under their own laws, or in circumstances where their trials – which were conducted in English according to an alien system of law – were so obviously unfair as to verge on the preposterous.

Wells and segregation

In November 1928, two Aboriginal men – Arkirkra and Padygar – were put on trial in Alice Springs' Supreme Court for the murder of a white station hand, Fred Brooks. It was a sham trial, and the judge, Ross Mallam, knew it. Brooks had been killed on Randall Stafford's cattle station, Coniston, in early August. In response, William Murray, a police constable who had recently been appointed Protector of Aborigines, led a series of punitive raids against Warlpiri, Anmatyerre and Kaytetye people at nearby locations. Those raids are now known collectively as the Coniston Massacre.[14] Murray and his posse killed at least thirty-one people, probably twice that number, and possibly many more. When he gave evidence as a witness in Arkirkra and Padygar's trial, he repeatedly justified his decisions to kill people on the basis that they were suspects in Brooks's murder. Justice Mallam wouldn't have a bar of it. 'Constable Murray,' he asked at one point, 'was it really necessary to shoot to kill in every case? Could you not have occasionally shot to wound?' 'No, your honour,' Murray replied. 'What is the use of a wounded blackfellow hundreds of miles from civilisation?' Mallam asked him how many people he killed. Murray admitted to seventeen. 'You mean,' Mallam replied, 'you mowed them down wholesale.'[15]

Murray was never charged or tried for his mass murders. He survived a whitewashed inquiry, which was set up to conclude that his actions were defensive and justified; the inquiry even recommended greater police patrols to establish better control over Central Australian Aboriginal people.[16] Murray emerged with a reputation (among settlers) not as a mass-murderer, but as a 'hero of the Central Australians', at least according to Adelaide's *Register News-Pictorial*.[17] He went on killing Aboriginal people, and boasting about it, until he retired to Adelaide in 1945. The only time he ever faced trial was in 1938, for fraudulently selling a stationery cupboard said to be owned by the Commonwealth government.[18]

Ross Mallam, the judge who presided over the trial of the two men accused of murdering Fred Brooks, was furious that his courtroom was being used in this way. He angrily ordered the jury to acquit Arkirkra and Padygar, which it did. But Mallam didn't stay long on the bench. In 1933 he fell ill at the age of fifty-five and retired to Adelaide. His successor was Thomas Alexander Wells, a barrister who had been a court reporter in Sydney before World War I.

Wells was not like Mallam, who had practised law in the Top End for twelve years before becoming a judge. Wells arrived in Darwin entirely ignorant of local Aboriginal laws, language and culture, at a time when racist beliefs among white people were at their zenith.[19] He expected Aboriginal people to submit to settler laws, or simply stay out of the way. In line with the Privy Council's implicit rejection of Aboriginal culture in 1889, Wells saw no place for it whatsoever. He also didn't believe Aboriginal witnesses when they contradicted settler witnesses. It didn't matter to him why Aboriginal people did things; if they broke settler law (or were said by settlers to have broken settler law), they had to be punished. He didn't think Aboriginal people were capable of reform or rehabilitation, which is what prison was designed to induce. Instead, he preferred to sentence Aboriginal defendants to death. This was despite a 1939 amendment to Northern Territory law that gave courts the power to avoid the death penalty for Aboriginal people convicted of murder by imposing 'such penalty as, having regard to all the circumstances of the case, appears to the Court to be just and proper'.[20]

One very famous case, which came into Wells's court the year after he arrived in Darwin, serves to illustrate the problems his approach created. In mid-1933, a group of four police and four trackers went to Woodah Island (in Blue Mud Bay, off East Arnhem Land) to investigate the deaths of five Japanese trepangers (sea cucumber fishermen), who'd apparently been killed by Yolngu people in Caledon Bay the previous September. In the southern capitals and London, some people asked what right the Japanese fisherman had to be there in the first place. In the Top End, a different question dominated among the settlers: what was to be done about the dangerous Aborigines?

The investigating party landed on the island and soon came across a deserted camp, where they stopped for lunch. The police sent the trackers to investigate further. One of them returned soon afterwards, letting them know there was a group of Aboriginal women nearby. The officers hand-cuffed the women, brought them back to their lunch spot and 'questioned' them. Three of the constables then went to meet some Aboriginal men who were landing a canoe, leaving the fourth constable, Albert McColl, in charge of the women. When the other officers returned, McColl and the women had disappeared. The next day McColl's dead body was found. He'd been speared.

Darwin learned of McColl's death on 7 August and erupted in rage and concern. Three weeks later, Thomas Wells arrived from Sydney. And the very next day, Robert Weddell, the Territory's administrator, demanded that a 'fairly large' party of police enter Arnhem Land to capture McColl's killer. Canberra signed its approval and arranged for a boat carrying twelve policemen and an arsenal of ammunition to leave Sydney. But this was just five years since the massacres at Coniston Station had made international news. London's *Daily Herald* reported that the Australian government had approved a 'punitive expedition'. Former prime minister Stanley Bruce, in London as high commissioner, demanded that Canberra 'please explain immediately'. John Perkins, Minister for the Interior, recalled the boat.

Meanwhile, a white trepanger claimed that he'd learned the identity of McColl's murderer: a Yolngu man, Dhakiyarr Wirrpanda. But with the world watching Australia it was difficult to justify sending police to make an arrest on such a flimsy basis. Two missionaries went instead, and convinced Wirrpanda and five other men to return with them to Darwin. Who knows what they were told, but as soon as they arrived in April 1934, they were immediately arrested. They'd never seen a city, and they'd never been locked up. They reportedly yelled for hours in their police cells.

As preparations were made for Wirrpanda's committal, two of the other men who'd come with him claimed that he'd told them his version of how he'd killed McColl. One of these hearsay witnesses, Parriner, had Wirrpanda throwing his spear at McColl to allow the women to escape; the other witness, a mission boy called Harry, had McColl shooting first at Wirrpanda, who then threw his spear in self-defence. Harry's version also had McColl raping one of the women. When Harry gave this account in court, Wells made it clear that he didn't appreciate the impugning of an officer's moral character, and improperly allowed the prosecutor to call a (white) witness, who said McColl would never do anything like that. But this was the sum total of the Crown's evidence. None of the trackers or Aboriginal women who might have known more about McColl's death was called to testify.

Clearly worried that the prosecutor hadn't led enough evidence to convict Wirrpanda, Wells decided to help him out. He told the jury:

You must think very carefully about that aspect of the matter and not allow yourselves to be swayed by the fact that you think the Crown has not done its duty. If you bring in a verdict of not guilty it means that this man is freed and cannot be tried again, no matter what evidence may be discovered in the future, and that may mean a grave miscarriage of justice. Another aspect of the matter that troubles me is that evidence has been given about a man who is dead, and if the jury brings in a verdict of not guilty it may be said that they believed that evidence, and it would be a serious slander on that man. It was the obvious duty of the Crown to bring all the evidence procurable and to have all these matters cleared up entirely, but you must not allow the fact that the Crown has failed in its duty to influence you to bring a verdict of not guilty if there really is evidence of guilt before you on which you can rely.[21]

For Wells, the acquittal of a possibly guilty Aboriginal man and the impugning of a white officer's moral character was a graver miscarriage of justice than the conviction – and likely execution – of a probably innocent Aboriginal man. Wells also told the jury to disregard Harry's hearsay evidence entirely, which he described as 'so utterly ridiculous as to be an obvious fabrication', and to only accept Parriner's evidence insofar as it confirmed that Wirrpanda speared McColl. This was, almost to a letter, the precise opposite of how the law authorised Wells to direct the jury, which is supposed to make its own findings of fact based on the evidence it hears. When the (all-white) jury returned a guilty verdict, Wells sentenced Wirrpanda to death – the same sentence he'd already imposed for eight other Aboriginal men in the few months he'd been in Darwin. (Minister Perkins had since commuted all eight sentences to life imprisonment.)[22]

After a campaign led by the anthropologist A.P. Elkin, the High Court quickly heard Wirrpanda's appeal and unanimously quashed his conviction on 8 November 1934. The next day, Wirrpanda was removed from Fannie Bay Gaol in Darwin and placed in the Kahlin Compound for stolen children. It's unknown why that happened; after all, he was free. At Kahlin, he simply vanished. Weirdly, there was no investigation. Historian Peter Read has found a deeply suspicious absence of comment about Wirrpanda's disappearance in bureaucratic documents. The clear implication is that he was killed by police avenging McColl's death, and nobody wanted to know very much about that.[23]

Justice Thomas Wells did not change his approach in light of the High Court's rebuke. Throughout 1934, he'd been causing headaches for Perkins and the government of Joseph Lyons in Canberra, due to his fondness for sentencing Aboriginal people to death, especially when their victims were white. When Attorney-General John Latham introduced laws that would allow courts to consider anthropological evidence, for instance to allow them to better comprehend actions by Aboriginal people, Wells described them as 'just another case of ill-considered legislation', and made it clear that, despite what the statute provided, anthropologists had no place in his courtroom.

But Wells's racism, his manipulation of juries and his unwillingness to defer to the limits set by legislation did not amount to 'proven misbehaviour or incapacity', which was necessary for a judge's removal. He provided the judicial support for the prevailing policy of 'protection' given effect by the Aboriginal Acts, which segregated Aboriginal people on missions and reserves and generally sought to 'smooth the dying pillow', as one chief protector infamously put it. Wells kept on executing Aboriginal defendants as the resident justice of the Northern Territory Supreme Court until he suffered a stroke in 1951, aged in his sixties, and retired the following year.

Kriewaldt and assimilation

Wells's replacement was Martin Chemnitz Kriewaldt, the son of a Lutheran pastor who had 'settled' in the Adelaide Hills. For the decade he sat on the Territory's bench between 1951 and his death in 1960, Kriewaldt was a firm believer in the emergent government policy of assimilation, which assumed that the future for Aboriginal people lay in coming to live like settlers. Heavily influenced by the work of the Lutheran missions he'd known in his youth, he kept a portrait of Martin Luther next to paintings by Albert Namatjira – who had grown up at the Lutheran mission at Hermannsburg – in his chambers.[24]

Eight months before the artist died in 1959, Kriewaldt would reduce, but confirm, the prison sentence imposed on Namatjira for 'supplying' alcohol to a fellow Aboriginal artist after he left rum on the back seat of a taxi.[25] 'All my life,' Kriewaldt told the court during his judgement, 'the duty of Christians toward heathens, and the duty of the more fortunate towards the less fortunate has been impressed upon me.'[26] Unlike his predecessor, Kriewaldt firmly opposed the death penalty. When he convicted two young Czech men for the robbery-motivated murder of a taxi driver in 1952, he was upset when they were executed.[27] (Theirs proved to be the Territory's final executions. Police described the driver's murder as 'the most brutal in Territory history', which was only true if one ignored all the more brutal murders of Aboriginal people over the previous century.)

Whereas Wells favoured segregation, Kriewaldt anguished over how best to effect the goal of ensuring that Aboriginal people would one day live like white people. After his death, a magistrate described him as 'a missionary, not a judge': and that he 'considered the native Aborigine as the white man's burden'.[28] The only possible future for Aboriginal people was that they learn to obey settler laws and not their own.[29] Killing them wouldn't help. But imprisoning them might. Kriewaldt believed that for assimilation to succeed, settlers first had to learn more about who they were assimilating. To this end he used other white 'experts' – primarily anthropologists – who made Aboriginal culture 'knowable' to colonisers.

In the 1950s, the problem that had bedevilled colonial law in Sydney 120 years earlier remained unresolved: how to apply the assumptions and expectations of settler law to people who did not share them, especially when the law assumed that all defendants were equal before it? When an Aboriginal man, Patipatu, killed his wife in 1951 by throwing a spear at her after she'd left their child on the road, Kriewaldt told the jury to think about Patipatu's criminal responsibility 'as if the act of throwing the spear had been performed by a white man'.[30] This was obviously nonsensical, yet it was what Kriewaldt firmly believed the law required. Like Dashwood before him, Kriewaldt's solution was to use leniency in sentencing as a demonstration of his (and the settler law's) 'fairness': while Aboriginal people must be shown the consequences of criminal behaviour, they must also be treated more leniently to take proper account of their cultural backwardness and 'disadvantage'.[31]

> Where tribal law or custom might possibly be relevant I have in every case endeavoured to inform my mind on these topics either by hearing evidence in court or perusing any material available to me which seemed to bear on the point. In general, it has been my practice, since I have been the occupant of this office, to impose on natives sentences substantially more lenient than the sentences imposed on white offenders for similar offences.[32]

This was no more than what he would do for everyone, to the extent that the common law required him to take account of personal characteristics of all accused when sentencing them. It would have been considerably fairer to have allowed Aboriginal people to deal with offenders in their own ways, of course, but this was inconsistent with the logic of assimilation and colonisation.

After he'd served almost a decade on the bench, Kriewaldt wrote: 'The plain fact is that in the Northern Territory the trial of an [a]borigine in most cases proceeds ... as if the accused were not present.' He thought Aboriginal defendants rarely understood much, if anything, of the court process. Courts must be satisfied that a defendant understands the court process: this is part of ensuring a fair trial, which is fundamental to the British Constitution. But if this rule were actually applied in the Territory, Kriewaldt said frankly, 'many [a]borigines could simply not be tried.'[33]

In 1953, a young Pitjantjatjara man, Charlie Mulparinga, killed another Aboriginal man, 'Selly', by knocking him on the head and twisting his neck. While the evidence of what happened and why was somewhat opaque to Kriewaldt, he believed he'd been able to piece together enough of the story with the help of (white) Native Affairs Branch officials. Selly had revealed secret men's business to women, which was a crime punishable by death in Pitjantjatjara law. Elders at Ernabella had ordered Selly's death, and two men – 'Captain' and 'Tiger' – commanded a group of young men to carry it out. (Both Captain and Tiger were acquitted by juries for their parts in Selly's death.[34]) While most of the young men were unwilling – probably, Kriewaldt thought, because they feared punishment from settler authorities – Mulparinga obeyed. Kriewaldt thought this was probably because Mulparinga had 'less knowledge of white people'. The judge accepted that Mulparinga 'felt bound to obey the commands of Captain and Tiger and that he regarded the killing as being required by tribal law and as justified by that law'. Kriewaldt thought it likely that 'at no stage did the thought of punishment by white people occur to him'. Yet none of this was relevant for the (all-white) jury. 'Wherever white people impose their civilisation upon a native race,' Kriewaldt told the jury in summing up after Mulparinga's trial, 'that native race is subject to the same laws as the white man is.' That wasn't an adequate summary of the law anywhere other than Australia. If the jury believed Mulparinga killed Selly in accordance with Aboriginal law, 'that is no excuse in this court for his act'. Rather, that was a matter for sentencing.

After the jury dutifully found Mulparinga guilty of murder, Kriewaldt applied his own interpretation of the 1939 amendments allowing Aboriginal people to avoid the death penalty. Given the likelihood that Mulparinga had acted in accordance with Pitjantjatjara law, retribution wasn't an appropriate basis for punishing him. Nor was reform or rehabilitation. But Kriewaldt did think Mulparinga should be punished as a deterrent to other Aboriginal people. If not, all tribes who met regularly at Areyonga 'will believe that white law approves of the killing of a native who reveals tribal secrets'. Kriewaldt sentenced Mulparinga to eighteen months' hard labour: an outcome significantly more lenient than death.[35]

The closer Aboriginal people appeared (to Kriewaldt) to being 'civilised' into white norms, however, the less deserving of leniency they became. In March of 1954, a white woman was walking home in Alice Springs when a twenty-one-year-old Aboriginal man, Anderson, ran up behind her, dragged her onto the Todd River bed and tried to rape her. She screamed, and her attacker ran away. A passing motorist helped her to the Alice Springs hospital. She made a police report and identified Anderson, who eventually confessed. 'I was silly with the grog,' he told police, 'and wanted to treat a white woman like the white men treat the black gins.' White men had been helping themselves to Aboriginal women on the frontier for 150 years and prosecutions were almost unheard-of: it was hardly surprising that Kriewaldt knew of only 'very few cases' of crimes of violence by white people against Aboriginal victims since 1910.[36]

Kriewaldt saw Anderson's case as different to those he normally dealt with, though not because the victim was a white woman instead of another Aboriginal man. 'The prisoner is about twenty-one years old and has throughout his life been in touch with white people and subject to the influences of white civilisation,' Kriewaldt observed. 'He was described in evidence by the Acting Superintendent of Native Affairs as "sophisticated" and as "substantially civilised". He has had some education and is fairly well conversant with the English language.' So, Kriewaldt arrived at his formula: 'The nearer his mode of life and general behaviour approaches that of a white person, the closer should punishment on a native approximate punishment proper to a white person convicted of a similar crime.' He sentenced Anderson as he would have sentenced a white man: to two and a half years' prison.[37]

In Kriewaldt's mind, Aboriginal people could be found on a spectrum between 'tribal' and 'civilised'. Engagement with white civilisation, especially

on missions and in schools, tended to reduce the strength of Aboriginal people's 'tribal' beliefs and propel them toward a white worldview. Of course,
Aboriginal people didn't simply drop their entire cultures when exposed to
white culture, and Kriewaldt himself developed a more nuanced view the
longer he remained on the bench: by 1958 he accepted that Albert Namatjira,
for instance, had an outlook on life that in some areas was similar to that of
white people, and in other areas was predominantly Aboriginal.[38] He concluded that Aboriginal people were only entitled to leniency in sentencing
to the extent that they were 'disadvantaged' by their tribal backwardness.[39]

Kriewaldt dearly wanted Aboriginal people to become 'civilised'. 'The
Aboriginals concerned in this affray,' he declared about two men who'd fought
with weapons, 'have reached a sufficient stage of civilisation that they can be
made to understand that the use of knives or other instrument which may
cause wounds in a fight will merit punishment.'[40] The obvious problem with
the way he used his 'uncivilised–civilised' spectrum in sentencing Aboriginal
defendants was that the impact of British 'civilisation' on individual lives and
community relations had in many cases been utterly destructive. The 'whole
pattern of Aboriginal life' among the Gurindji, for instance, had (according to
young anthropologists Catherine and Ronald Berndt) been disrupted by the
'white man's economy' – namely, the demands of the Vesteys' cattle station at
Wave Hill – and by 'the belief of missionaries that they were gradually civilising the Aborigines and making them into God-fearing men and women ...'[41]
And often, it was the *destruction* of Aboriginal society associated with the
coming of British 'civilisation' that drove the kind of criminal behaviour for
which Kriewaldt issued the greatest penalties and punishments.

Kriewaldt's approach was no better exhibited than when he heard Albert
Namatjira's appeal against his conviction for supplying alcohol to a ward.[42]
For the judge, Namatjira provided evidence for both a capacity for assimilation – his watercolours – and the reality that a person who had adapted
to 'white' ways had not necessarily abandoned their Aboriginal culture. On
26 August 1958, Namatjira shared a taxi with his cousin, fellow watercolour
artist Henoch Raberaba. Raberaba was in his forties, but like 99 per cent of
the Territory's Aboriginal population, he'd been declared a 'ward' under Paul
Hasluck's *Welfare Ordinance*. Wards were prohibited from drinking alcohol,
and everyone else was prohibited from supplying it to them. 'Our considered
opinion,' Hasluck explained, 'is that intoxicating liquors are often a cause of
the degradation of primitive natives.' Namatjira, however, had enjoyed full

citizenship for over a year.[43] At least twice on its 125-kilometre journey to Hermannsburg, the taxi stopped so that Namatjira could relieve himself in nearby bushes. On each occasion he left an opened rum bottle inside the taxi, and on each occasion Raberaba helped himself to it while Namatjira was outside. By the time they arrived at Hermannsburg, Raberaba was apparently drunk. Namatjira was arrested and charged with 'supplying alcohol to a ward'.

For 'supplying' Raberaba in their shared taxi, the sentencing magistrate imposed the minimum six months' imprisonment. Namatjira appealed, arguing that the *Welfare Ordinance* was invalid. The Aboriginal Protection League in Victoria paid for the senior constitutional lawyer, Maurice Ashkanasy, to represent him in Alice Springs. Ashkanasy launched an all-out assault on the *Welfare Ordinance* in Kriewaldt's courtroom. His argument was that the *Ordinance* offended the fundamental rights and dignities at the core of British-Australian law. The ward system was never about 'protecting' Indigenous people. Researcher Colin Tatz later went looking through the Welfare Branch's records for any occasion on which it had litigated on behalf of 'civilly wronged "wards", for the legions swindled out of wages and rations on some cattle stations, those underpaid and underfed on most mission stations, those wrongly held in custody, exiled or otherwise punished on government stations'. He found not a single case.[44] Ashkanasy told Kriewaldt that a law that effectively abolished the civil rights of most Aboriginal people couldn't possibly be one for the 'peace, order and good government' of the Northern Territory.[45] Even if it was valid, the decision to declare Raberaba a ward could not be. Clearly, Ashkanasy said, Raberaba didn't meet the definition of 'ward' in the legislation – he wasn't 'in need of such special care or assistance' – so he should never have been made one. Kriewaldt described Ashkanasy's attack as 'trenchant', but the lawyer did not do much more than list the provisions of the *Ordinance*.[46]

So, said Kriewaldt, the *Welfare Ordinance* was valid, and Raberaba was lawfully a ward. The only question left to decide was whether Namatjira had 'supplied' rum to him by simply leaving an open bottle on the taxi's back seat. Kriewaldt had some sympathy for Ashkanasy's argument that he had not. Recently, while he and his wife were away, an Aboriginal house boy Kriewaldt 'employed' had 'helped himself' to some grog the judge kept at home, and had then driven and crashed his government car. 'My failure to keep my stock of liquor in a more secure place did not,' Kriewaldt hoped, 'constitute a "supply".' Despite this, the 'only possible' inference that could be drawn from Namatjira's decision to leave the open bottle of rum on the back seat was that he intended Raberaba to drink from it.

Namatjira was guilty of supplying alcohol to a ward, and had to be punished. The minimum penalty was six months' prison unless the Supreme Court thought there were 'mitigating circumstances'. Ashkanasy led evidence suggesting that Arrernte people were under an ongoing obligation to share property with other Arrernte, and Kriewaldt – who 'from time to time read such books on the Australian Aboriginal as come under my notice' – agreed that this traditional rule had indeed been well documented. After digressing into a weird discussion of the anthropological literature on wife-sharing, he said he didn't think that the Arrernte sharing rule was all that relevant. Missionaries had been busy converting Arrernte people since 1877. Namatjira himself had been born on a mission. Kriewaldt thought most Arrernte people probably retained very little traditional law. On the other hand, Namatjira was a generous guy, and he wasn't fully assimilated. Kriewaldt concluded that he had grounds to mitigate Namatjira's sentence from six months to three.[47]

Namatjira instructed Ashkanasy to lodge a further appeal, so Kriewaldt didn't immediately enforce the imprisonment order. The artist went bush to paint and wait. The High Court refused to hear the appeal.[48] After Namatjira went briefly to the Alice Springs gaol, Hasluck intervened to ensure he served the rest of his sentence at Papunya, northwest of Hermannsburg. But Namatjira was dejected. His health declined rapidly, and he died following a heart attack in August 1959, just five months after he was imprisoned.[49]

Exclusive domain

Settler courts aren't static. What happens in them changes according to the attitudes and beliefs of, and approaches taken by, judges, juries, prosecutors and defence lawyers, all of whom are subject to prevailing cultural ideas and policy environments. Nowhere is this more evident, due to the limited number of judges who sat there, than in the Northern Territory during the twentieth century.

The most powerful of all prevailing ideas among settlers about the applicability of their courts and their laws in Australia is that their laws *should* apply universally and exclusively, including to the actions of First Nations people. This idea, which developed during the first fifty years of British settlement, continues to prevail as strongly as ever in the present century.

WINDS OF CHANGE

How the First Nations tried to get settler institutions to listen

It's a typically wintry June day in Melbourne, where the damp cold wind feels like it's come straight off the Antarctic. It's mid-2012, and I'm living in one of Preston's many multiplying apartment blocks, each of which is built by developers and purchased by investors, who clearly have no intention of enduring the lack of soundproofing and high heating costs themselves. But it's only a five-minute walk to where I'm interning, in an old Centrelink office on High Street that's been recently repurposed by the Victorian Aboriginal Legal Service (VALS) after it outgrew its Fitzroy origins and chased its clients through Melbourne's rapidly gentrifying northern suburbs.

The first voice callers to VALS hear is that of the teenaged trainee downstairs; she hasn't been here very long herself, so she'll invariably call one of the lawyers or legal secretaries upstairs for advice about where to direct the call. Today that's me, which I like to think helps out the lawyers who are rushing in and out with briefcases and folders and stories of law at the coalface of the magistrates' courts. 'I've got a bit of a strange one,' she says in a voice even more unsure than usual. 'I think it might be crime? Some guy wants to sue the government because he got charged with trespass or something.'

Suing the government would be a civil matter, but a trespass charge is definitely criminal. He might just be unhappy about being charged, or maybe police were unnecessarily rough when they arrested him. 'I'll talk to him,' I say.

The voice on the other end of the line is that of an older man, perhaps in his fifties or sixties. 'I'm pleading not guilty and I want VALS to help me sue the government,' he confirms emphatically. I ask whether he was arrested. 'My oath I was arrested!' He tells me his story.

> There's a house the government owns, it's boarded up now. Long time back, they used it to keep kids in, Stolen kids. Our mob. I got wind they're going to try to flog it off, maybe to a developer. So I set up camp there. I changed the locks. It's owned by the government, right? So it's Crown land. Well, there's no such thing as Crown land. The Queen of England owns nothing on Wurundjeri land. We never gave it up to that British mob. We never sold it. Nobody ever paid us nothing for it. So it's Wurundjeri land. How can I trespass on my own land? That's like me going to England and putting the Queen in lockup for trespassing in Buckingham Palace!

Self-determination

The relationship between Aboriginal and Settler Australia, which had been on a footing not that far removed from slavery, began to change in some fundamental ways during the 1960s.[1] There were many reasons why. The movement for civil rights among African Americans provided ideas and tactics, which were adopted and adapted by Aboriginal activists.[2] White Australia began to reject overtly racist ideology in the wake of the Nazi atrocities, and was increasingly obliged to extend its liberal language of rights to people who weren't white. Slowly, governments began to reflect this change.

As a result, Aboriginal people gradually won full civil rights: the right to vote at all state and federal elections; the right to be counted in the national Census;[3] the right to access social security; the right to not be discriminated against on the basis of race, ethnicity or culture.[4] And the right to be paid ordinary wages, equal to the wages earned by settler Australians. Like all civil rights milestones, equal wages were won at different times in different places, though among the most celebrated are those won by Aboriginal workers in the Northern Territory's cattle industry. One of the largest cattle stations, Wave Hill on Gurindji land, had been owned for half a century by a British family, the Vesteys, large-scale tax-avoiders who for decades hadn't been paying their Aboriginal workers much more than very basic food – and often not even that.[5] Dexter Daniels, an indomitable organiser originally from the Roper River Mission, convinced the North Australian Workers' Union to challenge discriminatory provisions of the pastoral award. The Commonwealth Conciliation and Arbitration Commission famously agreed in March 1966 but the Vesteys and other pastoralists then convinced the Commission to give them three years' grace before the new non-discriminatory award would be enforced.

And so, what at first appeared (to settler Australians) to be a campaign for civil rights – the right to be treated *equally* to settler Australians – was also something quite different. Being paid equally wouldn't change the fact that the Vesteys owned the land on which the sprawling Wave Hill cattle station was situated. The Vesteys would continue to profit from that land, which the Gurindji had never sold or ceded. The Gurindji had been forced into dependence on Wave Hill when their waterholes were fenced off and cattle destroyed their food sources. It was the Vesteys, not the Gurindji, who had the legal right to use the land and to say who could come and go. Vincent Lingiari led two hundred stockmen, servants and their families off the Wave Hill station in August 1966. 'We want them Vestey mob all go away from here,' striker Pincher Manguari told writer Frank Hardy at the time. 'We bin here long time before them Vestey mob. This is our country, all this bin Gurindji country ... We want this land. We strike for that.'[6] The famous strike lasted nine years, until the new prime minister, Gough Whitlam, negotiated the return of a small proportion of Wave Hill to the Gurindji in 1975.

Upon becoming prime minister in 1972, Whitlam asked Edward Woodward – who'd represented the Yirrkala plaintiffs in the Nabalco case (discussed later in this chapter), and was now an additional judge of the Territory's Supreme Court – to investigate how best to legislate Aboriginal land rights in the NT. Out of Woodward's recommendations came Aboriginal Land Councils and Australia's first land rights bill, which was later carried through by Malcolm Fraser's government (using the federal parliament's new post-1967 powers) after Whitlam's dismissal.[7]

Land rights were part of an even broader campaign for what can be called 'Indigenous rights'.[8] This campaign wasn't aimed at the right to be merely treated *equally* to settler Australians. It was, at its core, a campaign to have Settler Australia recognise that the First Nations had rights inherent in their status as first owners and occupiers who had never ceded their lands or their sovereignty to the settler invaders. It was of course important that settler law stopped discriminating *against* Indigenous people: that was what civil rights were about. But it was just as important that settlers began allowing First Nations to determine their own futures, in accordance with their own cultures and their own laws. Canadian First Nations activists began using the term 'citizens plus' to articulate their similar demands.[9]

International law, itself drawn almost exclusively from Western European norms, didn't explicitly recognise a principle of 'self-determination' until it was included in the United Nations' new charter in 1945.[10] Most of humanity, especially in the northern hemisphere, had become accustomed to an almost entirely opposite idea over the preceding millennia: the 'rights' of the conqueror to the spoils of a successful invasion and to impose his own laws, culture and language on a vanquished people.[11] But the right of a people to freely determine both its political status and its economic, social and cultural development is surely at the core of the very idea of peaceful coexistence of different communities of people.

Suddenly, settler institutions in Australia – parliaments, governments, even courts – were open to arguments they and everyone else, including historians, had been studiously avoiding for nearly two centuries. Whitlam's government did away with Menzies and Hasluck's old policy of assimilation, and ushered in an era of 'self-determination', underpinning which was the then-radical recognition that Aboriginal people have a right to make decisions, or at least participate in them, about matters affecting their lives. But the First Nations wanted something even greater. An important aspect of cultural practice was the maintenance and enforcement of cultural norms, including through the punishment of transgression. Would Aboriginal people at last be able to live according to their own laws? What would this mean for the application of the criminal law?

As the 'winds of change' swept through Africa and Asia, nations that had been colonised by imperial European powers during the preceding centuries asserted their right to independence – and were prepared to take up arms in the cause. The journey to independence was often long and more than occasionally bloody, but the process was relatively straightforward: it involved the removal of small elite groups of European administrators. By the 1980s, most former European colonies had won or otherwise gained independence.

But in places where colonial powers had practically taken over – like in Australia – things were much more complicated.

Holding the line

In August 1963, parliament in Canberra tabled bark petitions from Yolngu people and communities asking that it put a halt to a planned bauxite mine near Yirrkala. It was, after all, their land: they'd never sold it, or given it away, or leased it, or given any kind of permission for minerals to be dug out of it so that settler shareholders could get rich. It wasn't the first time Aboriginal people had petitioned settler lawmakers, but it was the first time that lawmakers took anything like real notice. Parliament didn't accede to the petitioners' requests, but it did create a committee that recommended the Yirrkala people be compensated.[12] If that had led to compensation being paid, it would have been another first: for nearly two hundred years, land had been stolen from Aboriginal nations without the merest hint of redress. But the Northern Territory's parliament ignored the compensation idea when it legislated its approval of Nabalco's mine in 1968.

In another first, representatives of the Rirratjingu, Gumatj and Djapu clans then brought a lawsuit in the Supreme Court. They argued that if the common law of Britain did in fact apply to the Gove Peninsula, where the Territory government had authorised Nabalco to establish its mine, then that same common law necessarily had to recognise the form of 'communal native title' held by the clans around Yirrkala since time immemorial. If there was a form of property right, and it was being usurped by the mine, then the Yolngu were entitled to compensation.

Justice Richard Blackburn disagreed. He was presented with many cases showing Britons making agreements with 'native peoples' all around the world, from Africa and India to the American colonies. But those cases assumed there had been people with the capacity to make agreements about the use of land. Australia, however, had been 'settled', not anything else; the Yolngu plaintiffs were haunted by the ghost of *Cooper v Stuart*. Therefore, only the common law of Britain applied in Australia from the date of settlement, in addition to any applicable legislation passed by parliaments. He referred to another archaic (1919) decision of the Privy Council – the same body that had decided *Cooper v Stuart* – also decided at a time when racist ideas were thought to be scientific:

> The estimation of the rights of aboriginal tribes is always inherently difficult. Some tribes are so low in the scale of social organisation that their usages and conceptions of rights and duties are not to be reconciled

with the institutions or the legal ideas of civilised society. Such a gulf cannot be bridged. It would be idle to impute to such people some shadow of the rights known to our law and then to transmute it into the substance of transferable rights of property as we know them.[13]

On the other hand, just two years later, the Privy Council had issued a caution to judges throughout the British Empire who may have cause, from time to time, to determine 'the real character' of native title. 'There is a tendency ... to render that title conceptually in terms which are appropriate only to systems which have grown up under English law,' wrote Viscount Haldane in 1921. 'But this tendency has to be held in check closely.'[14] Yet Blackburn concluded that the common law had *never* recognised any form of 'communal native title'. And neither the British parliament, nor any Australian parliament after self-government, had created such a title.

Blackburn also found, paradoxically, that while the plaintiffs' clans had 'a government of laws, and not of men',[15] there was no evidence they had a *proprietary* interest in the land, which he thought would be required to show a form of title. Although he found against the Yirrkala plaintiffs – the bauxite mine went ahead, and is still there today – Blackburn's judgement left a narrow legal gap through which Eddie Koiki Mabo, from the island of Mer in the far east of the Torres Strait, subsequently threaded his own challenge. Mabo's decade-long case concluded in June 1992 with the High Court's finding: the common law *does*, after all, recognise native title.[16]

Blackburn's 1971 judgement signalled something important about how the new arguments based on self-determination would play out in Australia. Much of the success of those arguments elsewhere depended either on weight of numbers (in Africa and Asia) or on the pre-existence of some code of rights (like the United States' Bill of Rights) to which advocates could appeal. Those conditions were uniquely absent in Australia. Anyone hoping that the institutions of settler law might dramatically overturn decades of accepted principle, even if that principle was drawn from what we might kindly describe as alternative facts about First Nations' cultures and societies, was to be disappointed.

Plural expectations

Yirrkala was at the vanguard of efforts by Aboriginal people in the 1960s to have their laws recognised by settler authorities. Sustained contact with settlers was relatively recent. The Methodist Missionary Society had arrived in the wake of the deaths of the five Japanese trepangers and Constable McColl in 1932–33. The settler population on the peninsula exploded in 1968 as Nabalco developed its bauxite mine, and with the company and its workers – who lived in the new mining town of Nhulunbuy, less than 20 kilometres up the road from Yirrkala – came alcohol in large quantities. By 1970, the last groups had 'come in' permanently to Yirrkala, and the people there were now 'almost entirely economically dependent on wages received' for working on the mission station, though growing numbers also worked for Nabalco.[17] The community sent petitions on bark to Canberra demanding a halt to the mine; by 1968, as we've seen, that dispute had escalated to the Federal Court. Yirrkala was making waves, nationally and internationally. As such, it was a frequent destination for researchers.

One such researcher was Nancy Williams, a doctoral student in the University of California's department of anthropology. For extended periods between 1969 and 1971, Williams lived among the people of Yirrkala and learned not only about their interactions with settler law, but also something of how their own law and dispute-resolution mechanisms worked. Despite these decades of upheaval, Williams found at Yirrkala a political community with a well-functioning system of dispute resolution that was effective at maintaining social order. This was the community Blackburn found – after Yolngu leaders invited him to spend time there – governed by a rule of law, not of men. In her thesis, Williams described what she learned of Yirrkala's authority structure, based on traditional kinship relationships and seniority and modified to the town-like environment of the Yirrkala settlement. A 'village council' of senior men met regularly to decide matters of concern to the community as a whole. Its meeting procedure drew from that used in clan meetings, from speaking order to its consensus decision-making model. Among the matters discussed at meetings were disputes, offences and sanctions.

During the time Williams was there, most of the grievances discussed at public meetings were over contractual obligations of bestowal, betrothal, marriage and women. Although these appeared to outsiders to be disputes over the control of women, the obligations were tied to underlying land

obligations. There had been an increase in these grievances since people
had permanently settled at Yirrkala, and the recent introduction of alcohol
seemed to cause some men to become angry over 'old troubles' – grievances that were supposed to have been resolved – when they were drunk.

The response to individual offending was invariably the imposition
or expectation of a form of redress. Williams observed that most physical
assaults, even where they led to serious injury or death, were not seen as
offences in and of themselves, but rather related to underlying issues. 'Their
perception of the underlying issue determines liability for the assault, and
the nature of appropriate redress,' Williams wrote. Sanctions were publicised,
and ranged from physical assault and ritualised revenge (including death if
the offence was serious enough) to temporary exile, religious ceremonies and
restitution, which by 1970 had taken the form of cash payments. Ultimately,
sanctions directed at individuals were aimed at the restoration of group harmony, and justice was tied to the equitable allocation of land among clans.

All of this took place alongside, and almost regardless of, any involvement by the settler justice system, which Yolngu people assumed operated
in parallel with their own. Unlike the settler system, the Yirrkala community had no expectation of total or perfect sovereignty. In 1967, the president
of Yirrkala's Village Council prepared a written statement aimed at con-
firming or establishing legal pluralism. Settler and Yolngu laws 'will stand
together and work together for the people's benefit and for country because
the white Australian law is too hard and too far from the Aborigines law,' it
said. 'If we are going to let down our laws,' it continued, 'that means we are
lost because we will lose a part of our life.' Later, the council also wrote a
letter to the Northern Territory's police commissioner to express Yirrkala's
displeasure regarding the recent behaviour of officers. 'We like them – all
the constables,' the letter said, 'and we'd like to understand and be friendly
with them, and to make a good relationship between the constables and the
Aborigines.' The council hoped that, in future, officers would be 'friendly,
kindly and will talk to people in a Christian way before they are taken to
the police car or to the gaol here at Nhulunbuy'.

Unsurprisingly, just as settlers see and interpret Aboriginal law and
culture through their own cultural lens, Yolngu people looked for equivalent structures and authorities in settler institutions. When Williams was
in Yirrkala, settlers had imposed their law in eastern Arnhem Land for
fewer than four decades. She observed that Yolngu people still had little

comprehension of the principles that underpinned settler law, namely sanctity of the person and of private property, although settlers tended to assume either that these principles were universal or that people in Yirrkala had been adequately instructed in them. Often these principles conflicted with those that underpinned Yolngu law. When Yolngu people wanted to challenge settler interests they were forced to do so in settler courts, because the settlers didn't recognise Yolngu law or its dispute-resolution systems. But they were at an insurmountable disadvantage because settler courts rarely placed significance on factors most important to Yolngu people. The land rights case was an instance of this injustice; another occurred when the Yirrkala community tried to contest a hotel liquor licence for Nhulunbuy. Both cases were inevitably decided by settler institutions in favour of settler interests, and against Yolngu interests.

Settler court proceedings were seen by the Yolngu as variations of particular kinds of clan or council meetings, which Williams called 'moots'. But the procedure in a clan moot bore little resemblance to that of a criminal court, where represented defendants don't participate directly, where charges are discussed separately even though they might emerge from a single incident, where rules of evidence precluded certain material from even being discussed, and where admissions had consequences drawn from a practically invisible code. In clan moots, there's usually no question that everyone in the room knows what a 'defendant' has done wrong, so questions of proof aren't significant. Clearly, Yolngu people were at a severe disadvantage in courtrooms. Even when they were represented, their understanding of court procedure – while much more advanced than settlers' understanding of Aboriginal law – was rudimentary at best.

Williams spoke to many Yolngu people who wanted to use police to enforce Yirrkala's existing system of temporary exile: to have police officers escort people out of the community in accordance with the decisions of the moots. Police, of course, couldn't do that. Their job was simply to uphold the settler law, regardless of what the Yirrkala community or Aboriginal law demanded. As a consequence, Williams observed that for most Yolngu people, police were inextricably linked with jail. Perhaps because prison had no equivalent among the sanctions imposed by Aboriginal law, or perhaps because Yolngu people could clearly see that police officers didn't respect them, 'a number of Aborigines professed to be disdainful of imprisonment'. It remains the case in many parts of north Australia that an offender who spends time in prison must yet face a much more meaningful cultural sanction following his release.

But settler law had long since unilaterally claimed total sovereignty over the entire continent. Its institutions – its courts and parliaments – guarded that sovereignty zealously. Even in the era of self-determination, settler law was not about to let any cracks open up.

The sovereignty challenges

In 1971, two men stood trial for murder in Victoria's Supreme Court. One of them, Trevor, was Aboriginal. The court settled on the requisite twelve jurors. Through his lawyer, Trevor then challenged the jury. None of the jurors was Aboriginal, so the jury couldn't possibly be said to be made up of Trevor's peers. Justice Murray McInerney ruled that was irrelevant. It was the sheriff's responsibility under the *Juries Act* to compile a random list of names from the roll and to issue summons. Nobody in the parliament who had created the *Juries Act* in 1967 had been Aboriginal, and the Act said nothing about jurors' race or ethnicity or culture. Trevor's challenge failed. His right to be tried by a jury of his 'peers' did not mean that he had a right to be tried by people who shared his upbringing, cultural expectations and experiences.[18]

The legal challenges became more radical. One man charged with murder in 1976 argued that the NSW Supreme Court had no jurisdiction to try him, because New South Wales was neither settled, conquered nor ceded. The judge, Arthur Rath, found the argument 'untenable' and that these questions had been settled by the nineteenth-century decisions in *R v Murrell* and *Cooper v Stuart*. The Privy Council's Lord Watson 'would have been fully aware of the presence of Aborigines in New South Wales at the time of settlement', Rath wrote, so second-guessing his conclusions a century later was futile. Rath continued the conspiracy of silence about *R v Bon Jon*, decided by Judge Willis five years after *Murrell*.[19]

Paul Coe, a Wiradjuri man who had co-founded both the Aboriginal Legal Service in Redfern (1970) and the Aboriginal Tent Embassy in Canberra (1972), travelled with fellow 'members of the Aboriginal nation' to England where, in the presence of its 'natives', he planted Harold Thomas's new Aboriginal flag on a Dover beach in November 1976 and proclaimed sovereignty over the whole of the United Kingdom. The following April, he did the same thing at Kurnell, where James Cook had first landed and encountered the Gweagal people more than two centuries earlier. Settlers dismissed them as stunts, but they served a serious point, which became clear when he tried to sue both Australia and Britain on behalf of 'the Aboriginal community and nation of Australia'. He argued that Aboriginal people had 'enjoyed exclusive sovereignty' over the Australian continent 'from time immemorial', that Cook had wrongfully claimed sovereignty in 1770, and that Phillip had wrongfully claimed possession in 1778.

Coe never had the opportunity to have his claim considered. Three settler judges – Harry Gibbs, Anthony Mason and Keith Aickin – said the claim was too deficient, and refused his request to amend it. Gibbs – who would later conclude that the *Racial Discrimination Act* was unlawful,[20] presided over the arch-conservative Samuel Griffith Society and remained a staunch monarchist – was particularly unimpressed with Coe's claims to have asserted sovereignty over both Australia *and* Britain, which was 'quite absurd and so clearly vexatious as to amount to an abuse of the process of the Court'. Clearly he'd missed Coe's point entirely. Again, Gibbs and Aickin believed that legal questions about Australia's origins had been settled by the Privy Council in *Cooper v Stuart*: the colonies had been acquired by Britain by settlement, not conquest.[21]

Others built on Coe's challenge, and learned from its perceived deficiencies. Carlemo Wacando, a resident of Erub in the Torres Strait (also named Darnley Island by William Bligh in 1792), went to court asking for a declaration that the island was not legally part of Queensland or Australia. Wacando wanted to establish a trepang fishery and explore for petroleum without complying with state or federal legislation. It turned out that Wacando had a pretty good argument in settler law. The 1494 Treaty of Tordesillas, which had apparently assigned Erub (along with the entire eastern half of the Australian continent) to Spain, was hardly more preposterous than Cook's possession claim in 1770. Documents were created during the second half of the nineteenth century which contained what one High Court judge called 'gross inconsistencies and ludicrous errors of geographical description' in the way they described Queensland's boundaries. But then the British parliament – more than 14,000 kilometres away – created the *Colonial Boundaries Act* in 1895, and smoothed away any problems by allowing governments to 'alter' colonial boundaries at will. If Erub hadn't been part of Queensland before, it was now.[22]

Carlemo Wacando wasn't the only challenger from the Torres Strait Islands. By the early 1980s, Eddie Koiki Mabo was working as a groundskeeper on the Townsville campus of James Cook University. Henry Reynolds was working on the same campus as a historian. With his students, Reynolds had begun collecting oral histories from Indigenous people. Mabo told Reynolds about his homeland, the island of Mer – which had been known to Britons as Murray Island since 1791 – on the eastern edge of the Torres Strait. The London Missionary Society arrived in 1872, and by the end of that decade Queensland had annexed all the islands in the Strait, including Mer.

'Don't you realise it's all Crown land?' Reynolds asked. Mabo was stunned. Over sandwiches and tea, Reynolds encouraged Mabo to speak to lawyers and claim land rights over Mer.[23] When he did, Queensland's parliament, then controlled by Joh Bjelke-Petersen's National Party government, immediately legislated to explicitly and retroactively extinguish – without compensation – any claim the Islanders might have had since the 1879 annexation.[24]

In the first *Mabo* case, the High Court – with Mason now as its chief justice – decided that Queensland's law was inconsistent with the *Racial Discrimination Act*, passed by the federal parliament a decade earlier in 1975, and was therefore invalid.[25] That decision paved the way for Mabo's substantive land claim. Queensland's government argued the position as it had been in Australian law to that point: that upon settlement of a territory, the law of England became the law of that territory, and the Crown automatically acquired the 'absolute beneficial ownership' of all the land in that territory. That was the effect of *Cooper v Stuart*. Sensationally, though, this time the Mason court found *against* Queensland. It rejected the nineteenth-century doctrine of *terra nullius*, held that Australia's common law did, after all, recognise a form of property known as 'native title', and found that the Meriam people were entitled to the possession, use, occupation and enjoyment of most of Mer and the surrounding islands.[26] Sadly, of course, Koiki Mabo had died six months before the decision. On its third anniversary, his grave in Townsville was desecrated with racist and Nazi graffiti.[27]

Mabo (No 2) looked and felt to many people like a thunderous blow to the foundation myths of the settler state. So Paul Coe and his family thought the time was ripe to have another go at the sovereignty argument. If *Cooper v Stuart* did not reflect the factual circumstances, either at the time Cook claimed sovereignty over the eastern coastline or at the time Phillip arrived to 'settle' what was clearly not an empty land, then surely it followed that the British claims to sovereignty would quickly unravel? In 1993, Paul's sister Isabel sued on behalf of the Wiradjuri nation, claiming sovereignty over its lands – a significant proportion of what is now known as New South Wales – only. They once again drew Anthony Mason, who thought their description of the boundaries of the territory they were claiming was too imprecise. It was a neat way of setting them up to fail: precise and fixed territorial boundaries had been a relatively recent invention of the modern Westphalian nation-state,[28] and had not demarcated Aboriginal lands. In any event, Mason reminded the Coes that all the judges involved in the 1979 case *and* all the judges involved in the *Mabo* decision had firmly rejected the suggestion that Aboriginal people had a legitimate claim to *sovereignty*. Mason did so again.[29]

The Coe siblings weren't the only ones looking for a crack in the settler state's defences. In June of 1988, the year that Settler Australia was celebrating the 200th anniversary of Phillip's arrival, Denis Walker appeared in a Queensland court charged with burglary. Walker's mother was Oodgeroo Noonuccal, the Quandamooka Murri poet, educator and activist who had joined the Communist Party during the 1940s because it was the only Australian political party that opposed the 'White Australia' policy. Influenced by the Black Power movement, which emerged out of the American civil rights struggle of the early 1960s but rejected its commitment to nonviolence, and which achieved global notoriety following Tommie Smith's and John Carlos's raised fist salutes on the dais at the Mexico Olympics in 1968, Walker established one of Brisbane's first tent embassies (in 1969) and, with Sam Watson, founded the Australian Black Panther Party in Brisbane in 1972.[30] Representing himself, Walker told the judge, Tony Skoien, that he refused to plead guilty or not guilty. He said the court had no jurisdiction to try him. It was a jurisdiction born of Cook's illegal claim of sovereignty. If he were to go to trial, it wouldn't be before a jury of his peers, because most or all of the jury members would be white. Ignoring these arguments, Skoien set Walker's case down for trial. Walker was later found guilty of causing damage (though not of burglary).

Walker engaged lawyers, including Bryan Keon-Cohen, who was already working on the *Mabo* cases. They appealed to the High Court, which sent his case back to the Court of Criminal Appeal. There, the

Queensland government conceded that Walker's people, the Nunukul, *had* occupied Stradbroke Island before and since 1770. They also agreed that Cook's instructions had authorised him to take possession of 'convenient situations' on the Australian continent only 'with the consent of the native' peoples, and that he'd obviously acted outside that authorisation. The court itself could see how Cook's original sovereignty claim raised questions about how it was, exactly, that judges apply Queensland's criminal laws to Stradbroke Island, and also why the Nunukul people are 'now expected and obliged to laws not of their own making'. Unable to answer these questions, the Queensland court's judges fell back on circular reasoning: 'the fundamental fact, be it historical, political or social, is that we as judges recognise the authority in Queensland of laws having their source in the Imperial, Colonial, State and Commonwealth statutes'. Put another way: constitutions tell judges to apply laws made by parliaments, and that's the end of the story.[31]

In the wake of Walker's challenge, Justin Malbon, who later became a professor of law at Monash University, thought that the Queensland court's reasoning was open to 'a well thought out jurisdictional challenge' by an Aboriginal plaintiff.[32] After the High Court decided *Mabo* in mid-1992, Denis Walker had the opportunity to try again. Members of the Bundjalung nation had invited him to Nimbin, to help prevent the local municipal council from digging up a sacred site. In July 1994, council workers felled a huge laurel tree in the park. Local Aboriginal people reacted with grief and rage. Fights broke out, including at the Rainbow Cafe, where Walker was. A police officer arrived and, Walker said, assaulted him. Walker retaliated, and managed to take the officer's gun from its holster. Walker pointed the gun at the officer, made a brief speech, and then pointed it up and fired until it was empty of bullets. He then presented his wrists to be handcuffed, and they were. The officer charged him with resisting arrest, assaulting police and discharging a firearm. In court, Walker explained that his own life experience had caused him to fear what could eventuate if the gun remained loaded and in the officer's possession, and observed that nobody had been hurt.[33]

Walker also appealed to the High Court, claiming that parliaments 'lack the power to legislate in a manner affecting Aboriginal people' without their consent: the Crown had no sovereign law-making power over Aboriginal people. Like Paul and Isabel Coe before him, Walker drew Anthony Mason, who called his claim 'untenable'. Mason's judgement is striking for its tone of sneering contempt. Nimbin was 'said to be' on Bundjalung Country. Walker was 'said to be' a member of the Nunukul nation. 'Nation' was placed inside inverted commas, as if to indicate Mason's view that neither Bundjalung nor Nunukul can really be described by that word. New South Wales' parliament had the power to make laws 'for the peace, welfare and good government' of that state and everyone in it, 'in all cases whatsoever'. The chief justice said nothing about the facts of Walker's arrest, and only that he'd been charged with 'an offence'. For Mason, the facts that brought Walker to court were irrelevant. For Walker, of course, those facts were key to his whole argument.

And Mason took the opportunity to clear up what might have been a misconception among Aboriginal people and their supporters in the aftermath of *Mabo*:

> There is nothing in the recent decision in *Mabo v Queensland (No 2)* to support the notion that the parliaments of the Commonwealth and New South Wales lack legislative competence to regulate or affect the rights of Aboriginal people, or the notion that the application of Commonwealth or state laws to Aboriginal people is in any way subject to their acceptance, adoption, request or consent.

Mason said that such notions 'amount to the contention that a new source of sovereignty resides in the Aboriginal people'. He reminded Walker, and everyone else, that his court had specifically rejected that idea in its *Mabo* decision. He quoted himself: '*Mabo (No 2)* is entirely at odds with the notion that sovereignty adverse to the Crown resides in the Aboriginal people of Australia.' Mason said Aboriginal people had no rights or interests other than those created or recognised by legislation (made by settler parliaments) and the common law (imported from Britain). For Mason, Walker's statement of claim disclosed 'no reasonable cause of action'. There was simply no such thing as Aboriginal sovereignty in settler jurisprudence. *Full stop.*

Mason also disposed of any concept that an Aboriginal criminal law survived colonisation, an argument that recent cases from the Northern Territory and Western Australia had clearly been flirting with (see chapter 5). In their submission, Walker and Keon-Cohen had quoted from

Blackstone's *Commentaries* – 'colonists carry with them only so much of English law as is applicable to their own situation', an idea which had been approved by the Privy Court in *Cooper v Stuart* – to argue that the New South Wales criminal law didn't apply to Aboriginal people. 'That proposition must be rejected,' Mason said flatly, reverting to axiom in the absence of reason. 'It is a basic principle that all people should stand equal before the law.'

'Just as all persons in the country enjoy the benefits of domestic laws,' Mason went on, 'so also must they accept the burdens those laws impose.' (Walker, and many Aboriginal people, would have been entitled to ask: 'which benefits?') Even if Aboriginal criminal laws survived after 1778, Mason said, they were 'extinguished by the passage of criminal statutes of general application', namely the various Crimes Acts and Criminal Codes.[34] So again, the circular argument: the British did something a long time ago, without asking Aboriginal people, and now that it's done it can't be undone. Why? Because it was done.[35]

Most recently, this circular argument has included a new component: that Australian courts – even the highest court in the land, the High Court – are not competent to even *hear* challenges to the sovereign rights of the Crown, because it is those rights which also created the High Court, in the *Commonwealth of Australia Constitution Act*, passed by the House of Commons on 5 July 1900. There's something of the original sin to this circular argument: because the mistake was made *before* the Australian Constitution was created, there's nothing that can be done about it. The practical effect of this argument is that sovereignty challenges must be heard outside the legal system established by the Constitution. The obvious option is the Privy Council, to which the Constitution originally allowed appeals, and which dates in its current form from the *Acts of Union* in 1707. Despite repeated efforts to shut down appeals from the High Court to the Privy Council, such an avenue remains, as long as the High Court issues a certificate.[36] Conveniently, however, the High Court declared in 1985 that it would no longer be issuing such certificates because it wishes to protect Australia's sovereignty.[37] The circular argument thus takes on the logic of a petulant child, or a gaslighting bully: the High Court won't hear your sovereignty challenge because it can't, and it also won't give you a certificate to allow the Privy Council to hear your sovereignty challenge because it doesn't want to.

Mason's language – 'said to be', 'no reasonable cause of action', 'enjoy the benefits', 'accept the burdens' – was clearly inflammatory, and it's hard to believe he wasn't aware of that. If it's difficult to reconcile the Anthony Mason of the *Mabo* decisions with the Anthony Mason of his rejection of the claims made by Paul and Isabel Coe and Denis Walker between 1979 and 1994, it should be observed that the second *Mabo* decision, while revolutionary within the context of settler law, is actually a very limited one. The form of title it recognised – native title – is weak and easily extinguishable by settler parliaments. If it was considered radical in 1992, that's really because Australian courts had (radically) ignored the development of the common law for two hundred years. The decision provided retrospective justification for many of the terrible – and illegal – acts of dispossession that settlers had perpetrated over the previous 216 years. And, as Mason emphasised, it confirmed that the settler state – of which the High Court itself was an integral part – did not recognise Aboriginal sovereignty. Ultimately, *Mabo (No 2)* was a highly compromised decision. If *terra nullius* was a myth because Aboriginal people did actually live here before 1770, and if they did so under 'a government of law, and not of man', and if Aboriginal people resisted the British when they stole their lands, then how was it that the British 'settled' (rather than 'invaded' or 'conquered')?

To avoid answering that question, the High Court's judges in *Mabo* stretched logic beyond its limits. Gerard Brennan and the other five judges in the majority had no problem overturning most of the old fictions – that Aboriginal people were too 'low in the scale of social organisation' to occupy land; that the Crown automatically acquired complete title over all lands over which it claimed sovereignty; the idea of *terra nullius*. The High Court was no longer bound by decisions of nineteenth-century courts concerned with empire-building. But it baulked at the next logical step in the argument. To fully recognise Indigenous rights in Australia would 'fracture a skeletal principle of our legal system', as Brennan put it.[38] In other words: while it was no longer constrained by *particular* decisions made by past judges, the High Court remained bound by an opaque and undefined *general* sense of the law's historical development. Brennan might equally have appealed to 'the vibe', as Dennis Denuto would five years later in the film *The Castle*.

By the time it was pulled and stretched through the settler legal system, *Mabo* had become a case not about *whether* the Crown had acquired sovereignty over Mer: in the High Court, Koiki Mabo and his lawyers ultimately didn't challenge that (mostly because they would have lost if they had). For the courts it was a case about the *implications and consequences* of the Crown's (apparently undisputed) acquisition of sovereignty. The High Court abandoned *terra nullius*, but created a new fiction in its place: that any 'native title' rights to continue using and occupying land *following* the Crown's acquisition of sovereignty could be subsequently 'extinguished' by the Crown, whether or not the native title holders consented. In the end, *Mabo* was a slightly more palatable justification for what happened after 1788 than *Cooper v Stuart*.

Australia's 'mainstream' media didn't trouble itself with these questions when it reported Denis Walker's 1994 challenge. Mason's judgement didn't need them to because it said nothing about what had occurred in Nimbin. A reporter reading Mason's words would have come away assuming that the story here was one of an Aboriginal criminal trying to get off scot-free by trying it on with a preposterous argument. Echoing the *Sydney Herald*'s description of Sidney Stephen's very similar (and equally unsuccessful) argument in 1836, the Fairfax papers reported in 1994 on Walker's 'extraordinary claim that Aboriginal people are beyond the reach of the law'.[39]

○

I knew something of this legal history in 2012, when I took the call at the Victorian Aboriginal Legal Service from the man who'd got himself charged with trespass and wanted to challenge the Crown's claim of ownership over Wurundjeri land. I knew of *Walker v The Commonwealth* and a little of Paul and Isabel Coe's challenges. The Coes had been instrumental in establishing the first ALS in Sydney in 1970. It sparked the creation of similar services in other places, including VALS in Melbourne. There is a strong argument that continued challenges to the Crown's defensive claim that it is the single sovereign owner of the Australian continent is, or should be, a core mission of the Aboriginal Legal Services.

As it happened, we explained what the High Court had said in *Walker* and declined to run his challenge. We advised him to plead guilty, and said we'd help him enter a plea in mitigation that would make his punishment more lenient. Given the prevailing attitude of settler courts to sovereignty challenges, it was sound legal advice.

BENDING

How the settler criminal justice system began to make accommodations

Just before Christmas in 1958, the mutilated body of an eight-year-old white girl, Mary Olive Hattam, was found in a small cave just off a beach near Ceduna, South Australia, where she'd been playing with her brother and a friend. Aboriginal trackers led police to where a travelling fair, the Fun Land Carnival, had been stationed when Mary was killed. A twenty-seven-year-old Arrernte man, Rupert Max Stuart, had been with the carnival, operating its darts stall. He'd been out drinking on the fateful day, which led to his arrest at 9.30 p.m. He wasn't drunk, but this was the era of 'protection'. Although he'd had full drinking entitlements in the Northern Territory (where he was born) since 1953, in South Australia he was permitted to drink only if that state's Aborigines Protection Board had explicitly exempted him from the provisions of its *Aborigines Act*. Among Aboriginal people, such exemptions were commonly known as 'dog licences'. Stuart didn't have one.

Stuart was arrested and interrogated by police, following which he signed a typed confession written in advanced English, even though he was illiterate. Without the confession the case against him was entirely circumstantial. Police later said they'd read each line of the statement back to Stuart to make sure he agreed with it before he signed it. A taxi driver said he dropped him off at the murder scene the very afternoon Mary had been killed, and trackers said Stuart's feet matched the footprints that led away from the cave. Stuart told his lawyer police had used physical violence to force him to confess. But if Stuart gave evidence and submitted himself to cross-examination, the prosecutor would have asked him to confirm – in front of the jury – that he'd been convicted of sexually assaulting another nine-year-old girl in Queensland two years earlier.[1] That fact was likely to overwhelm any chance that the jury might engage in nuanced analysis of the evidence from the Ceduna beach. To avoid that, Stuart made what was called an 'unsworn' statement:

> Mr Jones [a police officer] said: 'Come we know you did it.' I said: 'No.' He said: 'Yes, come on tell me the truth.' I said: 'I didn't do it.' Mr Jones punched me over my eye. I nearly fell off the chair. When I stood up he hit me again on the side of the throat and on the ribs. He tried to punch me again. I stopped it with my elbow. Then Sergeant Walker grabbed me round the throat with two hands. He kept pushing his thumbs into my throat. I could not breathe. I thought I was going to die. The other police-men were all around me. The Sergeant said: 'You had better tell us the bloody truth, now you know.' The Sergeant let me go. The policeman with the typewriter said: 'You killed the little girl.' I was frightened. My head and my throat were hurting. I could hardly breathe . . . One of the police-men . . . said: 'If you don't tell us I will skin you' . . . I thought they would kill me if I didn't say what they wanted. Then I said 'Yes' all the time.[2]

Stuart wasn't allowed to make the statement in court himself, but the judge read it out to the jury. The jury didn't believe him. It convicted, and Justice Geoffrey Reed sentenced him to hang. Through his lawyers, Stuart appealed.

The anthropologist Ted Strehlow, who had been raised in Hermannsburg speaking Arrernte along with English and German, had known Stuart as a child. Strehlow visited Stuart in prison and translated his alibi from Arrernte: Stuart had taken the taxi to a hotel where he'd paid a woman for sex, and where he'd stayed until he was arrested later that evening. Strehlow, also a linguist, formally tested Stuart's command of English. It was nowhere near the standard of the typed confession. Strehlow formed the view that the con-fession was false, and told the High Court. Strehlow was 'apparently . . . not without authority in such matters', the High Court observed. But nobody – including Stuart's trial lawyer – had ever suggested before now that Stuart needed an interpreter. 'This case has caused us a good deal of anxiety,' the court concluded, but it dismissed Stuart's appeal. So did the Privy Council.[3]

By then, journalists and editors at *On Dit* (Adelaide University's stu-dent paper), *Nation*, *The Sydney Morning Herald*, the Melbourne *Herald* and especially Rupert Murdoch's Adelaide paper, *The News*, had been covering Stuart's case in some detail. Murdoch's editor was Rohan Rivett, a grandson of Alfred Deakin and an outspokenly progressive liberal critic of Robert

Menzies and the White Australia policy. Most of the coverage took the view that Stuart's conviction was a miscarriage of justice, and that to execute him would be a travesty. Petitions demanded the commutation of his sentence to life imprisonment. New evidence took Stuart even further away from the crime scene. The conservative premier, Thomas Playford, called a royal commission, which endorsed the courts' decisions – probably because two of the commissioners, Geoffrey Reed and Mellis Napier, were judges who had made those decisions.[4] The commissioners dismissed Strehlow's evidence, declared that Stuart 'understands and speaks … reasonably good English', and were 'quite unable to accept' Stuart's allegations of police brutality.[5] By then, though, Playford's government had already decided – in response to growing public disquiet – to commute Stuart's sentence to life imprisonment.[6]

Max Stuart did fourteen years before he was released in 1973. He spent the next decade in and out of Adelaide's Yatala prison on parole breaches, mostly of the condition to not consume alcohol. Inside prison, he became literate in English and learned to paint watercolours. Upon his final release in 1985, Patrick Dodson, who was then director at the Central Land Council, gave Stuart part-time employment. He eventually became an Arrernte Elder and a significant figure in Central Australian land rights and native title politics, rising to chair of the Central Land Council in 1998.

Stuart may well have murdered Mary Hattam. But his trial and appeals exposed such gaping problems for settler law in trying Aboriginal people who hadn't been socialised into that law or its language that it remains impossible to know for sure. Evidence uncovered after the trial was unable, in 1959, to be considered by appeal courts; this terrifying situation wasn't rectified until 2013 in South Australia.[7] In 1959, Stuart's defence was conducted by a lawyer who was essentially acting pro bono on behalf of the Law Society, and who had no training and little experience in defending Arrernte clients. Nobody interpreted Stuart's Arrernte for settler ears, or settler legalese for Stuart's ears. Settler courts could not fathom the idea of a conspiracy among six police officers to lie about the voluntariness of a confession. Yet during his research for the screenplay of what became the film *Black and White* (2002), writer Louis Nowra spoke to one of the officers, Paul Turner, just before he died. According to Nowra, Turner told him that police had 'jollied' or 'laughed' the confession out of Stuart, and that they'd then bashed him.[8]

The Max Stuart case became a cause célèbre for a new generation of post-war civil rights activists. The problems it highlighted in settler law – many of which had been there from the very beginning of settlers' efforts to apply it to Aboriginal people – were unacceptable to a growing cohort of lawyers throughout the 1960s and 1970s. 'It is a sobering discovery,' wrote High Court judge Michael Kirby following the release of *Black and White*,

> to learn … that the real saviour of Max Stuart's life was not the Austra-
> lian court system. It was not our Constitution. It was not the learned
> judges or the barristers. It was not even our professor of linguistics. To
> a very large extent, it was the chance decision of an exceptional editor-
> in-chief of the Adelaide *News*, Rohan Rivett, endorsed at the outset by
> the new chief proprietor of the *News*, the young Rupert Murdoch, to
> support Max Stuart's cause, that saved his life.[9]

Over the decades that followed, the settler criminal justice system began to make some accommodations to Aboriginal defendants.

Language and understanding

As far back as 1896, Justice Charles Dashwood had thrown out murder charges against Aboriginal defendants where the evidence against them was solely in the form of their own confessions. Four years later, settlers were scandalised by what the *Northern Territory Times and Gazette* called 'a deed unique in the annals of outrages perpetrated by natives': the sei-zure of a boat, the *Wunwulla*, as it was voyaging down the Daly River, and the killing of its settler crew. The following month, two police constables arrested two Aboriginal men, known as 'Cammerfor' and 'Mungkum', near the river's mouth. When the case came to Dashwood's court, the only evi-dence against them was their confessions to police, as filtered through an interpreter. But other available evidence proved that neither men could have been involved. When they were arrested, Aboriginal people 'all along the river' were amused by the white officers' mistake. Dashwood threw out the charges. It was a 'striking example', he said, of the danger of convicting Aboriginal people 'on evidence out of their own mouths'.[10]

Many of Dashwood's successors adopted his approach. When Justice Ross Mallam was confronted with apparent evidence of Padygar's and

Arkirkra's apparent confessions to their murder of Fred Brooks – the act Constable William Murray used as justification for the Coniston Massacre in 1928 – Mallam refused to admit it.[11]

But there had been slippage from this approach by the mid-1970s. Geoff Eames, a senior lawyer at what was then the Central Australian Aboriginal Legal Aid Service (CAALAS), noticed that police were relying solely on confessional evidence to charge and try Aboriginal defendants for serious crimes. He briefed barristers to run a series of criminal trials in which they would specifically challenge confessional evidence. The first four were before Justice James Muirhead (who would later become well known to Settler Australia as Lindy Chamberlain's trial judge). The barristers asked their clients questions like 'are you an airline pilot?' Invariably, their clients would respond: 'yes, I am an airline pilot.' The barristers also called evidence from linguist Jim Downing. In court, Downing told Muirhead: 'I have not been able to get across [to an Aboriginal suspect] the idea of not having to answer if he doesn't have to.' But Muirhead didn't budge. He accepted the officers' testimony: in their own experience, they said, they had no trouble communicating with Aboriginal suspects, and their confessions were reliable.[12]

o

Paula Sweet was an Aboriginal woman who was living the tragedy of dispossession. According to the welfare department, she had been selling sex since she was twelve years old. In 1974, she lived with a white man, Bernard Grondman, who acted as her pimp, and who was known to knee her in the stomach during arguments. One night, when she'd gone missing, Grondman was, he later told police, driving around looking for her. He found her, he said, as she was running from the Todd River. He saw five Aboriginal men chasing her. He did a U-turn as soon as he could, and by the time he returned – about thirty seconds later – he saw an Aboriginal man having sex with Paula in some long grass, apparently against her will. He then rescued Paula, he said, and drove her home. She was very drunk, he said, and she didn't say much except that she'd lost her underwear. She slept through the night, and the next morning declined his offer of a cold hamburger. She said she was a bit sore, but she didn't want to go to the hospital or complain to police. He went to work and returned at lunchtime, when (according to him) she still didn't want to go to the hospital. He returned to work. Grondman finally took her to the hospital at 5.45 p.m. His account was uncorroborated.[13]

Immediately, Paula was rushed to surgery at the point of death. She had a ruptured spleen, four fractured ribs and injuries to her liver, her kidney and her intestines: what is known in medicine as a 'crush' injury. She survived a few days, but died of acute pancreatitis caused by the crush. She never spoke to police. Medical evidence showed that she wouldn't have survived more than about six hours following the kind of assault that could have produced those injuries. Grondman said it had been eighteen hours since her assault by a group of Aboriginal men. After providing a statement, Grondman took police around town and pointed out Nari Wheeler and Frankie Miller Jagamara, whom he said looked a bit like two of the men he'd seen with Paula. Police 'invited' both Wheeler and Jagamara to the station, where they were interviewed and their responses typed up and read back to them, each saying 'yeah' to every assertion.

Transcripts recorded each man's detailed confession to his involvement in a gang rape of Paula in the Todd River bed, during which they'd jumped on her stomach and kicked her in the ribs to stop her screaming. Police charged both Wheeler and Jagamara with rape and murder. The detective sergeant who interrogated Jagamara was cross-examined during the trial about the caution he'd given before asking any questions. The officer had interrogated 'possibly a hundred' Aboriginal suspects during his time in the force. He'd issued cautions to every one of them. 'Can you tell me one occasion on which a full-blood Aboriginal has declined to answer your questions, having been warned that he didn't have to?' The detective sergeant replied: 'I can't remember any, sir.' The officers confirmed that they didn't do any investigating beyond interrogating their two (Aboriginal) suspects, who were pointed out to them by (white) Grondman. Police even claimed not to know anything about Grondman's history of using violence against Paula. In court, both Wheeler and Jagamara said the words on the transcripts weren't theirs.[14]

At around the same time, police had also obtained signed confessions from four other Aboriginal men – including Angus Anunga – admitting their involvement in another gang rape of a woman known to history only as 'JB'. As with Wheeler and Jagamara, the confessions were the only solid evidence of their guilt. In August 1975, William Forster, the Supreme Court of the Northern Territory's first senior judge (his title was later changed to chief justice), refused to admit any of the typewritten confessions into evidence, and threw out the cases against the six men. It was important, he said, 'that the court should put on record general guidelines for the conduct of police officers when interrogating Aboriginal persons'. The Supreme Court's other judges, Dick Ward and, in an about-face, James Muirhead, agreed. Legal English and its concepts often translated poorly into Aboriginal languages. Many Aboriginal people answered questions by trying to provide the answer sought by the questioner.[15] The 'Anunga guidelines' as set down by Forster are still supposed to formalise how police should interview Aboriginal suspects: they should use interpreters, invite a 'prisoner's friend' into the interview, ask the suspect to repeat what they understand of the right to remain silent, and avoid questions which invite a 'yes' answer.

Limited recognition

When an Aboriginal man, Patrick, set fire to a classroom at Bamyili (now Barunga) in early 1975, he was charged with arson – a serious crime. Patrick had done some work for the school and hadn't been paid. He got drunk and decided to make his own justice. Ordinarily, Patrick would have gone straight to prison. But because 'your people had suffered [from the damage to the school] as well as the Australian government', Justice James Muirhead wanted to hear from the local Bamyili Council. It had decided that Patrick wouldn't be subject to payback, but would banish him to Maningrida, 450 kilometres north, on the Arnhem coast. 'They tell me you are a good man and a good worker', Muirhead told Patrick during the sentencing hearing. Muirhead suspended Patrick's prison sentence and released him. 'When an Aboriginal offends against his own community', Muirhead explained, 'we will wherever practicable always be interested to hear the views of that community expressed through the Councillors before deciding on sentence.'[16]

Muirhead was willing to entrust Aboriginal offenders' communities with their rehabilitation, especially in the wake of Cyclone Tracy, which had flattened Darwin at the end of 1974 and created a shortage of prison accommodation. So, when another man, Frank, raped a two-year-old child at the Bagot Reserve, Muirhead ordered that he be released from prison after only five months. Muirhead explained that if Frank had been 'European or an educated person', he would have requested a psychiatric report. 'But because of the difficulties inherent in your lack of so-called sophistication and language and because of the most limited facilities at present available in Darwin, I cannot avail myself of this help.' Muirhead explained that he'd heard from a member of the town council of Milingimbi, Frank's home community. 'I am satisfied that whilst your people do not view the matter lightly and they will talk about it upon your eventual arrival, you are unlikely to sustain physical injury by way of community punishment, although it may be you will be sent "bush" for some time.'[17]

Judges and magistrates were also more willing to take into account – and even occasionally defer to – any punishment inflicted by offenders' communities under Aboriginal law. By the time twenty-five-year-old Andrew pled guilty to indecently assaulting a nine-year-old girl, she had fully recovered – at least physically – and Andrew had been punished. Senior people had beaten him severely, including around the testicles. The evidence in court was that Andrew would continue to endure 'tribal' punishments during ceremonies, regardless of whatever penalty of imprisonment the court imposed. 'As you have already spent two months in jail and you will be punished further by your own people,' Stipendiary Magistrate Towers said, 'I don't propose to pass any sentence on you at all.'[18]

Gordon, twenty-three, had been drinking at a hotel with his eighteen-year-old wife, when she approached and kissed some other men. 'I took her out and beat her up because she went with another man,' Gordon said later. After the assault she was found dead in a drainage ditch. Gordon was immediately remorseful, inflicted sorry cuts on himself and made a full confession to police. A meeting of relevant clans on Groote Eylandt resolved to convene a full-scale minungudawada: a 'trial by spears'. While Gordon was remanded in custody the community threw spears ceremonially at Gordon's brothers and other family members. This worked to dissipate tension in the community and allowed Gordon to return. Justice John Gallop suspended Gordon's prison sentence. The punishment had already been carried out, he explained. 'Imprisonment is not expected by the community in relation to this offence,' he said.[19]

These were extraordinary accommodations. For 150 years, settler authorities had been guarding their singular sovereign right to make the rules. *Cooper v Stuart* meant outlawing First Nations' laws and dispute-resolution systems. Yet here were judges and magistrates affording recognition – albeit limited – to empirical reality, especially in places far away from established cities and settler towns, where Aboriginal people lived under the day-to-day governance of local councils of Elders and respected persons. It was a fraught balancing act.

'There is a possible argument that the law should not concern itself with disputes and crimes which are purely Aboriginal in origin,' William Forster acknowledged in 1979, 'and of which the participants are Aborigines, living a tribal or semi-tribal existence in their own country.' It was one side of an old debate, as we've seen. But Forster made it clear that he didn't personally subscribe to this view. 'Whereas I am certain that crimes, if committed, should be punished, it would be unjust to take no account of social or other pressures which exist in Aboriginal society.'[20] Here was the old compromise again: *sentence, but leniently.*

In the late 1970s there was an ongoing dispute between the Gurindji and Mudburra, who at that time lived mainly in what is now Daguragu (Wattie Creek), and the Warlpiri who lived at what is now Kalkaringi (which had been part of the Wave Hill station). Leaders of those communities arranged a fight in an effort to settle the dispute; during the fight, one man was struck in the head with a traditional weapon and died. When he came to sentence the defendant, Forster was torn. He knew that imposing a specific penalty was likely to be futile. 'Whatever the outcome of these proceedings may be, the matter will not be settled and the hostilities [will] continue and will periodically lead to violence,' he predicted. Forster didn't approve of this, but he also thought the court 'should be realistic'. In the end, though, the crime was serious. 'Without wishing to destroy your essential Aboriginality,' Forster concluded, 'the court must do what it can to discourage the resort to dangerous violence to settle differences.'[21] The defendant went to prison for three years, and was eligible for parole after eighteen months. *Sentence, but leniently.*

Sometimes, communities made it clear they didn't want any part of rehabilitating or punishing offenders, and were happy to leave that to settler institutions. When twenty-two-year-old Godfrey climbed into a Darwin hostel and attempted to rape a six-year-old girl, his Elders at Galiwin'ku (Elcho Island) pointedly refused to have him returned there and let the court know that they expected a significant period of imprisonment, which is what he got.[22]

Limited reform

The year 1976 was something of a watershed in the willingness of settler authorities to reconsider their approach to and treatment of Aboriginal people. Federal parliament created the *Aboriginal Land Rights Act* for the

Northern Territory. Elizabeth Eggleston published her groundbreaking study into how settler criminal law applied in practice to Aboriginal people (see chapter 9). Three Federal Court judges laid down their expectations of minimum standards for police when interrogating Aboriginal suspects. And in mid-September, Neville Bonner, parliament's first Aboriginal senator, introduced a private member's bill that aimed to codify Forster's guidelines.[23]

Bonner's second reading speech was, for its time and its context, extraordinary. Although he'd been in the Senate for five years and had asked a few pointed questions, most of his contributions during the Whitlam government's term in office (including his famous 1974 motions, asking the government to 'admit prior ownership' of the Australian continent by Indigenous people, and to compensate them for land theft) had been motivated by party politics.[24] He'd never let fly like he did on 15 September 1976:

> This Bill can be likened unto the mythical phoenix, as it rises and triumphs from the ashes of oppression, discrimination and mistrust, which for too long has been the lot of my people; a cruel lot, thrust upon them by almost two centuries of harsh, unthinking and, generally, uncaring European rule.

Bonner took the opportunity to 'digress' from the subject of his bill to 'inform the uninformed as to the events which have caused the very real problems that exist for the Indigenous and Island peoples in their contact with the law, that is, European law':

> After some 40,000 years of peaceful possession of this vast continent, living under a culture so totally different from, and in many respects much better than, that of their conquerors, many of my ancestors were unceremoniously butchered. Those far too few who escaped the guns, knives and poisons of your so-called civilised ancestors were herded in droves into reserves and missions, there to live in enslavement ... Those who avoided death and the subsequent great round-up, and others who escaped from the missions and reserves, came to the cities and towns, there to be completely shunned by white society and forced to lead the life of pariahs in tin shanties, in bark humpies and in other degrading accommodation ... and indeed in any place sufficiently far

from the cities and towns so that they would not offend the delicate senses of their so-called superior white masters. These of my race were the fringe-dwellers, the legion of the lost, the dirty, ignorant, mentally inferior, 'Abos', 'Boongs', 'Blacks' as you were wont to call us, and treat us accordingly. It was within this deprived society that I grew up; within these harsh confines of human degradation that I, Neville Bonner, suffered the cruel barbs of discrimination and depravity at the hands of my white brother. Is it little wonder that there is suspicion and mistrust? As our culture was systematically destroyed and the tribal laws and customs which had sustained us for aeons were deliberately eroded, my forefathers were subjected to the white man's law, laws which were incomprehensible to them.

Bonner appealed to his fellow senators' sense of justice and fairness. 'Now, can honourable senators see the need for reform, the need for greater protection of my Indigenous and Islander brothers in their dealings with the law?' Apparently they could not. The bill lapsed, and Bonner doggedly reintroduced it, unaltered, in 1978 and 1981, before he was dumped from the Liberal Party's Senate ticket ahead of the 1983 elections, at which he narrowly lost his seat.[25] Perhaps because they sensibly couldn't, no other senator ever responded to Bonner's eviscerating historical analysis.

Meanwhile, Whitlam's minister for the Northern Territory, Rex Patterson, had commissioned two Sydney criminologists to produce a series of reports into the Territory's criminal justice system. These reports made it patently obvious that the Territory's justice system was inadequately serving Aboriginal people. Three-quarters of all prisoners in Territory prisons were there because of public drunkenness. Therefore, the report's authors concluded, public drunkenness should be decriminalised and replaced with a system of well-resourced detoxification centres. Due to a faulty and discriminatory recruitment system, everyone involved in the administration of criminal justice in the Territory was white. There were no youth-specific services. Remandees were treated like convicted prisoners, and there were very few alternatives to imprisonment. All of this had to change.[26]

But the reports' most significant recommendations addressed the question of *whose* law should apply in Aboriginal communities, many of which were newly self-governing, or soon would be, and were asking for a decentralised system in which they would have primary responsibility for settling disputes and deciding punishments. Yirrkala, which had famously petitioned the federal parliament on bark to stop the Nabalco mine in 1963, had been requesting greater power to manage its own offenders for some time. The reports to Patterson recommended decentralisation along these lines.[27] In 1975, the Council for Aboriginal Affairs – a three-man, all-white committee established by Harold Holt in the wake of the 1967 referendum – visited Yirrkala, where the community expressed 'strongly held objections to direct action by European police, to the incarceration of Aborigines at [the nearby town of] Nhulunbuy, to the hearing of Aboriginal cases in a European setting, and to the kind and scale of penalties imposed according to European standards'. The council endorsed these views and the Yirrkala community's alternative proposals, which would have seen it assume much greater responsibility for dispute resolution and justice.[28]

If ever there was a time to revisit the question of whose law applied in Aboriginal communities, it was now. The era of self-determination had already produced seismic shifts in settler thinking about land rights, community control and racial justice. Why not expose the legal system to the same philosophical shift?

Ian Viner, a barrister who'd been appointed Aboriginal affairs minister in Malcolm Fraser's first post-election government, thought the time was ripe. Although it was hardly the main focus of the campaign, the 'Aboriginal affairs' policy Fraser had taken to the December 1975 election aimed to dramatically increase Aboriginal people's civic freedoms: a soundly liberal objective. Viner repeatedly made it clear that the 'freedom' he was interested in for Aboriginal people was not merely formal. Land rights, improved housing and health-care, and Aboriginal people's involvement in decisions that affect them were all requisite components of Viner's liberalism. So, too, was the capacity for Aboriginal communities to practise their own cultures and their own laws.[29] Viner convinced his attorney-general, Bob Ellicott, to, in turn, ask the new Australian Law Reform Commission (ALRC) to inquire into and report on whether what he called 'Aboriginal customary law' should be properly recognised by the settler legal system.[30] Ellicott himself had a genuine sense that Aboriginal people were poorly served by Australian justice. As solicitor-general, he'd represented the federal government in the Nabalco case of 1977. Following Blackburn's judgement, he wrote a paper to Prime Minister Billy McMahon urging him to take some action to recognise, however belatedly, the obvious relationship Aboriginal people had to their lands.[31]

The ALRC and its commissioner in charge, future High Court judge Michael Kirby, quickly saw that Ellicott's reference would take some time to investigate and complete. In fact, its report didn't appear until June 1986, nearly a decade later. By that time, the ALRC had undertaken seventeen field trips, conducted thirty-seven public hearings, considered 506 written submissions and produced twenty-eight research papers (many of which were written by Bryan Keon-Cohen, Koiki Mabo's junior counsel throughout that decade-long litigation). The ALRC produced two draft bills aimed at recognising Aboriginal 'customary law' on matters as diverse as marriage, the placement of Aboriginal children removed from their parents and environmental regulations.

And in the arena of criminal justice, the ALRC's proposed bills would have recognised, for the first time in Australia's post-contact history, a kind of formal legal pluralism. When deciding whether an Aboriginal person *intended* to commit an offence, or had acted 'reasonably', courts and juries would be required to have regard to any relevant customary laws that applied in a defendant's community. Courts would be unable to accept pleas from Aboriginal defendants unless satisfied they sufficiently understood the nature of the court proceeding. It would be a defence to a charge of statutory rape if a defendant could show that the alleged underage victim was both consenting and traditionally married to the defendant. And judges would be required to take into account evidence of any applicable customary laws when sentencing Aboriginal defendants.[32] The ALRC didn't go so far as to suggest pluralising settler Australians' exclusive sovereignty, but its bills would have been a start. As we'll see, they didn't see the light of day.

Settler courts in the era of self-determination

While the ALRC pressed on with its inquiry, Aboriginal people, of course, continued to be charged with crimes. One week before Christmas in 1979, a group of Aboriginal men and women were sitting down, drinking, at a camp at Borroloola, a town on Yanyuwa Country just inland from the Gulf of Carpentaria's southern coast. Two women began fighting. One accused the other of making moves on her husband. The jealous woman later argued with her husband, Harry, who became enraged. He chased her. She took shelter inside a car. He picked up a stick and smashed its windscreen. She fled and hid inside a humpy. He pursued her. Then she grabbed the stick from him and whacked him with it. Harry fell to the ground. Harry's wife's uncle, Oliver, was sitting nearby on a chair. 'That's my niece,' he called out. Harry picked up a jerry can and hit him on the head, to little effect. Harry then picked up a six-foot piece of 2x4 timber and had another go. This time, Oliver fell off his chair. He never regained consciousness. He later died of a subdural haemorrhage. Police charged Harry with manslaughter.

At least, that was how the Crown prosecutor originally put the facts when Harry appeared in Darwin's Supreme Court charged with manslaughter. Harry's lawyer told the court that the facts were a little more complicated. The prosecutor conceded that they were. It turns out that Oliver had made a number of comments to Harry that were full of innuendo and were deliberately provocative and culturally taboo. Oliver considered himself Harry's wife's promised husband, but that view wasn't widely shared. A witness told the court that the Yanyuwa community – to which both Harry and Oliver belonged – was of the firm opinion that Oliver's death was his own fault. Harry would not face payback upon his return to Borroloola.

James Muirhead had been a resident judge in the Northern Territory for five years when he sentenced Harry for manslaughter. Killing a man by cracking his head with a 2x4 could have meant a life sentence in jail, Muirhead told Harry. 'But fortunately, it seems to have been the sort of accident where you were forced to take some sort of an action according to your tribal customs and traditions, and that other man . . . should not have intervened in what was essentially an argument between you and your wife.' Muirhead imposed a three-year prison sentence, suspended it immediately on the condition that Harry stay out of trouble, and freed him. *Sentence, but leniently.*

Scandalised at the 'manifest inadequacy' of the sentence, prosecutors appealed to the Federal Court. The prosecutor tried an argument that would have worked in front of Martin Kriewaldt. Harry was not a 'tribal' Aboriginal person. He'd worked consistently as a stockman, and even spent some years in a leprosarium. He'd had plenty of contact with white people and, therefore, he had good knowledge of white laws and expectations. But that argument didn't work in front of the Federal Court's chief justice, Nigel Bowen, in 1980. 'Association with white people does not necessarily erase deep-rooted customary fears or beliefs,' he said, 'nor does it eradicate the sense of what is, or what is not, acceptable or appropriate.' The Federal Court allowed Muirhead's sentence to stand.[33]

There wasn't much the courts could do at the level of intention: if Harry intentionally assaulted Oliver and was reckless as to whether the assault would kill him, then settler law said he was guilty of at least manslaughter. But if the *reason* Harry picked up the 2x4 in the first place was tied up with the Aboriginal worldview he'd been socialised into, the settler courts had to acknowledge it. So, when another Aboriginal man, Charlie, speared another man to death after he'd been ordered to do so in accordance with the law of his Aboriginal nation, James Muirhead found him guilty of manslaughter but entirely commuted his prison sentence.[34] This 'sentence but leniently' approach wasn't likely to radically reduce the rates at which Aboriginal people were being locked up. But something was better than nothing.

The settler courts struggled for consistency during this period. On Sunday, 4 April 1982, a group of Aboriginal men went to Timber Creek to buy alcohol. They all worked at the massive Victoria River Downs station (VRD), then the Northern Territory's second-largest cattle station. The group returned to Centre Camp, where they lived, and began drinking. One of them, the head stockman at VRD, was a thirty-one-year-old Ngarinyman man called Billy. He and his wife of fourteen years began a drunken argument. He picked up a piece of wood and hit her, breaking her left arm. Later in the evening, he also hit her repeatedly on the back with a piece of plastic piping. One of those blows ruptured her liver. She died of internal bleeding shortly afterwards. Police charged Billy with manslaughter, to which he pled guilty.

At his sentencing hearing in the NT Supreme Court, Billy's lawyer (from the North Australian Aboriginal Legal Aid Service, NAALAS) led evidence that it was not unusual, in Aboriginal society, for women to be beaten if they didn't obey their husbands' commands. The court didn't like this argument, and of course had no real way of being able to gauge its truth. 'We are of the opinion,' the appeal court's (all male) judges concluded instead, 'that the court should approach the matter on the basis that the [stockman] beat his wife in anger when they were drunk.' The Supreme Court imposed something like the sentence it would have given a white person: four years' prison, with an eligibility for parole after one year.

But if Aboriginal cultures – that is to say settler lawyers' and judges' (very limited) *understanding* of Aboriginal cultures – couldn't excuse the manslaughter, perhaps it could be relied on to take care of the punishment? Billy appealed to the Federal Court. His lawyers argued that the original sentence had failed to account for the fact that 'the appellant is a full-blood Aborigine, who has undergone and is likely to undergo further traditional punishment'. Indeed, Billy's father, a senior Gurindji man, told the court that 'payback has already been done by the local people here and [at] Yarralin'. The lawmen had nominated one person to beat Billy with a boomerang. 'The local people are now satisfied that honour has been met.' What's more, the dead woman's family was yet to arrive from all over the Top End – 'from Daly River, Port Keats, Kununurra, Hooker Creek and Wave Hill' – and would 'tribally encircle Billy and on cue will be allowed to let fly with boomerangs, nulla nullas and spears'. Billy's father thought it was a punishment that was likely to lead to serious injury, evacuation to a hospital and permanent disability. It was also likely that Billy would be banished for some years. If he wasn't available for this punishment – if he was in prison, for instance – then the punishment would be inflicted on his family members instead.

The three Federal Court judges – Robert St John, John Toohey and Francis Fisher, all white men – were clearly troubled by the extent of 'extra-curial' punishment that Billy (or his family) would incur. But as outsiders, they couldn't know for sure. Aboriginal law was entirely outside their social-isation and lived experience. What little they knew of it came from what they'd read in (white) anthropologists' accounts and from the testimony of Aboriginal people in their courtrooms, (who may have been restricted in what they could say to men who were both uninitiated and white) and, often, from the submissions of (white) ALS lawyers. Settler law required that extra-curial punishment be taken into account when determining a sentence, otherwise an offender would be punished twice, which isn't fair. But how, when that punishment was itself illegal under settler law? In the end, the judges fell back on the approach taken by the original sentencing judge. 'It cannot be said that His Honour was oblivious to what had hap-pened to the appellant or what was likely to happen to him and his family.' All things considered, they thought it was best to send Billy to prison for a year, and then let him face his tribal punishment when he came out.[35]

But courts continued to admit evidence about 'traditional' or 'cus-tomary' punishment. A drunken argument between two Aboriginal men in Umbakumba in mid-1981 left one of them dead, from a stab wound. Immediately, other men pelted the surviving fighter, Ethan, with spears, causing injuries that required two operations at the Nhulunbuy hospital.

His NAALAS lawyer asked the Supreme Court judge to consider this 'pay-back' when sentencing him. But was this particular payback punishment in accordance with Aboriginal 'custom' or 'law'? Or was it simply the 'angry reaction of friends of the deceased'? Prosecutors tendered a letter signed by the Umbakumba Community Council. The letter asked the sentencing judge for Ethan to be punished, not in prison, but on a mainland outstation 'for three years or more'. The letter explained that Ethan had four wives and twelve children. 'At the moment they get by with child endowment money but [if they were allowed to live] with Ethan they could manage better'. This argument didn't work for the trial judge, but it did when Ethan appealed.[36]

Settler courts were flirting with two ideas during the 1970s, each of which followed when they took seriously the fact that many Aboriginal people had been socialised into worldviews rather different to that of Western modernity. One was the notion that settler law *could* recognise the empirical reality of First Nations' communities' cultures and laws, which operated in parallel with, or even regardless of, whatever police and courts were doing. The terms judges used to mark this recognition – they referred to Aboriginal 'custom' and 'culture' but not, pointedly, to 'law' – suggested they weren't quite prepared to acknowledge the whole reality. The second idea was that First Nations' communities may actually hold some kind of restorative or rehabilitative value for Aboriginal offenders: that efforts to assimilate and 'civilise' had led to what researcher Charles Rowley called 'the destruction of Aboriginal society', and that if there was a solution to the growing problems of drunkenness, criminality and imprisonment, it lay at least in part *within* Aboriginal cultures and communities themselves. Each idea was radical in the context of settler law and history, and each provoked significant controversy among settler opinion.

Restorative culture

As Thalia Anthony, professor of law at Sydney's University of Technology, explains in her remarkable study of the shifts in the NT Supreme Court's attitudes between the 1930s and the present century, in the era of self-determination the court came to see the 'civilising process' as a *cause* of Aboriginal disadvantage. This was an extraordinary development following the post-war approach taken by Martin Kriewaldt, who was unequivocal in his view that Western civilisation was inevitable and good for Aboriginal people and believed wholeheartedly in assimilation. Anthony writes that the 'devastating effect' of Western civilisation could be overcome, according to the court and its new thinking, by encouraging the revival of 'authentic' cultural practices. Offenders could be brought 'back into the fold' of Aboriginal communities, whose customs and culture held greater restorative promise than prisons. This would in turn 'restore Indigenous community harmony' and, of special relevance to the work of the court, reintegrate offenders and reduce recidivism.[37]

In 1976, Justice Andrew Wells released a Pitjantjatjara man from prison after he'd killed a woman by bashing her with a stick and a bottle. The man, Joseph, was drunk. So was the woman, Judy. Joseph was a 'tribal Aborigine', in the settler courts' language, and spoke very little English. Police had chased him through the bush, arrested him, charged him with murder and conveyed him to Adelaide for the trial, where Wells faced a problem now very familiar to settler courts: how to approach the trial and, if necessary, the sentencing of a person who has lived very much outside the world imagined by the legal system he's now caught up within?

According to Joseph's defence lawyer, Judy had repeatedly taunted and insulted Joseph by mentioning tribal secrets she shouldn't have known about. The open discussion of such secrets in court provided grounds, Wells concluded, to make an order banishing all women from the court, including from the jury. Joseph formally pled 'not guilty' to murder through an interpreter. (Unfortunately, that interpreter was uninitiated, and it emerged that Joseph, who *was* initiated, was unable to speak to him.) Wells decided that the woman's actions amounted to provocation and accepted Joseph's plea to manslaughter rather than murder. *Sentence, but leniently*.

Joseph's lawyer then went further. He told Wells that Pitjantjatjara Elders would take him back onto Country, punish him according to their law and instruct him in traditional ways for about a year. Wells agreed that, where possible, tribal justice should be 'reinforced' rather than simply 'replaced' by settler concepts of justice, especially in a case where the defendant spoke little English. Wells sentenced Joseph to two years' prison with hard labour, but suspended it immediately. This took into account the three months he'd already served on remand. For the next year, Wells ordered, Joseph had to 'submit himself to the Tribal Elders' and to obey their 'lawful directions'. He also had to refrain from committing any further offences for two years. If Joseph breached those orders, there was a good chance he'd need to serve the remaining twenty-one months of his prison sentence.[38]

Joseph was then duly released into the authority of his Pitjantjatjara Elders, one of whom speared him in the leg. Settler opinion erupted in a brief panic when this 'punishment' was reported. Both *The Australian*'s editorial and the secretary of what would become Liberty Victoria condemned the 'barbarism' of the Elder's punishment.[39] *The Age* praised Wells for his 'serious and sensitive attempt' to deal with the problem of sentencing a 'tribal Aborigine', but worried about the implications of a sentence that provided authority for an action (spearing) that was otherwise illegal. Didn't that mean, by extension, that 'there is not only one law in the land but two'? More progressive settler opinion extolled the virtues of Wells's approach, including La Trobe University's Alan Ward (an historian of colonial settler–Māori relations in colonial New Zealand),[40] the young legal academic Andrew Ligertwood[41] and Fraser's Aboriginal affairs minister, Ian Viner.[42]

Aboriginal culture was no longer the disadvantage Kriewaldt had seen it as. Instead, culture was potentially the salvation – though never to the extent that judges could abandon the field and leave the management and punishment of offenders entirely to Aboriginal communities themselves. Aboriginal culture became relevant only insofar as the agents of settler justice deigned to recognise it. In practice, culture's salvational role mostly meant slightly shorter prison sentences. The formula didn't change. *Sentence, but leniently.*

In October 1994, a group of Aboriginal people had come to Darwin from Milingimbi – one of the Crocodile Islands off the north coast of Arnhem Land – for a football carnival. They went to a few pubs before ending up at a house party in Palmerston. An argument broke out between one of the couples. The woman, Lisa, in her mid-thirties, was holding a knife. With it, she stabbed her husband, Rodney, in the chest, puncturing his lung. He was rushed to Darwin hospital, and survived. Lisa pled guilty to a serious assault. It was the second time she'd seriously hurt her husband in the space of about five months.

Rodney wrote a letter to the sentencing judge, Brian Martin. His two mothers wrote another one, and there was also a petition carrying the names of 140 other people. Rodney didn't want Lisa to go to prison, because he was afraid that would effectively annul their marriage in the eyes of the Milingimbi community. He also explained that Lisa had already been dealt with under Yolngu law. She'd been forced to attend meetings among Milingimbi, Ramingining and Gatji leaders, who had talked about whether to subject her to payback. She and her husband had stopped drinking alcohol and had detoxed at a dry outstation. According to Yolngu law, the matter was finished. 'If traditional law has resolved this issue,' Rodney asked, 'why can't balanda law respect this?' He went on: 'If the prosecution proceeds, not only does it discredit our decision to deal with our own problems according to our cultural law, but Lisa would be tried twice for the same alleged offence. To me, this does not seem fair.'

Indeed. And for Brian Martin, it was a compelling resolution. He released Lisa on a good behaviour bond. But Martin had to explain himself. In line with the view that prevailed in settler courts at the time – that the victim's wishes weren't usually relevant to sentencing – he wasn't simply being led by Rodney. Rather, he was recognising the wishes of the Milingimbi community. And he wasn't outsourcing his court's responsibilities *to* that community. Rather, he was taking the community's wishes into account 'as a mitigatory factor'. He wasn't imposing no punishment. Rather, he was recognising the reality that most of the lawful purposes of punishment under settler law – including rehabilitation – had already occurred. Threading his sentence through the narrow gaps left by legislation and previous cases was a delicate task. 'To send her to gaol would serve no compelling purpose,' Martin concluded.[43]

Judges appointed to the Northern Territory's Supreme Court in the 1970s and beyond never became so radical that they overturned *Cooper v Stuart*. And they never deferred to Aboriginal law to the point that they were prepared to entirely excuse violence done in accordance with it. But they did accept evidence of Aboriginal law much more readily – and extensively – than ever before. Whereas Martin Kriewaldt had gleaned most of what he knew of Aboriginal law and culture – generally, and in particular cases – from white anthropologists, the Northern Territory Supreme Court toward the end of the 1970s, and throughout the 1980s and beyond, was increasingly happy to hear about Aboriginal culture from Aboriginal leaders themselves. Thalia Anthony calls the approach that emerged in these decades a 'valorisation' of Aboriginal cultures.[44] It was an approach that was to spark its own reaction.

BACKLASH

How the implications of self-determination unsettled settlers

The inconsistent, occasional and very limited recognition of Aboriginal law and culture by settler courts during the period of self-determination was not to last. Internationally, the right of Indigenous self-determination was being asserted by activists – and increasingly recognised in international law (see chapter 9). In Settler Australia, however, 'self-determination' was an umbrella term governments gave to a vague policy approach which emerged following the end of formal discrimination. It had little to do with the internationally recognised right, and only ever allowed a very limited autonomy, always firmly within the tight bounds of total settler sovereignty. In Australia, the Labor governments led by Gough Whitlam, Bob Hawke and Paul Keating broadly supported the limited approach to what they sometimes called 'self-determination', as did Malcolm Fraser's Coalition government, at least philosophically.

But Settler Australia's cultural politics had no room for even the very limited form of so-called 'self-determination' allowed by governments. A vicious campaign against Aboriginal land rights was orchestrated by small groups of influential – and often very wealthy – white business and political leaders, especially from the early 1980s, among them Hugh Morgan (the CEO of the Western Mining Corporation) and Joh Bjelke-Petersen, the premier of Queensland. This campaign, which made extraordinary claims about Aboriginal plans to reclaim the entire continent, generated fear and concern among groups of settlers, now being presented, in the language of politicians and media outlets, as 'ordinary people', the 'silent majority' or the 'mainstream'.[1] These were racial categories, and euphemisms for the (largely) white settlers who felt threatened by the disturbing challenges being made by Indigenous activists to their assumed place in the world – and on these lands.[2]

This political backlash against land rights produced a new way of explaining Aboriginal disadvantage, which settlers could see in their cities and towns. The drunken, violent Aboriginal welfare bludger, among the most vicious – and clearly racist – stereotypes created by settlers in the neo-colonial era, was presented as the predictable failure of self-determination, which was re-cast as 'the whiteman's dream'.[3] Per head of population, fewer Indigenous people drink alcohol than 'white' people in Australia.[4] But the stereotype performs an important function for settlers. If self-determination, with its irresponsible and unrealisable demands for equal pay, equal rights and land rights, was what had made Aboriginal people homeless, alcoholic and incarcerated, then settlers, their ancestors and their governments are off the hook.

Justification and doubt

Lawyers representing Aboriginal people accused of violent crimes in the era of self-determination found that courts were now much more willing to accept arguments based on what they called 'tribal law'. Quite often, the accused person was a man and his victim was a woman. Through their lawyers, who were mostly white and who often worked for the new Aboriginal Legal Services, Aboriginal men were asking white judges to excuse their conduct, or to reduce their sentences, on the basis that 'tribal law' justified the beatings they'd inflicted on women, or that 'tribal law' did not regard the rape of women as seriously as it was treated in settler law. As we'll explore in the next chapter, these arguments are no longer accepted by settler courts, and there's been a lot of consternation at the actions of lawyers and their clients during this period. But it's difficult to blame individual lawyers for these arguments. In such a system, lawyers must make whatever arguments are in the narrow interests of their clients.

Again and again, settler court records of the 1970s and 1980s show white, male judges accepting that horrific brutality perpetrated by Aboriginal men against Aboriginal women was partly justified by 'tribal law'. Prison sentences were shortened, suspended or avoided entirely. William Forster – the judge who had established the *Anunga* rules for police interrogations – gave a non-parole period of only twelve months to a man, John, who had shot his de facto partner while he was drunk. John's wife had died in tragic circumstances; his new relationship, unsanctioned by Aboriginal law, was turbulent (because of alcohol abuse and what Forster called 'her sexual conduct'); she'd refused to leave their child with him; for that, he shot her. In court, his lawyer claimed John had a right under tribal law to 'punish' her for taking their child and for 'her past misconduct'.[5] On the same day, Forster released another Aboriginal man, Danny, on a suspended sentence. Danny was charged with the attempted murder of his wife after he'd assaulted her while he was drunk. Forster accepted that Danny believed his wife 'had been misbehaving herself in some way', and that Danny was 'almost required to punish her' in 'obedience to tribal custom'.[6]

On Groote Eylandt, Tom Pauling (now a stipendiary magistrate) released a man, Timothy, on a good behaviour bond after he'd stabbed his wife in the shoulder, chased her when she ran away, and then stabbed her another five times. Timothy had suspected his wife of infidelity, and other men gave evidence that tribal law required she be punished severely. In response, her family had ritually speared Timothy, and the community considered the matter finished.[7] To acknowledge the exclusive sovereignty of settler law, Pauling imposed a token punishment – a good behaviour bond – which also acknowledged the reality that Bernard's main punishment had been 'tribally' inflicted.

James Muirhead released a twenty-six-year-old man, Charles, back into his community at Yuendumu after he'd killed his seventy-year-old stepmother with a digging stick. He was drunk, and it was accidental: the evidence suggested he'd probably intended to use it on his wife. In the aftermath, Charles had been ritually speared, 'properly according to custom'. As such, the community considered the matter dealt with, so Muirhead felt justified in fully suspending the prison sentence he imposed.[8] 'Tribal payback' also allowed Muirhead to substantially reduce the prison time he gave to another twenty-six-year-old man who had returned to Wave Hill Station drunk and beaten his wife to death.[9] And a South Australian judge condemned another man, Morris, to prison for just under sixteen months after he beat his wife – causing injuries from which she later died, owing in part to a lack of adequate medical facilities in Yalata – after finding her sitting and drinking with other men.[10]

There were obvious problems with the way that settler courts had begun, in the 1970s, to pay limited deference to Aboriginal law. Much of the furore in the national press following the case of Joseph Williams (discussed in the previous chapter) – who'd been ordered to 'submit himself to the Tribal Elders' apparently as 'punishment' after he'd bashed Judy to death – focused on the 'barbarity' of the punishment the Elders would enforce. But outraged settlers had got it wrong. Wells hadn't ordered the Elders to spear Joseph as some form of 'tribal punishment'. 'The real reason I was disinclined to impose an immediate custodial sentence,' Wells later told the Australian Law Reform Commission, 'was that he was worried about the effect of prison on Joseph's health. 'The fact was that he had very little English: it would have been impossible for him to have communicated with the staff of the prison or with any fellow prisoners, or to have related to them in any way. He would, in effect, have been in solitary confinement. To condemn a tribal Aborigine to such a fate was something which I wished, if possible, to avoid.'

In the end, the whole thing – arrest, charge, trial, sentence, media furore – had taken place almost entirely within the worldview and the minds of settler Australians. 'The Elders did not want a "tribal" thing made of it,' claimed Barry Lindner, who was then superintendent of what remained of the Lutheran mission after Yalata – near where Joseph had killed Judy – was reconstituted as an Aboriginal community in 1974. Judy's death 'had not occurred in anything resembling tribal circumstances', Lindner continued:

The Elders were perplexed by [Joseph's] defence counsel's aggressive intrusion into tribal matters … The whole matter had become a white-fellow exercise. I met the plane, and was handed a copy of [Joseph's] bond. [Joseph] returned with me to the village … He was later ritually speared by an Elder. Penetration was not deep, and the spear was not barbed. [Joseph] came to the clinic soon afterwards, and received very minor medical attention. He then returned to the camp. I have no reason to believe that the spearing was considered by the Aboriginal people as being 'punishment' for the woman's death. Tradition demanded subjection to this practice prior to resumption of normal community associations. It also signalled the end of the matter. [Joseph] was not taken 'to areas beyond the Musgraves for about a year' [as Wells had ordered]. I heard nothing to indicate that this suggestion came from the [Old] Men. I gained the impression that [Joseph] thought it a bit of a joke.[11]

Lindner's was yet another settler account. Anangu voices remained silent, at least to the ears of settlers and their justice system. But Joseph was imprisoned again, two and then four years later, for further assaults on women. Apparently, the great showpiece of settler law – the criminal trial – had not produced the substantive justice it promised. In large part, this was because settler law had never satisfactorily dealt with the question of whether, how and to what extent it should recognise Aboriginal law. On the one hand was the line of racist and obviously erroneous authority, which culminated in and flowed from *Cooper v Stuart* in 1889; on the other was a line of compromise, which stretched from the House of Commons' 1837 inquiry and George Grey's 1840 recommendations, through to Charles Dashwood and Martin Kriewaldt's 'lenient' approach to sentencing in the twentieth century. And within a few years, settler courts' approach would again be revised by arguments introduced by both Indigenous and settler women.

Women speak up

In Alice Springs in 1980, John Gallop found what seemed to him good reason to reduce what would have been a life sentence of imprisonment after Fred, a 'traditional Aborigine', had participated in the gang rape of a woman in the bed of the Todd River and then bashed her to stop her screaming, leaving her with injuries from which she later died. 'I am required to take account of native law and custom,' Gallop said. 'I cannot ignore the fact that whether the European society likes it or not, rape is not as seriously regarded in the Aboriginal community as it is in the European community.'[12] Gallop's conclusion on this point was drawn from evidence given by the Australian National University's Noel Wallace, an anthropologist who had worked with Western Desert people for over a decade. Wallace told Gallop's court that 'the crime of rape in Aboriginal society is definitely regarded as being different from the way that European people regard rape.'[13]

'Unfortunately,' wrote another anthropologist, Catherine Wohlan, later, 'courts often receive a fragmented or one-dimensional impression of the type of behaviour sanctioned under Aboriginal law':

> This can occur at the expense of Aboriginal women and children. More often than not, these arguments are used in an adversarial attempt to

either divert Aboriginal males from entering the criminal justice system or as mitigation during sentencing.[14]

A second (white) anthropologist had given expert evidence in Fred's case.
Diane Bell had gone to what is now Ali Curung in Central Australia in the
late 1970s specifically to research the lives and experiences of women.[15]
With lawyer Pam Ditton, Bell published a collection of interviews with
Aboriginal women. 'Women said that under the old law,' Bell and Ditton
wrote in *Law: The Old and the New: Aboriginal Women in Central Australia
Speak Out*, 'sexual violence was punishable by death.' In Fred's case, Bell told
Gallop's court that the traditional punishment for rape in Central Australia
was 'usually very severe'.[16] For settler courts, this was quite a new idea.
Settler courts interpreted it to mean that Aboriginal women *needed* settler
law and its institutions to protect them.

In part, that was because there *were* many Aboriginal women who
were calling out for help. By 1986, the national concern over the number of
Aboriginal people who were dying in police and prison cells reached such a
crescendo that the Hawke government established a royal commission. But
beginning in the 1980s, there were suggestions that the number of Aboriginal
women who were killed by partners and family members may have been even
greater – at least in some places – than the number of Aboriginal people who
died in custody, most of whom were men.[17] The Federation of Aboriginal
Women reported in 1980 that 'Aboriginal women's pleas for assistance from
drunken attacks have fallen coldly on deaf ears.'[18]

Settler Australia was very much ready to hear reports of extreme
violence inside Indigenous communities. Also in 1982, a high-profile
(white) criminologist published a book which made startling claims about
Queensland's communities.[19] In 1982, a nineteen-year-old Gurindji woman
claimed that male Elders were ordering – and leading – bashings and gang
rapes of young girls so as to ensure that they were being married according
to the traditional skin system.[20] (The skin or moiety system is the complex
system of relationships that governs many Aboriginal societies.) It was by
now being regularly reported that rates of homicide in Aboriginal communities were *ten times* greater than the national average, and that when
women were the victims – which was often – their killers were men.[21] Of
course, this says nothing necessarily about who exactly the killers were.
Canada's National Inquiry into Missing and Murdered Indigenous Women

and Girls (2016–2019), for instance, was unable to determine perpetrators in many cases, but did conclude that an 'often-cited statistic that Indigenous men are responsible for 70 per cent of murders of Indigenous women and girls is not factually based'. A similar inquiry is yet to take place in Australia. But Marcia Langton, descendant of the Yiman and Bidjara peoples and Australia's first Indigenous anthropology graduate, told the deaths in custody royal commission, 'the death of women and constant assault, both sexual and physical, of women and children, in Aboriginal communities far exceed in sheer numbers and the enormity of suffering the problem which custody and deaths in custody pose for men'.[22] Subsequent research confirmed that the reason so many Aboriginal men were dying in prison was because they were there for serious crimes – murder, manslaughter, rape, serious assault – often committed against their wives or other women.[23]

This renewed concern for the female victims of Aboriginal male violence spoke to – and in many cases emerged from – two related social movements, which had also emerged at about the same time that Australian governments opened themselves to Aboriginal cultural and land rights: 'second wave' feminism and victims' rights. The victims' rights movement, which had grown out of the United States in the 1970s and soon caught on in Australia, claimed – with no small justification – that the ordinary procedures of criminal law excluded and disempowered victims. By focusing on offenders, their rights, their punishments and, now, their tragic childhoods and upbringings, victims' rights activists claimed courts had lost sight of what should have been their purpose all along: the protection of victims and the broader community.

There were obvious implications for the tentative steps settler courts had taken, during the self-determination era, toward recognising Aboriginal law. In 1989, Diane Bell and Topsy Napurrula Nelson, a woman she'd met a decade earlier during her Territory fieldwork and whose mother's first husband had been killed in the Coniston Massacre, wrote of 'the resounding silence of social scientists' about what they called 'intra-racial' rape. 'Acknowledge the facts,' they demanded: 'Aboriginal women are being raped by Aboriginal men.'[24] The paper – later published in *Women's Studies International Forum*, a feminist journal – provoked sustained intense criticism from other Indigenous women, most notably in the form of a letter to the journal (which refused to publish it) by Bidjara, Birri Gubba and Juru academic Jackie Huggins and a now-classic analysis by Goenpul researcher Aileen Moreton-Robinson in her own book, *Talkin' Up to the White Woman*.[25] The Bell–Huggins debate then played out within Australian feminist circles as a proxy for a much broader conversation about the experiences and place of women of colour in feminism.[26] But by the end of the century what Settler Australia understood – accurately or otherwise – was that Aboriginal women were copping it from their partners, their fathers, their uncles and their sons, and they weren't getting any help.

Settler Australia was a very willing receptor for a range of claims which implicated Indigenous culture in the violence it was reading about in newspapers. Traditional cultural attitudes, it was claimed, meant victims were unlikely to report violence to police.[27] And when they did, police wouldn't take any action.[28] Or if they did, their assailants got excellent defence lawyers through Aboriginal Legal Services, and victims had no representation, limited support and were often shamed in court.[29] Courts either found in favour of defendants or imposed inadequate sentences. And in response, the charged or imprisoned perpetrator – or his family – might 'punish' his victim for reporting him.[30] Meanwhile, settler governments had, under the rubric of self-determination, privileged male-dominated councils and corporations and marginalised women's authority. The problems were worst in remote Aboriginal communities, where traditional authority structures had been undermined by missionaries and bureaucrats and, finally, washed away by rivers of grog.[31] Whatever devastation had been wrought on communities historically, Lowitja O'Donoghue said in 2001, 'simply excusing violence on the grounds that the perpetrator is a victim too is not on'. In *The Age*, she declared that Indigenous violence was 'everyone's business'.[32]

One analysis went even further. It wasn't only in *contemporary* Aboriginal communities that women were subjugated, violated, attacked and killed. Some settler feminists and anthropologists claimed that women had *always* been the victims of men's brutal violence in Aboriginal societies. Joan Kimm, a (white) lawyer, pointed out that the records created by the earliest European explorers and settlers contained observations of the violence Aboriginal men regularly or even routinely inflicted on Aboriginal women.[33] In his journal, for instance, John Hunter noted occasions on which Bennelong had hit his wife on the head with a weapon. Hunter observed that the women around the Sydney area 'are certainly treated with great cruelty'. Watkin Tench, too, had noted that 'the women are in all respects treated with savage barbarity'. The time had come, insisted experienced anthropologist Peter Sutton, to accept the reality that a large part of the problem was emanating from *within* Aboriginal cultures. 'If people are in any doubt as to whether serious armed assaults on women and men took place in Australia over the thousands of years prior to conquest,' Sutton wrote, 'the archaeological record of prehistoric human remains settles the question decisively.'[34]

These readings of the historical and paleopathological records were unfortunately literal and selective, and open to various interpretations.[35] Accounts of wanton brutality among 'native savages' had routinely been twisted, exaggerated and even fabricated for an imperial London readership that simply couldn't get enough of stories of Pacific cannibalism, violent bride-capture and general heathen barbarism.[36] Even if we assume that the settlers' accounts are accurate, to focus exclusively on them – as Kimm did – means that British men's violence against women at the same time can be conveniently ignored. Any Aboriginal person who saw women convicts thrashed with the cat-o'-nine-tails, as was Nance Ferrel on board the *Lady Juliana* in 1789, or hanged, as were four women in Van Diemen's Land after 1830, may have reached similar conclusions about the colonists' treatment of women.[37] As judge advocate, David Collins himself had ordered twenty-five lashes for a convict woman who had gone to his court in December 1788 to complain that her husband had beaten her.[38]

But many of the accounts of Aboriginal men's violence against women in 'traditional' societies simply weren't accurate. When anthropologists began to spend time observing and learning from women living traditionally – which didn't happen until Phyllis Kaberry went to the Kimberley in the 1930s – they found economic interdependence rather than male domination and exploitation. The violence Kaberry directly observed defied simple classification. 'I, personally, have seen too many women attack their husbands with a tomahawk or even their own boomerangs,' she wrote in *Aboriginal Woman Sacred and Profane,* 'to feel that they are invariably the victims of ill-treatment.' First Nations and settler researchers have since demolished these claims about innate or traditional violence.[39] Drawing from the American anthropologist Lloyd Warner's study of Yolngu communities during the late 1920s, Marcia Langton pointed out that women often used weapons in fights with each other, which were among 'the organised forms of social interaction in the traditional Aboriginal societies.'[40] As Langton, by then a Melbourne University distinguished professor, told the National Press Club in 2016: 'If these practices were [based on] traditional laws, there would be no Aboriginal society in existence today.'[41]

The problem of settler law

A prime ministerial taskforce, established as the result of sustained political action by Aboriginal women, visited two hundred communities in 1984 and sought women's views.[42] Two years later, its report found that Aboriginal women were very concerned about the extent to which crimes like murder, rape and assault were being perpetrated in their communities. But they saw alcohol, *not* Aboriginal law and culture, as the principal driving factor. They were just as concerned about the extraordinary levels at which Aboriginal people – and especially young men – were being locked up. Settler law's unwillingness to accept Aboriginal law created ongoing conflict and confusion. Aboriginal women wanted settler police, parole officers, lawyers and judges to be educated about Aboriginal law and culture. But they also wanted the right to practise their law. Often, they said, settler courts' punishments for very serious crimes like rape and murder were 'significantly milder' than punishments offenders would receive under Aboriginal law.[43]

The forced disruption and breakdown of women's traditional culture meant that knowledge about land responsibilities, nutrition, food preparation and especially sex education wasn't being passed down. Traditional gender relationships were transformed, and among the practices the settlers introduced was a standard of violence and a culture of abusing alcohol. This, women felt, had made them very vulnerable to sexual exploitation and victimisation. Continued child removals by settler authorities were only compounding existing problems by adding to the reasons women feared going to police.[44] 'Aboriginal women have no faith in the criminal justice system,' observed Judy Atkinson, though not because it wasn't locking men up enough. Settler courts and governments had both undermined Aboriginal women's efforts to maintain Aboriginal mechanisms of social control, while at the same time accepting submissions about 'bullshit law' that somehow authorised men's violence against women. 'The tragedy is that some of our men are now starting to believe such garbage,' Atkinson lamented.[45]

Many Aboriginal women pointed to the destructive effects of alcohol, solvents and the policies that had increased their availability since the late 1960s. Marcia Langton famously described alcohol as 'white poison', invoking past practices by many settlers on the frontier. The right to drink alcohol had been one of the first civil liberties granted to Aboriginal people, Langton recalled, when laws prohibiting Aboriginal people from consuming alcohol in the Northern Territory were repealed in 1964. Since then, she observed, it had been 'the widespread Aboriginal view that alcohol abuse and petrol sniffing' and inadequate policing – *not* Aboriginal law and custom – were 'the main obstacles to attaining good health, to the orderly development of communities, and to the safety and welfare of women and children'.[46] Langton led the Northern Territory Aboriginal Issues Unit for the Royal Commission into Aboriginal Deaths in Custody. Her unit's lengthy report, *Too Much Sorry Business*, focused extensively on violence against Aboriginal women and children, often by Aboriginal men, but recommended that part of the answer must lie in an *increased* willingness by settler law and government to recognise Aboriginal law.

Instead of continuing to deny and decry Aboriginal law, settler authorities needed to involve Aboriginal communities in their own justice mechanisms. With Bonnie Robertson and Barbara Miller, both also Aboriginal women working in senior roles in settler institutions, Judy Atkinson approached Queensland's attorney-general with law reform proposals that would empower Aboriginal women in their own communities, and allow Aboriginal people to sit in judgement of each other, rather than submit to the settler court system, which was largely a male domain.[47]

Women weren't saying they didn't need help. But they *were* saying that police and courts and prison rarely provided it. Again, this was complicated. Langton's unit recorded some women lamenting the fact that Aboriginal law had no answers to the level of violence in some communities, especially against women, and that they needed police to intervene more often. But these women explained the offending itself by the fact that settler law and government did not allow communities to properly initiate Aboriginal children in their own law and responsibilities. There was even a suggestion that some young men were taking 'advantage' of prison through deliberate acts of vandalism or vehicle theft in order to avoid unpleasant initiation rituals (such as subincision).[48] Then, when Aboriginal women did seek help from the settler justice system, they faced additional barriers. Aboriginal Legal Services offered the most culturally appropriate (or the least culturally inappropriate) services, but women – often as the victims of men's violence – were regularly conflicted out of them (because the same legal service can't simultaneously act for both victim *and* offender). Intervention orders, if they had any effect at all, sometimes increased the risk of violence in communities where police didn't have a regular presence. And when settler courts expected women to give evidence in public courtrooms, they didn't account for the fact that by doing so, women were often being asked to divulge matters that custom, tradition or law required be kept secret.[49]

Yet the myth that Aboriginal law traditionally authorised violence against women proved extraordinarily durable in Settler Australia. The ALRC's recommendations needed a champion in Bob Hawke's Labor government. The Aboriginal affairs minister was now Clyde Holding, a former Victorian lawyer who wanted to extend the existing land rights legislation from the Territory to the whole of Australia. But a strong backlash from the mining and pastoral industries in Western Australia and Queensland forced that plan to the backburner. And police unions vigorously opposed the ALRC's recommendation to codify the Federal Court's *Anunga* guidelines for interrogating Aboriginal suspects. Neville Bonner's bill (which had the same aim) 'seems to restrict alarmingly police powers in the state of Queensland', the Queensland Police Union's general secretary claimed, 'and would render virtually impossible the upholding of law and order amongst the coloured members of our community'. The implication behind the proposal was that police were regularly obtaining false confessions from Aboriginal suspects.[50]

Holding put the ALRC's recommendations in the bottom drawer. While agreeing that 'our law and Aboriginal society have demonstrated that they are ill-fitted to each other', he noted that the scope of the proposals was 'formidable'. There would need to be consultation with multiple Commonwealth, state and territory government departments, and with various industries, not to mention Aboriginal communities themselves.[51] The departmental reviews sank into bureaucratic quicksand. When the Department of Aboriginal Affairs was wound up and its functions were transferred to the new Aboriginal and Torres Strait Islander Commission (ATSIC) in 1990, the ALRC's proposals were virtually shelved, despite their endorsement by the commissioners who had inquired into Aboriginal deaths in custody ahead of their 1991 report.[52]

By the late twentieth century, Settler Australia was looking for reasons to explain Aboriginal violence in terms of Aboriginal cultures, customs, social practices and laws. The multigenerational effects of frontier violence, land theft, missionaries' social engineering and government policy paled, it was said, against the terrible role played by Aboriginal cultures themselves. Government policy and courts were now, apparently, deferring to those cultures – with disastrous results. Many concluded that self-determination had failed abysmally. Aboriginal people were killing each other, and themselves, in such staggering numbers that – according to Peter Sutton – 'everything, including the question of artificially perpetuating "outback ghettos" ... the encouragement of corporatism as against the pursuit of individual needs and aspirations, de facto laissez-faire policing policies ... even separate Indigenous service delivery, should all be on the table'.[53]

Aboriginal violence was everyone's business, including, eventually, that of state and federal governments. John Howard's government adopted a National Crime Prevention strategy, as part of which a major report titled Violence in Indigenous Communities (2001) concluded that 'violence in Indigenous communities and among Indigenous people is disproportionately high'.[54] In the same year, an inquest into the suicide of a fifteen-year-old girl in the Swan Valley Nyoongar community camp had heard shocking evidence of sustained child abuse and other forms of violence. The state's premier, Geoff Gallop, immediately commissioned Western Australia's first Aboriginal magistrate, Sue Gordon, to inquire into allegations of child abuse but also family violence in Aboriginal communities.[55]

Dysfunctional communities

What Settler Australia understood as 'self-determination' was predicated on the assumption that Aboriginal leaders were competent enough to govern their own communities. But the stories of violence and abuse that were pouring out of these communities by the 1980s helped to revive an older narrative in Settler Australia, one which presented a person's Aboriginality as an inherent disadvantage. The earnest, young, generally white lawyers working for Aboriginal Legal Services were finding that courts were again open to that narrative. With more than occasional success, ALS lawyers submitted that their clients should receive sentencing discounts due to their membership of Aboriginal communities defined by poverty, unemployment, little or no education, alcoholism, drug abuse and myriad other forms of deprivation. Indeed, this remains a standard sentencing submission made by lawyers – the vast majority of whom are not Aboriginal – on behalf of Aboriginal clients today. That's because it's a submission that has for decades worked, at least in part, to reduce their clients' prison sentences. Settler law requires that offenders are treated as individuals; where anyone has been born and raised into neglect and abuse, that becomes a relevant factor when a court is later deciding how 'morally culpable' they are for their criminal behaviour. It's an idea that has its origins in fields like psychology, psychiatry, sociology and child development studies, whose empirical research findings have clashed with the criminal law's traditional insistence that individuals choose their own actions. No longer were Aboriginal communities and cultures being 'venerated' as sources of restoration and rehabilitation.

On 1 July 1988, Graham, a twenty-year-old man who had just been released from prison on parole, returned to Wadeye where there was, in the words of judge David Angel, 'widespread aimlessness, drinking, unemployment and a climate of violence'. Graham was a member of one of two rival clans, whose long-running dispute in the former Catholic mission southwest of Darwin had already brought much work to the courts. When Graham returned, there was (according to Angel) 'a lack of effective leadership and governance', which was difficult to avoid interpreting as a comment on Wadeye's achievement of self-government a decade earlier. Graham went to the social club, drank some beer and got into a violent argument with another man, whom Graham stabbed to death with a fishing knife. He was quickly evacuated by plane to Darwin for his own protection.

Angel wasn't one of those judges who wanted to see the breakdown of society and culture in Aboriginal communities as a consequence of colonisation and dispossession. Graham had 'indulged' in what Angel described as the 'dreadful practice' of petrol sniffing as a teenager, but his actions were in no way excused by the 'setting of domestic conflict, clan conflict and general social upheaval' in which they took place. 'You are responsible for this crime,' Angel told Graham. 'It is not the case that you were driven to it by your circumstances.' Angel lectured the whole of Wadeye about 'the misguided view that violence is a necessary consequence of differences of opinion. The fact is,' he went on, extolling the virtues of tolerance as if to unruly children, 'people do not have to agree or, to use a word fashionable in some circles, be in "consensus", in order to be reasonable or to avoid violence.' Absurdly, he went on to quote both Lord Russell and the Mexican poet Octavio Paz. 'It is only through tolerance of individual differences that life, as Paz and as our law see it, can go on.'

It was a sermon unmoored from history. After the Catholics arrived there in the mid-1930s they – and government policy – brought in people from seven distinct language groups, and imposed conditions of scarcity, which promoted conflict. Much of that conflict was managed during the mission decades, but civic freedoms and self-determination unleashed it again under conditions of poverty and unemployment. Wadeye and its problems are in large part settler creations. But even under self-determination, settler authorities have prevented Wadeye from managing its conflicts internally.

Angel ignored most of this history, but he was constrained, at least in part, by settler law as it was then understood. He accepted that Graham was at 'real risk' of payback, and may be unable to ever return to Wadeye. He weighed the need to deter violent crime and protect victims with what another judge, Roger Derrington, had recently described as 'the social difficulties faced by Aboriginals in this context where poor self-image and other demoralising factors have placed heavy stresses on them leading to alcohol abuse and consequential violence'.[56] This was something of a return to Martin Kriewaldt's focus on the disadvantages of Aboriginality. Angel imposed a ludicrously convoluted prison sentence (which is now typical of Territory sentences): seven years' prison, backdated twenty-one months to the time of his arrest, to be served concurrently with the unexpired portion of the sentence for which he was still on parole, and then to be suspended after three years on an order to be of good behaviour for four years while being supervised on strict conditions by the Department of Correctional Services.[57]

A series of cases in senior courts across Australia from the late 1980s, which themselves were built on submissions by ALS lawyers, re-established Kriewaldt's legal 'reality' that urban and then remote Aboriginal communities were dysfunctional, and that Aboriginal people living in them were severely disadvantaged – which entitled them to a reduced prison sentence (though never an *excuse* for criminal behaviour). These cases culminated in a decision by the NSW Court of Criminal Appeal in 1992, *Fernando*, which became for a generation the standard precedent for any lawyer representing an Aboriginal client.

Wilson and Amanda were in an on-again, off-again relationship. They lived in western New South Wales. One night there was a party. Everyone had lots of beer and port. Amanda stayed up listening to music. At about

6 a.m. she went into their bedroom for some cigarettes. Wilson was lying on the bed, awake. As soon as he saw Amanda, he jumped up and screamed, 'I'm going to kill you!' Amanda fled to another bedroom. In a psychotic rage, Wilson retrieved a butcher's knife from the back door – where it was used as a wedge to keep it open – and followed Amanda into the bedroom. He knocked her onto the bed and stabbed her in her neck and her leg. Fortunately she survived, and needed only stitches at the hospital. Wilson later told police he couldn't remember much about the assault, saying he was too drunk.

It was a horrific assault, obviously terrifying for Amanda, and it wasn't Wilson's first. His police history showed a steadily worsening rap sheet from the time he served six months' imprisonment for driving someone else's car without permission in 1962. During the 1980s he'd begun to serve prison sentences for assaults, including assaults on Amanda. Clearly the short prison terms were doing nothing to curb his behaviour. At the time he stabbed Amanda in a drunken rage he was already on a good behaviour bond for a drunk and disorderly conviction. Judges had ordered him to stop drinking alcohol. He'd tried rehab. He'd even tried abstaining for a while before the house party. But if anyone could be said to be a born alcoholic, Wilson could. His parents and his siblings all had major drinking problems. The welfare department had sent him to a remote property to be trained as a station hand when he was fourteen; within two years he'd fled to Queensland where, although he was barred from entering pubs because he was Aboriginal, he developed a dependency on alcohol that he was never able to shake. At eighteen, he joined a tent-boxing troupe and suffered repeated concussions in poorly supervised fights over the course of a year. He'd take work when he could find it, and spend whatever he'd earn on grog. Wilson's lawyers arranged psychometric and psychiatric reports, which found brain damage consistent with repeated concussions and heavy alcohol abuse and a possible personality disorder, all of which meant that his level of impulse control was not high – especially when he was drunk.

James Wood, the judge, found sentencing Wilson a 'very difficult problem'. On the one hand, there was his terrible record of violence and the 'objectively very serious' assault with a knife. But Wood, a Knox Grammar old boy who believed in doing what he could for disadvantaged and underprivileged people, could see Wilson wasn't evil. He had a big problem, and any reasonable person could see that he was only partly responsible for it. On the back of the deaths in custody royal commission, which had reported its findings the previous year, Wood knew that prison was useless in deterring both the abuse of alcohol by Aboriginal people and 'their resort to violence when heavily affected by it'. But he also believed that their victims – who were often Aboriginal themselves – needed the 'protection' prison offered them. What to do?

In the end, Wood felt he had to recognise that 'the problems of alcohol abuse and violence, which to a very significant degree go hand in hand within Aboriginal communities, are very real ones' and require 'more subtle remedies than the criminal law can provide by way of imprisonment'. Wood thought that courts should accept that alcohol was 'endemic' in Aboriginal communities, a fact which had to mitigate the degree to which offenders like Wilson were 'morally culpable' for the various compounding disadvantages – 'poor self-image, absence of education and work opportunity' – of their birth. All in all, a long prison sentence would be experienced by an Aboriginal person who has come from a deprived background or 'who has little experience of European ways' as 'unduly harsh'.[58] Wood sentenced Wilson to four years' prison, but allowed him to apply for parole after just nine months, which was seen as remarkably lenient given the assault and Wilson's record.

Wood's judgement signalled a return to Kriewaldt's assimilationist assumptions about the innate disadvantages of Aboriginality, presented now through prisms of psychology and child development studies. Courts across Australia repeated Wood's balancing act countless times over the years that followed. Defence lawyers trotted out *Fernando* to paint a picture – often in graphic detail – of the deprivations that marked their clients' tragic lives. They also used the deaths in custody royal commission's findings and recommendations to argue that courts should keep their clients out of prison wherever possible.

General deterrence

Fernando was new authority for the old formula: sentence, but leniently. But over the decade that followed, the Northern Territory's Supreme Court judges were among those who lost patience with what they increasingly saw as 'dysfunctional' self-governing Aboriginal communities. When in July 1997 a magistrate in Alyangula, on Groote Eylandt, sentenced an

Aboriginal man, Jason, to prison for a sustained, alcohol-fuelled assault on his wife, the magistrate emphasised the 'extreme prevalence' of domestic violence on the island. On *Fernando*'s logic, that could have been a reason to sentence Jason more leniently. Instead, the magistrate thought it made 'general deterrence' the most significant sentencing objective. (Whenever 'general deterrence' is seen as more important than 'rehabilitation', prison sentences are invariably longer. Yet by the late twentieth century, there was plenty of evidence that criminal behaviour isn't 'deterred' by the threat of prison, especially where that behaviour is driven – as it often is – by mental illness, adverse development or intoxication.) On appeal, Jason wife wrote a letter saying he'd stopped drinking alcohol and she didn't want him going to prison. But by now, there was awareness that some Aboriginal women wrote such letters as a result of pressure applied by their husband's families. The Supreme Court judge, William Kearney, thought the focus on general deterrence was right. To prison Jason went.

Kearney's judgement showcases the power of a new narrative. He repeatedly dismissed factors that would militate against a prison sentence on the basis that there was no hard evidence for them. But when Jason's NAALAS lawyer tried telling Kearney that domestic violence had actually been *less* prevalent in recent years in Alyangula, Kearney preferred to rely on his 'own general experience over the years', even though he'd never lived in Alyangula. Kearney thought there was a 'widespread belief' among Aboriginal communities that 'it is acceptable for men to bash their wives in some circumstances', though he cited no evidence. (In fact, a number of people had tried to stop Jason assaulting his wife.[59])

What can be seen in William Kearney's 1998 judgement is evidence of a growing concern for victims among judges in settler courts. By the late 1990s, most courts were compelled – by laws created by parliaments – to think much more about victims of crime, their experiences (through new 'Victim Impact Statements' submitted during the sentencing process) and community protection than they'd been doing for a generation. But in their new regard for victims of crime, judges in settler courts tend to listen to them only if they play a particular, idealised role: that of a vulnerable sufferer who needs protecting by a paternal authority figure. Many observers have pointed out that this is hardly empowering for victims, and regularly means they're ignored entirely when they don't play their proper role, as when William Kearney disregarded Jason's wife's letter. The new focus on this 'idealised' victim meant, in practice, that judges zeroed in on the *seriousness of the offence*. The crime itself became the most important thing – more important than any mitigatory factors, and more important than the victim's actual wishes (where the victim didn't want the offender to go to jail).[60]

The Territory's Supreme Court confirmed its new approach in 1999, in an appeal by the Crown against a sentence imposed on another young man who had been born and raised on Groote Eylandt. Twenty-three-year-old Harold had committed some terrifyingly violent crimes – he'd stabbed his wife during an argument, and attacked another man with a machete in retaliation for an earlier incident. Accepting Harold had no previous criminal history and was very remorseful, the sentencing judge imprisoned Harold for three and a half years, but suspended the last two-thirds of it. Prosecutors thought that sentence was 'manifestly inadequate'. The appeal judges agreed. They began their reasons with an exegesis on 'Violence in Aboriginal communities', about which courts and governments had been 'consistently expressing concern' in recent years. They cited a range of (white) judges who all shared that concern. The prevalence of this violence in Harold's community made general deterrence *the* most important sentencing principle. And Harold's particular violence was so 'horrifying' and 'disturbing' that it rendered the mitigatory factors practically irrelevant. In what was highly unusual for twentieth-century appeal court judges, they *increased* Harold's sentence.[61]

'The Supreme Court made it very clear [in 1999] that they felt that violence had got out of control in Aboriginal communities,' Glen Dooley – then NAAJA's principal solicitor – told the ABC in 2010. 'As a direct result of that decision, the jail population in the Northern Territory has doubled since then.'[62]

Incarceration. This was the consequence of the new, paternalistic focus on idealised victims and black violence which also prompted greater police numbers and powers. The deaths in custody royal commission's recommendations had become all but obsolete within a decade. It wasn't just the Northern Territory's courts that had changed their attitude. Canberra shared the concern.[63] And settler courts across the country were participating in the same project.

The new paternalism didn't square with the *Fernando* principles of deprivation, enunciated as recently as 1992. So the NSW Supreme Court set about restricting the kind of Aboriginal person who could rely on them. In January

2000, police charged Paul, a twenty-year-old man of Aboriginal heritage, with trafficking cocaine. He'd been paid $50 each time he agreed to receive mysterious packages through the post and then hold them until someone collected them. Paul's parents were both addicted to drugs. He'd seen them hit each other. He'd known his mother did sex work. He'd lived mostly with his grandparents, but his grandmother died when he was ten years old. The following year he watched first his father and then, only two weeks later, his mother, die of drug overdoses. Then his grandfather died when he was fourteen. Paul dropped out of school early to care for his younger brother and cousin. If he went to prison, they'd obviously suffer. The only reason he was part of the importation racket was to supplement his paltry Centrelink income. Applying the *Fernando* principles, the sentencing judge did send Paul to prison, but 'only' for three years – which was lenient for this kind of involvement with importing cocaine – and allowed him to apply for parole after eighteen months. But the Director of Public Prosecutions (DPP), Jason Cowdery, thought that wasn't nearly enough. Cowdery appealed.

Sitting on the bench of the Court of Criminal Appeal was none other than James Wood, who was now chief justice. But a decade after his judgement in *Fernando*, Wood thought it was probably being applied too broadly. 'As I endeavoured to explain in *Fernando*,' Wood said now, the principles he set down then 'were not intended to mitigate the punishment of persons of Aboriginal descent, but rather to highlight those circumstances that may explain or throw light upon the particular offence, or upon the circumstances of the particular offender which are referable to their Aboriginality.' No doubt that had been what Paul's original sentencing judge thought he'd done. But Wood imposed a new restriction. 'The present case is not such a case,' he said, 'nor is it one which needs to be understood as having occurred in a particular local or rural setting, or one involving an offender from a remote community for whom imprisonment would be unduly harsh because it was to be served in an environment that was foreign to him.'

It was a staggering judgement. What James Wood was now saying, in 2001, was that all those things he'd said in 1992 about Aboriginal people and the relevance of their disadvantages and deprivations to the task of sentencing them really only applied to Aboriginal people living in 'remote' places whose problems were tied up with alcohol abuse. Paul lived in Sydney and he didn't drink much, which meant Wood now thought he could effectively ignore the rest of his tragic story. Could anyone be sure that Paul's story had no antecedents in the broader history of dispossession and racial discrimination? It didn't matter that Paul himself had never been to prison; somehow, Wood concluded that because Paul was an urban Aboriginal person, prison was not 'foreign' and would therefore not be 'unduly harsh'. Wood's new position seemed dangerously close to the discredited settler distinction between 'real' Aborigines, who lived remotely according to tribal law, and urban Aborigines, who'd apparently lost whatever Aboriginality their ancestors had. The idea that dispossession and loss of culture was many urban Aboriginal people's experience of their Aboriginality didn't strike Wood as relevant. Ultimately, for Wood, Paul just wasn't Aboriginal enough. His grandfather was, in Wood's words, only 'part aboriginal', so *Fernando* just didn't apply.[64]

From there, James Wood and the NSW Court of Appeal doubled down. An Aboriginal offender originally from Shepparton, Darren, who'd missed a lot of school whenever he'd run away from his 'intimidating, violent and alcohol-dependent' father and who'd seen one of his brothers killed by a car, drifted into drug abuse and criminality. In April 2001, he approached a man outside a hotel, knocked him to the ground, and stole his wallet. In July, he broke into a house and accused one of its occupants of sleeping with his girlfriend. He cut the occupants with a kitchen knife before forcing them to leave with him in a stolen car. The sentencing judge accepted that the *Fernando* principles applied. In the Court of Criminal Appeal, James Wood said that was wrong. Darren wasn't alcohol-dependent. Shepparton wasn't 'remote' enough. He wasn't 'unfamiliar with the justice system'. Despite his childhood and his violent father, Darren wasn't 'particularly disadvantaged'. Again, Wood increased Darren's original prison sentence.[65] His successor as chief justice, Peter McClennan, further narrowed *Fernando*'s applicability when he held in 2007 that, regrettably, 'alcohol abuse is a factor in many violent crimes, whatever the racial background of the offender'.[66]

Suddenly, at the turn of the millennium, the approach that had guided settler courts since the 1830s and earlier – *sentence, but leniently* – no longer applied. Evidence of community dysfunction, which should have reduced offenders' moral culpability and therefore their prison sentences, was being used to *increase* sentences on the basis that it created too great a risk of recidivism. In doing so, the courts were taking their cues from settler culture more broadly, which had now decided that the 'experiment' that was self-determination – albeit in a very limited form – had demonstrably failed.

SAVIOURS

How settler courts and governments 'saved' First
Nations women and children from First Nations
cultures – and then locked them up anyway

In 1990, Nanette Rogers moved to Alice Springs from Sydney, where she'd been a Legal Aid lawyer for a decade, and began working for the Central Australian Aboriginal Legal Aid Service (CAALAS). Before long, she found herself being 'weighed down' by what was a significant part of her job: frequently having to defend men who abused and assaulted women and children.

In 1992, Rogers co-wrote a paper with her friend Jane Lloyd (who would later manage a domestic violence service in Alice Springs) on problems facing Aboriginal women who are victims of rape in Central Australia.[1] Both women are white. She resigned from CAALAS to establish the Central Australian Women's Legal Service (CAWLS) and commence a PhD through Sydney University before, in 1998, becoming a prosecutor. Her doctoral thesis, which studied the ways in which the Northern Territory Supreme Court at Alice Springs dealt with Aboriginal law between 1986 and 1995, identified what she saw as Aboriginal law's consistent role in prioritising the position of male offenders above the voice and interests of their female and child victims. She concluded that Aboriginal law was a large part of the problem in Aboriginal communities: it all but endorsed the violence men commit against women and children, she claimed, and made it incredibly difficult for victims to report crimes.[2]

It was a conclusion that dovetailed with broader concerns being expressed in Settler Australia, which was increasingly prepared to listen to First Nations voices – as long as those voices were delivering the message settlers wanted to hear. In June 2003, Mick Dodson told the National Press Club of the 'extreme' violence that was 'shattering our communities', and called for 'extreme action' in response. John Howard invited sixteen leaders and experts to Canberra. Four Aboriginal leaders and researchers – Lowitja O'Donoghue, Jackie Huggins, Ian Anderson and Alison Anderson – prepared a report for the Council of Australian Governments (COAG), which nominated a number of causes for the violence plaguing many Indigenous communities, including colonisation, inadequate housing and continued mass unemployment. It took nearly a year for COAG to finally agree on a framework, which cherry-picked from the solutions the paper proposed.[3] Unemployment and housing were problems governments could fix, at least in theory. But doing so without addressing the colonial relationship would risk augmenting the problems it created and sustained.

Child abuse

First Nations cultural practices, rules and laws had remained opaque to settlers since they first began to observe them in 1788. From the earliest days, Indigenous people expressed shock and horror when they saw settlers beat children. By the twentieth century, settler authorities had turned those concerns on their head. Courts during the self-determination era occasionally tried hard to grapple with practices and laws they knew very little about, and which more than occasionally caused great consternation. None would cause more concern in the late twentieth century and beyond than sexual contact between adults and children. In particular circumstances, such contact was either endorsed by First Nations law or it wasn't, and courts had no reliable way of reaching a sound judgement. In the end, all that mattered was that such contact was and is illegal in settler law, and courts found it easy to slip into a civilising role on the issue. In 1975, judge William Forster released an Aboriginal man on a good behaviour bond after he'd had sex with a ten-year-old child in Oenpelli (now also known as Gunbalanya). The evidence suggested the child had been a willing participant, and Forster said he knew enough of the 'sexual precocity in young Aboriginal girls'. But he also had the duty to impose settler law, which defined the man's conduct as statutory rape. 'This is a serious offence,' Forster said, 'and young girls like this one must be protected against themselves.' Forster applied the usual formula – *sentence, but leniently* – and fully suspended the man's prison sentence.[4]

Human history is replete with examples of sexual contact between adults and children. As late as 1947, the anthropologist Ronald Berndt recorded what to settler eyes appeared to be precocious sexualised behaviour among children in Arnhem Land, and what in reality were play and performance with ritual and sacred significance to Yolngu culture. But those Aboriginal societies that had significant contact with settlers – of the missionary or secular kind – were more likely to have lost much of the ritual and sacred dimensions of sexuality in favour of its eroticism.[5] However, by the end of the twentieth century, settler law and culture – increasingly aware of research findings, and increasingly shocked by the revelations pouring out of churches and other places of supposed sanctuary – had accepted that all such contact is exploitative, abusive and harmful to the child. It is impossible to know to what extent the child's experience of trauma depends on cultural preconditions, such as post-industrialisation (which creates ideas such as 'childhood' and its 'innocence') and sexual repression (especially prevalent in Anglo-American and Christian cultures).[6] What is known is that none of these conditions was present in pre-contact First Nations societies.

By the turn of the century, Settler Australia was primed to accept that self-determination – which had never really been allowed – had failed, either because Indigenous communities were dysfunctional, or because Indigenous cultures were inherently violent, or both. Two cases became emblematic. In August 2001, a fifteen-year-old girl was temporarily at an outstation 120 kilometres east of Maningrida. A forty-nine-year-old man, who later told the court he was the girl's promised husband, had sex with her and forced her to stay with him for two more nights.[7] Police arrested him, charged him with statutory rape, and took him to Maningrida. He was incensed. Her maternal grandmother and uncle – the appropriate people to identify the correctness of the relationship – had consented to the union. Indeed, he said they'd been pressuring him to consummate the union for some time. She hadn't been going to school, she'd been using ganja, and (he believed) she was already sexually active. 'It wasn't my idea,' he said. 'I was just forced to take her; I been told so many times.' There was ample evidence, including anthropological evidence, that supported his assertions. He was unjustly being treated as a criminal, he maintained, just because settler law refused to accommodate his people's law and culture. The court sent him to prison for four months, following which he was to be released and show good behaviour for a year and a half.

With the help of his NAALAS lawyers, he appealed. John Gallop, Supreme Court judge, agreed that the sentence for statutory rape was excessive. The sentencing magistrate hadn't taken First Nations 'custom' into account. The girl 'didn't need protection' from settler law, Gallop concluded. 'She knew what was expected of her. It's very surprising to me [he] was charged at all.' There was nothing Gallop could do about the conviction – statutory rape was illegal under settler law – but he reduced the prison sentence to twenty-four hours. *Sentence, but leniently.*

Darwin, and the Settler nation, erupted. The man had earlier served a seven-year prison sentence for the manslaughter of his wife, so the headline of Paul Toohey's front-page article in *The Australian* read: 'A wife-killer forces sex on a 15-year-old betrothed to him by traditional law and escapes punishment.' Prosecutors appealed. The man's jail time was increased to a month before he could be released on a suspended sentence.[8] Amid a media storm, ATSIC refused to fund his further appeal to the High Court. Aboriginal women's groups also said Aboriginal law couldn't be used to excuse or mitigate crimes against children. The Territory government rushed amendments through parliament removing any ambiguity: underage sex was prohibited, even in traditional Aboriginal marriages.[9]

It wasn't just Aboriginal law's role in apparently excusing violence against women and the statutory rape of underage girls that offended settler sensibilities. It was also its inherent 'barbarism', as *The Australian*'s editorial put it. An Alice Springs magistrate had granted bail for seven days to an alleged murderer so that he could travel to a community 450 kilometres away to undergo payback. Police stood by while relatives of his alleged victim ritually speared him thirteen times in the legs and broke his ankle.[10] At the same time, a regular practice in Wadeye whereby police officers observed and sanctioned community-organised one-on-one fistfights on the main oval there as a means of keeping the broader peace, spiralled out of control and ended with an acting sergeant shooting an eighteen-year-old man dead (see chapter 12).

A review into 'Aboriginal customary law' by the Territory's standing Law Reform Committee, which comprised eight additional Aboriginal members including Galarrwuy Yunupingu,[11] made recommendations broadly consistent with those the ALRC made in 1986. Legislation and courts *should* recognise Aboriginal law as a source of law.[12]

It wasn't at all what Nanette Rogers and *The Australian* wanted. (Indeed, no newspaper or TV station even covered the report's release.)

Rogers despaired. The Territory's amendments banning promised marriages weren't enough to protect another girl, a Year 9 student in Darwin
who, when she was four, had been culturally 'promised' to a Ngarinyman
man, 'GJ', who was now fifty-five. His was to become the second emblematic case in the settler panic about Indigenous laws.

In June 2004, the girl went to Yarralin to stay at her grandmother's
house for the school holidays. Her grandmother came to believe the girl
had become sexually active with a boy. As punishment, her grandmother
and GJ hit her with a boomerang and a stick. She then packed the girl's
bag, insisted that she go with GJ to his outstation, and made her get into
his car. He drove her to his outstation and forced himself on her, causing
a significant injury to her anus. GJ, who had lived mostly outside the ever-
expanding reach of the settler state, made her stay with him for four days
before he drove her back to her grandmother's. From there, the girl complained to police, who charged GJ with statutory rape and assault (for the
beating). Just as prosecutors had, the Supreme Court's chief justice, Brian
Martin, accepted that GJ believed that both acts were appropriate according
to Ngarinyman law. On that basis, he reduced the sentence he would have
otherwise imposed to two years' imprisonment, suspended after a single
month. Outraged newspapers and TV news reports all over the country
condemned what was seen as an inadequately short sentence, and prosecutors successfully appealed.[13]

For Rogers, whose husband managed the Territory's child welfare department's Alice Springs office, forced sex in promised marriages
between middle-aged men and teenagers was only the tip of the iceberg. In
October 2005, two months after Martin's sentencing of GJ, she presented
a paper to the Police Commissioners' Conference in Sydney, which contained even more explosive allegations. Indigenous children – some as
young as seven months old – were being raped by men in their communities, she declared. Australians 'knew' these communities were violent
places, but this was next level. Why hadn't they been told? The vast majority of these horrific crimes were not being reported. 'Violence is entrenched
in a lot of aspects of Aboriginal society here,' Rogers told the police commissioners. 'Aboriginal people choose not to take responsibility for their
own actions.'[14]

In the twelve years between 1994 and 2006, fewer than 1 per cent of
Indigenous offenders sentenced by the NT's Supreme Court – just thirteen

matters out of 1798 – made submissions arguing that their culpability was mitigated because Indigenous law had imposed particular restrictions or requirements on them to act as they'd done. In five of those cases, the crime being sentenced was actually (the defendants argued) a punishment sanctioned by Indigenous law. In another four, the defendants argued that they'd been provoked by another person's breach of Indigenous law. And in just two cases in total – those of the Ngarinyman man and GJ – Aboriginal law was invoked in attempts to explain or excuse charges of statutory rape.[15] This recent history might suggest that Rogers was exaggerating the extent of the problem. But for Rogers, it was evidence of the opposite. According to her, Aboriginal law was being invoked well before sentencing courts became involved: it was being used by violent and abusive men to head off complaints before police ever learned about crimes, and to silence witnesses who did consider making reports.

After talking to ABC reporter Suzanne Smith over the period of a month, Rogers handed over her conference paper and agreed to talk about it on air. 'I just fell over,' said Smith after she read the paper. Tony Jones, by then among the ABC's most senior reporters, flew to Alice Springs to meet Rogers. He came away from that meeting convinced of her bona fides.[16] Rogers appeared on *Lateline* during the evening of 15 June 2006, a Monday. Rogers made a number of sweeping statements about 'Aboriginal society': it was punitive; it intimidated and punished people who reported child abuse; its members 'fail to take responsibility for their actions.' Jones then asked her to describe the particulars of three shocking cases, and she did, giving graphic detail. *Lateline*'s audience wasn't told whether these cases were representative or outliers; whether perpetrators had mental health issues or intellectual disabilities; even whether these cases had been proven.

The solution? Ultimately, Rogers said, Aboriginal victims and witnesses had to be better at telling their stories in Northern Territory courtrooms. Rogers wanted Aboriginal children, girls and women to 'take responsibility for the kinds of violence that is happening in and around themselves and their communities'. The way to do this would be to give 'correct evidence' – the evidence contained in their original statements to police – when they came to court.

In that first interview, Rogers set alight a national media firestorm that would burn for months.[17]

Settler law resurgent

Lateline and other outlets went to Central Australia to check Rogers' claims. Many Aboriginal people – including the old women – gave very different accounts. They blamed alcohol, not Aboriginal law, for the violence now being perpetrated against women and children.[18] Australian governments and its legal system had corrupted Aboriginal law,[19] and its (white) judges had too often accepted bogus claims about it, which had been fashioned by (often white) defence lawyers.[20] The problem was not Aboriginal culture, within which women had senior roles – it was that too many men had lost it,[21] or had developed a traumatised 'bullshit culture' from spending too much time in prison, or were prevented by the Australian justice system from being held accountable to it. Indigenous leaders and researchers pointed to the fact that governments had not acted on earlier recommendations to help communities improve their living standards – housing, infrastructure – which were implicated in the crimes now being complained about.[22]

Meanwhile, Rogers' claims became the basis of sensationalised media reports, nationally and internationally. Journalists demanded to know what politicians were going to do about the urgent problem of customary law–condoned child sexual abuse in communities. This was now the only urgent issue in Indigenous affairs as far as Settler Australia was concerned. *Lateline* broadcast additional claims of babies, children, adolescent girls and women being subjected to horrific violence at the hands of Aboriginal men during subsequent reports. Newspapers did the same. During the days and weeks that followed, more and more non-Aboriginal people denounced Aboriginal law.[23] Former prime minister Malcolm Fraser was among the very few non-Indigenous people who advocated an historically informed approach that would see the present crisis in the context of the 'terrible crimes' committed against First Nations people and communities by white people and the colonising state, and that would address 'underlying causes' such as unemployment and overcrowding.[24] But most settler commentators angrily rejected any approach other than immediate, punitive action. Self-determination had been a tragic and violent failure. The good intentions behind such landmark reports as the deaths in custody royal commission and *Bringing Them Home* had paved the road to hell for too many First Nations children and women.[25] From within the Howard government came calls for *more* child removals and even 'exit grants' for people who wanted to leave violent communities.[26]

The calls for urgent action, made within days of Rogers' first *Lateline* appearance, bore all the hallmarks of a moral panic: the inevitability and widespread nature of the harm to children in First Nations communities was being exaggerated as part of an effort to define First Nations culture as 'a threat to societal values and interests'.[27]

Mal Brough was Howard's minister for Indigenous affairs. 'There's no culture in the world which should accept babies being raped,' he declared. He urged the Northern Territory government to send more police into Aboriginal communities, to rein in 'mafia-style' customary law. He proclaimed that self-determination had failed. He appeared on *Lateline* and declared that 'paedophile rings' were operating in remote communities.[28] He backed away from that claim the next day, but by then everyone in Australia had heard it. From the United States, Howard asserted the need for greater policing and more prosecutions without deference to Aboriginal law. 'I hold a very clear view on things like this,' he said emphatically. 'There is one law in this country.'[29] Brough declared that housing, overcrowding and other problems caused by governments would need to wait until 'law and order' was restored.[30]

The initial panic was just beginning to subside when, on the evening of 21 June 2006, *Lateline* broadcast an interview with what it described as an anonymous 'former youth worker' in Mutitjulu. Following the broadcast of Rogers' interview in May, *Lateline* said it had been contacted by senior women in Mutitjulu, who told of an old man who traded petrol for sex with young girls in their community. The former youth worker had been told 'by a number of people' about a group of men in the Central Desert Region 'who are systematically abusing children' by keeping girls as 'sex slaves'. The youth worker had made reports to police, he said, but he'd withdrawn his statements after he and his wife had been threatened with violence. 'The people who are in control,' said the former youth worker, 'are the drug dealers and the petrol warlords and the paedophiles.'[31] In response, Clare Martin – the Territory's chief minister – commissioned Pat Anderson, an Alyawarre woman and executive of Aboriginal health organisations, and Rex Wild, a senior (white) lawyer and the Northern Territory's outgoing Director of Public Prosecutions, to inquire into claims of child sex abuse in Aboriginal communities.[32]

Everyone now agreed there was a problem; the question was what to do about it. On the one hand were the calls for a 'law and order' response, which would see more police and perhaps even the army sent into Aboriginal communities to 'restore civil order'. On the other hand were the calls by a panel *Lateline* convened toward the end of June – Marcia Langton, Sue Gordon and Fred Chaney, then chair of Reconciliation Australia – for genuine partnerships between communities and governments aimed at addressing decades of neglect and abuse by government agencies in a way that also addressed the terrible legacies of colonisation, genocide, dispossession and racial discrimination. 'You can arrest as many people as you like,' Chaney told Tony Jones. 'You can jail them, you can go through all of these things which have to happen when people abuse children. But the fact of the matter is if you don't address these long-term underlying issues you're simply fiddling at the edges.'[33]

John Howard's federal government was leaving few people in doubt about which approach it favoured. In July, justice minister Chris Ellison backed a monstrous proposal to force rape victims to testify against perpetrators or risk being jailed themselves.[34] At a COAG meeting, Brough told states and territories he would withhold $130 million in additional funding for service delivery to First Nations communities unless they also prohibited Aboriginal law.[35] Pat Dodson pointed out that the proposal was racist and signalled a return to the old assimilation policy. Aboriginal law 'does not condone abuse', Dodson said. 'It's absolute nonsense to suggest it does.'[36] But the proposal was applauded by Jodeen Carney, a (white) Victorian lawyer who was now a Country Liberal Party (CLP) politician in Alice Springs: she'd twice introduced bills that would have made the same changes.[37] 'Let's be clear,' Carney declared in an opinion piece published in *The Australian*. 'Customary law is a shield behind which violent Aboriginal men hide.'

The 'former youth worker' whose appearance on *Lateline* had reignited the panic was then, rather sensationally, outed as a Canberra-based public servant. While working in Central Australia, Gregory Andrews told an inquest into the deaths of two men and a teenage boy, all of whom had died of suffocation after sniffing petrol, that 'stronger policing' was one of the answers.[38] In February 2006, Andrews moved to Canberra to become an assistant secretary in the Office of Indigenous Policy Coordination (OIPC). The role meant that he was effectively advising Mal Brough. Two months after arriving in Canberra, Andrews gave evidence to a Senate inquiry:

I was at Mutitjulu for about 18 months and I lived in the community for about half of that time. It was desperate for intervention to address the really serious dysfunction that was occurring there. People were being raped, being bashed, killing other people and killing themselves. I was chased by psychotic petrol sniffers and threatened by people with violence for challenging some of the people who were engaged in sexual violence against women and children and in drug dealing. Young people were hanging themselves off the church steeple on Sunday and their mothers were having to cut them down … Sadly, to drink alcohol, smoke marijuana, sniff petrol, beat your wife and abuse your family and yourself is to be an Aboriginal person in that community, and if you do not participate you are socially excluded, which is one of the reasons why I was threatened with violence on a number of occasions when I tried to support the very few people who were brave enough to do something about it.[39]

But no child had ever hanged themselves from the church steeple in Mutitjulu, police clarified, and no mother had ever had to cut her child down. Andrews later apologised in writing to the Senate for misleading it, an offence that can carry (but never has) a term of imprisonment.

How, then, within two months of misleading parliament, did Andrews show up on *Lateline* as an anonymous 'former youth worker'? *Lateline*, it turned out, had approached him – not the other way around. They knew what he'd said to the inquest and to the Senate committee, and they wanted him to say something similar to the ABC's audience. Andrews thought it over. He provided his minister with briefing notes about what he intended to say. 'Living in a remote Indigenous community in the Central Desert Region is like living in a war zone,' he told Brough.[40] Unsurprisingly, Brough took no issue with that. Andrews told *Lateline* he would appear on their story, but only if he remained anonymous. After giving evidence at the inquest in 2005, he said in a statement to the ABC, 'I was threatened with violence and intimidated on a number of occasions.'

But what of the specific claims Andrews made on *Lateline*: the hearsay about 'sex slaves' and 'petrol warlords' and 'paedophiles'? And the complaints he'd made to police and subsequently withdrawn after being threatened with violence? While he was at Mutitjulu, Clare Martin later told parliament, Andrews had relayed allegations to the Northern Territory government that children were prostituting themselves for alcohol. Those allegations found their way into a memo Martin herself sent to her police minister in 2004, and the government encouraged Andrews to report specific allegations to police. But Andrews never reported anything to police. He'd never *withdrawn* any complaints after being threatened, because he'd never *made* any in the first place. Subsequent investigations found 'no evidence whatsoever' for what Andrews had told either the government or *Lateline*.[41] Martin described his time at Mutitjulu as 'very disappointing.'[42] (That didn't slow Andrews' career in Canberra. He later moved into biodiversity conservation, and in 2014 Greg Hunt appointed him Australia's first threatened species commissioner.)

In mid-September, Brough's promised legislation appeared in parliament. When considering bail and passing sentence for people accused of committing federal crimes, courts in the Northern Territory would be absolutely barred from taking Aboriginal law or cultural practice into account as a mitigatory factor.[43] In the very same month, Western Australia's Law Reform Commission concluded a six-year inquiry into Aboriginal 'customary laws' with recommendations similar to those made by the ALRC twenty years earlier.[44] And this time, Alan Carpenter's Labor administration wanted to act on them.[45] But Brough had already threatened to block tens of millions of funding dollars if it did. The proposed Western Australian reforms were swept aside. Labor, the Greens and the Democrats voted against Brough's bill, and even the Coalition's own Senate committee members agreed it was fundamentally flawed.[46] But the Coalition had the numbers in both houses. The bill raced through parliament and was law in December.

By the beginning of 2007, the idea that First Nations law and culture was to blame for family violence and sexual crimes in remote communities had well and truly taken root in the settler imagination. Perhaps the most startling expression of this idea was a book that appeared in March 2007 by playwright Louis Nowra, who just six years earlier had worked on *Black and White*, the film about Max Stuart's case in Adelaide. *Bad Dreaming: Aboriginal Men's Violence Against Women and Children* and its sister essay, 'Culture of Denial' (published in *The Australian*'s literary review at the same time), both hit the same notes that everyone from Nanette Rogers to Mal Brough to Peter Sutton had been thumping for months and years. 'Tradition is no excuse for the epidemic of male violence and sexual abuse that is obliterating indigenous communities,' Nowra declared.[47]

Pat Anderson and Rex Wild then delivered their 320-page report, *Ampe Akelyernemane Meke Mekarle* (which translates from the Arrandic languages of the Central Desert Region as 'Little Children are Sacred'). The report identified a number of what its authors termed 'myths' that underpinned the moral panic that had led to the report being commissioned: that men are the only abusers; that Aboriginal law somehow causes or justifies the abuse; that Aboriginal culture somehow causes the under-reporting of violence and abuse. As far as Aboriginal law was concerned, incest and intra-familial child abuse was 'an extremely serious breach of traditional law and punishable by death'.

This was a very different account to the story that was now dominant in settler media, politics and culture. There *were* 'paedophiles' operating in some Aboriginal communities, Anderson and Wild found. But they were often outsiders, including a Christian Brother, acting in ways by then depressingly familiar to many settler Australians living in cities and towns. In fact, people in communities had been trying for years to get authorities to take action against these men. Now, communities were being blamed by practically everyone in journalism and government for the crimes they'd tried to report. And what did they find of those 'promised' marriages, which media reporting had depicted as little more than old men gratifying themselves with young girls? Anderson and Wild found that instances of forced sex within traditional marriage were extremely rare, because that was a crime often punishable by death under Aboriginal law. Promising brides to men was a cultural practice that was possibly thousands of years old, and was part of complex kinship systems designed to protect genetic integrity and ensure group survival. If kinship marriages, in which neither party could choose their partner, offended Western liberal conscience, they did so in the same way that arranged marriages do. The two court cases that had been held up by Nanette Rogers and in media reporting as emblematic of the urgent problem of traditional marriage – those involving GJ and the Ngarinyman man – had in fact involved sex that had *not* been sanctioned by Aboriginal law.[48]

Overall, Anderson and Wild concluded, the picture was much more complicated than media reports and politicians were making it out to be. Child sexual abuse was a problem in the Northern Territory's Aboriginal communities, they confirmed. But it was the breakdown of traditional laws and customs, rather than their continued observance, that created the

conditions for abuse. Little would be achieved by crisis intervention following each episode of abuse. Rather, the solutions required greater investment
in prevention and 'the structural forces of factors that impact on the health
and wellbeing of a community': better, more adequate education; tackling
substance abuse; more and better housing; and, most importantly, reinforc-
ing cultural and community strengths.

Brough and Howard were disappointed by *Little Children are Sacred*. So
was everyone else who wanted to blame Indigenous communities for their
own deprivations. Brough called the report's recommendations 'totally weak
and totally inadequate'.[49] He wanted the report to make the case for radical
intervention. It didn't. He wanted the report to back his claims of paedophile
rings. It didn't. He wanted the report to confirm Nanette Rogers' revelations
about what was happening in communities. It didn't.

In April 2007, three twelve-year-old girls were evacuated from the old
Catholic mission of Kalumburu in the East Kimberley – 'for fear of tribal
retribution', as *The Australian* put it – after the deputy chair of the local
Aboriginal corporation and another man were charged with 'dozens' of
child sex offences.[50] By the end of the year, local Western Australian police
had charged more than thirty men and boys across the Kimberley.[51] At last,
Brough and Settler Australia's news media had found the case of their imaginations. It was a thousand kilometres from where Nanette Rogers said they'd
find it, but no matter. 'I do not believe that this is the only community where
children are being abused,' Brough said. He declared that paedophilia was 'rife'
in First Nations communities across Australia.[52] Brough, who had grown up
believing he may have had Aboriginal ancestry, was now determined to act.[53]

The Northern Territory Emergency Response (NTER) – 'the Intervention' – has been written about many times, so a detailed recount is
not necessary here.[54] Two months after the first child sex arrests in the
Kimberley, and three weeks after declaring child sex abuse was 'rife' in other
communities, Brough made the major announcement on 21 June 2007.
There would be alcohol restrictions and pornography bans on Aboriginal
land. There would be more police. Welfare payments would be quarantined
and linked to children's school attendance. All Aboriginal children would
be subject to compulsory health checks. The NTER would be 'overseen' by
a taskforce led by Sue Gordon.

Brough claimed the NTER was the federal government's response to
Little Children are Sacred. Yet the whole thrust of the report's ninety-seven

recommendations required that communities be *empowered* to address problems. The Intervention ignored this entirely. Recommendation 1, for instance, was that child sexual abuse in the Northern Territory 'be designated as an issue of urgent national significance' by both Territory and Commonwealth governments. The Intervention certainly did that, but it ignored the rest of the recommendation: 'It is critical that both governments commit to genuine consultation with Aboriginal people in designing initiatives for Aboriginal communities.' Brough consulted with almost nobody before rolling out the NTER – *via army tanks*, which entered Aboriginal communities within a week of his press conference.

'The Intervention' is shorthand for a raft of top-down measures imposed on Aboriginal communities in the Northern Territory, on the premise that the women and children in those communities needed saving from their violent men. Some certainly did, and on that basis the Intervention attracted the support of some influential Aboriginal public figures, including Marcia Langton, Noel Pearson and Bess Price.[55] But as legal academic and Eualeyai/Kamillaroi woman Larissa Behrendt pointed out a year into its rollout, the Intervention was 'a textbook example of why government policies continue to fail Aboriginal people': it was ideological rather than evidence-based; it was paternalistic rather than consultative and collaborative; it undermined communities' control over their own resources. As well as tighter restrictions and greater penalties for the possession and supply of alcohol and pornography in Aboriginal communities, the Intervention imposed a number of other restrictions and greater levels of surveillance. Under 'Operation Themis', it introduced eighteen new police stations in Aboriginal communities, and gave police increased powers – for instance, the power to enter people's houses and cars and search for alcohol. The Intervention dissolved Aboriginal community councils and replaced them with government 'shires'. It imposed Australian government 'business managers' on dozens of Aboriginal communities and town camps. It prohibited courts in the Territory from taking into account Aboriginal law or cultural practices in mitigation when imposing criminal sentences.[56]

And the Intervention did nothing, apparently, to prevent significant crimes being perpetrated against children. In February 2018, a two-year-old child who had been the subject of thirteen substantiated child protection investigations was raped in Tennant Creek by a man in his twenties. (Police initially arrested the wrong suspect, who spent months in prison until DNA evidence revealed the perpetrator.) As Prime Minister Malcolm Turnbull flew into Tennant Creek for much-publicised 'crisis talks', the child's family expressed fury with authorities who had ignored their reported concerns.[57]

Incarcerate faster

The Intervention never found those paedophiles hiding behind Aboriginal law. But the increased surveillance it created – with more police on the ground – did have an impact. Two researchers who studied driving offences in the Warlpiri communities of Yuendumu, Mutitjulu and Lajamanu between 2006 and 2010 concluded that the Intervention led to a dramatic *250 per cent* increase in traffic offences being detected by police.[58] In the decade following the Intervention, the number of Indigenous men in prison doubled. The number of Indigenous women in Territory prisons more than tripled. And most ironically, the number of Indigenous children locked up in Don Dale and the Alice Springs youth detention centres more than doubled. Most tragic of all is the spike in suicide and self-harm among First Nations children. The Intervention had been about protecting children. Yet, compared with the five years leading up to the Intervention, suicide rates over the following five years among First Nations children aged between ten and seventeen *increased by 160 per cent.*[59]

The Intervention was a watershed moment in Indigenous–settler relations in Australia. More than a decade later, its legacy is clear: if the idea of 'self-determination' had survived the Howard government's attacks on land and native title rights and on the very concept of representative Indigenous politics (following ATSIC's abolition in 2005), it was practically killed off under the NTER. The prospect that Indigenous law would play any more than a tokenistic part in communities' efforts to heal following generations of traumatic intervention by governments and churches receded further.

o

In 2018, I was talking with a prosecutor in the foyer of Katherine's courthouse. We were both white, both from 'down south'. She'd 'done her time' as a defence lawyer, but she now worked (for significantly better pay) for Darwin's Director of Public Prosecutions. She was more eager than most to talk about the reasons she practised. She was a socialist, she declared. I asked her how she squared her politics with her role in sending Aboriginal people to prison at alarming rates. That was only a by-product, she told me, of her primary role. 'I represent the people who are truly without a voice,' she said. I looked at her quizzically. I thought that's what *I* was doing, working as a defence lawyer for an Aboriginal legal service. Prosecutors represent the state, which is hardly powerless.

'I represent Aboriginal *women*,' she clarified. 'Women and children. Aboriginal men are protected by their land councils and their customary laws and their Elder system. Women and their kids are completely silenced in that whole system. It's our role to give them a voice, help them to stand up to the bully men who are maiming and killing them.' I could have been in a conversation with Nanette Rogers herself, and it suddenly dawned on me that her views might be pervasive within the Territory's DPP. Of course, women and children are entitled to help if they're being attacked. But Rogers' view was that the DPP and the settler state was best-placed to provide that assistance … how? By locking up as many men for as long as possible?

Nemarluk and Jandamarra

Two small black-and-white photos hang, framed, on a wall of the council meeting room which doubles once a month as a courtroom on the main street of Wadeye. The photos are easy to miss, especially in the chaos of court days, where the speed at which people are processed has led to comparisons with a 'cattle yard'.[60] In one photo, mounted constable Ted Morey sits astride a horse on the Moyle River flood plains, looking like a figure out of a Western, during his pursuit of a man called Nemarluk. In his account of the last three years of his life, author Ion Idriess presented Nemarluk as a feared 'savage', determined to repel 'the Japanese and white intruders who had come, unasked, into his people's tribal lands of which he was chief'.[61] Nemarluk was notorious in the Top End during the 1930s. He'd killed uninvited newcomers to Wadeye (a Catholic mission then known to settlers as Port Keats, and to Aboriginal people as Wentek Nganayi), escaped from Darwin's Fannie Bay Gaol by dragging himself through 7 miles of mangroves after being shot in the side, and evaded police and trackers for some time before being recaptured.[62]

Nemarluk's recapture is shown in the second of the photos on the wall. The resistance leader is standing, chains and shackles prominent against his bare skin, next to another Aboriginal man of much smaller stature and in the khaki uniform of the tracker. The photos assume a powerful symbolism in the 'white space' of the Wadeye courtroom.[63] Resistance to settler law is futile. Nemarluk, who is said to have provided the inspiration for Robert Tudawali's character in *Jedda*, contracted pneumonia in Fannie Bay Gaol and died, aged about thirty, in Darwin's hospital.

Nemarluk has been practically forgotten by Settler Australia. Bunuba man Jandamarra, is more well known, thanks largely to Paul Kelly's song 'Pigeon/Jundamurra' and also Banjo Woorunmurra and Howard Pedersen's remarkable book, *Jandamarra and the Bunuba Resistance*. Idriess had also written about Jandamarra, albeit as 'a criminal who defied the legitimate laws of white society'.[64] But in the 1890s, after police ordered him to track and capture other Bunuba men, Jandamarra continued in the Kimberley the guerrilla resistance that Pemulwuy and Tedbury had begun in Sydney and on the Hawkesbury a century earlier. 'Jandamarra died on his own soil defending his country', Paul Kelly says, and describes him as 'a true Australian hero'. But these heroes have never been part of Settler Australia's mythology.[65] Settler 'justice' branded them criminals, and got them all in the end.

Criminalisation has been at the very heart of the settler-colonial project in Australia. That was easy to spot when the criminal law was one of the weapons settlers were brandishing on the frontier. But now, its colonial role gets buried beneath the epidemic of violence and grog and sexual abuse, which are its very legacies. Anyone who doubts this only needs to suggest – to settler politicians, to judges, to bureaucrats – that there are alternatives to prison, and that some of those alternatives might already exist within First Nations communities.

Significant swathes of Settler Australia remain staunchly resistant to that idea, and prefer an analysis which ignores to the point of absurdity the ongoing structural barriers governments *continue to impose* in their efforts to deny Indigenous sovereignty. Nearly a century after Nemarluk's resistance, if Wadeye is known to Settler Australia at all, it is because of its reputation as one of the most violent places in the country.

In large part, that reputation is due to the fact that ongoing clan conflict is regularly reported in news media without reference to the fact that settler governments have maintained Wadeye's dispossessed population – through decades of under-investment in basic infrastructure – in conditions of poverty and inadequate housing[66] and prohibited Wadeye from engaging in its own dispute-resolution processes. When conflict erupts, settler authorities insist on responding to it in a way which individualises the problem – police single out individual 'offenders' and charge them with particular crimes – and precludes local resolutions.

Yet in parts of Settler Australia, an extraordinary ignorance prevails. 'It is disheartening to read yet another account of a dysfunctional Indigenous remote community', wrote Dr Peter Balan of St Peters, Adelaide, to *The Australian*, where he read an account of weeks of escalating violence in April 2022 which left dozens of houses 'extensively damaged' and caused hundreds of people to flee to surrounding outstations. 'It is evident from this report that the local population is not able to turn [Wadeye] into a "true town" without unaccountable millions of taxpayer dollars thrown into this settlement each year.' Balan is an adjunct senior lecturer in the University of South Australia's business school, has a PhD in business innovation, and was awarded an Order of Australia in 2016 for services to tertiary education. Postgraduate research generally encourages people to defer to informed opinion on subject matters outside their areas of expertise, but Dr Balan OAM felt able to pontificate on little more, apparently, than a single newspaper article.[67] And Balan's solution to Wadeye's problems? 'Residents should be actively encouraged to move to a better life in a better-serviced community.'[68] It's unclear where such a hypothetical community is (it's unlikely to be Balan's exclusive inner-Adelaide suburb of St Peters, where the median rent for units is higher than the entire Jobseeker payment).[69] Apart from the innate importance of being On (or close to) Country, a major rationale for the Homelands Movement, which began in the 1970s, was to build a life away from the devastations of capital city fringe-dwelling.[70] Settler authorities have often imagined Indigenous people as rootless. Dr Balan OAM apparently continues to do so.

By himself, Balan is hardly significant in this story. But views similar to his are still held by enormous sections of the settler population. Settler Australia's response to the problem of anomic violence within Indigenous communities remains to lock up as many people as possible. The state has continued its intrusive involvement in Indigenous lives. It's an intrusion that behaves differently to that during the so-called protection era, but it has the same character. In Wadeye, police are available 24/7 to lock people up, but people can't access the clinic at night or on weekends, even during emergencies Incarceration presents the political answer to all the social and other dilemmas posed by Indigenous disadvantage and associated crime.

So far, we've investigated the history of how settlers came to apply their criminal law to First Nations peoples and communities. The second half of this book shifts gears. It still spends time in the past, but it looks more directly at prison itself and the law that supports and sustains it. How fair, really, is Australia's justice system?

INCARCERATION

How settler justice threw up its hands and decided prison was the only answer after all

Roebourne is a small, sparse and hot collection of buildings on the highway between Port Hedland and Carnarvon, in the Pilbara.[1] During the gold rush there it was the largest settlement between Darwin and Perth. By the 1980s, it had become home to many First Nations people who had drifted in from surrounding stations, camps and reserves in the wake of the Equal Wages decision. Mining companies had moved in, but they weren't yet taking on Indigenous workers. The companies built their own towns – Dampier, Wickham – where their white employees lived.

Half of Roebourne's residents were Indigenous. Blocked from employment in the mining and pastoral industries, and from their traditional lands, many sank into welfare dependence and alcoholism. Clashes with police were commonplace. Indigenous people were living with nightly – sometimes hourly – police surveillance. Over the course of eighty-nine days in 1983, police made 730 arrests, mostly of Aboriginal people. Most of those arrests were for minor alcohol-related offences. One senior officer temporarily stationed at Roebourne in 1983 was shocked at 'the enormous amount of blood splattered all over the place' inside the police cells.[2]

During the evening of Wednesday, 28 September 1983, an Aboriginal man, Ashley James, went to buy a drink at the Victoria Hotel's bottle shop. A drunk, off-duty, white police officer swore at and threatened him. The officer was sitting with four of his colleagues, all white. They were all drunk, having returned earlier from a police union meeting at Karratha, half an hour's drive west. Later, on the footpath outside, the officer again accosted James. James fought back, and the off-duty officers attacked him. Before long, the off-duty officers were fighting as many as eight Aboriginal men.

A sixteen-year-old Aboriginal teenager, John Pat, was one of those who leapt into the fray in James's defence.

At one point during the fight, one of the officers punched John Pat in the head, possibly his face. John fell backwards, his head hitting the concrete. Another officer fell on top of him: this may have been how his ribs fractured. He lay there, possibly unconscious. Later, some witnesses said they saw an officer kick John in the head, twice. When the fight was over, at least two of the officers dragged John up and threw him into a police van – 'like a dead kangaroo' according to witnesses – along with other Aboriginal men. John's head may have connected with the van. Police intended to charge them all with assault. The vans were then driven back to the station. There, police opened the van and dragged each of their Aboriginal prisoners out. Witnesses saw the officers punching and then kicking the prisoners before dragging them into the police cells. Two of the other Aboriginal prisoners also fell to the ground. The prisoners and a witness said later that the police systematically beat each of the prisoners as they dragged them out of the vans. John was by now mostly unconscious. The officers thought he was playing what they called 'doggo': pretending to be asleep. In their paperwork, the officers described John as 'bleeding'.

An hour later, when police checked on the teenaged Pat, he was dead; an autopsy revealed a fractured skull and bruising and tearing of the brain. The officers refused to give evidence at the subsequent inquest, and the coroner committed them all for trial. They were charged with manslaughter, but an all-white jury in Karratha – a town established by Hamersley Iron in 1968 – returned a unanimous acquittal.[3] The Crown prosecutor recommended they then face internal police discipline. Brian Bull, in charge of internal police discipline at the time, disagreed. On the very same day that Bull submitted his report, all five were reinstated to full duty. None of those responsible incurred any official sanction for John Pat's death. Within a year of recommending no further action against the officers involved, Brian Bull was appointed commissioner of Western Australia's police force.

In the history of police violence against First Nations people, this latest episode was not particularly noteworthy. But in 1983–84 it had the sense of 'last straw' about it. John Pat's death prompted a number of senior First Nations people to form the National Committee to Defend Black Rights (NCDBR). Over the next few years, NCDBR took every opportunity to call for a major public inquiry into why so many Indigenous people were dying in prisons, police cells and police vehicles. 'There seems to be a conspiracy on behalf of the police, prisons, pathologists and courts,' said NCDBR chair Helen Boyle in 1986, 'to stop the truth coming out.'[4] John Pat's became one of six emblematic deaths of young Indigenous people whose families suspected were murdered by police. By September 1986, the NCDBR had succeeded in convincing Charles Perkins, descendant of the Arrernte and Kalkadoon peoples and the federal Department of Aboriginal Affairs' first Aboriginal secretary, to call for a royal commission.

Six apparent suicides by hanging over the summer of 1986–87 – all inside police cells on North Queensland Aboriginal communities by Aboriginal people arrested ostensibly for drunkenness or other minor 'social order' offences – initially prompted the federal minister, Clyde Holding, to order a parliamentary inquiry limited to suicides in north Queensland lockups.[5] Bob Katter, then a young minister in Queensland, refused the cooperation of Joh Bjelke-Petersen's state government.[6] Two more deaths on 11 June – in Brisbane's Boggo Road jail and in the Warragul police cells in central Victoria – led Holding to order a national inquiry by the Human Rights and Equal Opportunity Commission.[7]

But First Nations people continued to die in police and prison cells throughout 1987. The fourteenth in just seven months was nineteen-year-old Kingsley Dixon, hanged by a sheet within half an hour of entering the Adelaide Gaol in July after being arrested for possessing marijuana.[8] His grieving mother was convinced Kingsley had been murdered.[9] The family of the sixteenth – twenty-eight-year-old Lloyd Boney, who had apparently hanged himself with his own sock in the Brewarrina police station (in New South Wales) after being arrested in breach of his bail conditions in August – similarly rejected suggestions of suicide.[10]

Within a week of Boney's death, the new Minister for Aboriginal Affairs in the Hawke government, Gerry Hand, ordered what the NCDBR had been demanding for nearly four years: a nationwide royal commission that would investigate every single one of the ninety-nine deaths of Aboriginal people in custody since 1980.[11] When it finally reported in 1991, the commission didn't find what the families of Kingsley Dixon and Lloyd Boney, and many others, had anticipated. In the vast majority of cases – all but five – it found that people had not died at the hands of police or custodial officers. John Pat's probable homicide was not representative.

What was happening was that Indigenous people were being arrested far, far more often than were non-Indigenous people. The main reason so many First Nations people were dying in prisons, police cells, juvenile detention centres and police vehicles was that they were in those places so often. The five commissioners' recommendations were wholly focused on getting custody and arrest rates down.

Crime and punishment

The Royal Commission into Aboriginal Deaths in Custody became one institutional expression of a reform movement whose aim is to *reduce* the modern justice system's reliance on prison as a punishment for criminal behaviour. This movement to 'decarcerate' – the opposite of 'to incarcerate', to imprison – is a contemporary expression of a much longer reform movement in Western culture. Plato in his *Laws*, written in the early 340s BCE, was among the first to suggest punishment could rehabilitate as well as merely avenge. If retribution and deterrence are the only goals for a system of justice, then torture, spectacle and death might well make sense. But if a criminal is to rehabilitate, they should not only survive but be afforded an opportunity to become a better person. Francis Buller, an English judge, complained in 1782 that 'offenders come from [the hulks on the Thames] more hardened than they went, form themselves into gangs, are ripe for all kinds of iniquity, and engage in it immediately on their discharge'.[12] Transportation and modern imprisonment were supposed to address this 'crime school' effect: it works (at least in theory) by taking the criminal's liberty, and by affording them 'time out' to reflect and to grow.

It's a nice theory, and occasionally it even succeeds. But for most prisoners the reality of imprisonment is about as far from the reformers' ideal as it's possible to be. The fantasy of quiet reflection is overtaken by a reality in which the monotony is noisy and claustrophobic and authoritarian, demanding a constant vigilance against an ever-present threat of violence. Ever since the modern prison was born in the eighteenth century, reformers have wanted prisons to be clean, hygienic and oriented to the rehabilitation of their inmates.[13] That's rarely been the case. Alexander Maconochie, a Scot (and former geography professor) appointed by the Whig government in 1836 as John Franklin's private secretary on Van Diemen's Land, observed that 'the amount of suffering is much greater than it appears to be', and that the 'essential and obvious error' in the system of transportation was 'its total neglect of *moral* reasoning and influence, and its exclusive reliance on mere *physical* coercion'.[14] For a brief period, Maconochie was made governor on Norfolk Island, where he transformed a place where 'the worst of the worst' had been ruled with tyrannical brutality into a place which aimed to restore the twice-convicted convicts' dignity through a system focused on rewards for good behaviour rather than punishments. Maconochie reported extraordinary results: 'crime diminished ... on the island to nearly one-half of what it had previously been'.[15]

But Maconochie's ambitions ran into the forces of reaction, which are ever ready to thwart any reform that shifts the focus too far away from deterrence and retribution. Robert Peel's Conservatives regained power in London, so despite a favourable report on Maconochie's penal experiments by (Whig-appointed) New South Wales governor George Gipps, Maconochie was pulled out of Norfolk Island after nearly four years there. His replacement, Joseph Childs, reintroduced more traditional discipline, which sparked a riot that killed four officers.[16]

The interplay between reform and reaction has continued ever since to define Settler Australia's system of criminal justice. Reformers have succeeded in defeating the death penalty (it was practically abolished everywhere by 1985)[17] and corporal punishment, creating non-custodial punishments, which can be served in the community, and improving prisoners' ability to exercise their limited rights. By the late twentieth century, reformers – armed with the findings of studies in fields as diverse as criminology, psychology and anthropology – became increasingly convinced that prisons often militated *against* rehabilitation. Prisons are authoritarian and traumatic institutions, and spending time in them seems, if anything, to *increase* the likelihood that a person will commit future crimes.

Fifty years ago, reformers – armed with new sociological and criminological data – began agitating openly for decarceration, or prison abolition. When Thomas Mathiesen, a Norwegian sociologist, published *The Politics of Abolition* in 1971, he believed an end to prisons was in sight. In Australia, the aims of settler reformers dovetailed with a new expression of Indigenous resistance politics which had been defying colonisation for two centuries (see chapter 13).[18] The Aboriginal deaths in custody royal commission became a flashpoint. Instead of mitigating the enormous toll vioence was exacting on Indigenous families and communities, mass incarceration was adding to and multiplying that toll. Nearly every review by settler institutions into Indigenous incarceration rates during the past half-century – by royal commissions, departmental and parliamentary inquiries, law reform commissions, ombudsman and coronial investigations, academic studies – has urged governments to do whatever they can to reduce the numbers of people going to prison.

Yet, these reviews and recommendations have been overwhelmed by the forces of reaction. Movements in support of the rights of victims, which have emerged over the same period, have often devolved into simplistic campaigns for longer and tougher prison sentences, or for changes to the law which make it easier to secure convictions in courts.[19] Victims' rights campaigners tend to emphasise deterrence, retribution and incapacitation over rehabilitation, often professing a belief that dangerous criminals can't be rehabilitated, and that victims and the broader community can only be protected by longer prison sentences for perpetrators of crime. They also tend to focus on the responsibilities of individual perpetrators, rather than of broader forces that create conditions for criminal offending. Although victims are often drawn from the same communities as offenders, and the same people frequently oscillate between victim and offender, victims are inherently more sympathetic figures than offenders, and political leaders quickly discover that promising to be 'tough on crime' by lengthening prison sentences is infinitely more popular than promising to be tough on the *causes* of crime, which include poverty, trauma and state failure. While institutional reviews carry on in the background, popular tabloid media – newspapers, commercial television, social media and mass-market books and movies – generate and fuel 'hot' moral panics about particular crimes and inadequate sentences. A decade and a half after Mathiesen's book, most countries – including Australia – had commenced massive prison-building programs.[20]

Mandatory sentences

Since the 1990s especially, the forces of reaction have held sway in Australia's parliaments. Both major parties – Liberal and Labor – have been committed to longer maximum sentences, and even mandatory minimum sentences. The Northern Territory's attorney-general, former police officer Daryl Manzie, pushed through new laws in 1989 which made it mandatory for second-time drug offenders to serve prison time.[21] Two years later he extended the same principle to anyone who breached a domestic violence order a second time, even if it involved no actual violence.[22] These were the first of what would be many efforts by governments and parliaments around Australia to remove from courts and judges discretion over whether or not to send particular offenders to prison.

Such solutions had many motivations. In the late 1980s and early 1990s in the Territory, for instance, there was growing frustration among victims' rights campaigners about the prevailing 'remission' system, under which prisoners were being more or less automatically released earlier than their sentence dictated if they'd demonstrated good behaviour. A campaign for so-called truth in sentencing led in 1994–95 to a new *Sentencing Act*.[23] The Territory's corrections department estimated 'truth in sentencing' would add between eighty and 130 additional prisoners to the already overcrowded prison population within the first year.[24]

In Western Australia, five children who'd stolen cars were killed in high-speed police pursuits in an eighteen-month period from April 1990. Another eleven *non*-offenders were also killed. Most kids arrested by police for stealing cars were Aboriginal. A moral panic about a 'youth crime wave' ensued.[25] In a desperate (and unsuccessful) attempt to avoid defeat at the 1993 election, Carmen Lawrence's Labor government created new laws aimed at what it called 'hard core' youth offenders.[26] Kids who committed a *fourth* violent crime had to be locked up for at least eighteen months, with no guarantee of release. That provision only lasted two years and – some suggest because it was designed to – caught nobody.[27] But it heralded what was to come. In 1996 – just five years after the royal commission – the new Liberal government legislated Australia's first 'three strikes' law.[28] Anyone convicted of a third burglary – now described as a 'home invasion' – would go to prison for at least a year. The new law was obviously targeted at First Nations kids: it was introduced into parliament by the Minister for Aboriginal Affairs, and four in every five children dealt with under the laws in the first five years were Indigenous.[29] During the second five years that proportion rose to 87 per cent.[30]

Inspired by the Western Australian law, Shane Stone's CLP government in Darwin introduced its own version of 'three strikes' the following year, under a policy it called 'compulsory imprisonment'. *Any* property offence, no matter how minor, meant at least two weeks' prison. A second meant ninety days' prison. And a third finding of guilt for a property crime meant courts had no choice but to sentence a person to at least *one year* in prison.[31]

Among the early offenders who went to prison under the new regime were a forty-year-old woman who'd stolen a chicken from an Alice Springs supermarket and also damaged a timber barrier (owned by the council) when she used it to light a fire to keep warm, a twenty-three-year-old Kalkaringi woman who stole a can of beer worth $2.50, and a teenager who scratched a tag on a shop window. Three Supreme Court judges confirmed that 'compulsory imprisonment' meant *actual* imprisonment and not, for instance, suspended imprisonment or home detention.[32] The rate of Indigenous incarceration in the Territory shot up immediately. The Territory government – still obliged to do what it could to *reduce* the First Nations prison population, after the deaths in custody royal commission – denied that had anything to do with mandatory sentencing laws.[33]

In May 1999, a homeless Aboriginal man, 'James', took a towel from a clothesline to use as a blanket. The towel went back to its owner. But it was James's third property crime, and he faced a year in prison. 'It seems to me that we haven't come very far from transporting people for stealing a loaf of bread,' his lawyer observed. But the chief magistrate, Hugh Bradley, saw things differently. 'It may be that it's for a person such as you the mandatory sentencing law was enacted,' Bradley told James, and sentenced him to one year in jail. Bradley had been appointed (by Stone) after his predecessor resigned in protest at the new laws.[34] Darwin lawyer Jon Tippett agreed that the law was indeed for people like James: 'It was enacted to put poor, homeless, drunken Aboriginal people who commit petty offences against property in prison for inordinate and quite unjustified periods of time.'[35] Most youth offenders weren't subject to mandatory prison, but that didn't stop magistrate Greg Cavanagh – briefly known to Settler Australia as Lindy Chamberlain's Legal Aid lawyer in her murder trial – sentencing fifteen-year-old Benjamin, a Warnindhilyagwa boy from Groote Eylandt, to two stints in Don Dale in 2000 for theft of minor items. 'Did you like it in there or something?' Cavanagh asked the second time. Benjamin did not. Less than a decade since the deaths in custody report, Benjamin hanged himself with his bedsheet twenty-four days into his second 'mandatory' sentence.[36] Cavanagh was also the Northern Territory's coroner, a role which required him to investigate systemic causes of deaths in custody .

In opposition, Labor – led by former ABC journalist Clare Martin – promised to repeal the mandatory sentencing laws, and won the 2001 election in a landslide. It did repeal the CLP's three-strike laws, then simply replaced them with its own brand of compulsory sentencing for property crime.[37] And late in its first term, Martin's government introduced a mandatory minimum non-parole period of at least twenty years for most murder convictions, regardless of the circumstances.[38] This would later see nineteen-year-old Aboriginal teenager Zak Grieve jailed for at least two decades, despite having backed out of a murder plot before his victim was killed, while his co-accused, who repeatedly hit the victim in his head with a spanner, was entitled to the benefit of 'exceptional circumstances' and had his non-parole period reduced.[39] And in its third term, the Martin ALP government also replaced the CLP's mandatory sentences for violent offending with its own. From December 2008, anyone who committed a second 'aggravated assault' had to go to prison for three months, unless there were 'exceptional circumstances'.[40] These laws remain on the books, despite the recommendations of multiple inquiries and even despite government promises to repeal them.[41] I've represented people in cases involving such 'aggravated' assaults as throwing an empty cigarette lighter or a Biro at another person ('threaten with offensive weapon'), a man slapping or pushing a woman ('male assault female'), and smacking a kid's bottom ('adult assault child').[42]

Other states have also since experimented with various types of mandatory sentencing legislation, though with one or two exceptions – such as the mandatory one-year prison sentence for assaulting police in Western Australia[43] – such sentences have largely been confined to very serious crimes where courts are already imposing lengthy prison terms. But nowhere outside the Northern Territory are people subject to *minimum* prison terms for such 'crimes' as possessing cannabis, breaching a DVO or merely pushing another person in the chest. And nowhere else in Australia is the Indigenous population so great a proportion of the total population – both generally, and in prisons – as it is in the Northern Territory. Unsurprisingly, the people who are 'caught' by mandatory prison sentences in the NT are overwhelmingly Indigenous. There are no mandatory sentencing laws, for instance, for middle-class crimes like fraud, embezzlement and corruption.

Bail 'reform'

Being convicted and sentenced in court is only one of the ways a person can be ordered to spend time inside a prison. The other is to be remanded there if bail is refused. At the point a person is arrested by police, they're merely a suspect: they're innocent right up until the point they're found guilty by a court. Innocent people are ordinarily entitled to their liberty. Sometimes there are very good reasons we might want someone who hasn't yet been found guilty in court to be locked up: alleged serial killers and compulsive child sex offenders are the most obvious cases. But what about less obvious cases, like someone accused of an assault or a break-in? Imprisoning a person without a trial is a big deal. What if someone spends months or even years remanded in custody, and is then found not guilty in court? And what happens when someone dies on remand, as Gunditjmara, Dja Dja Wurrung, Wiradjuri and Yorta Yorta woman Veronica Nelson Walker did at Melbourne's Dame Phyllis Frost Centre – despite calling out for help twelve times – in January 2020? It's a terrifying prospect. Advocates of strict bail laws say dangerous people roaming free is sometimes much more terrifying.

Before Adrian Bayley raped and murdered ABC employee Jill Meagher in a lane off Melbourne's Sydney Road in Brunswick in September 2012, he'd been convicted and jailed for an assault in Geelong that left his victim with a broken jaw. But he'd immediately lodged an appeal against his sentence and was bailed.[44] (The conviction should also have triggered the cancellation of his parole, which was part of an earlier prison sentence for five rape convictions, but didn't.) When it was discovered that Bayley could and should have been in custody at the time he killed Meagher, there was outrage. *The Age* published a timeline under the heading: 'How the justice system left [Bayley] free to stalk Melbourne's streets.'[45] Victoria's parliament rushed through changes to the state's parole laws,[46] and spooked magistrates denied bail to more and more alleged offenders.

Originally, explains Deakin Law School's deputy dean Marilyn McMahon, whether to bail or remand someone depended mostly on how likely it was that they'd show up to court on a future date.[47] When she was completing her surveys in the mid-1960s, Elizabeth Eggleston noticed that magistrates and justices of the peace assumed Aboriginal people were inherently unlikely to return if released, so they often weren't: in one Western Australian town, not a single Aboriginal person was released on bail during the first nine months of 1966; and one police officer in South Australia told her he'd only seen two Aboriginal people bailed in the previous two *years*.[48]

But in the last thirty years, parliaments have shifted the focus to community protection. As well as assessing the likelihood of a person answering their bail, police and magistrates also need to assess the risk they'll commit another crime if they're released. It's an impossible task: the vast majority of people don't reoffend while they're on bail.[49] Should everyone charged with a crime suffer imprisonment without trial so that the community can be protected from a few? In recent decades, Australian parliaments have said 'yes'. State and territory Bail Acts now create presumptions against bail for people charged with a whole host of offences.

McMahon cites a common pattern in public debates about bail laws. Victoria's former attorney-general Robert Clark spoke in 2018 about 'the growing contempt for the law' and 'the huge amount of offending by those who have been granted bail'.[50] 'The Victorian community is seeing effectively a revolving door bail system for people who are charged with violent offences,' declared Gordon Rich-Phillips, an upper house politician, in the same year.[51] The problem is that these perceptions, while deeply held, don't reflect reality, especially among people charged with violent crimes. McMahon explains that *perceptions* of a 'huge amount of offending' comes from what she calls the 'William Horton effect'.[52] Horton was serving a life sentence for murder in Massachusetts when, while on a weekend furlough in mid-1986, he escaped and later assaulted, bound and gagged a man before twice raping his wife. We might also talk about the 'Adrian Bayley effect' now. Cases like this are so big, and get so much media coverage, that they overwhelm all other information – particularly dry, statistical information – in the minds of voters. The 'huge amount of offending' is actually a small amount of offending, most of which is relatively minor. Veronica Nelson Walker – who died in Melbourne's women's prison – had been arrested on theft charges and outstanding warrants, and could hardly be described as a threat to anyone. Adrian Bayley is a statistical outlier, but no magistrate wants to be the one who lets the next statistical outlier out on bail.

Victoria's laws *were* already 'tough' enough when Bayley murdered Jill Meagher. His case was an extraordinary study in repeated failures of authorities to apply *existing* laws. Yet his crime has had ripple effects throughout the country. Activists observe another distortion. While Victoria Police apparently left no stone unturned in their hunt for Bayley following Meagher's disappearance, police and prosecutors in New South Wales had to be dragged kicking and screaming to lay charges after an Aboriginal woman, Lynette Daley, was brutally raped and killed in January 2011. Prosecutors, who had dropped charges against two white men and declined to re-lay them even after a coronial recommendation, were eventually prompted into action after a *Four Corners* report aired in May 2016. A jury took just over half an hour to convict the men after a lengthy trial.[53]

As a result of the Bayley-inspired law changes, remand populations – people in prison before their trials – are swelling well beyond prisons' and courts' capacity to deal with them. There were more people on remand in Victorian prisons in February 2020 than there were convicted prisoners in mid-2006.[54] Other states and territories report similar statistics. 'Record high prisoner numbers' is a headline which appears with almost monotonous regularity in various newspapers. The proportion of Australian prisoners on remand almost doubled from 17 per cent in 2000 to 33 per cent in 2019, before Covid-19 restricted people's movements and led to a decrease in prisoner numbers for the first time this century.[55]

In 1976, Elizabeth Eggleston drew attention to what were then extreme cases of people serving 'long periods of pre-trial detention' – she cited cases where people spent four, six and ten months on remand – before their trials.[56] These remand periods may have been noteworthy in the 1970s, but they're more or less standard now. People charged with very serious charges spend a year or even two on remand while they wait for their trials in a district, county or supreme court. Even courts of summary jurisdiction – which are supposed to prioritise efficiency and churn – are making people wait extraordinarily long periods in prison while they're still legally innocent. The Local Court in Darwin and Katherine, for instance, routinely lists hearing dates for charges such as assault and theft many months, and up to an entire *year*, after the accused was first charged.

Defence lawyers often get blamed – by magistrates, judges and politicians – for contesting too many charges and clogging up the court system. From a court's point of view, guilty pleas are much more efficient. They can be all over in fifteen minutes or less. But if you're a defendant who wants to exercise your right to have the case against you proven in court, you'll cause the courts to set aside hours, perhaps a whole day or two (or more). Jury trials – reserved for the most serious charges – can take weeks. But in my experience, most defendants will plead guilty if there's evidence that will prove their guilt in court. Where there isn't evidence, they shouldn't be prosecuted. Prosecutors, who are public servants, have a duty to make sure the cases they take to hearing or trial have a reasonable prospect of success. But it's not uncommon for defendants to come to court for their contested hearing, only to find that summonses haven't even been served on witnesses. Often, the DPP prosecutor agrees on the day of the hearing to a deal the defence lawyer offered months earlier – a deal that reflects the evidence on the brief. As a result, many defendants are spending an unprecedented amount of time on pre-trial remand, or on bail.

When a First Nations person is bailed from a Territory court, it will typically impose a long list of conditions, a single breach of which can see bail revoked. 'There's a stack of people in here who are being induced into pleading guilty,' a client of mine tells me. He's in Darwin's prison. It's euphemistically called a 'Correctional Centre', though there's not much 'correcting' that happens there. People on remand wear bright orange clothing, which distinguishes them from sentenced prisoners who wear other colours – yellow, green, blue, red – depending on their level of assessed risk. Low-security sentenced prisoners get access, at least in theory, to work and rehabilitation programs. 'Orange-shirts' get almost nothing: they're innocent until proven guilty, authorities say with what must be a sly bureaucratic wink, so they don't need to be rehabilitated. It's far from uncommon for people to spend much longer on remand – in an orange shirt with nothing to do – waiting to defend a charge at a contested hearing than serving the sentence they'd receive if they simply pled guilty. After being refused bail, many defendants over the years have instructed me that they want to plead guilty and 'get it over with', so that they can get a green shirt, do some work and plan for their release date. These instructions come despite the paucity of evidence against them, in circumstances in which they would very likely beat their charge. This is a curious form of 'justice'.

During the two years I worked as a defence lawyer in Katherine, the most common type of contested hearing was what is known as an 'oath-on-oath DV hearing'. I'd meet an Indigenous person – generally a man, though not always – in the cells after they'd been charged. He'd be charged with assault. The (alleged) victim would have given a statement to police naming the defendant as the perpetrator. There might be photos of bruises or wounds. But there were no other witnesses. My client, the defendant, might also have injuries. They'd give me a version of events that casts the complainant as the aggressor, or which is consistent with a legal defence. We'd go into court, where I'd tell the judge my client is pleading not guilty, and we'd apply for bail. It's invariably refused, because at that point all the judge has is the evidence *against* my client. My client would go to prison on remand, in an orange shirt. Three months later he'd come back to court. One of two things would then happen. Either the complainant would turn up and give his or her version under oath, following which my client would also give his version under oath. As long as my client's version was reasonably plausible, and it generally was, he'd be acquitted and would walk free. Or the complainant would *not* turn up, in which case the charges would be dropped. It's difficult to avoid concluding that three months of remand – conveniently the mandatory minimum sentence for most people convicted of assault in the Northern Territory – is being used as a de facto punishment for people whom courts can't convict.

It's possible to mount a pragmatic defence of this practice. If you break the law, what difference does it make if your prison time happens before or after your trial? The difficulty with this argument is that it assumes that a charged person is guilty. But in the settler justice system, a court is the only institution capable of finally determining a person's guilt. Campaigners for victims' rights who look to the criminal courts for 'justice' are regularly disappointed by them and their insistence on rules of evidence and proof beyond reasonable doubt. In her bestselling 2018 memoir *Eggshell Skull*, Bri Lee, prominent campaigner for the rights of sexual assault survivors, recalls her first few weeks as a judge's associate in the Queensland District Court. 'I'd been researching how widespread sexual assault against girls is,' she writes. 'At law school the first and most sacred principle they teach you comes from Blackstone: that it is better that ten guilty men go free, than for a single innocent man to be imprisoned. Benjamin Franklin said it was one hundred. I doubted that Franklin had been confronted with the rapes of one hundred girls, but my tally was stacking up.'[57] I've heard many defendants say they used to share Lee's scepticism of the value of Blackstone's principle until they found themselves locked up for something they didn't do. Australia's bail laws make that scenario much more likely than we assume it is.

Indigenous people are bearing the brunt of Australia's ongoing crackdown on bail. Of the 147 Indigenous people who died in custody in Australia during the decade to 2018, more than half were on remand, being arrested or were in 'protective' custody.[58] If we recall the key recommendations of the Royal Commission into Aboriginal Deaths in Custody thirty years ago – to keep more Indigenous people out of custody – that represents an abject failure.

Does prison work to reduce or prevent crime?

The whole premise of this book might be blown apart if the answer to this question is 'yes'. And at first glance, the data is promising. Together with most of the Western world, Australia experienced steepening crime rates during the 1970s and 1980s, especially as heroin flooded the streets of cities and towns. By the end of the century, Australia had the highest rate of crime victimisation among a survey of eighteen developed nations, including the United States. John Hewson, as federal opposition leader during the early 1990s, described Australia as the crime capital of the world.[59] In response, governments promised to get 'tough on crime'. Parliaments funded more police, set longer maximum and then minimum prison sentences, made it more difficult to get bail and parole, and made sure a lot more people went to and stayed in prison. Then, toward the end of the last century, the crime rate began to fall. At first, commentators in tabloid media – who'd sold a lot of advertising space by covering crime – refused to believe it. But subsequent data confirmed it. Why shouldn't this be seen as an endorsement of the policy of mass incarceration to control crime?

This is certainly the popular view, and it's one that courts and judges (and politicians and tabloid media and most voters) accept as an almost self-evident truth. The idea that sending a criminal to prison both prevents his own future crimes *and* gives pause to a phalanx of potential offenders is such a fundamental belief in criminal law that it's barely questioned. But in his latest book, *The Vanishing Criminal*, co-authored with research statistician Sara Rahman, the retired criminologist Don Weatherburn rejects that logic as one which confuses correlation with causation.

It turns out that the related but separate concepts of *arrest risk, imprisonment risk* and *sentence length* are rarely studied by criminologists. There's only one published Australian study – in 2012 – which has looked into all three factors and their effects on crime rates. Weatherburn himself participated in it, with three colleagues. They did find that, over the long run, imprisonment showed a small benefit: for every 1 per cent increase in the imprisonment rate, there was a corresponding 0.115 per cent reduction in property crime and a 0.17 per cent reduction in violent crime. In other words: small fry. To get even a single percentage point reduction in the rate of violent crime, you'd need to increase the incarceration rate by 6 per cent. (As a way of demonstrating just how miniscule this is, Weatherburn and his colleagues found that simply *increasing average incomes* by a single percentage point generated much greater effects on the crime rate: property crime dropped by 1.894 per cent, and violent crime dropped by 1.46 per cent.)[60] As New South Wales' former chief prosecutor Nicholas Cowdery concluded in his 2001 book, *Getting Justice Wrong*, imprisonment is an extraordinarily expensive and inefficient way of controlling crime. It costs more than $2100 a week to keep a single prisoner in prison in Australia. Locking up young people in youth detention centres costs double that.

It turns out that the main way in which policing and courts affect the crime rate is through a combination of shame and containment. Prison does have what's known as an 'incapacitating effect' for people who commit multiple crimes, though, again, it's extraordinarily expensive.[61] Most crimes are committed by teenagers and people in their early twenties – in other words, before their brains are fully developed – who then mellow out with age. And most people who commit crimes aren't compulsive criminals, so incapacitation isn't necessary most of the time. Many first-time offenders experience such shame when their crime is detected by police that they never offend again. Often it's not even the punishment that's decisive here: it's the very fact of detection and all that entails, including being charged and formally interviewed by police, being forced to disclose sordid details to friends and family, and so on. Prison is no more effective than non-custodial punishments – including community work, fines and electronic monitoring.[62] By the time most people have been arrested and charged, the criminal justice system has probably already done most of what it will ever do to deter them and others from offending in the future.

The specific prospect of going to prison isn't what deters most people from committing crimes. We've known this for a long time. If prison *did* work to deter anyone from committing a crime, then even more brutal punishments – like transportation or torture or the death penalty – would presumably work even more effectively. Yet, even as Britain's parliament quadrupled the number of crimes that attracted the death penalty throughout the eighteenth century, peasants and paupers continued to pick pockets and steal food (which were both capital crimes). If the prospect of severe punishment *did* deter anyone from criminal acts, then the United States – which imprisons its population at a rate that dwarfs every other nation – would be one of the safest places on the planet, because nobody there would be committing crimes. But despite imprisoning people at almost double the rate of the next most prison-happy nations (Brazil,

Russia and Turkey), and at almost four times Australia's rate, the United States has seen only slight reductions in crime this century compared with Australia, Canada and New Zealand.[63] This is also despite the fact that the United States continues to execute prisoners by lethal injection and electric chair. A similar phenomenon can be found in the Northern Territory, where rates of violent assault have not reduced since the introduction of mandatory prison sentences in 1999.

Why doesn't the threat of prison prevent people from committing crimes? Because the theory of 'deterrence' is really just a variation on what's known in public policy as 'rational choice' theory, which itself misunderstands why humans act in the ways they do. It assumes that people rationally weigh up benefits and costs before choosing to act. The deterrence hypothesis predicts that by making the costs of criminal behaviour higher (in the form of longer prison sentences) or more likely (by increasing the number of police available to detect criminal behaviour), we'll cause more and more people to decide *not* to behave criminally. Unfortunately for proponents of deterrence theory, most people who commit serious crimes like assault, homicide, rape, burglary, robbery and theft aren't behaving rationally while they do so. Rather, they're likely to be intoxicated or enraged or desperate or traumatised. Their 'executive functioning' – the part of the brain that regulates our emotions and behaviour – is either temporarily or permanently disengaged. Sociologists suggest that the main reason most people *don't* do the wrong thing is that they've successfully 'internalised' social rules and norms, and that most of this internalisation occurs in early childhood, well before rational choice – or legal responsibility – comes into it.

While 'choice' as an explanation for criminal behaviour might have something going for it if the behaviour we're talking about is a highly elaborate insider trading scheme, it's been found wanting for many more impulsive crimes, such as assault and property damage. As a well-educated, middle-class white guy with reasonable mental health (most of the time) and a stable childhood, I might strongly believe I've 'chosen' to avoid letting my emotions get the better of me in situations when I've felt angry enough to hit people. But what's probably closer to the truth is that I was afforded the opportunity to develop just enough skills of emotional regulation I'd need to function effectively in a highly bureaucratised and regulated world. Deferred gratification and impulse control don't require much effort from me. That I've never assaulted anyone, or criminally damaged someone's property in anger, or 'lost control' behind the wheel, or developed a dependency on alcohol or other drugs probably has nothing much to do with the deterrent effects of punishment and prison, and more to do with my adequate development and socialisation, and, no doubt, the privileges afforded to me by my racial and class power. For someone whose childhood was less stable – perhaps it was violent, or abusive, or neglectful – impulse control and emotional regulation may be much more difficult to attain, especially if they're under the influence, and/or experiencing desperation due to poverty or homelessness, which is also more likely.

Bri Lee's memoir, *Eggshell Skull*, provides an excellent contemporary example of the popular narratives that hamper reform of the criminal justice system. As the survivor of a childhood sexual assault by her older brother's fifteen-year-old friend when she was nine, Lee gives a harrowing account of the way the assault has continued to affect her, especially after she begins sitting through rape trials as a judge's associate following her graduation from law school. Understandably enraged by the justice system's failure to find the vast majority of accused rapists guilty, she files a formal complaint about her own assault with police. To induce an admission from her assailant, she phones him – it's what's known as a 'pretext call'. She doesn't tell him it's being recorded. Now in his thirties, he apologises to her for what he'd done to her fifteen years earlier, and tells her he'd also been sexually abused by an adult cousin when he was a child.

Prosecutors lead the recorded pretext call as evidence against him in his criminal trial in the Queensland District Court, which finally occurs two years after her initial complaint. Lee directs most of her rage at her assailant (for daring to plead not guilty) and at the system for subjecting her to extreme stress just for trying to seek justice. 'He literally can't go any lower,' she tells her boyfriend (and her readers). 'He's denying the second count *and* he's running a defence.' The jury finds him guilty and he's convicted, sentenced to nine months' imprisonment (fully suspended), and placed on the sex offenders' register. 'So while he didn't have to do any time, it would be on his record forever,' Lee writes. 'It was all I'd ever wanted.' Consistent with prevailing 'three act' thinking, Lee encourages her readers to believe that the main injustice lies in the various ways the system blocks many victims from experiencing the validation that accompanies a guilty verdict. That Lee *did* experience this kind of validation owes a significant amount to her own racial and class privileges, which aren't enjoyed by the vast majority of sexual assault victim-survivors.

What Lee doesn't tell her readers is that her assailant successfully appealed his sentence. Three Court of Appeal judges agreed that because he was a child himself at the time he assaulted Lee, and one who had himself been sexually abused, he shouldn't have been subject to a conviction or a prison sentence, albeit suspended.[64] Lee is critical of the court system for making it so hard for her to secure justice, and *Eggshell Skull* brilliantly expresses the rage and powerlessness many victims experience when they encounter it. As a trained lawyer, though, Lee could have introduced her readers to the many structural critiques of the justice system's failings. Often, it's the very significant *penalties* for crimes like sexual assault that incentivise people accused of them to plead 'not guilty': Lee's assailant – who was training to be a nurse when he was tried – knew that pleading guilty would have virtually guaranteed he'd be disqualified from ever working with children, which in practical terms means he could never work in most jobs (including nursing), because of something terrible he'd done when he was a teenaged survivor of child sexual abuse. His only chance of avoiding that outcome was to plead 'not guilty' and hope to beat the charges. Ignoring his apology to Lee during the pretext call, both the sentencing and appeal courts concluded he'd demonstrated no remorse because he'd pled 'not guilty'. It's one of the many convenient fictions courts perpetuate. There are many ways offenders could take responsibility for the harms they cause, but the system itself precludes most of them.

The criminal justice system, which creates significant penalties and therefore insists on a trial that's fair to the accused, makes it difficult to secure convictions on the evidence of a sole complainant, and is often – for those reasons – an inappropriate forum for many sexual assault victim-survivors seeking justice. Many victim-survivors tell researchers that they want offenders held accountable for their actions, but not necessarily through imprisonment or the criminal court system.[65] Various alternatives to the 'crime and punishment' approach, which encourage offenders to take responsibility for their actions, and to participate in both rehabilitative programs and (where appropriate) therapeutic processes to assist their victims' recovery, have been abandoned by governments determined to lock up as many offenders for as long as possible, despite the proven success of such alternatives in preventing reoffending.[66] The criminal trial aims to determine whether an alleged offender is guilty beyond reasonable doubt, and the courts then determine punishment – including prison – based on a philosophy of 'rational choice', which isn't backed by research.

The criminal justice system blunders along according to its own institutional logic, which often holds few answers for victims, offenders or the broader community.

Ultimately, as Andrew Leigh – a former economics professor and now Labor MP – demonstrates, any claimed correlation between rising imprisonment rates and falling crime rates is illusory.[67] Australia followed the United States into a new era of mass incarceration of the poor and the marginalised, one not seen since the industrialising nineteenth century with its laissez-faire policies encouraging 'free' capital markets – which to many simply meant the several freedoms (from jobs, from home ownership, from anything to lose) associated with poverty. Between 1985 and 2009, Australia's rate of incarceration – the proportion of its population who go to prison – rose by a spectacular 64 per cent.[68] But that was nothing compared with the phenomenal spike in imprisonment rates after 2012. In South Australia and the Northern Territory, the rate of imprisonment has now almost *doubled* just since the beginning of this century.[69] Australian courts are now locking people up at a rate not seen since the end of the nineteenth century. Leigh calls ours the 'Second Convict Age'.

What does prison actually do?

Among the greatest of the challenges that social and medical science present to the criminal law is that which suggests that punishing an already traumatised person may induce *more* of the unwanted behaviour, not less of it. While prison has an incapacitating effect for the period an offender remains inside one, we also know that spending time in prison is one of the factors that seems to *increase* the likelihood that a person will commit a crime in the future.[70] Why would this be?

The Northern Territory has the highest rate of recidivism – reoffending – in the country. It's not a coincidence that the Territory's prisons offer very few rehabilitation programs, especially since Covid-19. Authorities there are prepared to pay nearly $600,000 every day to keep about 1700 people locked up in Darwin and Alice Springs, knowing that the lack of any meaningful rehabilitation programs inside prisons, and the lack of much social support outside it, mean that nearly three in every five ex-prisoners will reoffend within two years of their release. 'The community should be outraged that we're spending so much money on these prisons without it reducing crime,' NAAJA's principal lawyer, Beth Wild, told the ABC in July 2022.[71]

The costs of prison are enormous, and go well beyond the spectacular amounts we're spending on keeping a small but growing proportion of people locked up. Prison creates a 'crime school' effect. When we send an individual offender to prison, he or she mixes with other offenders, is forced into an 'us-and-them' relationship with authorities, and has an unparalleled opportunity to acquire tips, hints and tricks from more experienced criminals. An even greater problem is that, despite policymakers' hopes and intentions, each prisoner is quickly resocialised into a 'criminal' identity. The intense prison environment – in which the constant threat of violence from other inmates and prison officers invokes a 'fight-flight' response while affording no opportunities for 'flight' – is likely to weaken protective relationships with friends and family, and strengthen relationships with those who display hardened criminal tendencies.[72] Prisoners lose their jobs and, frequently, their job prospects. Spending time in prison tends to damage people's health, often severely. Ex-prisoners are frequently homeless, which is a major factor in recidivism. In Australia, people lose their ability to earn an income – either from employment or social security – when they go to prison. That often has significant flow-on effects for their families, who may depend on it for rent or mortgage repayments. Children of prisoners have poorer outcomes on every measure imaginable.[73] The idea that a prisoner pays his debt to society and is then released to make a fresh start may have always been a myth. It's now a fantasy.

To say that these costs of imprisonment are augmented in Indigenous communities would be to badly understate the point. Prison does very little to assist communities who are already struggling with dispossession and disenfranchisement, poverty, housing insecurity, mass unemployment, alcohol dependency, child removals, suicide and violence. In many cases it merely exacerbates those problems. Prison has become such a fact of life among many Indigenous communities that it's a more common experience than full-time work. It's what researchers Bruce Western and Catherine Sirois call 'pervasive'.[74] Nearly a *quarter* of all Aboriginal and Torres Strait Islander men who were born in the 1970s have gone to prison at least once in their lives.[75]

After the Royal Commission into Aboriginal Deaths in Custody reported in 1991, every state and territory government voluntarily signed up to implement its recommendations, all aimed at reducing the chances that Indigenous people would spend time in prison. Yet in the three decades since, nearly everything state and territory governments have done has *increased* the chances that people go to prison. They've tightened bail and parole laws. They've lengthened maximum sentences and legislated minimum sentences. They've dramatically increased the numbers of police on the beat. These changes have been sold as ways of responding to criminal behaviour, but they're just reactions. And even as governments have supercharged the ability of the justice system to put people in jail, they've underinvested in the *capacity* of courts and Legal Aid and prosecutors. There are now enormous bottlenecks all around the country – augmented by Covid-19, but not caused by it – which keep defendants on bail and on remand for month after dragging month.

Meanwhile, governments have also done just about everything they could have to destroy the social safety net which people who can't compete in the employment market depend on. They've sold off public housing and created waiting lists in some places – like the Northern Territory – as long as *ten years*. They've abandoned the economic policy goal of full employment. They've created hurdle upon hurdle for people who need to access social security. They've refused to ensure that paltry dole amounts keep pace even with inflation. They've pursued policies which have created a multigenerational underclass. These policy decisions have had an enormous impact on Indigenous people living the legacy of dispossession. It's not middle-class people – Indigenous or settler – who are feeding Australia's prisons. Australia's prisons have become twenty-first-century warehouses for First Nations poverty and disempowerment.

DEBATE

How settlers could not agree on which story to tell about Indigenous incarceration

'My son's not a bad, evil man,' the late Ruby Langford Ginibi told the federal government's *Australian Biography* project in November 1995. 'He's done some stupid things and been easily led and stuff like that, but we're all human, but nobody's been murdered or maimed…' Langford was born on a mission in New South Wales, and later wrote and lectured on Aboriginal – especially Bundjalung – history. She's best known to Settler Australia for her 1988 memoir, *Don't Take Your Love to Town*. She was referring to her son who had been in and out of prison through his own life, and was the subject of her later book, *Haunted by the Past*. 'We don't have any justice because Aboriginal people always had to conform to the laws of the invading powers of our country, because we were never allowed to be ourselves,' she said. 'How can we be the most bad, evil people in the whole of this now multicultural Australia … ?'[1]

The fact that Australian prisons are filled with many more First Nations people than is proportionate to their population size has become part of the background noise in contemporary Australia. Some people are trying to change that fact, but there are many more who aren't particularly exercised by it. Langford's simple question – *why is prison used so often against Indigenous people in Australia?* – has some simple answers. Settler Australia, however, can't agree on them.

Uncovering the data

While the bare statistics of Indigenous incarceration were available in most state and territory government annual reports, the person who first drew them to the attention of lawyers and academics was Elizabeth Eggleston.

As a young lawyer in the mid-1960s, Eggleston went to California to do a master's degree. While there, she visited an Indian 'reservation' – a parcel of land set aside for or transferred back to a First Nations tribe, which manages it under the federal Bureau of Indian Affairs. The United States recognises a limited form of what it calls 'tribal sovereignty', one practical effect of which is that tribal councils, rather than federal or state governments, have jurisdiction inside reservations, where laws often differ from those outside. There was (and is) nothing like an Indian reservation in Australia. Eggleston got to thinking about the rights of Australia's First Nations to their traditional lands.[2] After returning to Melbourne, she enrolled in a doctoral thesis at Monash Law School's new Centre for Research into Aboriginal Affairs (CRAA), just as a new type of activism emerged among young Aboriginal people and their supporters. The thesis was eventually published as *Fear, Favour or Affection* in 1976 – just two months before her death, from cancer. By then, Eggleston had become CRAA's director and co-founded the Victorian Aboriginal Legal Service in 1972.

Before Eggleston's surveys, there simply wasn't any sustained criminological research into First Nations people's engagement with and experiences of the criminal law in Australia. Lawyers and others had published anecdotes based on their superficial observations, which often served as ethnocentric humour.[3] And there were occasional attempts at research,[4] and particular cases – none more so than Max Stuart's (see chapter 5) – were occasionally the subject of sustained analysis. Colin Tatz had been among the few settlers not directly employed in the system to observe the special kind of criminal 'law' that operated on Queensland's missions and reserves under its 'protection' regime – law which saw Indigenous people who were forced to live on reserves imprisoned for such 'crimes' as 'failing to observe habits of orderliness and cleanliness', 'failing to cease dancing before midnight', leaving the reserve without permission, and 'evading' or refusing to work for no pay.[5] In an astounding conflict of interest, the 'judges' of these 'courts' were none other than the superintendents of the reserves – who'd often brought the charges in the first place. Obviously, no white person was subject to laws and punishments like these.

At the other end of the decade, a group of Sydney University students, energised and radicalised by the campus politics there, used their May vacation in 1969 to travel to Walgett in northern New South Wales, through which Charles Perkins' Freedom Ride had sensationally passed four years earlier. The discrimination against First Nations people there was well known. Over the previous year, 70 per cent of everyone arrested had been Indigenous. 'Police often open the bar door and beckon to regulars to come over,' Peter Tobin reported, and 'they are then locked up for drunkenness.' They heard many allegations by Indigenous people of police brutality. An Aboriginal stockman was 'brutally beaten' by a white publican when he tried to enter the segregated lounge bar. Instead of charging the publican, the police arrested the stockman for drunkenness. The nearly unconscious stockman spent nine hours in a cell, bleeding from his nose, eyes and mouth, before he was taken to hospital. 'The law in this town is like a wrestling match,' one man told the students. 'It's all pre-arranged.'[6]

But Eggleston was the first to attempt a systematic analysis. *Fear, Favour or Affection* didn't spark public concern when it appeared in 1976, but it was among the influences on the Australian Institute of Criminology – established by the Whitlam government in 1973 – when it began publishing its annual prison census during the 1980s. As she began her research in the mid-1960s, Eggleston expected to find a 'high rate of involvement' by Aboriginal people with legal institutions in Victoria, South Australia and Western Australia. The statistics confirmed it, overwhelmingly. So she adopted a 'further and more important objective': 'to find explanations for the imbalance.' Was it simply because Aboriginal people committed more crimes? Or was it due to 'discrimination in the administration of justice'? This question has divided criminologists ever since.

Eggleston set about trying to work out whether there was some kind of systemic bias in the justice system. What did she find? The charges most commonly accrued by Aboriginal people were disorderly conduct, driving offences, stealing, offences against what were then known as the *Native Welfare* Acts (which were essentially offences of bringing, drinking or supplying alcohol on Aboriginal reserves) and, overwhelmingly, public drunkenness. By itself, this didn't say very much: minor charges are always much more common than serious charges across all populations.

What explained the clear over-representation of Aboriginal people in prisons across all three states? One reason was that many of the fines ordered by courts ultimately became prison sentences because Aboriginal people couldn't pay them.[7] An obvious reason for the high number of public drunkenness and public order offences was that Aboriginal people were outside – and visible to police – far more often than white people were. Given limited resources, police officers were much more likely to charge the offenders they could see as opposed to those behind walls and doors. One country officer told Eggleston that he would have been able to prosecute many more white crimes with an assistant; as it was, the lowest-hanging fruit was public order offending by Aboriginal people.[8]

'A typical aboriginal,' one police officer wrote in a report intended for court, 'rarely works but gets drunk very often and gets himself and others into trouble.' Based on her interviews with fifty-five officers, her observations of police behaviour and her perusal of police documents, Eggleston concluded that this attitude was common among police. She observed 'the enthusiasm and zeal with which the police proceed' against such offences as 'Native receiving liquor'.[9] 'These figures can be read,' Eggleston concluded, 'as an index of police harassment rather than of police efficiency.'

Eggleston found that Aboriginal people drew the short straw at practically every point of police discretion: the decision to charge or warn; the decision about which charge to lay; the decision to issue a summons or to arrest. 'Some policemen have attempted to justify the use of the arrest procedure on the ground that Aborigines would not understand what a summons meant,' Eggleston reported. Aboriginal victims were believed when the alleged offender was also Aboriginal, but not when the alleged offender was white. On the one hand, a white staff member at a remote Western Australia mission who caned Indigenous children severely enough to warrant an assault charge was given a 'stern warning'; on the other hand, Indigenous children had been charged with very trivial offences, including the theft of three oranges or a bottle of milk.[10]

Eggleston found the same biases in the attitudes of officials all the way through the criminal process. Police harassment was regularly condoned by magistrates and government bureaucrats. When police tried to force their way into a First Nations man's home and he was 'cheeky' to them, they arrested him on a charge of public drunkenness and assaulted him on the way to the police station. ('Cheeky' was, and occasionally still is, a term used by white officials to describe an Indigenous person who doesn't 'know his place'.) A subsequent analysis showed no alcohol in the defendant's blood. Nevertheless, the magistrate believed the officers who all said they'd observed signs of drunkenness. Another case in the same town saw an Aboriginal man convicted of public drunkenness, despite evidence given by two witnesses who swore he hadn't been drinking.[11]

In one Western Australian town, Eggleston observed that not a single Aboriginal person had been released on bail during the first nine months of 1966.[12] Courts compounded charge, arrest and bail discrepancies by convicting Indigenous people more often and sending them more often to prison. Squalid remand conditions became clear incentives for defendants who'd been refused bail to plead guilty.[13] In the 1960s, many charges – especially in remote locations, with significant Aboriginal populations – were still heard by justices of the peace (JP), who weren't legally trained, and tended to be local shopkeepers and farmers whose interests were often directly threatened by criminal behaviour.[14] JPs advocated flogging First Nations offenders because they thought jail was no deterrent,[15] declared that 'natives must be kept under the thumb' and decided that 'being called a black bastard is not sufficient cause to strike a white man'.[16] Indigenous defendants were often 'represented' in court not by lawyers but by bureaucrats from the native welfare departments. And in some cases, charges had been initiated by the same welfare bureaucrats who later 'represented' defendants in court![17]

The longer a defendant's criminal record, the greater the likelihood they'll go to prison for a new crime. Eggleston thought part of the reason Indigenous people had longer records was because of the 'cumulative effect of past injustices' – namely, discrimination at each earlier stage in the process.[18] But longer rap sheets didn't fully explain the sentencing discrepancy. Eggleston observed some hefty sentences dished out to First Nations people in perplexing circumstances: an Aboriginal woman with no priors sentenced to prison for 'Aboriginal drink liquor'; and an Aboriginal boy, also with no priors, sentenced to ten years' prison for rape in a year that nobody else convicted of rape got anything close to that.[19]

Eggleston concluded in the mid-1970s that the Western ideal – equality before the law – simply hadn't been achieved in Australia. But self-determination had (very) recently become official government policy, and there was cause for optimism about the future of First Nations incarceration rates: if racial discrimination in settler government policy and the administration of settler justice was a substantial cause of the high number of Indigenous prisoners, then, thought Eggleston, that number should drop as discriminatory policies and attitudes fell away.

But the numbers did not drop. There was a royal commission and dozens of other inquiries whose reports declared that the numbers were too high.

Still they rose higher. As we've seen, incarceration rates among Indigenous people in Australia are now the highest in the world. Why? Criminologists haven't been able to agree.

The deprivation thesis

In July 2019, Don Weatherburn retired from New South Wales' Bureau of Crime Statistics and Research (BOCSAR), where he'd been director for more than three decades. BOCSAR is arguably Australia's best criminological research agency, and Weatherburn is a kind of god in the field. His trademark stubble, now snow white, is familiar to thousands of Australians who have seen him during one or more of his countless TV appearances. He's good copy. Producers learned over the years that he was not afraid to contradict ministers and premiers – including owners of hands that fed him.

Arresting Incarceration: Pathways Out of Indigenous Imprisonment is his third book. Published in 2014, it takes as its point of departure the 1991 deaths in custody royal commission report. Weatherburn reminds us that the commission's conclusion – that the main reason Indigenous people were dying so often in custody was simply that they *were* in custody more often – was 'courageous' at the time, given the 'overwhelming belief' held by many people that First Nations people were dying at the hands of violent or criminally neglectful police officers.[20] In *Arresting Incarceration*, Weatherburn sets out to discover why incarceration rates among Indigenous people have gone up – way up – instead of down since 1991.

Very little research into the 'causes' of Indigenous incarceration had been done when the commission began its work in 1987. Into this statistical vacuum, what Weatherburn calls 'interested parties' – he means anti-racist campaigners – dropped hundreds of submissions alleging racial bias in every cog of the criminal justice system. Weatherburn says that given what it had to work with, the commission did a good job of beginning the data-gathering process, by setting up a 'very effective' research unit inside the Australian Institute of Criminology. The unit's findings led the commissioners to conclude that 'Indigenous disadvantage', rather than racial bias, was the principal underlying cause of First Nations people's over-representation in the entire criminal justice system, which includes prisons.

'But the lack of good data on Indigenous offending and contact with police,' Weatherburn argues, 'meant that the Commission was more than usually dependent on, and influenced by, the submissions made to it.' And this is what led the commissioners to make what Weatherburn calls a 'fateful leap':

> Instead of evaluating the relative importance of the various forms of disadvantage – an assessment that would have been of enormous help in focusing the attention of policy makers expected to carry the Commission's recommendations into effect – it decided to proffer a theory about the root cause of Indigenous disadvantage.[21]

The root cause, the commissioners found, was to be found in the history of colonisation:

> Aboriginal people have for two hundred years been dominated to an extraordinary degree by non-Aboriginal society and ... the [solution] requires an end of domination and an empowerment of Aboriginal people ... control of their lives [and] of their communities must be returned to Aboriginal hands.[22]

This was, of course, an expression of the logic that many First Nations activists and their supporters had been using for decades: colonisation had wrecked lives and communities by removing control and agency, so the solution was its radical opposite – self-determination. And by the early 1990s, indigenous peoples around the world had already been remarkably successful at asserting and establishing their moral right to self-determination, by adapting to their own struggles within 'settler' states what had been a principle of international law that legitimised nationalist movements of subjugated nations inside traditional empires – such as Arab nationalism within the Ottoman Empire or Kenyan nationalism within the British. By the time the commission reported, drafting of the United Nations' Declaration of the Rights of Indigenous Peoples – which included a right to self-determination – was well underway.[23]

But the argument that Indigenous disadvantage is a product of Indigenous disempowerment is a contention, and contentions need supporting evidence. For Don Weatherburn, that evidence simply doesn't exist. It's not that he doesn't accept the basic facts of Australia's colonial history. He does. But he rejects the idea – propounded by many – that authorities continue to treat Aboriginal and Torres Strait Islander people in variants of the ways they did following their invasion in 1788. Weatherburn argues that Arabanoo's capture on that first New Year's Eve acts as a kind of original sin for those who see First Nations incarceration as a consequence of institutional racism that began in 1788 and has more or less continued.

Weatherburn doesn't buy this at all. Especially in Western Australia and Queensland, but to some extent nationally, Indigenous incarceration rates actually *fell* between the late nineteenth century and the 1960s, as many Indigenous people were herded onto reserves (which restricted opportunities for cattle theft and for other conflict with white people) and 'employed' (albeit for paltry or no wages) in the cattle industry. But then came the civil rights victories. The Commonwealth Conciliation and Arbitration Commission's Equal Wage decision in 1965 and the lifting of alcohol prohibitions had transformative consequences for many Indigenous people, who were forced into a marginal, welfare-dependent subsistence on the edges of white towns, where many people and communities sank into alcoholic poverty. From that point, it's unsurprising that people increasingly showed up in criminal courts and prisons.

Weatherburn observes that Indigenous people are more likely to be charged, more likely to be refused bail, and more likely to be imprisoned if convicted. But he says this has very little to do with bias on the parts of police or courts, and much more to do with the fact that Indigenous people commit more crimes that are serious enough to lead to incarceration. More offending means longer criminal histories, which lead to bail refusals and longer sentences for subsequent convictions. And *why* do Indigenous people commit more crimes? His positivist analysis provides the statistical answer, namely, that the four key risk factors for criminal behaviour can be found in very high proportions among First Nations communities: 'poor parenting'; 'poor school performance'; 'unemployment'; and drug and alcohol abuse.

The problem isn't Indigenous people's lack of self-determination, Weatherburn concludes. Nor is it worth locating the source of the problem in the history of dispossession, genocidal massacre, assimilation, child-removal and discrimination, because we can't do much about all that now. The problem, rather, is the conditions of severe disadvantage in which too many children now grow up, regardless of why that is, and in which too many adults eke out lives on the fringes of modernity. Criminologically speaking, Weatherburn argues that the way we think about First Nations disadvantage and criminality shouldn't be all that different to the way we think about disadvantage and criminality generally. It's just that Indigenous people are much more likely to experience the kinds of disadvantage statistically associated with criminality. The question *why are there so many Indigenous people in prison?*, for Weatherburn and the positivists, has the same answer as to the question *why is criminal behaviour so prevalent among Indigenous people?*

The solution, then, is for governments and organisations to get in there and help First Nations people overcome their disadvantages – by encouraging them to finish school, get jobs, avoid abusing alcohol and drugs, and be better parents. In his final three chapters, Weatherburn makes the case for more and better 'services'. What he calls 'culturally sensitive' approaches should of course be pursued, he says, in circumstances where they increase the likelihood that necessary services – run by experts – will be better taken up among Indigenous clients.[24] But as Weatherburn sees things, along with the majority of criminologists working in Australia today, 'culturally sensitive' approaches are simply those which help service and client alike to achieve the end goal.

The discrimination thesis

The first time Weatherburn made this argument explicitly was in 2003, when he and two of his colleagues at BOCSAR published an essay in the *Australian Journal of Public Administration*. Titled simply 'Reducing Aboriginal Over-Representation in Prison', the essay was a missive aimed at everyone – from the royal commissioners down – who sought to place the blame at the feet of a discriminatory justice system. In particular, Weatherburn was frustrated at what he saw as the continuing output of a group of academic researchers who remained wedded to the idea that there was ongoing discrimination in Australia's courts, police forces and justice system, and that this substantially explained the high rates of Aboriginal incarceration. As we've seen in chapter six, this was a time – the early 2000s – when violence in Indigenous communities had overwhelmed all other concerns for Settler Australia.

One of the academic researchers in Weatherburn's sights was Chris Cunneen, then a professor of criminology at Sydney University. In 1987, Cunneen had co-authored a study of First Nations people's interactions with the settler justice system in north-west New South Wales – where Charles Perkins' Freedom Ride had passed through two decades earlier – and found two prevailing explanations for Indigenous over-representation. The first was that Indigenous people committed more crimes because of their socio-economic circumstances: this is Weatherburn's explanation. The second was that Indigenous people were *policed* in very different ways to settlers.[25]

Many researchers argue that there *is* evidence of direct discrimination in the justice system, or something like it. Courts in New South Wales and South Australia were increasingly more likely to send Indigenous offenders to prison between 1998 and 2008, for instance. To try to explain why, one study used the framework of what's called 'focal concerns': a theory that suggests the act of sentencing is heavily influenced by the factors the sentencing *judge* considers most important at that particular moment. White magistrates who are focused on attributes particular to First Nations offenders – perhaps because those attributes are less familiar or more threatening to those magistrates – are likely to justify their decisions to use imprisonment by reference to those attributes.[26] There's also clear evidence of 'indirect' discrimination. Laws that criminalise drinking alcohol in public, for instance, obviously disadvantage Aboriginal people, because for various reasons (including culture, custom, poverty) Aboriginal people drink in public spaces far more often than white people. So even though the proportion of Aboriginal people who drink alcohol at all is smaller than the proportion of white people who drink alcohol, Aboriginal people tend to show up far more often as 'offenders' against public drinking laws.

Weatherburn's starkly statistical analysis assumes that the settler criminal justice system is basically neutral. Statistics can never adequately show how a court conducted in the English language disadvantages people who don't speak English at home, and whose cultural priorities and worldviews are substantially different from the judges and lawyers and juries who make the decisions. Whereas Weatherburn insists that the system does not, statistically speaking, treat Aboriginal people any worse than settlers, Cunneen's group points to a more fundamental issue: that from within many Aboriginal communities, the whole settler system is inherently alien.[27] This problem can perhaps be better seen by settlers in reverse. Imagine, for instance, that Yolngu law had asserted its sovereign right to regulate the behaviour of settlers, and as a result, that settlers were frequently subject to sanctions and punishments for breaches of kinship rules, and were denied even the right to resolve settler-to-settler conflicts according to settler law. Settlers would no doubt experience this arrangement as deeply unfair, and would be unlikely to be placated by Yolngu analyses, which insist that settlers are dealt with no less harshly – and, if anything, slightly more leniently – than Yolngu offenders.

Weatherburn, Cunneen argued in 2006, had created an artificial binary. He'd assumed that evidence of Indigenous people's greater offending rates and their poor performance across multiple indicators automatically worked to knock out the argument that First Nations people were subject to systemic bias, indirect discrimination or institutional racism. Other researchers have disagreed with Weatherburn's conclusions on this point: Samantha Jeffries and Christine Bond at the Australian Institute of Criminology looked at sentencing decisions in various states and found that, after controlling for all other factors, Indigenous defendants 'were more likely to receive a prison sentence, compared with non-Indigenous defendants in comparable circumstances …'[28] But for Cunneen it was no longer good enough – and hadn't been for decades – for researchers to point to simple causal factors such as poverty, or poor parenting, or even racism. Cunneen argued that the focus needed to be on *why* Indigenous people attracted so much deficit data (I'll explain this term shortly). 'An adequate explanation involves analysing interconnecting issues, which include historical and structural conditions of colonisation, of social and economic marginalisation, and institutional racism,' Cunneen insisted, 'while at the same time considering the impact of specific (and sometimes quite localised) practices of criminal justice and related agencies.'[29] To stop at the point Weatherburn does is effectively to authorise more of the same: governments telling Indigenous people to behave differently.

Weatherburn responded in the journal *Current Issues in Criminal Justice* with a spirited defence of his own argument.[30] But the Weatherburn–Cunneen debate proceeded as most academic debates between quantitative researchers do: as one apparently focused on definitions, interpretations, misinterpretations and errors. As the debate continued, Weatherburn became more and more certain of his own position. To the consummate statistician, arguments about history and unprovable claims of institutional racism seemed woolly-headed, especially when propped against the clear and unambiguous record of Indigenous violence. Weatherburn and Cunneen, along with practically everyone else in this area of research and government policy, share a common goal: to reduce the numbers of First Nations people going to prison. For that to happen, Weatherburn reasons, First Nations people need to stop committing serious crimes. In a very real sense, everything else is secondary. And for *that* to happen, First Nations people need help to – what? Address their statistical disadvantages.

Implicit in Weatherburn's analysis – and in that of most criminologists working in Australia today – is an assumption that the colonial project is well and truly in the past. Yes, terrible things happened in the nineteenth century, and into the twentieth. But they can't be undone. Everyone working in government and NGOs today is committed to Indigenous people's equal civil rights. There is no formal discrimination anymore. Whatever the 'distal' causes of over-representation in prisons, we need to focus on the social problems as they present today, and address them – by improving parenting, education and self-sufficiency in a market economy.

The postcolonial[31] and critical race theory critiques

At this point in the story, we need to take a brief departure into the history of ideas, and into Lyon, France, where a middle-class student from the Caribbean island of Martinique was studying psychiatry and medicine after World War II. The descendant of African slaves, Frantz Fanon was constantly encountering and battling the assumptions white French people made about his race. For his doctoral thesis, which he published in 1952, Fanon argued that 'blackness' was a racial identity that had been constructed by those in power – 'white' people – to justify treating black people as inherently inferior to them. Fanon used insights from psychoanalysis to explain the feelings of inadequacy and dependency prevalent among many black people, and identified some of the techniques white people used to ensure black people retained an 'inferior status within a colonial order'.[32] Fanon's most famous book is his third, *The Wretched of the Earth*, which appeared in English in 1963, when the 'winds of change' were blowing through African and Asian colonies. Other thinkers took Fanon's torch and ran with it, including the French existentialist Jean-Paul Sartre, the Palestinian-American critic Edward Said and the Indian feminist thinker Chakravorty Spivak.[33]

At the same time, scholars of colour in the United States and elsewhere were formulating theoretical critiques – including Critical Race Theory

(CRT) – which aimed to identify, name and overcome the various ways in which Western law, which claims to be formally colourblind, works in subtle and not-so-subtle ways to privilege the experiences of middle-class white people over those of racialised minorities.[34] By the 1980s, new schools of critical and postcolonial scholarship had emerged in university humanities departments across the world, and were challenging the received wisdom in a range of disciplines.

Meanwhile, Indigenous people in Australia were continuing to formulate their own postcolonial critiques – in a very real sense, they'd been doing so for two centuries. Movements for Black Power (adapted from the United States) and the Tent Embassy (see chapter 13) generated such works as Wiradjuri man Kevin Gilbert's *Because a White Man'll Never Do It* (1973) and *Living Black* (1977). And as Indigenous people entered the universities – they'd been formally excluded until the 1950s, and structural barriers continued to the point that the second and third doctorates to Indigenous students weren't awarded until as late as 1989 – groups of activist-intellectuals have generated their own critical race scholarship.[35]

It was only a matter of time before the postcolonial and CRT-based critiques challenged the received wisdom of Australian criminology, especially insofar as it sought to explain criminal behaviour by Indigenous people. Seen through a postcolonial lens, Indigenous people in Australia are among the clearest example of a subjugated, suppressed, 'colonised' population. The history that had caused their subjugation – the massacres; the land thefts; the deliberate destruction of social, economic, cultural and religious structures; the breakup of families and communities – wasn't something First Nations people could simply 'move on' from. Even in the era of so-called 'self-determination', they were still being presented with an impossible choice by settler authorities: behave more like white people, or suffer the consequences.

Among those heavily influenced by postcolonial ideas are Thalia Anthony and Harry Blagg, both now professors of law at, respectively, the University of Technology Sydney and the University of Western Australia. For them, any criminological analysis of Indigenous offending *must* begin with an analysis of settler colonialism and the total expropriation of land. 'Settlement', after all, requires not only that Aboriginal and Torres Strait Islander people are moved off their land, but also that the history of that land is rewritten: rather than lived on by people for countless generations, it was empty and 'discoverable' by Europeans. The real-world consequences of settlement – genocide, forced assimilation, dispossession, concentration, confinement – flow inevitably from the original expropriation. Aboriginal people were forcibly deprived of their economic and spiritual resources. The settlers made money and fortunes from the land they took, fortunes that were passed on through generations. The children of those first dispossessed First Nations people remained dispossessed; so did their children, and so on.[36]

But the dispossession associated with settler colonialism doesn't merely deprive the First Nations of material resources. It also allows the settlers more or less complete freedom to determine what is and isn't important. What was important for the Australian settlers was the protection of 'their' property so they could generate income and wealth from activities such as farming, pastoralism and mining, the continuation of their culture via institutions (churches, schools, parliaments), and the maintenance of their worldview, informed by Christian theology and liberal philosophy. What was important to the dispossessed – called by settlers 'natives' or 'Aborigines' or 'lubras' or 'myalls' or 'piccaninnies' instead of their proper tribal or clan names – was unimportant to the settlers. So, as Munanjahli and South Sea Islander woman Chelsea Watego, professor of Indigenous Health at the Queensland University of Technology, observes in her book *Another Day in the Colony* (2021), practically the entire canon of Australian literature is written exclusively by and for white settlers. First Nations people, where they appear at all, are seen through a 'white lens'. The same can be – and is – said of Australian jurisprudence and criminology.

If Indigenous people had roles in Settler Australia, it was as cheap or free labour and sources of sexual gratification for settlers, and as demonstrations and reminders of British or 'Western' superiority. The criminal law of the settler state proceeded from that beginning. It continues to protect private property and punish those who damage or steal it by depriving them of liberty. The acts it criminalises are those that settlers deem transgressive; if Indigenous people do too, that's merely coincidental. But if Aboriginal and Torres Strait Islander people perceive an act as transgressive that settlers don't (for instance, a romantic relationship with someone of the wrong skin or moiety), then it's not in the criminal law. And by insisting on a totalising role for its criminal law – everyone is subject to it equally, and everyone is protected by it equally – the settler state continues to suppress a significant aspect of Indigenous cultural practice, namely, dispute resolution and socialising punishment. This all goes to maintaining First Nations people's 'inferior status' in the settler-colonial order.

For postcolonial critics, the problem inherent in standard criminology is its implicit acceptance of prevailing orthodoxy. Perhaps the simplest way for us to see this problem is to focus on that foreign country, the past. As the Thames filled up with rotting ship hulks full to bursting with growing numbers of 'criminals' in the wake of the American War of Independence in the 1780s, most contemporary thinkers weren't asking why so many trivial offences were listed among the crimes that had to be punished by way of commuted executions and transportation. They were asking why there was so much crime, especially among Britain's lower classes, and what to do about the criminals.[37] Most criminology in our time works the same way. It's unlikely to ask *whether* imprisonment as a form of punishment is an adequate policy response to a social problem, and even less likely to ask why particular types of behaviours are criminalised and others aren't. Most of today's criminologists instead ask variations of the question: what causes some people and not others to commit crimes?

What do these insights mean for contemporary Australian criminology? In their 2019 book *Decolonising Criminology*, Anthony and Blagg identify its 'deficit approach': it goes looking for the problems in and among Indigenous people, while assuming that the criminal law and the police and courts that enforce it are implicitly neutral. 'The facade of neutrality emerges in statistical inquiries into Indigenous crime,' they write.

Maggie Walter is a member of the Briggs/Johnson Tasmanian Aboriginal family, and is a palawa woman, who is descended from the pairrebenne people of north-eastern Tasmania. She's also a professor of sociology at the University of Tasmania, where she has spent years challenging what she calls the 'established practices' involved in the collection of statistics about First Nations people. Simply collecting statistics showing that Indigenous people perform worse than white people on parenting and school performance, she says, leaves researchers and readers – including governments – with the idea that there are many deficits within Indigenous people which, if they could only be corrected, would lead to better 'outcomes' for them. Most data collected about First Nations people 'proves' that they are deprived, disadvantaged and dysfunctional, compared with settler Australians. Walter calls this 'deficit data'. *All* the main statistics institutions and surveys produce deficit data, she says: the Australian Human

Rights Commission; the Australian Bureau of Statistics; the Australian Institute of Health and Welfare; the National Aboriginal and Torres Strait Islander Social Survey; even the annual Closing the Gap reports.

The function of statistics like these, Walter says, is to 'rationalise our dispossession, marginalisation and even our right to be Indigenous'. It's all well and good to say that First Nations people should determine their own futures. But settler governments inundated with never-ending streams of deficit data must do something about it. Within the prevailing order, which settler governments vigorously defend, the only thing that governments insist they *can* do is to 'close the gap' between Indigenous people's data and that of the rest of the country. Indeed, they have a 'responsibility' to do so. If the deficit data shows that First Nations children don't attend school as often as other Australian kids, then governments threaten Indigenous parents with social security suspensions. If the deficit data shows that Indigenous people are diagnosed with heart disease younger and more often than other Australians, then governments send dieticians and exercise physiologists into First Nations communities to teach them healthier habits.

It can't be a bad thing to want to bring down the incidence of heart disease among Indigenous people. So what's wrong with this analysis? What ends up happening is that governments with good intentions pursue programs of assimilation or dispossession. Walter isn't saying the deficit data is inaccurate (though it is sometimes conveniently selective). What she is saying is that deficit data obscures the causal relationship. In what she calls the 'deficit data/problematic people' correlation, 'the problematic people are the ones who, through their behaviour and their choices, are ultimately responsible for their own inequality'. One only needs to follow the logic of that correlation to reach conclusions which look for all the world like policies Settler Australia believes are relegated to the past. Walter explains that this is how policy responses like the Northern Territory Emergency Response can occur in the 'enlightened' twenty-first century. One of the main functions of deficit data in contemporary Australia, Walter says, is to reinforce the impression among ministers, bureaucrats and policymakers (and journalists, the general public and even many First Nations people themselves) that *Indigenous people*, and *not* settler society and its structures and assumptions, need to change.[38]

An even more fundamental critique of mainstream criminology and the role and function of the carceral settler state is now being made by a group of Indigenous activist-scholars informed by Foucauldian, subaltern and Critical Race Theory, as well as the long history of First Nations' struggle for decarceration.[39] Gomeroi researcher Alison Whittaker observes that those with interests in the maintenance of the status quo – police surveillance and violence, high rates of incarceration and regular deaths in custody – include not just police and jailers, but also the lawyers who represent Indigenous defendants in courts and their families at what are now more-or-less rolling inquests into custodial deaths. Wiradjuri, Kuringai and Māori researcher Latoya Aroha Rule is a PhD student and active in both academic and community circles. Their brother, Wayne 'Fella' Morrison was twenty-nine when he died after being aggressively restrained by fourteen guards at Yatala prison in Adelaide, who bound his wrists and ankles and covered his head with a spit-hood before placing him in a prison van with seven guards for a three-and-a-half minute journey to the prison's high-security section. There's no video footage of that journey, following which Morrison was 'found unresponsive', and the guards have refused to give oral evidence to the inquest. Rule and their family have so far succeeded in having South Australia's parliament vote unanimously to ban spit hoods.[40]

Amanda Porter, an academic lawyer and a descendant of the Yuin people, and Chelsea Watego argue that criminology is inherently too complicit in the maintenance of the carceral state to be of very much potential benefit to incarcerated Indigenous people.[41] Watego was invited to contribute a research paper to the Queensland Sentencing Advisory Council as part of its government-ordered review into penalties for people found guilty of assaulting police and other frontline emergency services workers. 'We looked for news stories in which assaults against public officers could be traced,' Watego said. 'And in examining those reports, we concluded that over-representation [by Indigenous people in 'assault officer' statistics] … might be explained by the fact that Aboriginal and Torres Strait Islander peoples are falsely accused of serious assaults against public officers. We found numerous examples where Indigenous peoples were before the court on assault charges which were found to be false or unfounded, and in fact where Indigenous peoples had been assaulted by first responders.' Watego and her colleagues also theorised that Indigenous people were subject to 'routine racialisation' by public officers, so that Indigenous peoples seeking *care* from the state were met instead with *violence*. After some initial resistance from one Queensland Sentencing Advisory Council (QSAC) member, QSAC published Watego's report – but went on to recommend higher penalties anyway.[42] 'This [was] in Queensland in 2020,' Watego recounted later, 'when the rest of the world [was] bringing into full view the violence of police on black people.'[43]

Watego and Porter are uncompromising in their explicit demand for the de-funding and dismantling of the carceral state and of its constituent agents, the police. For Watego, the over-representation of black people in prisons and police cells is primarily a function of their over-surveillance by police and their racialisation by the state. She vigorously rejects analyses which suggest that higher rates of violent offending are a significant cause of higher incarceration rates. 'Here we see young black people framed as the antagonists in police relations,' Watego said of a recent study into offending rates among a particular ethnic minority in Victoria. 'This is what criminogenic factors do. They blame black people for their own brutalisation.'[44] Decarceration would mean implementing a range of alternatives – many of which First Nations communities have been offering for decades – which divert the opportunities for police involvement.

Several communities have created 'night patrols', staffed by their own men and women who (as the name suggests) patrol their own communities, offering people lifts – including to sobering-up shelters – and intervening to prevent violence. Night Patrols typically have no authority from the settler state and no power to arrest (other than that shared by all citizens). What they do achieve with their community-based responses is to prevent people's engagement with police and the line of carceral responses which flow – including 'assault police' charges, arrest, detention and imprisonment. Night Patrols are vulnerable to interference by the settler state, which tends to have very little patience for any perceived or actual indiscretion by them. The state's patience for police, on the other hand, is limitless. Governments never act to abolish police forces following an act of police violence. On the contrary, governments spend enormous resources defending police actions at inquests and inquiries.[45]

Australia is not the only settler colony in which Indigenous people are heavily over-represented in crime and incarceration statistics. A similar statistical story is evident in Aotearoa/New Zealand, where Māori people make up 17 per cent of the population but more than half of the total prison population. And in Canada, where First Nations and Métis people are imprisoned at about six times the rate of non-Indigenous Canadians.

And also in the United States, where Native American and Alaskan Native people go to prison at five times the rate of white people. Australia is by far the worst in terms of the rate at which it imprisons Indigenous people compared with settlers, but the deficit-based analysis of positivist criminology and sociology is consistent across all four settler states: to be Indigenous, regardless of where, is to be far more likely to be poor and to have experienced negative interactions with the criminal justice system.[46]

The Indigenous populations of the former British colonies are different in many ways, but they share important experiences in common, as summarised by the Canadian anthropologist Noel Dyck: the sovereignty they held over their lands was appropriated by settler-colonists; they are a minority of their present-day nation-states; their culture has been stigmatised by the dominant cultures within those nation-states; they have continued to struggle for social justice, self-determination and control of traditional lands and resources; and they remain economically and politically marginalised.[47] Zooming out to consider the entirety of the European imperial project, as historian Lisa Ford has done in her magisterial book *The King's Peace* (2021), allows us to see that law and the agents of its enforcement – police – were used everywhere as tools in the creation and maintenance of the colonial order. During the 1980s, communities and nations who shared these experiences began to be referred to as 'fourth world'. Surely, asks Maggie Walter, these experiences have something significant to do with their present status? Instead of asking 'why are Indigenous people criminals?', she suggests the better question is: 'what is it about the lived reality of fourth-world peoples in first-world Anglo colonised nation-states that leads to and results in their dramatic over-representation within their respective criminal justice systems?'[48]

Telling true stories

Weatherburn is right, of course. If there were fewer struggling, traumatised Indigenous parents; if those Indigenous people who drink alcohol at unhealthy levels cut back; if fewer Indigenous men used violence against their wives; if more Indigenous people finished school, got 'good jobs' and became productive members of the market economy at the rate that settler Australians do – if all that happened, Indigenous people might well be going to prison about as often as settler Australians. We can see this conclusion borne out among the Indigenous middle class which has emerged since the attainment of equal civil rights.[49]

And therein lies the conceptual difficulty at the heart of the debate between the Weatherburns and Australian governments, on the one hand, and the Chris Cunneens and Thalia Anthonys and Maggie Walters and Chelsea Wategos on the other. One group can't see why First Nations people shouldn't be given every assistance to overcome their disadvantages. The other group can't see why Settler Australia and its legal and justice systems shouldn't change, perhaps quite drastically, to allow for communities that have been at the mercy of some terrible government and settler practices to heal, to more honestly reflect the factual and legal realities of Australia's history, and to allow the kind of cultural autonomy that is commensurate with the right to self-determination.

This conflict can often be seen even *within* settler institutions. As we've seen, the Northern Territory's Supreme Court has oscillated between positions like these since the post-war era. And it can also be seen in the trajectory of individuals' thinking. When Colin Tatz arrived at Monash University from South Africa in the 1960s, he was determined to work toward self-determination. But by 1990 he was too confronted by the 'reality' of Indigenous violence, and concluded that self-determination had failed and that the 'solution' must lie in better government policies and greater levels of public assistance.[50] Lee Sackett, a younger anthropologist, pointed out that self-determination hadn't actually been tried. Even, or especially, under policies governments called 'self-determination', First Nations people had remained entirely dependent on the settler state and its priorities. 'I see Aborigines as in a very real way having been barred from managing their own affairs,' Sackett said.[51]

And this gets at what is potentially an even deeper vein of conceptual disagreement. People who enjoy autonomy and the freedom to determine their own futures – including government ministers, policy bureaucrats and judges and magistrates – tend to value those things only in the abstract. People who are denied autonomy and the right to self-determination tend to value them extremely highly, or succumb to depression, shame or rage. What we recognise as 'rights' – privacy, movement, asylum, equality, ownership, assembly, freedom of thought – are actually fundamental human *needs*.

Self-determination is no different. Over and over again, empirical research demonstrates the human need to be self-determining. The more people perceive that they have some measure of control over their lives, the healthier they tend to be – and the less often they experience or perpetrate violence, self-harm, suicide, mental illness.[52] In British Columbia, where suicide rates are much higher among First Nations children than among white children *on average*, researchers in the 1990s wanted to know why some communities exhibited youth suicide rates at *800 times* the national average while others appeared to have no incidents of youth suicide at all. They concluded that, unsurprisingly, youth suicide rates were 'strongly associated' with the degree to which each community, or band, was actively engaged in generating group pride and cultural continuity.[53] One study of the differing rates of crime in six Aboriginal communities in New South Wales suggests similar factors at play.[54]

In concluding that the solution lies in ever-greater government intervention and control in the lives of Indigenous people, the 'Weatherburn view' necessarily devalues the fundamental human need for self-determining autonomy. The price of being poor, traumatised and criminalised – the legacy of settler colonisation – is that many First Nations people, families and communities are forced into dependence on a highly bureaucratic, impersonal, inflexible surveillance state, the likes of which those who aren't forced to experience it would never be able to cope with. The clarion calls to simply *get more services in there* avoids, or ignores, the reality that such 'services' are provided on terms unilaterally imposed by the state or its agents.

This paradox can be seen across the full gamut of government-provided services to people on the margins, from social security and housing to public psychiatry to community corrections to child protection. All are created by (mostly) benevolent policymakers with good intentions, provided by middle-class professionals who are (mostly) motivated by a desire to help by lending their expertise, and are regularly experienced by their 'clients' or 'customers' as oppressive and intrusive. On top of this general level of service oppression, First Nations people also experience the added oppression associated with being members of communities whose entire cultures – or significant aspects of them – have been outlawed by the settler state for generations, and whose land and resources – the very basis of economic livelihood – has literally been stolen. The Weatherburn view may be motivated by the best of intentions, to intervene with expertise and resources to help Indigenous people achieve better outcomes. But that's also been the motivation behind all interventions by Australian governments since the original acts of dispossession.

'Western' medical and psychological science is only just beginning to comprehend the full consequences of what is now known as trauma on individuals, families and communities.[55] People who survive a single traumatic experience – a violent assault, a molestation or rape, the unexpected death of a loved one – can remain hostage to that experience, often for the rest of their lives, as it manifests in all kinds of disturbed behaviour and psychiatric labels. It's almost impossible to imagine, then, the consequences of what are often entire lifetimes of trauma experienced by many First Nations people in Australia – and then to go further, to imagine the effects of more than *ten consecutive generations* of extreme trauma inflicted not 'merely' by an individual (a significant other, family member, violent stranger), but by the state itself and its many agents.

Acknowledging the sheer scale of this trauma is what Judy Atkinson invites us to do in her remarkable book *Trauma Trails: Recreating Song Lines* (2002), which documents the transgenerational effects of trauma in Indigenous Australia. The people who survived massacres, dispossession, rape and torture on the frontier had children and grandchildren who were rounded up into missions and reserves, and forced to work under slave-like conditions making wealth for white settlers; their children and grandchildren were then stolen and abused in settler institutions and told to stop being Indigenous; and *their* children and grandchildren, carrying the legacy of intergenerational injustice in a country that continues to deny its responsibility for what it did, are locked up by that country's 'justice' institutions at ever-increasing rates.[56]

Imprisonment is not a fact of nature, like the sun or oxygen or pain. It didn't exist in Australia before 1788. It is a state and a force, created by humans on the belief that it works as a behavioural corrective: people placed in a state of imprisonment will be less likely to act in the way that caused their imprisonment in the future. This is an old belief, and one that's been increasingly challenged over the course of the last century. If personal and intergenerational trauma is causing, or driving, much of the behaviour that we describe as 'criminal' and we punish accordingly, does it make sense to compound that trauma by sending people to prison?

WOMEN

How protection isn't working much better this time around for First Nations women

I'm already sitting at the single desk in the small, sparse, professional visits room in Darwin's prison when 'Lucy' is ushered in by a tattooed officer.[1] She's wearing a prison-issue orange T-shirt, which denotes her status as a remand prisoner: she hasn't been sentenced, but a judge has refused her bail. Lucy is an Aboriginal woman in her late forties. She's been in and out of prison since she was a teenager.

She's happy to see me. She's overly deferential. She knows I'm her only ticket out, and she's anxious to keep me onside. All I know about Lucy is her name, her charges and her history of criminal convictions and 'antecedents', a curious document which lists every court outcome she's ever had – including the times charges against her have been withdrawn by prosecutors, and the times she's been found 'not guilty'. There have been a large handful of those, all for assault charges. There are also lots of breaches – of bail, of suspended sentences, of good behaviour bonds. That doesn't bode well for her bail prospects. One of the factors judges must consider is her record of obeying court orders.

Lucy has six charges. The easiest way of finalising a charge is to plead guilty to it. After a week, Lucy's already sick of remand. 'Can I just say "guilty" and do my time?' she asks me. But she'd still need to wait. One of her charges – 'cause serious harm' – can only be heard in the Supreme Court. To get there, she'll need to go through a series of fortnightly mentions in the Local Court, endure a Committal and wait for a Supreme Court mention, when her case can finally be listed for a plea. That could take months.

But I don't want Lucy to plead. Her assault charges – as well as 'cause serious harm', there's also 'reckless endanger serious harm' and a mere 'aggravated assault' – all arise from the one incident. Police allege she picked up a rock and clobbered her partner, 'Jimmy', with it, apparently damaging an eye, while she was accusing him of being with another woman. That version comes directly from Jimmy's statement, made the day after the assault. There were no witnesses. When police arrived, according to their own statements, they found both Jimmy and Lucy with significant injuries. The officers' own statements record what must be Lucy's defence: that Jimmy was thumping her with a stick when she punched him to get him to stop. The police called ambulances for them both, and a doctor's notes confirm injuries consistent with Lucy's version. When Lucy's charges eventually go to trial, the police and medical evidence will be more than enough to establish a bona fide self-defence case. Prosecutors will then have to 'negative' that case beyond reasonable doubt. It's already clear that they won't be able to. Lucy will be found 'not guilty' of each of the assault charges. Given all this, Lucy should never have been charged with the offences of violence. Yet they're the reason she's been refused bail.

Lucy confirms my reading of the evidence, and fills it out. *Jimmy* was the one accusing *her* of infidelity, she says. It's something he does whenever he's drunk, which is often. He picked up a large stick – more like a tree branch, she states – and started belting her with it, mostly on her back and her side. She was telling him to stop, but he was too angry. When one of his blows landed on her head she fought back. She punched him in his face. She doesn't think she used a weapon, but she can't be sure: she was very drunk, too, because (she says) Jimmy had aggressively demanded she drink with him, even though each has a domestic violence order forbidding them to drink with the other. Jimmy stopped hitting her, and threw the stick away. He calmed down. They eventually went to sleep. When he woke up the next morning, Lucy saw that Jimmy's eye had puffed up badly. She wanted to call an ambulance. Jimmy wouldn't let her. He slapped her, said he was going to get her locked up 'for blinding him', and went off to call the police. I try to explain to Lucy that she should take the assault charges to trial; legally speaking, she has a very strong case. When I tell her how long she might need to wait, Lucy's eyes widen. She can't stay in prison a whole year, she says, panicking. So we start making a plan for bail.

I ask Lucy about her most recent assault convictions. Those in the last few years are all for hurting Jimmy, she confirms. I ask her about a couple of 'not guilty' verdicts. Those were when lawyers convinced her to fight assault charges. One time, Jimmy didn't show up to court. Another time, Jimmy did show up but the judge didn't believe him. I stop to consider this, then ask: has Jimmy ever been in trouble for hurting *her*? Lucy nods vigorously. He'd just come out of an eight-month prison stint for bashing her when this latest incident occurred. Lucy says she'd been sober all that time, staying with her sister and helping with her niece and nephew. But as soon as Jimmy got out he came looking for her. He was angry. He accused her of being with other men while he was inside. Jimmy's a nice guy when he's sober, Lucy assures me. But when he's drunk he gets violent. He hits her 'all the time'. But, Lucy tells me, she gives as good as she gets. She's not petite. She says she can look after herself.

I look more closely at Lucy's recent assault convictions. They're all within days or weeks of the offence date. That's not enough time to wait even for a contested hearing in the Local Court, so they would have been guilty pleas. I ask her about the most recent, about a year ago. That's when Jimmy was chucking stones at her, Lucy says, so she chucked a can of XXXX Gold at him and it hit him on his forehead. I tell her that sounds like self-defence. She says it was. Then why did she plead guilty? Because a judge refused her bail and she didn't want to wait around in prison for months waiting for a hearing. And, she adds, her lawyer got the story changed to say that the can hit Jimmy on his chest, not his head. The judge gave her a certain three months in a green shirt – the mandatory minimum – which was better than months of uncertainty in an orange shirt.

One by one, I ask Lucy about all twelve of her assault convictions. The recent ones involved Jimmy. An earlier set involved her ex, 'Wally'. And the first group, when she was a young woman, involved her first husband, 'Albert'. Some she can't recall in any detail. But she says all of them – *all* of them – were because she'd been fighting back against a man, got charged with assault, and then pled guilty in court, mostly after a judge refused her bail. I can't know whether Lucy's telling the truth about her past assault convictions. I can't even know whether she's telling the truth about the current charges. But I do know how the court – when it eventually considers the evidence – will decide her current charges, if it's allowed to. A terrible possibility invades my thoughts. *What if Lucy has never actually instigated violence, and has merely defended herself from a violent partner?* I blink, and look at her criminal record, which now goes back three decades. Any judge who reads this will assume she's habitually violent. *No wonder her bail keeps getting refused.*

The next day, I'm a man with a bail plan in Darwin's Local Court. Just before Lucy's case is called on, the prosecutor offers to drop all charges except 'reckless endanger serious harm', if she'll agree to plead guilty to it. Everyone waits while she's brought in from the cells in her orange shirt. I indicate that Lucy is applying for bail. I direct the judge's attention to those statements – on the prosecutor's own brief – which make out the self-defence case. The judge sees it clearly. At this point he could be putting significant pressure on the prosecutor to drop the charges, with reference to prosecutorial guide-lines that talk about 'reasonable prospects of conviction' and 'public interest'. But he merely calls the prosecution case weak, observes that Lucy would be looking at maybe a year on remand waiting for her trial, and grants her bail – but only if she'll agree to stay sober and completely away from Jimmy. I know that's setting her up to fail. I try to persuade the judge to remove those condi-tions. But they're practically compulsory in the Northern Territory for bailed Indigenous defendants. And, the judge points out, Lucy's record is terrible. In the dock, Lucy has a beaming smile: she's getting out. But as we leave the bar table together, I notice the prosecutor isn't exactly unhappy. He's been doing this for a decade. He's lost a minor skirmish, but the bail conditions mean he's likely to win the war.

Lucy goes back to her sister's. We speak twice during the next month, including when I call her after I get Jimmy's criminal history, which con-firms Lucy was the victim of his four most recent assaults. But the week after that, I learn that Lucy's been arrested again on two new charges: breaching bail and breaching her DVO. I meet her in the cells. She looks forlorn. Lucy's sister went to a funeral in Queensland, she says, and she was left alone. Jimmy came to the flat and threatened to hit her if she didn't come drinking with him. There's probably a defence to the new charges in there somewhere, but to run it we'd need to wait months for a hearing date. The judge refuses her bail this time, and I start thinking about asking the Supreme Court to review that decision.

As we leave the bar table again, the prosecutor tells me his offer is still on the table. He's happy to edit the rock out of the facts the judge will hear. This time, when I see Lucy in the court cells, she's distraught. She tells me she can't go back to remand. She instructs me – begs me, really – to take the deal. By the end of the day Lucy's case is 'finalised'. She'll do six months for punching Jimmy in the eye. A thirteenth conviction for violence appears on her record.

○

Lucy embodies a paradox of modern Australian settler law. As a frequent victim-survivor of what we now call intimate partner violence, Lucy demands – and deserves – our sympathy and the law's protection. But that same law frequently locks her up for being violent to her perpetrator.

Lucy is far from alone. Surveys of women in prisons frequently find that an enormous proportion of them have been assaulted – including sexually – by men. Indeed, during the very same period that we've become much more conscious of men's domestic and family violence against women, and much more prepared to act to protect women from men's violence, we've also begun to incarcerate women at ever-increasing rates. Between 2006 and 2016, incarceration rates for women in Australia doubled. Aboriginal and Torres Strait Islander women have accounted for almost that entire increase.

The Northern Territory Emergency Response – the Intervention – had as its justification to protect Aboriginal children and women from Aboriginal men's violence. How is it, then, that since the Intervention, the fastest-growing prison population has been Aboriginal women?

The punitive turn

Of all the 'deficit data' that records the living conditions of many First Nations people and communities, among the most terrifying is that concerning violence against Indigenous women. Our Watch, which campaigns for initiatives to prevent and end violence against women and their children, reported in 2018 that Indigenous women are *thirty-two times* more likely than other women in Australia to be hospitalised – and eleven times more likely to be killed – as a result of being assaulted.[2] Often, especially in the Northern Territory, the assailant is an Indigenous man. Many Aboriginal and Torres Strait Islander men are in prison for assaulting or killing a woman.

Settler Australian attitudes to domestic and family violence against women began to change during the 1970s, when feminists began to call out the prevalence and the consequences of 'wife-bashing'. Until then, men who assaulted their wives or girlfriends were rarely prosecuted. Although it was never written down anywhere, men were often said to have a de facto 'right' to use violence to keep their partners and daughters 'in line'.[3] Anne Summers, a pioneer of the Women's Liberation Movement who helped to establish and run the Elsie women's refuge in Glebe, wrote in the mid-1970s of the 'authoritarian' nature of the nuclear family, which supplied capital with free female child-rearing and domestic labour under what were effectively conditions of bondage: women who wanted to leave violent households were prevented from doing so by poverty and social pressures.[4]

During the decades since, the criminal law has remobilised to protect women, apparently, from men's violence. New laws were passed – first by New South Wales' parliament in 1982 – which allowed victims of violence to apply for court orders prohibiting perpetrators from certain behaviour that was otherwise lawful but which tended to lead to violence in particular relationships. Variously known as 'apprehended' or 'domestic' violence orders, or 'intervention orders', they're civil orders – which mean victim-survivors need to satisfy magistrates only on the balance of probabilities rather than beyond reasonable doubt. But *breaching* them is a crime. So, for example, a man who becomes violent to his wife when he's drunk can be ordered to stay away from her if he's been drinking. If he comes home drunk, she can request police protection *before* he assaults her.

Initially, DVOs were intended only to apply to relationships of 'coercive control' between men and women. In the language of the 1988 Queensland Domestic Violence Task Force:

> Couples may occasionally slap or shove one another. While violent behaviour is never desirable, no great harm may accrue in instances where partners regard and experience each other as equals and give as good as they get ... When the Task Force talks about domestic violence we are talking about one partner, usually the woman, being afraid of and being hurt by the other. Domestic violence like child abuse is about the abuse of unequal power relationships.[5]

The DVO system has expanded since the 1980s. In all states and territories, police now have the power to create 'interim' orders with just as many rules and restrictions as court-made orders – including full 'non-contact' restrictions. There are understandable policy reasons for this. Violence often doesn't wait until courtroom opening hours to express itself. When police are called to a violent domestic at 2 a.m. and don't quite have enough grounds to arrest the perpetrator for a crime, there might yet be good reason for ordering that person to stay away from their partner or house. Police can even make an interim intervention order – and apply to a court to make it longer-term – without a victim of violence requesting or even consenting to one. That's to address the problem in the worst cases, when perpetrators threaten their victims with further violence if they speak to police. Courts can now grant DVO applications – often simply on the basis of a statement written by a police officer – without even hearing from the alleged perpetrator.

In line with the general trend toward punitive solutions to social problems, governments have increased the penalties associated with breaching DVOs. DVO breachers in Queensland, for instance, originally faced a maximum twelve months' prison when the *Domestic and Family Violence Protection Act* was first legislated in 1989. In 2012, to 'increase the accountability of perpetrators', explained Minister for Women Karen Struthers, the Bligh government doubled the maximum penalty for a first breach offence (to two years' prison).[6] The Northern Territory, as we've seen, has had mandatory *minimum* prison sentences for repeat DVO breachers since 1992.[7] There's no evidence that the prison terms attached to DVO breaches (as distinct from the availability of DVOs themselves) have been at all effective at reducing violence against women. The number of family violence incidents reported to police continues to rise, as does the number of DVOs approved by magistrates' courts.[8] However, the rate at which people are killed by family members has declined.[9]

Among the first actions the women's movement took during the early 1970s was to establish refuges and safe houses for women to escape to. But the refuge model anticipates that the woman will be the one to leave her home in order to escape violence. But why should she be the one to leave? Feminists working with women who have survived violence insist that as part of holding perpetrators of violence accountable for their actions, the *man* should experience the consequences of his 'choice' to use violence. Why shouldn't *he* be the one who has to leave?

In practice, 'accountability' often simply means 'incarceration'. Countless studies have found that the men most likely to use violence against women are those who have been socialised into believing that men are naturally or inherently superior to women, or that men and women have fundamentally different social roles. Talk of 'socialisation' complicates the simplistic, three-act, bad-man narrative preferred by the justice system.[10] Some feminists have pushed very hard for recognition that the *only* problem that needs solving is gender attitudes. Talking about male violence as a consequence of 'psychological dysfunction', alcohol or drug abuse, or any other 'individual or socio-demographic characteristics', say the authors of a 2013 review of the published research on domestic violence, 'removes the responsibility of violence from the perpetrator'.[11]

But seeing domestic violence through a single lens is increasingly recognised as too simplistic. In Katherine, I acted regularly for a man in his forties, 'Eric', who was regularly charged with – and locked up for – assaulting his wife, 'Daisy'. They lived in a dilapidated, overcrowded housing department house in one of Katherine's Aboriginal town camps with their three children, who were always at risk of being removed, and with about fifteen other people. When they were sober, there was no violence. When they were drunk, both would use violence, and each would claim the other started it. But Eric invariably inflicted the most damage, and was nearly always regarded by police as the perpetrator. The expectations of 'perpetrator accountability' led to DVOs that required Eric to leave the house. But he had nowhere else to stay, so he often came back – especially during the wet season. Had Eric been provided with alternative accommodation it would have very likely been better than the camp house, which would have seemed too much like a reward. Eventually a social worker found Daisy somewhere else to stay with their three kids, and the violence between them stopped.

The kind of feminism that advocates longer prison terms for perpetrators of violence against women is often termed 'carceral feminism'.[12] Carceral feminism seeks justice for victim-survivors in the criminal courts, with success measured by the conviction and sentencing of the perpetrator: again, *Eggshell Skull* is a prime example. It's the expression of feminism that finds most favour with the state, probably because it shifts responsibility for violence sideways – onto individual perpetrators, who can then be punished in accordance with the criminal law's theory of rational choice – instead of upwards onto the state, which often has much more power to prevent violence. Carceral feminism builds on what American activists Judith Levine and Erica Meiners call the 'retributive impulse'. But in their book *The Feminist and the Sex Offender*, Levine and Meiners argue that imprisonment is 'no solution' to the problem of violence against women. More challenging forms of feminism can be found in the work of activist-thinkers such as Angela Y. Davis, who has agitated for women's rights, black rights *and* prison abolition since at least the 1970s,[13] and, closer to home, Aileen Moreton-Robinson and Chelsea Watego.[14]

For First Nations women in Australia, the structures that generate and support violence are overwhelmingly created by the settler state. The state had forced Eric and Daisy to live in substandard housing while charging them exorbitant rent for it. The state had inflicted the trauma of invasion, dispossession and child removal on generations of both Eric and Daisy's families. The state had forced both Eric and Daisy into long-term dependence on passive welfare, on terms stipulated by the settler state, rather than allow their communities to determine their own futures. And the state had made alcohol ubiquitous *and* criminalised Eric and Daisy's consumption of it. Only the most blinkered neoliberal ideologue would be able to excuse the settler state from its responsibility for creating and maintaining those conditions.

Meanwhile, Australian parliaments are looking for ways to enhance perpetrator accountability, mainly by increasing the penalties attached to domestic violence. Very often, the triggering event is a single, particularly shocking, case which is presented as representative rather than the statistical outlier it is. In Victoria it was the murder of Rosie Batty's eleven-year-old son by his father in February 2014. In Queensland it was Rowan Baxter's murder of Hannah Clarke and their three children in February 2020. Baxter's actions prompted a new round of efforts to criminalise 'coercive control', which is the conduct DVOs were originally intended to criminalise four decades ago. In response to a NSW government proposal, the Aboriginal Legal Service – among others – warned that the criminal law is a 'blunt instrument' for distinguishing between 'normal' and 'coercive' behaviour in relationships, and that a new offence of 'coercive control' would result in the arrest and imprisonment of more Indigenous men *and* women without doing much to prevent the behaviour.[15] Despite these warnings, a parliamentary committee, which didn't include any Aboriginal members, unanimously recommended criminalisation, and the government announced it would do so.[16] From opposition, South Australia's Labor introduced a bill that would have imprisoned 'coercive control' offenders for up to seven years, or up to fourteen if the offending involves a child, a weapon or the distribution of an 'invasive photo'.[17] Labor returned to government in March 2022, so a similar bill would now be expected to pass through parliament.

Sisters inside

Unsurprisingly, many First Nations women are critical of the most recent 'carceral feminist' push to criminalise 'coercive control' and lengthen prison sentences, primarily on the basis – as explained by Chelsea Watego and other researchers – that 'it results in an extension of power by the [settler] state'.[18] Many Indigenous women are distrustful of police, and there are ample reasons why. 'On police arriving,' Cathy Pereira told *Guardian Australia* in 2021, a male perpetrator may be 'calm and gives an account to police which is coherent'. His victim, who may have endured life-threatening assaults or repeated emotional abuse, is highly distressed. 'Police accept the male's version. He is more coherent and it is easier to record.' Pereira is principal solicitor at the Aboriginal and Torres Strait Islander Women's Legal Services North Queensland.[19]

When police arrived at the scene of a brutal domestic assault in Broome in 2013, officers found an Aboriginal woman, Tamica Mullaley, beaten, bloody, stripped naked – and agitated. She'd just been viciously assaulted by her partner, Merv Bell. But they insisted on questioning her against her wishes, and when – according to the officers – she spat at one of them, they decided to arrest *her*. Her ten-month-old child, Charlie, was left with two young girls on the street, and was later abducted by Bell. Police initially refused to search for Charlie, and when Tamica's father went to the station he was dismissed as drunk and aggressive – despite not having had any alcohol for three decades. The following day, Bell carried Charlie into a roadhouse, the child having died from horrific injuries including burns, broken bones and sexual assault. Bell was convicted of Charlie's murder and sentenced to life imprisonment; when he suicided in Perth's Casuarina prison, he was the third Aboriginal man to do so in as many years.[20] The carceral impulse might see a kind of justice in such an outcome. Bell, however, had lived a nightmare of his own. Both of his parents died when he was a child, and he was severely abused by his stepfather: Bell had then been imprisoned six times between the ages of fourteen and twenty-five before he killed Charlie.[21] Clearly, prison had been ineffective at 'correcting' Bell's behaviour.

Incredibly, authorities continued Tamica's prosecution for 'assaulting' police. A magistrate found her guilty and imposed a suspended prison sentence. He also convicted and fined Tamica's father. Police later appeared to lie to a Corruption and Crime Commission investigation, which nevertheless stopped short of finding 'serious misconduct' on the part of the officers.[22] Tamica's family sought an inquest into Charlie's death in order to explore the police response, but both the Coroner and the Supreme Court declined.[23] The attorney-general, who as a police union lawyer had defended the off-duty officers charged with the manslaughter of John Pat in Roebourne, refused to support a parliamentary inquiry.[24] It wasn't until June 2022 – following nine years of lobbying by the family – that the Western Australian government decided to pardon Tamica and her father, and apologised for the way they were treated.[25]

Critics including Hannah McGlade, a Kurin Minang Noongar woman and associate professor of law at Curtin University, point out that criminalising coercive control in part depends on the response of police. Criminalisation remains the preferred response among settler reformers, and (white) journalist Jess Hill – whose book and associated SBS documentary series, *See What You Made Me Do*, did much to bring stories like Tamica's to broader public attention – is prominent in the pro-criminalisation campaign.[26] The earlier Bell–Huggins debate has been reignited along similar lines. Chelsea Watego and other researchers expect the criminalisation of 'coercive control' will inevitably result in the imprisonment of more Indigenous women.

That is almost certainly right. When researchers Heather Douglas and Robin Fitzgerald examined the role DVOs play among Queensland's Aboriginal and Torres Strait Islander communities, they found that in 2013–14, more than a fifth of all DVO applications were taken out against Indigenous respondents – a huge over-representation, given that Indigenous people made up just 3.6 per cent of Queensland's population. Police applied for *nine out of every ten* DVO applications taken out against Indigenous respondents. Among all breachers, just over a quarter went to prison. But among all *Indigenous* breachers, *43 per cent* were sentenced to a form of custodial order.[27]

This kind of over-representation no doubt reflects, at least in part, the equivalent over-representation among Aboriginal and Torres Strait Islander women in rates of both hospitalisation and homicide as a result of domestic violence.[28] But it doesn't, at least at first glance, explain the over-representation of Indigenous *women* in prisons. During 2013–14 in Queensland, more than two-thirds of the women who were sentenced to prison for breaching a DVO were Indigenous.[29] Similar numbers exist all over the country. Why?

Heather Nancarrow was the director of Queensland's Centre for Domestic and Family Violence Research when she completed a PhD thesis investigating the many ways in which settler lawmakers have failed to consider matters of race and class when writing laws aimed at protecting women. Domestic violence laws – including DVO laws – may be written in gender-neutral language, but Nancarrow found they were intended to address 'a particular form of violence (an ongoing pattern of coercive control), with a particular kind of victim in mind (a subjugated, powerless woman)'. By casting the legislative net as widely as it has been cast, Nancarrow argues that DVO laws have produced 'a number of unintended consequences'. One major consequence is that women who are actually *victims* of violence are themselves being named as respondents in DVO applications – and then being breached, criminalised and imprisoned as a result.

The research is clear: while women can be violent, they rarely engage in the kind of coercive control envisaged by legislators.[30] Yet courts, unable to distinguish between situational violence and coercive control, are punishing and imprisoning women (and men) for the former. It's now recognised that a major factor in the rapid growth of incarceration among African American women in the United States is men's violence toward them: Douglas and Fitzgerald suggest the same link is apparent in Australia.[31] In 2009, Trevor Riley, a judge of the Northern Territory's Supreme Court, declined to overturn a two-week prison sentence for a fifty-year-old Aboriginal woman who'd breached her DVO but hadn't hurt anyone. 'I do not accept,' Riley said, 'that the gender of the offender is, per se, a relevant matter that should have been taken into account ...'[32] The following year, Riley became the court's Chief Justice. The punitive turn toward 'perpetrator accountability' during recent decades has actually seen an exponential rise in the imprisonment of Aboriginal and Torres Strait Islander *women* as well as men.[33]

In February 2016, criminal lawyers Jill Prior and Elena Pappas, who'd both previously worked at the Victorian Aboriginal Legal Service, established the Law and Advocacy Centre for Women (LACW) to advise and represent women charged with crimes, specifically in response to the extraordinary rise in the rate at which women were being imprisoned. Criminalised Indigenous women are often poorly served by the Aboriginal Legal Services (discussed in chapter 13): women are routinely conflicted away from them because they're representing the women's husbands or boyfriends or fathers or sons.[34] Indigenous family violence organisations don't represent anyone charged with crimes, and often refuse to even advise women who have experienced violence when they have their own criminal records for violence. In part because so many of its clients are Indigenous women experiencing violence, LACW's first location was on the ground floor of the Aboriginal Family Violence Prevention & Legal Service Victoria, in Collingwood (it's since moved to an RMIT building in Carlton).[35]

By seeking to enhance perpetrator accountability, DVOs risk overlooking the settler state's role in the perpetuation of Indigenous violence.[36] And they also risk conflating DVOs' intended targets – the relationships defined by coercive control – with relationships marked by situational violence, which are much more common. But it's notoriously difficult to tell the difference: *all* violence between family members meets the definitions of 'domestic violence' created by parliaments. It's no surprise that police and courts have slipped into granting DVOs whenever they see *any* violence between partners or siblings. It's now become very common for police and courts to simply make 'cross-orders' – to slap DVOs on both people in a relationship characterised by situational violence. DVOs have become a gigantic net in which authorities are catching all toxic or dysfunctional relationships in the hope they won't miss the minority of seriously abusive ones.[37] Lots of people have been going to prison as a result.

○

Two (white male) police constables, on patrol as part of an operation that promised a 'zero tolerance approach to domestic violence',[38] knocked on the flyscreen door of a public housing unit and peered inside. They saw 'Ellen' lying on the floor, asleep. They woke her and breath-tested her, even though nobody had called police or complained about her. When the test returned a positive reading they arrested her, drove her to the police station in the back of divvy van, charged her and bailed her. I met Ellen when she came to court in Katherine. I scanned through the evidence police had compiled. I wasn't aware of any law that gave police the power to check whether someone had committed an offence without any grounds for suspicion. We listed Ellens charge for hearing, and the Local Court judge agreed with me: police had acted outside their lawful powers, so Ellen was not guilty.[39] No doubt motivated by a desire to support proactive policing of domestic violence, prosecutors appealed. It was dismissed in the Supreme

Court by Acting Justice Dean Mildren. 'To hold otherwise would be an Orwellian intrusion into the fundamental rights of privacy that the common law has been at great pains to protect,' Mildren said.[40] Prosecutors appealed again.[41] Eventually, by a 3–2 majority, the High Court confirmed that Territory police *can* lawfully check on people in their own homes, in the complete absence of any complaint or suspicion, to make sure they're not breaching their DVOs.[42] In other words, under the guise of protecting victim-survivors, the High Court authorised an even greater level of targeting and surveillance of First Nations people by Northern Territory police.

Lucy, whom we met at the beginning of this chapter, tells me she doesn't know why police keep getting involved in her relationships with men. She'd prefer those relationships not to be violent, sure. But she has her own way of seeing the violence, and experiences the state's punitive and carceral involvement as far more distressing. 'We're not like white people,' she says to me. 'Aboriginal people have our own ways of being husband and wife, and our own ways of sorting out trouble.' I don't think Lucy is telling me she thinks Aboriginal relationships are naturally violent, or that Aboriginal women don't sometimes need help to protect themselves from dangerous men. I *do* think she's saying she doesn't think the punitive response from settler outsiders – police, courts, judges, prisons – helps her, especially when it means *she* gets locked up simply because – as often happens – her partner calls the cops first. 'I don't ever really think of going to police,' she says, 'unless it gets really bad. But sometimes Jimmy gets police involved just to punish me.' She believes he uses the institutions of settler law as an extension of the violence he uses against her. That's unsurprising. What's more surprising is how often those institutions allow themselves to be used like this. Despite everything, Lucy doesn't want to end the relationship. 'That's not for whitefellas to decide.'

Sisters Inside is a not-for-profit established in 1992 by Debbie Kilroy, who'd just been released from a prison term she served for selling cannabis to an undercover police officer. Kilroy earned a social work degree while inside, became a lawyer on the outside, and in 2017 was appointed to Queensland's Sentencing Advisory Council. Prisons, she told *Guardian Australia*, aren't the answer to anything at all. Brisbane's notorious Boggo Road prison was badly overcrowded in 1990 when Kilroy's friend was stabbed to death with sharpened barbecue forks. Kilroy had planned to retaliate by murdering the killer. 'Prisons are violent places, and the only way you respond to violence is with more violence,' she said. Prisons don't work. 'We built a new 260-cell prison at Wacol to stop overcrowding and now we've got over 700 women in prison.'[43] By 2016, overcrowding at the *new* Wacol prison had become such a problem that it sparked an investigation by Queensland's Ombudsman.

Kilroy knows that Aboriginal and Torres Strait Islander women do it particularly tough inside. For many women Sisters Inside engages with, prison is merely another stop on a revolving, settler state-run nightmare ride, which collects them from intergenerational trauma and poverty and pushes them through child 'protection' systems, punitive schools, punishing health systems, failing housing departments, and a near-complete absence of any actual help to navigate complicated and castigatory bureaucracies.[44] Meanwhile, the carceral response doesn't seem to be reducing the numbers of First Nations women being assaulted to the point of hospitalisation, or death. It's a curious system of 'protection' for Aboriginal women which locks so many of them up.

CHILDREN

How the settler justice system protects and rehabilitates Indigenous kids

Dylan Voller[1]

It's October 2010. Dylan Voller has just turned thirteen. Physically, never mind legally, he's still very much a child. His mother is a Ngarrindjeri woman from Victor Harbour in South Australia. But now, Dylan is in the 'behaviour management unit' (BMU) of the Don Dale Youth Detention Centre. The centre is named after a former police officer, who achieved fame when he recaptured seven escapees from the old Fannie Bay Gaol by wading neck-deep through mangroves, before going into parliament and serving as minister for both youth and 'correctional services' in the Northern Territory's government.[2]

The BMU is a purpose-built concrete block whose five austere cells open to a larger concrete room the staff call an 'exercise yard'. The cells have no air conditioning, fans, water, windows or ventilation. The only natural light in the whole unit comes from a very high window at one end of the 'exercise yard'. Dylan is only allowed out of his cell – and into the 'exercise yard' – for one hour every day. On his way back to his cell, he asks a staff member, Harold Morgan, if he can go to the toilet, or perhaps make a phone call. 'No,' Morgan says, and shoves Dylan forward. 'Fuck off,' Dylan replies. Morgan then lifts Voller by his neck, carries him into a cell, and chucks him a distance of about 2 metres onto a mattress. The pain causes Dylan to cry.[3] He complains to the Northern Territory Ombudsman. The incident is investigated, but it takes over a year for Morgan to be charged with assault. Legislation then in place explicitly requires that any charge against a youth justice worker be laid within six months of the alleged incident. (For anyone else who commits an assault, there's no expiry date.) A magistrate strikes out the charge, and Morgan walks.[4] Six years after the incident, Dylan says he still has a sore neck because of what happened.

By December 2010, thirteen-year-old Dylan had already spent well over 150 days locked up across six different stints in custody. One evening, in the Alice Springs Youth Detention Centre, he got into a fight with another kid. Staff marched him into an isolation cell. He threatened to hurt himself, which was 'something I did often, every time I got angry'. Dylan refused to change into an 'at-risk' robe, and calmed down. He had a deck of playing cards in his hand and was walking around his cell. Ten minutes went by. Then staff told him they were coming in. Dylan went and stood against the back wall, and Derek Tasker barged in with two other men. CCTV footage shows Tasker, who weighed perhaps as much as 115 kilograms, rush toward Dylan, grip him around the throat with both hands, and swing him down onto a mattress where he and his burly colleagues hold him face down while stripping him naked.[5] Tasker 'ground stabilised' Dylan by kneeling on his left shoulder.[6] This, said Tasker and the Northern Territory government later, was simply appropriate procedure whenever a child was declared 'at risk' of self-harm.

At this point, we can clearly see the oppressive madness at play in the carceral order. The staff, all adults, all trained to work with the kinds of kids who get locked up, could have de-escalated, observed, offered to speak with Dylan, to listen to him, to help him calm down. Indeed, that's what their relevant policy – contained in the *Youth Detention and Remand Centres Procedures and Instruction Manual* and the *'At Risk' Procedures Manual* – required. Those manuals instructed staff to maintain 'a humane and supportive attitude in their dealings with the detainee'. To work hard 'to dispel the impression that any part [of the procedures] is being applied for punitive reasons'. To try to 'calm the detainee and inform him regarding the "at risk" procedures'. To spend 'as much time as possible comforting the detainee'.[7] Plainly, none of this was ever attempted before Tasker and his colleagues burst into the cell, threw a kid onto a mattress and knelt on him while they stripped him naked. Where in the world would that be a 'reasonable' response to even a legitimate threat of self-harm?

In an Alice Springs courtroom, apparently. Prosecutors charged Tasker with aggravated assault. They alleged that the level of force Tasker used went way beyond what was reasonable or appropriate. When the charge was finally heard in an Alice Springs court in December 2013, Stipendiary

Magistrate Daynor Trigg accepted Tasker's explanations: that he needed to remove Dylan's shorts and to prevent Dylan from spitting on him. Trigg, who a few years earlier had jailed a seventeen-year-old for contempt after his phone rang inside the courtroom,[8] accepted that yes, it *was* reasonable that Tasker gripped Voller by the neck and throat, forced his head to one side, then 'ground-stabilised' the boy – by pressing a knee into his back – while his pants were forced off him. Trigg acquitted Tasker.[9] Prosecutors appealed to the Supreme Court, where Justice Peter Barr reconsidered the charge. Despite accepting that the staff members ignored their procedure manuals, Barr dismissed the appeal. He even added his view that Tasker's 'manoeuvre' was 'reasonably skilful and swiftly executed ... for ensuring the safe custody and protection' of Dylan Voller.[10]

While the courts were busy protecting violent workers, others saw things very differently. Martin Unger trains people employed to work in places such as youth detention centres. He's a director of MTU Training Concepts, the company that owns the training workshop Tasker told Magistrate Trigg he completed regularly. That workshop is called PART – for 'Predict, Assess and Respond To aggressive/challenging behaviours'. 'None of the techniques were consistent with any PART techniques or principles,' Unger said later, after reviewing the footage of the incident. 'The interventions were abhorrent and presented a greater level of danger to the young person than to the staff ... Specifically, PART Training warns against ... touching, making contact with or holding [a child's] neck and head area.'[11] So much for 'safe custody and protection'.

In April 2011, Dylan – still a very small thirteen – was sitting in the rec room inside the Alice Springs Youth Detention Centre. He used a phone mounted on one of the walls to call a friend. Dylan says the staff member then stood up, 'forcefully' kneed Dylan in the bum and slapped him in the face with such force that he was knocked over. Dylan was carried to an isolation cell. His cheek was swollen where the staff member had hit him, and there was blood. He complained to police, and the staff member was charged with aggravated assault. The footage got played on *Four Corners*. Surely, there was no possibility anyone could say the staff member's response was reasonable. Yet again, the assault charge was dismissed by a magistrate. And the staff member later returned to work at the Alice Springs Detention Centre.[12]

Dylan Voller lodged complaints every time he was assaulted by staff, first to the Ombudsman, occasionally to police, and eventually to the Territory's Children's Commissioner, Dr Howard Bath, who in 2012 commenced an investigation into complaints made by Dylan and other children. Bath was a trained clinical psychologist who'd held a range of positions in child welfare and youth justice. By April, he'd seen a number of incidents – all captured on CCTV – that he'd found 'most concerning'. He met with Greg Shanahan, then CEO of the attorney-general's department, and showed him some of the CCTV footage. Bath explained that whenever staff grabbed a child by the neck, or threw a child to the ground, or 'ground stabilised' a child by placing pressure on their lower backs, the staff member was engaging in 'highly inappropriate behaviour' that clearly violated their PART training. Somehow, courts were consistently reaching the opposite conclusion. Bath also questioned the 'at-risk' procedure, which involved force-stripping a child. That was a long way from therapeutic. Two detention centre staff, who were also in the meeting, explained that 'stripping and supplying the child with a rip-proof gown prevented him from choking on his underpants'. Bath scoffed. 'Quite apart from the illegal and dangerous physical intervention methods used,' he countered, choking on underwear was highly unlikely in an environment of constant surveillance. Shanahan agreed these practices were inappropriate, and assured Bath they wouldn't continue.[13] But they did.

Bad kids?

Dylan Voller has since become a household name in Australia. What made him famous was his preparedness to speak publicly to the ABC's *Four Corners* and then to the subsequent Royal Commission into the Protection and Detention of Children about his experiences in the Northern Territory's youth justice system. Dylan, now what the law calls an adult, is still in and out of prison. Many say that's evidence that he's a bad guy. His behaviour has had consequences for other people. He's created victims. Some say he deserves no sympathy for that reason. By extension, the same applies to all the other kids who get locked up in youth detention centres in Darwin, Alice Springs, and indeed in other states and territories.

On that line of thinking, prison is the place Dylan needs to be. Perhaps. But why must prison be violent and authoritarian? Let's go back to October 2009, when Dylan first went into the Alice Springs Youth Detention Centre, that time for a week. He'd just turned twelve, and he'd thrown a rock at the window of his mum's house. She'd taken Dylan and his sister up to Alice from South Australia two years earlier, apparently in an effort to get better help than what was being offered through Families SA.[14] She didn't get any more help in the Northern Territory. Dylan went to a handful of schools in Alice but they kept expelling him. He was a child with many challenges. Schools didn't want to deal with them. He says one school used to lock him inside a small room with no windows, and take his shoes and socks away. He was getting bounced around between caseworkers in what was then called the Department of Children and Families (DCF). We can only imagine how stressful this would have been for his mother. Dylan understands that a DCF worker encouraged his mum to report the rock-throwing incident to police, because that would mean she'd get more help with Dylan. Instead, Dylan got arrested. When he breached his bail, he was locked up for a week. 'I felt lost and alone,' he recalled later:

> They [the staff] would scream at me and tell me what to do, swearing at me and being abusive all the time. They would threaten to 'slam you', lock you down or put you 'at-risk'. I started to 'lose it' as I was not used to being spoken to like that. I felt like they were treating me like a dog.[15]

What does it do to a twelve-year-old, to be treated like that? This isn't just a peripheral question. It's a question that goes to the heart of Australia's systems of 'youth justice'. Just how *should* we respond to young people whose behaviour is so bad that we can start calling it criminal? The distinguishing feature of *youth* justice systems – as opposed to *criminal* justice systems, for adults – is their emphasis on what's called 'therapeutic' intervention. Very few kids commit serious crimes. Look into the short life stories of those who do, and it's not at all difficult to find reasons for their extraordinary, fatalistic rage. Most were victims of extreme abuse or neglect long before they began hurting others, and largely at the hands of adults – family members, teachers, foster carers – they should have been able to trust. Child protection systems are the tragic 'conveyer belts' that provide most of the young clients in each state and territory youth justice system – and, indeed, most of its adult prisoners. Most kids settle down eventually. Some keep bashing people and destroying property well into their adulthood. The ultimate KPI for any youth justice system is whether it makes that graduation more or less likely for the children it receives.[16]

In August 2014, Dylan Voller, now sixteen, chucked a bowl of spaghetti at his cell door and was transferred to the BMU. He was told he'd only be there for an hour. A week later he was still there.[17] Five other kids were there with him, in separate cells.[18] Locking kids in cells for twenty-three hours a day, as they were, tends to cause violent, even psychotic, outbursts.[19] The United Nations defines it as cruel, inhuman or degrading treatment or even torture. When Dylan complained, a staff member threw a pear at him and threatened to break his arm.[20] Not long afterwards, one of the other kids – aged just fourteen – exploded in pent-up rage. To subdue him, the authorities discharged as many as nine bursts of CS gas – commonly known as tear gas – into the BMU.[21] The gas causes an extreme burning sensation to the eyes, nostrils, throat and mouth, and makes breathing very difficult through massive coughing fits.

On 4 March 2015, at the Alice Springs Detention Centre, Dylan Voller experienced something new. After he briefly threatened self-harm, he calmed down and returned to his cell. That should have been the end of it. A little while later, staff came into his cell, fitted him with a spit hood and took him to the Alice Springs adult prison. He was seventeen. A prison officer said something insulting about Dylan's mother. Dylan swore at him, and blocked the camera in his cell. Staff came and put handcuffs on him, fit another spit hood, then dragged a 'restraint chair' to the corridor immediately outside his cell. They forced him into it, strapped him in and left him there for nearly three hours while they video-recorded him. 'I was busting and I asked to go to the toilet and they wouldn't let me,' he said later. He urinated on himself. 'I felt totally humiliated.'[22] The image of Dylan Voller, an Aboriginal teenager, his head cowled, his body strapped onto a mechanical chair, was among those Four Corners beamed into Australian living rooms sixteen months later. It evoked Abu Ghraib and Guantanamo Bay. It probably wasn't even legal.[23]

After the treatment of Dylan Voller and other teenagers in the Northern Territory's detention centres and prisons was broadcast on Four Corners in July 2016, Brian Ross Martin, who'd been the Supreme Court's chief justice between 2004 and 2010 and had continued to sit on an acting basis afterwards, claimed that he and his fellow judges had never known about it.[24] But that wasn't true. Four of the children who'd been gassed in Don Dale's BMU in 2014 had sued the government. In the Supreme Court, Justice Judith Kelly said she 'preferred the evidence of the [staff members]' to that of the detained children. She said she didn't believe the teenagers' evidence that the fourteen-year-old rioter had told the staff he wanted to surrender before the gas was deployed.[25] Yet footage of the incident clearly shows Jake asking to speak with a particular staff member, and staff saying it was 'too late' to do anything about motions that had been set in train.[26] The onus was on the Don Dale staff to explain how it was 'reasonable and necessary' to gas a fourteen-year-old kid in a youth detention centre, in circumstances where other kids were locked in cells close-by, some of whom had asthma. Kelly accepted that the authorities had no option other than to use CS gas to get the 'riotous and destructive' kids under control.[27] The teenagers appealed to the Court of Appeal, where another three Territory justices endorsed their colleague Kelly's original decision.[28] It was only when they appealed outside the jurisdiction of the Northern Territory, to the High Court, that they found judges who agreed it was illegal to use CS gas inside a youth detention centre.[29]

Almost half of all children in Australian youth detention centres are Aboriginal or Torres Strait Islander. And in the Northern Territory, where a third of all children are Indigenous, *more than 95 per cent* of the kids who are locked up at any given time are Indigenous. Frequently, that figure rises to 100 per cent. 'It is no longer adequate or meaningful to talk about a youth justice system,' wrote criminologist Harry Blagg as long ago as 2008. He was writing specifically about Western Australia, but the same applies to the Northern Territory. 'What we have is a system concerned almost totally with the habitual confinement of Aboriginal children and young people.'[30] In many youth detention centres across Australia, non-Indigenous kids are only occasional visitors.

Rehabilitation or harm?

There are two basic narratives about criminalised kids in detention. One is expressed by governments and detention centre authorities: these kids are violent and impossible to manage. They need much higher-security environments than those that presently exist. Staff who have to work with them are at constant risk. Force occasionally has to be used to keep them under control. It's unfortunate, they lament, but it's a reality. In recent months and years, this narrative has emerged at various flashpoints around the country. It gets expressed by ministers, police, staff unions and judges. In September

2014, the purpose-built Don Dale Youth Detention Centre was closed, its teenaged inmates transferred into the mothballed adult prison at Berrimah, which the government simply renamed 'Don Dale'.

The other narrative is often expressed by lawyers, children's commissioners and child development experts. Dr Jon Jureidini is a child psychiatrist at Adelaide's Women's and Children's Hospital. He also has a PhD in philosophy and conducts ongoing research in paediatric mental health at the University of Adelaide. In a past role, as director of adolescent psychiatry at the Royal Adelaide Hospital, he was responsible for mental health services in Kurlana Tapa, where kids in South Australia go when they're incarcerated. Kids who get locked up, Jureidini told the royal commission in June 2017, 'almost inevitably' have had traumatic lives full of broken trust. All efforts at rehabilitation, therefore, *must* start by trying to give them 'a sense of safety'. 'That's a challenge in that environment,' Jureidini acknowledged, 'but until and unless we can make children feel safe, then we can't do anything about rehabilitating them.'[31]

If you have kids, think about how much effort you've put in over the years to help them develop emotional resilience. You've probably had to 'punish' them from time to time, to reinforce the idea that there are consequences for poor behaviour. But whatever punishment you've inflicted has (hopefully) been scaffolded by a much larger reality of safety, stability and love. Without that context, experts say, punishments and even rewards won't work. And if a child's 'bad' behaviour is driven by internal responses to psychological trauma, harsh punishment – such as solitary confinement for hours or days, assault, humiliation, verbal abuse – is much more likely to compound existing trauma, exacerbate psychological harm and entrench, rather than overcome, the lack of emotional resilience that triggers bad behaviour.

Dylan Voller said some staff treated him okay, even quite well. Others played power games, gaslit him, yelled at him, humiliated him, abused him, assaulted him. He'd worked out how best to try to protect himself from these staff. But he was also still very much a traumatised kid. The realities of detention hadn't allowed him to develop, any more than life on the outside had, the kind of emotional resilience that becomes the basis, in well-regulated kids, for delayed gratification, self-reflection and all the emotional skills that we value in teenagers and adults we describe as 'well-rounded' and 'mature'. Often things got too much. Inside, his fight-flight response was continually conditioned to fight; there was no other option.

He didn't have caring adults who comforted him through distressing emotions. His tantrums would be violently punished. His cries for help would be ignored, or disciplined. He began harming himself, and was then punished for that, too. During his six years in and out of youth detention, he estimated later, he tried to kill himself perhaps as many as fifteen times.[32]

Child psychiatrists expressed horror at what was being done to kids like Dylan Voller in the Territory's youth justice system. 'What the kids need is for the staff to act in a parental way towards them,' Dr Jon Jureidini told the royal commission in June 2017. 'Self-harm is a communicative behaviour,' he said – one that signals that the child is in severe distress. Jureidini told the commission that in his opinion, isolating a child in a cell should never happen as a response to his threat of self-harm – yet that was routine practice at Don Dale.[33] For the trained adults working with Dylan and all the other damaged kids, *all* threats of self-harm meant, in practice, 'ground stabilisation', forced stripping and, invariably, solitary confinement. Each time a child exhibits distress becomes yet another opportunity to exert power and control over the carceral subject, rather than an opportunity to connect with and help that child. Dylan learns, probably on dozens of occasions every day for months and years, that he's at the complete and utter mercy of a system that seems designed to break him.

Escalation[34]

For the last decade, various forces have been at play which further entrenched the 'violent kids' narrative among governments across the country. In the mass youth detention facility at Banksia Hill in the Perth suburb of Canning Vale, children who'd been locked down in their cells because of staff shortages ran riot for nearly four hours on 20 January 2013, and trashed 108 cells.[35] The government had failed to heed multiple warnings before the riot,[36] and an independent report later concluded that a 'major security event' had been 'entirely foreseeable'.[37] But it was the kids who copped the consequences. They spent the next eight months in the Hakea men's prison while Banksia Hill was repaired. At Hakea, visits, education, recreation and remedial programs were significantly curtailed. Strip searches were frequent.[38]

Victoria's Labor government, led by Dan Andrews, responded in a remarkably similar way when a combination of major staff shortages, inadequately trained labour-hire staff and long lockdowns led to a major riot in November 2016 at the youth detention centre in Parkville, in Melbourne's inner north. Again, the government had ignored multiple warnings. Again, it responded by transferring the teenagers to the maximum-security unit of an adult prison. The boys were locked inside their cells almost constantly for the first weeks. Children weren't given even blankets for a week, despite air conditioning blasting cold air into their cells. They were hungry. There were rats. One boy self-harmed using porcelain from his cell's smashed sink. 'This is the most fucked-up place we've ever been,' one child is said to have told a worker. 'This is hell on Earth.' Ultimately, five Supreme Court justices – across two trials and an appeal – agreed with him, repeatedly declaring the Andrews government's actions illegal. That didn't stop them, however.[39]

Among authorities in most parts of the country, the idea that they were dealing with a novel 'type' of adolescent offender – physically larger, more violent and less manageable than anything seen in the past – quickly took hold among detention centre managements, their staff and their unions, police and their associations. It met receptive ears among right-wing politicians, tabloid media and some magistrates, and became a useful scapegoat for bureaucrats and ministers. But the idea that there is now a new, aggressive core of violent kids conflicts with what experts in youth offending have always known: that a small group of very troubled kids are responsible for a large proportion of youth offending, and then present with the most difficult-to-manage behaviour when they're arrested. 'Disadvantage, poverty, trauma – they've always been the drivers of criminal offending,' one insider told me just after the Parkville incident. Two-thirds of the kids in detention in Victoria have problems with drugs and alcohol. A quarter have diagnosed intellectual disabilities.[40] If statistics do show kids acting up more often than they used to, how can the changes that have occurred in youth justice systems – casualisation, cost-cutting, securitisation – be discounted as the main causes?

Reform and wind back

Advocates leaked the CCTV footage of the various assaults on kids in Don Dale to the ABC, whose *Four Corners* screened it nationally on 26 July 2016 on the episode 'Australia's Shame'. The result was instant. Malcolm

Turnbull, then prime minister, announced a royal commission. Within a month, the CLP government was dumped at election after just one term, and the incoming Labor government, led by Michael Gunner, promised to work with the new royal commissioners – Mick Gooda and Margaret White – to fix up the youth justice system.[41] The new government introduced new laws banning spit hoods and mechanical restraint chairs.[42]

For the next eighteen months, out of live-streamed public hearings poured revelation after revelation of what had been happening inside Don Dale and its Alice Springs equivalent. The commissioners' November report condemned the Territory's youth justice system. Practically no part of it, Gooda and White concluded, was any good. The very design of the detention centres made rehabilitation impossible. Staff working in the centres verbally and physically abused kids, and denied them food, water and toilets. Kids were regularly called 'stupid black cunt' and 'dumb black kid' by staff. A worker had kicked a girl in the stomach and called her a 'fucking slut'. Racist language was 'an everyday thing'. Kids had been prevented from going to the toilet or drinking water. Some kids had to defecate in their cells. Some staff members dared kids to eat bird faeces and cockroaches, or fight each other, or bash other kids, in return for rewards such as chocolates. One staff member video-recorded himself telling a child: 'come suck my dick, you little cunt.' Kids were frequently 'ground stabilised' in ways that departed wildly from the techniques staff had learned during training, sometimes having their heads slammed onto concrete floors. Again and again, kids – including girls who'd been sexually assaulted – told the commissioners they couldn't breathe when huge blokes were kneeling on their lungs.[43]

Similar reappraisals occurred when the actions of the Western Australian and Victorian governments were scrutinised by courts.[44] If the behaviour of kids in detention *had* been getting worse in recent years, it was most likely because they were being pushed to breaking point by management regimes that prioritised using ever-increasing force over the kinds of therapeutic interventions suggested by decades of evidence. The Gunner government passed additional laws that placed new restrictions on when staff could use force against kids in detention centres.[45] Dale Wakefield, a social worker who had run the Alice Springs Women's Shelter for eight years, was made youth justice minister and immediately set about reforming the system.[46]

But by the end of 2018, Wakefield and Gunner were under significant pressure from staff at the Don Dale and Alice Springs detention centres, who were complaining about working conditions they called 'unsafe'. They blamed the government's commission-inspired reforms, which banned many of the 'behaviour management' techniques staff had used before.[47] As evidenced in the *NT News*, settler opinion in the Territory had never really departed from the view held by the Country Liberal Party's sacked former corrections minister (and former cop), John Elferink: that the *Four Corners* report was a beat-up, and Turnbull had overreacted. When footage of another Don Dale tear gassing incident (from November 2018) emerged in January 2019, the government didn't merely condone the police response. New laws reversed many of the changes made just ten months earlier.[48] Staff using force against children no longer had to show it was objectively necessary or that it was a last resort. Restraints and solitary confinement could again be used simply to maintain order – and staff began doing so immediately.[49] Moreover, the changes were retrospective. And in May 2021, the Gunner government rushed through new laws designed to make it much harder for teenagers to get bail. Inevitably, First Nations children came flooding into Don Dale on remand. By October 2021, the number of children in youth detention in the Territory was the highest it had been in years, and at the time of writing, the government is pushing ahead with plans to expand Don Dale to accommodate even more children.[50] The numbers being held in Don Dale and its Alice Springs equivalent have reached record highs during 2022.

Running alongside this recent history of reform and reaction has been a national campaign – led by the Aboriginal-controlled organisation Change The Record – to increase the minimum age at which a child can be held criminally responsible for breaking the law from ten to fourteen, in line with the United Nations' standard. As part of the campaign, Archie Roach and other celebrities have shared photos of themselves aged thirteen. Governments in Australia have so far resisted the campaign's demands, so children as young as ten – most of whom having endured shocking abuse and neglect throughout their young lives – are frequently arrested, charged, subject to highly restrictive bail conditions and occasionally locked up for property crime. It's become very common for dysregulated kids to be forced into residential 'care' and then charged criminally for tantrums.

But the law has for a long time said that a child under fourteen can't be held criminally responsible *unless* prosecutors are able to prove – beyond reasonable doubt – that the child knew that what they were doing was not merely 'naughty' or 'mischievous' but actually 'morally' or criminally wrong.[51] It's almost impossible for prosecutors to prove that kind of knowledge, so most young children whose lawyers are prepared to fight their charges on this basis are acquitted. But before that can happen, prosecutors and courts in a lot of cases have conspired to ensure that many kids – who would never be found guilty at a contested hearing – spend months locked up or under very strict bail conditions. Often, children plead guilty just to get out of the bail nightmare.

'All I'm doing since the bail changes', one experienced youth lawyer tells me, 'is running bail apps for emotionally dysregulated and intellectually disabled kids who should never be locked up.' But despite the royal commission, the evidence-based psychological and emotional help kids need just isn't there. Don Dale becomes the only option. Another lawyer tells me that he's tried to have a teenage client referred into any kind of counselling or therapeutic treatment for nearly a year. The young man is open to it – indeed, is practically begging for it, because he knows he needs help to regulate his emotions to avoid reoffending. Yet none of the appropriate publicly funded government and non-government services have ever accepted a referral. He's in and out of Don Dale, and will likely be in and out of prison in a couple of years. And Northern Territory prosecutors are, at the time of writing, appealing a decision to acquit a thirteen-year-old girl of assault – on the grounds that she didn't have the capacity to understand that what she'd done was 'morally' or 'seriously' wrong – after she slapped her teacher during a schoolyard fight the girl was having with another student. To augment long-running failures of child protection and education systems, the Territory's prosecutors want even more young Indigenous children punished by courts – and locked up.[52]

JUSTICE

Who calls it a justice system anyway?

Every report into Indigenous incarceration rates in Australia looks the same. There are sections on arrests and detentions for public drunkenness, on policing practices, on child welfare policies, on teenagers, schooling, unemployment and poverty, on inadequate housing and mental health, on bail laws, on alternatives to imprisonment and on self-determination. The five-volume, 2000-page report of the Royal Commission into Aboriginal Deaths in Custody is remarkably comprehensive. It was issued in April 1991, and it's a testament to how little has changed about how the settler criminal justice system interacts with First Nations communities that most of it reads like it could have been written today.

There's an entire chapter in the deaths in custody report on 'The Legacy of History'. It was written by Elliott Johnson who, unusually for a judge, was politically radical: he only resigned his Communist Party membership in 1983 because he was required to on his appointment to the South Australian Supreme Court. 'Why is history relevant?' Johnson asked. Because at some point in history, an invader's justice system became the *only* justice system for the people already living here. Nobody can say exactly when that was in a way that makes sense to the First Nations, to international law or even to the internal rationales of British and then Australian law. Lawyers and judges have suggested various dates.[1]

If the sovereign territories of the First Nations weren't ceded to the newcomers, then how was their sovereignty extinguished? It can only be by application of the principle 'might is right'. If an alien people arrived and imposed their system like this on settler Australians and their descendants, we'd have no problem describing it as unjust. History matters because the convoluted logics that have satisfied imperial and settler courts and parliaments and governments for the last 235 years can't possibly satisfy anyone interested in justice and fairness. It is now a system which processes people – through surveillance, arrest, often multiple court appearances, remand, sentencing and imprisonment – for what must be its own reasons, comprehensible only to itself. For each of its agents – individual police officers, lawyers, judges, correctional staff – the small part of the system they work in might seem rational and even reasonable, though most are often perplexed by the other parts. Defendants, victims and witnesses – the system's 'users', in its own language – regularly find it disempowering and bewildering. If a justice system isn't 'fair' and it isn't 'just', then what is it?

Judging

In January 2017, Dr John Lowndes – then the Northern Territory Local Court's chief judge – upheld seventeen complaints against Greg Borchers, an Alice Springs judge who, among other tirades, had berated a fourteen-year-old Aboriginal girl for her parenting failures after she'd been raped. Lowndes warned Borchers formally that 'any repetition' of similarly inappropriate language 'would amount to serious misconduct'.[2] At around the same time, a woman was killed in Tennant Creek. The primary suspect in her alleged murder was her husband. The world of their child, 'Kyle', a thirteen-year-old boy, had been shattered. His school attendance dropped. He began to abuse alcohol and sniff petrol. The next month, Kyle pled guilty to damaging property, and came before Greg Borchers for sentencing. The judge told Kyle he'd 'taken advantage' of 'a bit of a breakdown in your family', and that he didn't know 'what a first world economy is'.[3] Central Australian Aboriginal Legal Aid Service (CAALAS) complained again to Lowndes,[4] who in December 2017 concluded that Borchers had 'engaged in inappropriate judicial conduct, which is unacceptable'. But his behaviour 'fell well short of judicial misconduct'. The January warning had apparently been forgotten.[5]

Borchers continued to let rip against First Nations defendants. 'One day,' he told 'Geraldine's' lawyer in Katherine in November 2018, 'we might read some literature, some important anthropological literature, we might learn something about what's called Indigenous laissez-faire parenting and I invite you to do so. Not that it will help your practice in any way, but it might get you to understand why it is that people abandon their children on such a regular basis.' Geraldine had left her kids with family in Lajamanu and boarded a bus into Katherine, where she was going to celebrate her birthday by having some drinks. She hadn't 'abandoned' her children. When she bumped into her husband's mistress, she became upset, found her husband in the hospital and punched him in the face. He hadn't wanted her charged, but authorities' discretion was exercised against her: staff called police; police charged her; prosecutors prosecuted her.

In April 2019, Borchers made similar assumptions about another Aboriginal woman, 'Evelyn', in Tennant Creek. 'Yesterday, probably, was pension day,' Borchers told her, 'so you got your money from the government, abandoned your kids in that great Indigenous fashion of abrogating your parental responsibility to another member of your family, and went off and got drunk.' Police found her asleep in the boot of a car that was parked outside a house she was banned from attending under the terms of a domestic violence order; the person the order was protecting, 'Fran', wasn't even at the house. Evelyn was arrested and locked in a cell. 'This morning, your eight-year-old will go to school and she will have to ask, "Where's my mother?" Her mother is in the lockhouse because she is drunk.'

Other judges might have asked why it was that police were locking intoxicated Aboriginal and Torres Strait Islander women in cells overnight, when very few white women experience the same treatment. Borchers, though, was more interested in lecturing Indigenous women about their parenting failures, even when they'd made arrangements to have their children cared for by family members before they'd gone out drinking. In March 2019, Borchers told an Aboriginal defendant that the way he'd assaulted his wife was 'just like a primitive person dragging his woman out of the cave ready to give her a further beating'.[6]

Perhaps inevitably, some of the Borchers transcripts were then leaked to *Guardian Australia*. The Criminal Lawyers Association of the Northern Territory (CLANT) lodged yet another formal complaint.[7] Lowndes retired in October, and his successor, Elizabeth Morris, completed the third formal investigation into Borchers in December. Surely this would be the third strike? Remarkably, it was not. While Borchers had 'improperly' conveyed 'a negative stereotype on the basis of race', Morris concluded that his behaviour again fell short of serious judicial misconduct. Morris observed that 'judicial stress and intemperance' can be a consequence of judges' heavy workloads and weekly exposure to 'hundreds of cases involving violence, neglect, drunken and abusive behaviour and often the effects that this behaviour has on children'. Judicial stress is a serious issue, and does lead to significant mental illness and suicide. But it was an odd remark for Morris to make. Nobody forces judges to sit on the bench. From 1 January 2020, the base salary of a Local Court judge was $361,534 – nearly *twenty-five times* as much as people on Centrelink received.[8] Whatever stress judicial officers experience when they hear *about* violence and neglect is nothing compared with the stress people experience by having to live it, and then by being forced through the criminal justice system. Was the Chief Judge suggesting that Borchers could be excused for his racist tirades because he was stressed? The stress of living with the legacy of dispossession, childhood trauma, poverty and racism is an argument that no longer gets defendants very far in Territory courtrooms.

First Nations people are systemically disadvantaged in courts and in the broader settler justice system. How did that system respond when one of its judges broke its own rules? It made excuses for him, three times. It failed to follow through on its own promise to consider *any* repeat behaviour as 'serious misconduct'. It told the community that racist remarks by a judge are, in the end, not unacceptable enough to make that judge unfit to continue sitting. More to the point, it told Indigenous people living in the Territory – who already make up most of its prison population and practically all of its youth detention population – that judges who make decisions based on racist and 'unjudicial' reasons go unsanctioned.

Greg Borchers isn't the first judge or magistrate to express racist views. In November 1977 a New South Wales Supreme Court judge, Gordon Carmichael, said during the trial of an Aboriginal man that he had 'lost his judgement and reasoning, and the veneer of civilisation having worn off'. 'Your race of people must be the most interfering race of people I have heard of,' magistrate Kenneth Quinn told three Aboriginal defendants in Wilcannia in March 1979. Apparently Quinn was unaware of the extent to which his own 'race' had 'interfered' over the centuries. 'You are becoming a pest race in Wilcannia, wanting to interfere in the job of the police.' Quinn's harsh sentence – imposed for 'unseemly words' – was confirmed on appeal.[9] And a Queensland magistrate's memoir published in 2016 – *Saltwater*, by Cathy McLennan – contains just about every vicious stereotype that has ever been ascribed to Indigenous people in Australia.[10]

Borchers is unlikely to be the last judicial officer to use this language. No judge in the Territory identified as Indigenous until NAAJA's David

Woodroffe was appointed in mid-2022. In the end, the system made it very easy for anyone to conclude that, ultimately, it looks after itself.

Protecting

Michael, a forty-seven-year-old Tiwi Islander, was living mostly in the long grass around Darwin. He got the majority of his meals at Vinnies. He'd been drinking heavily for two decades, and most days he drank until he was drunk. His brain had been damaged. He was a chronic alcoholic. One day in mid-2014, Michael was arrested after stealing food from Coles worth $4.20. The arresting officer slapped him with a three-month alcohol protection order, an instrument available in the Northern Territory between 2013 and 2016. The APO created for Michael his own private prohibition regime. If he drank, he faced three months in prison and an extension of the APO.[11] People on APOs could be searched or breath-tested at any time, for any or no reason. His APO didn't stop Michael drinking. He was arrested and charged no less than seventeen times, simply for breaching the APO by drinking, although police withdrew the original theft charge.

Of all APOs issued by police between December 2013 and July 2014, a whopping 86 per cent were issued to Indigenous people. That figure rose to *94 per cent* for second APOs.[12] Michael's lawyers at NAAJA appealed and challenged the law's validity, on the basis that while the APO law was racially neutral, it was practically and predictably discriminatory and therefore inconsistent with the federal *Racial Discrimination Act*. The Supreme Court's Justice Stephen Southwood didn't agree.[13] NAAJA appealed again. And again, the Court of Appeal – made up this time of not one white, middle-class judge but three – dismissed it. Michael's lawyer raised the ire of the Court of Appeal judges for arguing that a law that criminalised public alcoholism was necessarily a law that targeted Aboriginal people.[14]

The settler justice system's basic model is to criminalise individual behaviour while ignoring most of the social context within which it took place. Even when it's accepted that *particular* laws or policies are blatantly unfair, they tend to be replaced with variations of the same concept. Territory Labor stormed back into government in 2016 promising to repeal alcohol protection orders. But alcohol-related harm remained a huge political issue. It's a social and health problem, but governments' preferred response is to criminalise individuals. The new government commissioned a recently retired judge to report on alcohol policy. Trevor Riley recommended what most of these reports always recommend: volumetric taxation; unit floor pricing; a special alcohol court; and many more rehab and sobering-up options. Instead, the government amended the Territory's *Liquor Act* to give police even greater powers. It became lawful for a police officer to stop a car and search it for alcohol if it merely came within 20 metres of the *car park* of a shop that sold alcohol. No prizes for guessing who would be the main targets of these extraordinary powers. The government ignored more protests by NAAJA, and the bill became law in April 2019.[15] 'Territorians have had enough of the alcohol-fuelled crime and antisocial behaviour on our streets and in our communities,' the attorney-general told parliament,[16] even as her government declared its support for a new Dan Murphy's 'mega-store' in Darwin's geographical centre, within walking distance of three dry Indigenous communities.[17] Labor would get the Aboriginal grog-runners off the streets. And into prison.

Arresting

Between mid-2019 and 2020, Victoria – and the nation – was consumed by an inquest into the tragic death of respected fifty-five-year-old Yorta Yorta woman, Elder, mother and grandmother Tanya Day. She had been travelling by train to Melbourne from her home in Echuca in December 2017. Just past Bendigo, police arrested her for being drunk in public, which remained an offence in Victoria nearly three decades after the deaths in custody royal commission urged parliaments to repeal it immediately. Police took her to the Castlemaine Police Station and put her in a cell. After she fell and hit her head on the concrete cell wall, she was taken by ambulance to Bendigo Hospital where a scan revealed a massive bleed on her brain. She was airlifted to a hospital in Melbourne, where she underwent emergency surgery and died just over two weeks later. Day had been active in the movement to reform Victoria's public drunkenness laws since her uncle, Harrison Day, had died in an Echuca police cell in 1982 from an epileptic fit. He'd been arrested and locked up because he hadn't paid a ten dollar fine, and his death was one of the ninety-nine which the deaths in custody commission was tasked with examining. His original 'crime'? Public drunkenness.[18]

Coronial inquests (and internal police investigations, parliamentary inquiries and royal commissions) drag Indigenous families through the minutiae of their deceased loved one's last moments on the pretext that someone will be found accountable, or that the system which led to death will somehow improve. Mostly, that doesn't happen. Government agencies – police, prison authorities, hospitals, child protection departments – pour enormous resources into trying to convince coroners they aren't responsible. Even when coroners do make findings which implicate government agencies, they're not binding. Very often, what inquests do is to create an *impression* of openness and accountability while actually achieving the radical opposite.[19]

The coroner in Aunty Tanya Day's inquest, Caitlin English, found that her death was preventable had proper procedures – including regular welfare checks and earlier medical interventions – been followed. Such findings are common in coronial inquests. The inquest into four suicides by hanging – at least two of them by Aboriginal men – in Perth's Casuarina prison between October 2014 and November 2015 recommended that the prison increase the number of cells without hanging points 'without delay', even though a two-year construction project designed to reduce the number of hanging points should have been completed three years before the deaths.[20] Mainly because Day's family pushed so hard, however, the inquest also produced something almost unheard-of: an outcome. English also found that systemic racism played a major part in the decisions that led to Day's death. The train conductor had never called police for a sleeping passenger before. Victoria Police exhibited a continuing 'culture of complacency' regarding the medical risks of intoxication, and its welfare checks were 'illusory' and irregular.[21]

Public drunkenness offences clearly discriminate against First Nations people. White people regularly drink in public as well, though middle-class public drinking tends to occur in exempt spaces such as pubs, restaurants, beer gardens, wineries and festivals, or in private houses and backyards. There's no obvious reason why the state should be preoccupied with public drinking any more than private drinking, which causes much greater harm.[22] Day's family and supporters continued their campaign for change after the inquest. They used English's findings in a high-profile campaign to repeal Victoria's 'drunk in public' offence. The state parliament responded by passing a bill in February 2021, though it won't come into effect until November 2022.[23] Although it was often reported that this left Queensland as the only state where a specific offence of public drunkenness remained on the books, people who drink in public can still be at least fined in most places around Australia.[24]

Intervening

Even in those states and territories that have decriminalised public drunkenness, police retain 'protective intervenor' powers that authorise them to apprehend intoxicated people and slot them in police cells to 'sober up'. The people apprehended under these powers aren't accused of crimes. Though if you're placed in the back of a police divisional van against your will, driven to a police station and locked inside a cell, the legal distinction between 'arrest' and 'protective apprehension' may not seem all that meaningful.

'Edith' had been charged with assaulting police, apparently by kicking an officer in the shin after she'd been taken to the police station under 'protective custody'.[25] Edith permanently slurred her words and had trouble focusing. When she arrived at court I thought she was drunk. So had police when they'd detained her. But I soon discovered she *never* drank alcohol. These symptoms were what she was left with following a stroke some years earlier. My assessment of Edith's intoxication was entirely wrong. That's not surprising. I'd never been trained to detect symptoms of intoxication. But even first responders with medical training – doctors and paramedics – are often unable to spot the difference between intoxication, a head injury, sleep deprivation and mental illness.[26] Prejudice and unconscious bias can play a very real part in misdiagnosis. One study of trauma surgeons found that sober patients were more likely to be falsely suspected of intoxication if they were young, male, of dishevelled appearance, or had a low income.[27]

The law that gives police officers authority to apprehend intoxicated people in the Northern Territory also defines the word 'intoxicated': for the purposes of this protective power, a person is deemed to be intoxicated if their 'speech, balance, coordination or behaviour appears (to police) to be noticeably impaired', and 'it is reasonable in the circumstances' for police to *believe* that 'the impairment results from the consumption of alcohol'.[28] In other words, a person might be legally 'intoxicated' even if they're entirely sober.

Edith instructed me to help her fight her assault police charge. The CCTV footage showed the officers taunting and laughing at her at the station before she kicked out behind her, her foot glancing off one of the officers' left shin. If I couldn't prove to the court that police were acting unlawfully, she'd be found guilty. I argued that it wasn't 'reasonable' for a (white) police officer to stumble across an Aboriginal woman asleep on a bench and jump to the conclusion that she's drunk. The (white) judge disagreed. Finding First Nations people intoxicated and in need of 'protective custody' was regular police practice. In the end, Edith was acquitted of her charge on another basis: the officers weren't able to satisfy the court that it was 'impracticable for her to be cared for by someone else', which was part of the criteria. They took her straight to a police cell, which meant they were acting outside the powers granted to them by parliament.

Edith was understandably happy after her court 'win'. But the court had endorsed the politicians' very unsound idea that police officers are competent judges of whether Indigenous people are intoxicated. The ostensible intent behind section 128 – that people too drunk to look after themselves should be monitored or cared for by someone instead of being arrested and charged with public drunkenness – had morphed into a practice that sees drunk (or in Edith's case, sober) Indigenous people routinely locked up in police cells.

Disqualifying

Since at least the 1970s, people who are disqualified by courts from driving and who then get caught driving again face what amounts to a mandatory sentence of imprisonment. 'Imprisonment is the appropriate penalty save in exceptional circumstances', judge William Forster told an appellant, John Daniel, in 1976. The *maximum* penalty is a year in prison – the same as simply driving without a licence, or driving an unregistered vehicle, for which almost nobody goes to prison. Why is driving while disqualified so deserving of mandatory imprisonment? 'Such driving is a serious contempt of the court', Forster explained.[29]

That single declaration – 'a serious contempt of court' – has been repeated again and again by magistrates and judges all over the country.[30] But its effect on First Nations people in the Territory and Western Australia, often driving long distances on dusty, corrugated, flood-prone and very long dirt roads between communities in the absence of public transport, has been particularly cruel. In 2011, a quarter of the Northern Territory's entire prison population was there for driving offences.[31] One might assume that all breaches of court orders are taken as serious contempt, but prosecutors, police and prison officers who routinely breach court orders are barely admonished.

'Indigenous automobility' – a term coined by researcher Georgine Clarsen to describe Indigenous people's use of vehicles – often looks rather unfamiliar to settlers who have grown up in cities and towns, a category into which judges fit all but unanimously. Discordant with the settler state's bureaucratic demands for single registered owners and individual licences, vehicles in communities are often communally managed, their use governed by relations of kinship, gender and status, which seem bewildering to settlers. During her doctoral fieldwork at a Warlpiri family outstation west of Tennant Creek during the late 1980s, Gertrude Stotz described vehicles' importance for hunting, shopping, ceremonial travel and for visiting family in hospital and jail. Cars have mattresses and guns; windscreens are frequently cracked or non-existent; it's not uncommon to see dozens of kids crammed into – and on top of – Territory vehicles. 'There are no physical barriers to where a car can go and there are no limits to what a car can endure,' Stotz writes, evoking a usage more similar to the way settlers might use cars on private farms.[32]

But the Territory's Supreme Court has never wanted to know about the importance of vehicles to Indigenous mobility. It's no coincidence that William Forster's judgement emphasising John Daniels' 'serious contempt of court' took place amid the homelands movement – Aboriginal people's voluntary return to Country under the rubric of self-determination during the 1970s. Forster's response indicated that settler authorities would never cede sovereignty or state control over Aboriginal mobility to Aboriginal communities. 'The only practical method of obtaining maximum compliance with such [disqualification] orders,' Justice James Muirhead said in 1984, 'is to ensure that those subject to such orders understand that the consequences of a breach will almost inevitably be grave, and imprisonment must, in this regard, be the general sanction.'[33] Just three years later, Muirhead was appointed the first deaths in custody royal commissioner, a role which required him to ask why so many Aboriginal people were being locked up.

When parliaments created new, non-custodial orders intended to keep offending drivers out of prison, courts ignored them.[34] In 1991, the deaths in custody royal commission recommended that 'imprisonment should be utilised only as a last resort'. The following June, a Supreme Court judge, Dean Mildren, ignored that recommendation when he confirmed – citing 'the consistent policy of this court' – that an eighteen-year-old man from Yuendumu, Joey, had to spend four months in prison for disqualified driving.[35]

By the mid-1990s, Aboriginal people accounted for a remarkable 92.4 per cent of people imprisoned for driving offences in the Northern Territory. And then came the Northern Territory Emergency Response, which was the culmination of Settler Australia's backlash against self-determination. More cops on the ground meant that more offences – including regulatory and administrative offences – were detected.[36] Despite the proliferation of settler authorities in communities, there was no additional willingness to provide public transport alternatives.

Between 1995 and 2017, one study found, the Supreme Court decided thirty-six appeals involving Indigenous drivers and thirteen appeals involving settler drivers. (Not all were disqualified driving charges.) Most of the Indigenous drivers were imprisoned; only *one* of the settler drivers was. Indigenous drivers were consistently told to 'take responsibility' for their actions, while non-Indigenous drivers were often met with sympathy. When they excavated the ways in which drivers had come to be charged by police in the first place, the study's authors observed prejudice at work:

> Most non-Indigenous drivers were usually apprehended by police because the vehicle was speeding or erratic on the road, had caused an accident or the driver had been observed drinking alcohol while driving. The Indigenous decisions tell a different story. Most Indigenous drivers were 'found by the police', 'observed', 'stopped', or just 'driving' without any outward signs that the vehicle was in contradiction to settler state law. Only one Indigenous driver attracted police attention because of the external disrepair of the vehicle.

The Northern Territory doesn't keep statistics of how often First Nations people are pulled over by police, 'at random', and subjected to everything from a 'random' breath test to a full search for drugs and alcohol. Stops which don't find offenders or contraband and don't make it to court simply don't show up in stats. I've been randomly breath-tested – genuinely randomly, by going through established RBT stations – perhaps a dozen times in my life. My car has never been searched. But some of my Indigenous clients in Katherine had been pulled over for breath tests and had their cars searched multiple times in a single *month*. 'The suggestion,' the study's authors concluded, 'is that Indigenous drivers appear to [be] targeted by police simply because they are Indigenous and driving a motor vehicle; the phenomenon known in the United States as "driving while black".'[37]

Lying

While arresting 'Ross' for drink-driving, a police sergeant swears repeatedly at him. 'Are you fucking deaf or stupid?' the sergeant shouts. He hand-cuffs the offender. But while the sergeant is distracted by onlookers asking why that's necessary, Ross takes the opportunity to wander away. Ross is Aboriginal; the officers aren't. There's no objective evidence about what happens next because neither officer switches his body-worn cameras on until after they reapprehend him. Later, under oath in court, the officers claim that when they found him, Ross spat at one of the officers. For this, the officers charged Ross with assaulting police, which carries a maximum five years' prison. But Ross gives a different version in court after pleading 'not guilty'. He'd run up a hill and fell over because he'd injured his knee. As he was being dragged back to the police vehicle, Ross struggled to keep up because his knee was hurting. At one point the sergeant turned around, Ross says, and punched him, once, above his right eye. Ross says he never spat at anyone. There's no reference to spitting in the sergeant's notebook. The ser-geant denies punching Ross. But the sergeant had eventually activated his body-worn cameras. It records Ross complaining that he'd been punched, and it shows a cut above his eye and a bloodstain on his shirt. Unusually for criminal courts, the judge rejects the sergeant's evidence and finds Ross 'not guilty' of assaulting police. The sergeant had lied in court, used offen-sive language and very likely committed an assault: offences that would have seen Ross locked up had he committed them. But the sergeant is never even charged, and he continues to serve as a police officer.[38]

○

Ross's experience is both rare – being acquitted of assaulting police in the face of confident and cogent police testimony – and typical. The first por-tion of this book explored the settler justice system's legitimacy problem through a historical lens. Another 'test' of its legitimacy is to ask: how does the system deal with its own authorities' excessive and criminal violence?

Choking

David Dungay, a Dunghutti man, was born in 1989 and raised on the old Burnt Bridge Aboriginal Reserve, west of Kempsey, New South Wales. By the time he was seven years old, David had been diagnosed with type 1 dia-betes. He was just eighteen when he went to prison in January 2008. For breaking and entering, attempted sexual assault and another assault, the

Court of Criminal Appeal dealt him a crushing sentence of nine and a half years, one that would blow any chance that David might follow a different path.[39] David spent most of the first eight years of his adulthood being shunted around between various prisons. Unsurprisingly, his mental health declined. By mid-2013 he was diagnosed with schizophrenia. Four days after Christmas in 2019, David woke up in Cell 71 in G Ward, in the Mental Health Unit at Long Bay Hospital. His blood sugar levels were bouncing around. Officer D (their names have never been publicly revealed) reacted to David's request for biscuits – which he was given –by securing David inside his cell, and planning to forcibly take the biscuits from him again.

The acting assistant superintendent – Officer F – then decided, without medical authorisation, that David should be moved to another cell. Long Bay's Immediate Action Team (IAT) – which should only be used in emergency situations[40] – was called in to effect David's cell transfer. What was the emergency? David was eating biscuits. At about 2.35 p.m., five members of the IAT in full riot gear rushed into David's cell, pushed him back onto the bed, and piled on top of him. 'I can't breathe, please!' he called out. 'Let me up, please!' One of the officers told him: 'You brought this upon yourself, Dungay.' David started screaming repeatedly: 'I can't breathe! I can't breathe!' An officer told David, already handcuffed and pinned on the floor of a cell beneath at least three officers, 'Stop resisting with your feet.' Eventually they carried him into another cell and piled on top of him again.[41] A registered nurse injected midazolam – a benzo sedative – into David's buttock.

Later, the nurse told the inquest that David became increasingly aggressive during his administration of midazolam. But the footage shows David completely restrained and immobile, screaming repeatedly '*I can't breathe!*', with officers sitting or kneeling on him. The officers told David to stop resisting, but the footage clearly shows that David couldn't have resisted if he'd wanted to. (There are thousands of videos like this now, which show officers demanding that people stop resisting – while there's no resistance at all. It's only since the advent of body-worn cameras on police uniforms that defendants have begun to succeed in their challenges to charges of 'resisting arrest'.)

David, it turned out, was experiencing a cardiac arrhythmia – his heart started beating too slowly or too quickly – which in turn caused him to experience a shortness of breath. Within two and half minutes of getting the midazolam, his body went limp. A resuscitation attempt, the inquest heard, was shockingly bungled. Medical staff waited up to eight minutes before attempting basic CPR, and when they did, they left the cap on the resuscitation equipment and it came off in David's mouth. David never regained consciousness. He was pronounced dead at 3.42 p.m. Obviously, the officers didn't intend to kill David. (If anything, they believed they were trying to save him from diabetes-related complications.) But in barging into his cell, sitting on him and cuffing him, they may have brought on the arrythmia that killed him. And the inquest was told that by ignoring his desperate pleas – he said, '*I can't breathe!*' at least twelve times – for minutes, they almost certainly hastened his death. But none of the officers was charged with any offence, or even recommended for any disciplinary action.

The deputy state coroner, magistrate Derek Lee, concluded that the actions of the officers had contributed to David's death, and that the resuscitation attempt by the doctor and the two nurses 'was of a low clinical standard and lacking in several vital areas'. But Lee downplayed these findings even as he made them. It was 'not possible to quantify the extent or significance' of the contribution of the prone restraint to David's death. In the end, Lee recommended that policies and guidelines be reviewed, that staff be better trained, and that 'all necessary steps be taken' to make sure that an Indigenous person be available to assist, where required, 'in interactions with Aboriginal or Torres Strait Islander inmates in the Mental Health Unit'. He didn't recommend any sanctions against the prison officers involved.[42] Nearly every death of a First Nations person in a prison prompts similar findings in coronial courts. Policies are reviewed, training is provided. And Indigenous people keep dying.

R. Jongmin

Wadeye began as Port Keats, a Catholic mission established in 1935. People from seven different language groups 'came in' from the surrounding bush. After the missionaries left in 1978, tensions between those groups re-emerged. By the turn of the century, Wadeye had a reputation in Settler Australia as one of the most violent places in the country – though that reputation has managed to conveniently avoid implicating the substandard housing and healthcare, and enforced poverty, which pervades the community. The public violence played out between two rival groups known as the Evil Warriors and the Judas Priests.[43] On 23 October 2002, the violence flared up again on Wadeye's main oval, following a fight the previous week, which had put two people on care flights to Darwin hospital. An eighteen-year-old man, Tobias, lifted a rifle and aimed it at some Judas Priests men. He later insisted, repeatedly, that he didn't know it was loaded. One of the constables in Wadeye, Carmen Butcher, approached Tobias to try to talk him down. But the person closest to Tobias when he came running out from behind the house was his eighteen-year-old cousin, Robert Jongmin. He had no history of breaking the law, though that day he was carrying a tomahawk. Robert ran towards Tobias and threw his tomahawk at him. Tobias ducked, and it passed over his head. Robert kept coming. He grabbed the barrel of the shotgun Tobias was holding and pushed it downwards. It discharged.[44] Tobias dropped the gun. The shotgun *was* loaded. But Robert Jongmin had – heroically – neutralised its threat.

Meanwhile, Acting Sergeant Robert Whittington panicked. He'd failed a firearms instructor course the previous year.[45] It was his sixth day in Wadeye. He was about 40 metres away from Tobias and young Robert. Whittington aimed his Glock pistol – which he was only authorised to use on targets to a maximum of 12 metres – at Tobias. Later, he told investigating officers that he was repeatedly yelling, 'Drop the weapon!' Nobody corroborated that. He also told investigating officers that he thought he'd seen Tobias shoot Robert. That clearly did *not* happen. Whittington told investigators he calmly assessed the situation, knowing he had two houses as a backdrop. 'I aimed at this fellow and I fired.'[46] What actually happened was that Whittington discharged four rounds from his Glock pistol after the shotgun discharged into the ground. After hearing the first of Whittington's shots, both young men turned instinctively and ran away, in the direction of the house that was behind them.[47] Tobias was in front, Robert a couple of metres behind him. Tobias felt a sharp sting in his upper right arm. He'd been shot as he was turning to run away,[48] most likely with Whittington's first bullet.[49]

And Whittington kept firing. Some of the bullets ended up in one of the houses, entering through an open louvre. 'It was pure good fortune that no-one else was injured,' Coroner Greg Cavanagh later observed. Whittington's fourth bullet was one of those later found inside the house.[50] But before it ended up there, it entered Robert Jongmin's back, hit and fractured his fifth rib, travelled upwards through his right lung, then hit his windpipe before coming out the left side of his neck, just below his jaw.[51] For the bullet to have left Whittington's gun, passed through Robert Jongmin's body in the way that it did, and to have entered the bedroom in the house behind him, forensic evidence showed Robert would have been crouching or bending over, his back to Whittington, his head about a metre from the ground, at the time the bullet struck him.[52] In other words, at the moment he was hit, as Cavanagh later put it, Robert was most likely 'running towards the house crouching or bending down in order to try to avoid being shot at'.[53] Within twenty minutes, Robert Jongmin was dead.

Less than three months later, investigators concluded that 'not only were the circumstances where force causing death or grievous harm not justified, but that the discharge of [Whittington's] firearm was such that it caused serious danger, actual or potential, to the lives, health or safety of the public'. Whittington was formally charged with a kind of manslaughter in May 2003. He was also served with an internal disciplinary notice. His Supreme Court trial finally began in Darwin on 10 August 2006. Normally, there's no statute of limitations for indictable, or serious, crimes: that's how people can be convicted of historical murders and sex offences. For very minor offences, the law generally gives people immunity after six or twelve months. But in 2002, the law said police officers in the Northern Territory had immunity after just *two months* – even for murder. The lawyers all agreed that Whittington was acting in pursuance of his duty (albeit incredibly poorly).[54] In the Supreme Court, Dean Mildren concluded that Whittington was entitled to immunity based on time elapsed.[55] Whittington was free. He returned to active duty, though he was restricted to a desk job and his gun was taken away. The disciplinary charges were also withdrawn.[56]

Whittington was later promoted to sergeant, and was posted to Katherine in 2018 as that station's head of prosecutions. That role required him to appear in the Katherine Local Court and make submissions in favour of sending people to prison when they'd driven a car without a licence or committed a drunken assault.

o

It's a feature of the Settler Australian criminal justice system that no police officer has ever been held criminally responsible for causing the death of an Indigenous person. Perhaps the most notorious of these cases, owing to Chloe Hooper's remarkable book *The Tall Man*, is the violent death of thirty-six-year-old Mulrunji Doomadgee in a Palm Island cell in November 2004. Doomadgee had been arrested, allegedly for causing a public nuisance. An hour later he was dead. The autopsy revealed four broken ribs and ruptures to his liver, his spleen and his portal vein. Chris Hurley, then a senior sergeant, was arrested and prosecuted for assault and manslaughter. An all-white jury in Townsville found him not guilty.[57]

The apparatus dedicated to protecting police officers from being held accountable for their crimes against Aboriginal and Torres Strait Islander people is extensive, and includes secret internal disciplinary investigations, bullish police unions, a continued preparedness by magistrates, judges, juries, coroners and commissioners to give the benefit of the doubt to police officers and to downplay or overlook their lies in testimony and their fabrications of evidence, and a general bias in favour of police officers in popular media ('reality' TV shows which embed authorised camera units inside police patrols have all but replaced dramas and sitcoms on prime-time free-to-air TV). Even clear video footage isn't enough to ensure accountability: in 2018, one of four police officers who were surrounding a seated, handcuffed Indigenous boy dragged him onto the ground, causing the boy's head to hit the concrete; an internal police investigation found that the officer had used a level of force which was 'necessary and not excessive' because he'd formed a belief that 'the male juvenile had spat at them or was preparing to spit at them'.[58]

On 7 September 2019, twenty-nine-year-old Yamatji woman 'JC' was walking down a suburban street in Geraldton holding a large bread knife and a pair of small pink scissors. She was very unwell. Following her release from the notoriously overcrowded Bandyup Prison – on a sentence imposed for the theft of a mobile phone she'd believed was possessed by spirits – she was twice admitted to hospitals for self-harm. JC's sister called 000. Eight police officers arrived. None of them – *none* – was wearing a stab-proof vest or a body-worn camera.[59] Senior Constable Baker approached her, his hand held out in an effort to communicate with her. She stopped walking and stood still. Another officer, whose name remains suppressed, then ran at her and shot her in the abdomen.[60] Five months later he was arrested and charged with murder before being bailed. Members of the public were refused entry to the officer's trial in October 2021. Journalists were allowed in, but the trial was barely reported. After just a few hours' deliberation, the jury – which included no Indigenous people – found the officer 'not guilty'.[61]

Kumanjayi Walker

The Northern Territory parliament quietly removed the two-month time limit for police officers to be charged with crimes – the limit which saw

Whittington acquitted – in 2005 when it legislated to protect serving officers from the civil consequences of any decisions they make as long as
they're acting 'in good faith'.[62] More than a decade later, as one of the Mills-
Giles CLP government's final acts, it extended that 'good faith' protection
for officers from *criminal* liability as well, tucked inside a bill that aimed to
address police concerns about catching diseases from being spat on. Michael
Gunner, then opposition leader, acknowledged health-sector concerns that
the amendments were 'based on fear rather than information'.[63] Labor voted
for them anyway, and nobody seemed to notice the new bar on prosecuting
police. From September 2018, police officers in the Territory had an astonishing new defence available to them: if they committed what might otherwise
be a crime, they only needed to show that they honestly *believed* they had
acted reasonably.[64] In other words, unless an officer can be exposed as a liar
in court, they're likely to be practically immune from prosecution.

Just over a year later, nineteen-year-old Warlpiri man – known since
his death as Kumanjayi Walker – breached a court order imposed for (non-
violent) property crimes. Nearly three decades earlier, the deaths in custody
royal commission had recommended that such breaches be met with summonses, not arrests, yet Territory courts still routinely issue arrest warrants in
these circumstances. Walker travelled to Yuendumu to attend his great-uncle's
funeral. Funerals frequently prompt breaches of court orders in the Territory
because those orders – imposed by settler judges – routinely fail to account for
funeral obligations in Indigenous communities. Walker then evaded arrest by
two local officers in Yuendumu by threatening them with an axe. Those officers, who knew Walker, said they never felt he was going to hurt them, and
that it appeared that he'd mainly wanted to escape re-arrest. The local officers
revised their arrest plan and decided to wait until after the funeral.

In the Alice Springs police station, Constable Zachary Rolfe saw video
footage of the 'axe incident', which had been captured by the Yuendumu
officers' body-worn cameras. He thought they were 'greatly downplaying'
the incident. He recommended the Immediate Response Team (IRT), of
which he was a member, be deployed to Yuendumu. There's a difference
between local police, who live in communities and prioritise non-violent
methods, and the IRT. Rolfe later told the Supreme Court: 'I characterised
[Walker] as a high-risk offender, extremely violent, who was ... willing to
use potentially lethal weapons against police.' But he didn't speak with the
Yuendumu officers, and had never met Walker.

Rolfe's superiors developed a plan to arrest Walker at 5 a.m. on the day after the funeral. But this plan was not, it seems, communicated effectively to Rolfe and his IRT colleagues. They drove to Yuendumu the afternoon of the funeral, and after a very short briefing in the police station, they went looking for Walker. Rolfe entered one house – number 577 – and searched each room, with his hand on his Glock pistol. More senior officers, including those responsible for training NT police, later told the court that Rolfe wasn't acting consistently with his training or with documented procedures, especially with children in the house. Rolfe maintained otherwise. The officers moved to houses 511 and 518. Senior police told the court they should have formed a plan and established a cordon. Rolfe claimed that would have been 'impossible' with 'only' five officers and a dog. The IRT officers, it seems, responded to the axe incident not by planning Walker's safe arrest but by preparing to use greater force to effect it. Outside house 511, one officer was brandishing an assault rifle. A woman asked why and said it looked like police wanted to shoot someone. 'Someone probably shouldn't run at police with an axe,' another officer, Adam Eberl, replied.

Rolfe and Eberl approached the front door of house 511. Inside they saw a young man who, it would soon emerge, was Walker. Walker gave a false name, but Rolfe suspected he had his man. Despite characterising Walker as a 'high-risk' offender, Rolfe failed to notice Walker's hand in or near his pocket, which is basic police training. Rolfe moved up close to Walker to identify him using pictures on his phone he'd taken from a crucial email – the one detailing the Sunday arrest plan – he claimed he hadn't read in full. Senior police said Rolfe unnecessarily placed himself in a high-risk position. Deaths in custody are rife with evidence of police and guards escalating risk like this. New Zealand police don't routinely carry guns and tend to be better at avoiding situations in which they might need to use one.

When the officers moved to arrest him, Walker stabbed Rolfe in the chest with a pair of scissors, causing a small wound. Rolfe told the court he instinctively reached for his Glock and noticed Walker's hand already on it. When he made that allegation in court, it was the first time he'd done so. He hadn't issued commands to Walker, nor had he warned Eberl. He hadn't reported it to his colleagues afterwards. He didn't mention it in an interview he gave to Kristin Shorten, a journalist with *The Australian*, the following month. The prosecutor suggested he was lying to the court. Rolfe denied it. Eberl restrained Walker from behind. Rolfe said Walker was continuing to stab at Eberl with his right hand. That can't be made out on the footage and Eberl neither complained about it nor had any injuries, apart from a scratch on his left arm. Rolfe drew his Glock and fired one shot into Walker's torso.

Immediately after the first shot, Eberl tackled Walker onto a mattress and began 'ground stabilising' him. In the footage, Walker can be seen lying on his right side, with Eberl above him. Walker's right arm – the one holding the scissors – can't be seen. Eberl told the court he believed Walker's right arm was underneath his own body. A biomechanics expert said that even if it wasn't, any force Walker was able to muster would have been minimal and easily dealt with by Eberl. Rolfe told the court he saw Walker continuing to stab Eberl's neck, chest and shoulder. Nothing in the footage or any of the other evidence is consistent with this. Rolfe told the court he didn't have enough time to shout anything. He did, however, have time to place his left hand on Eberl's back, and shoot two more rounds into Walker's torso. When Eberl realised what had happened, Rolfe said 'It's all good, he was stabbing me, he was stabbing you.' In court, Rolfe explained he said those words not to justify what he'd just done but to help Eberl 'come down' from a state of 'auditory exclusion'. It seemed patently unbelievable. The second or third shot caused catastrophic injuries, and Walker died in the police station soon afterwards.

The footage captured by Rolfe and Eberl's body-worn cameras showed a shooting that appeared to be so obviously unnecessary and unlawful that the (then) Director of Public Prosecutions, Jack Karczewski, very quickly recommended that Rolfe be charged with murder. There would be no repeat of the delay that had led to Whittington's acquittal. At the trial, Rolfe contradicted his superiors on training and defensive tactics. Prosecutor Philip Strickland tied him in logical knots, leaving him unable to say why, despite apparently being so well trained, he failed to take even the most basic precautions against a person he'd determined was extremely violent. Eberl could easily have endorsed Rolfe's claims about Walker's right hand. He didn't.

The court system bent over backwards to ensure the fairest possible trial for Rolfe. Upon being charged with murder, Rolfe was immediately bailed – and allowed to leave the Northern Territory – by a (white) judge in a secret out-of-court session: nobody else charged with murder had ever received the same treatment. His trial was moved away from Alice Springs, which is relatively easy for Walker's family to travel to, and held in Darwin, whose population (and potential jury pool) includes proportionally many fewer

Aboriginal people. In part because of laws that erect multiple barriers to Indigenous participation on juries, all twelve members were settlers – and one even had a sister who was a serving police officer.[65] Most crucially of all, evidence that showed Rolfe's tendency to use unnecessary and even unlawful force when arresting Indigenous suspects was ruled inadmissible, as was evidence that would have damaged Rolfe's credibility in the eyes of the jury.

The jury wasn't told of an occasion in January 2018, when Rolfe had attended a house in Alice Springs and pursued a man who lived there – Malcolm, the *father* of the man police had arrived to question – into a bedroom, punched him in the head, grabbed his hair and slung him to the ground, knocking him unconscious. (This is what a judge – Greg Borchers, as it happens – found had 'likely' occurred.) Malcolm later needed sixteen stitches to close two head wounds. Rolfe then allegedly created false records claiming that Malcolm had repeatedly swung punches at him and his colleague, and had also – according to Rolfe's then-fiancée – asked a detective to scratch his face after the incident so that there was fabricated 'evidence' to substantiate his claims.[66] (Rolfe denies this.) Malcolm was arrested and charged with assaulting a police officer. He defended the charge, and Borchers acquitted him after seeing video footage captured by Malcolm's wife and by the officers' body-worn cameras. 'Constable Rolfe's evidence lacks credibility,' Borchers found. 'He lied.'[67] Nor was the jury told about another incident in April 2019, when Rolfe chased a seventeen-year-old Indigenous boy, Cleveland, until he stopped and voluntarily laid down. Cleveland said Rolfe then banged his head into a rock several times, causing a wound that needed four stitches.[68] Prosecutors alleged Rolfe again created false records to explain Cleveland's injury.[69] And nor was it told of other incidents, in April 2017, and February, September and October 2019, in which Rolfe used what a detective senior sergeant described as 'unnecessary force' against Aboriginal men, often causing them injuries – in one case a large gash on the forehead that required nine stitches – before, again, making what prosecutors alleged to be a false statement to retrospectively justify his actions. After reviewing the available evidence in relation to these incidents, the detective senior sergeant concluded that Rolfe 'uses quite heavy-handed tactics', 'consistently fails to use effective communication as a tactical option to defuse a situation' and had chosen tactical options that 'resulted in injuries to subjects and the potential for injury to himself, which could easily have been avoided'.[70] Rolfe's ex-fiancée, also a former police officer, claimed he'd told her 'numerous' times that he'd like to shoot someone so that he'd get a 'paid extended holiday' while they investigated him.[71] (Rolfe denies this too.) Had this material – which impugned Rolfe's honesty – been admitted into evidence, it would have been much more difficult for Rolfe to convince the jury he honestly believed he needed to shoot Kumanjayi Walker.

Rolfe was acquitted after the jury deliberated for less than a day. The tendency evidence remained suppressed for the next week, during which *The Australian* presented Rolfe as a good cop who, he said, had been 'thrown under the bus' by police command, which had 'sacrificed [him] to appease a crowd', namely, Elders and others in Yuendumu. By the end of the week, the police union and the opposition leader, the CLP's Lia Finocchiaro, were leading a popular campaign claiming that Rolfe should never have been charged. Once more, the settler justice system had engineered the acquittal of a white police officer. The particulars – *how* it did so – were remarkably familiar: a gun against an 'edged weapon'; a special law protecting police; a scandalised settler population; an all-settler jury; dubious claims of self-defence. It was as if the 234 years since Phillip's arrival was barely any time at all. After the trial, Aboriginal communities called for change. 'No guns in the remote community', insisted senior Warlpiri man Ned Hargreaves, who had attended every day of the trial. 'Enough is enough.' In July 2022, police confirmed Rolfe would be returning to work in Darwin.

All-white juries

Settler juries are nothing if not consistent when considering charges laid against white people for killing Indigenous people. A publican who choked Victor 'Binky' Simpson to death in Geraldton in 1986 was acquitted by an all-settler jury, which presumably concluded the publican had used 'reasonable force' to evict him.[72] Two white men who had found twenty-year-old Leslie Sampi, an intellectually disabled Aboriginal man, sitting on one of their cars and then dragged him off it, 'bashed him repeatedly on the head with a 3 kilogram lump of concrete', jumped on him 'with such force that the walls of his heart were torn' and 'stabbed him in the chest and then slashed his throat with a knife' were also acquitted of murder by an all-white jury (though one of the men was convicted of manslaughter).[73] On 29 August 2016, a white man in his fifties went driving around Kalgoorlie in his ute looking for two children's motorcycles that had been stolen from him. He found one being driven by fourteen-year-old Elijah Doughty. (There was no evidence he'd been the thief.) He chased Elijah, driving so closely behind him that (he said later) he had no time to react when Elijah swerved in front of him. He ran over the teenager, killing him: when Elijah's body was found 34 metres from the wreckage of the bike, his skull was split in half, his brain stem snapped, his spinal cord was severed, most of his ribs were broken, his pelvis was fractured, and his leg and ankle were 'mangled'.[74] The driver was charged with manslaughter and acquitted by an all-settler jury, which instead found him guilty of dangerous driving causing death. Although that charge carried a maximum sentence of ten years, he was sentenced to just three years' imprisonment and served nineteen months.[75] Hannah McGlade has described all-white juries as 'a symptom of structural racism'.[76]

○

This chapter has told a mere handful of the many thousands of stories the settler justice system generates every year. I would argue that they're representative rather than exceptional. Many, perhaps most, settler Australians who are drawn into the justice system's arcane processes find the experience disillusioning and alienating. Yet this is the system we continue to inflict on the people who were here first, who were (and must logically still be) the sovereign owners of this continent's lands.

'The poor bastards just need something to do.' Speaking to me is a sitting judge of the Northern Territory's Local Court. We're standing in the searing sun in one of the Aboriginal communities the court visits once a month or so, during the court's lunch break. Like all judges, this one isn't afraid to use prison, and probably uses it more often than others. 'It's got nothing to do with *self-determination* or whatever is the fashionable language in the southern states these days.' He lets the term drip with his disdain. 'It's about *jobs*, getting them to contribute to something meaningful. But they all get this bloody sit-down money and it's killing them.'

'But isn't the whole concept of self-determination,' I ask the judge, 'about the right of a community to decide what's meaningful for them, without having priorities forced on them?' I had in mind those Canadian studies which seem to show that suicide rates – tragically high among First Nations communities as a consequence of dispossession – were lowest among those with high levels of 'cultural continuity': language transmission, land rights, self-governance, control over services.[77]

'No, no, no, we went through all that rubbish in the '70s,' the judge scoffs, a generation wearier than my naive idealism. Less than half an hour ago, we'd been facing each other in the council meeting room, which doubles as a court-room, me throwing up reasons he's heard a thousand times before to urge him to keep out of prison a twenty-year-old who'd brought alcohol into his dry community, and a mother of three who'd driven a car to work eight months after she'd been disqualified. The other way of seeing what had been happening is that he and I had been colluding on the imposition of settler law onto a community that would no doubt decide its own disputes if it were allowed to.

'I'll tell you what self-determination looks like,' the judge said suddenly. 'It's Elders fucking little kids' faces through a fence. It's teenage girls being too afraid to take off their clothes when they shower. It's a pathetic people totally destroyed by grog and weed and syphilis.' Not for the first time, I wonder whether judges need time-limits built into their tenures. There must be a cost – emotional, even psychological – to hearing over and over again about the worst things people do. Immediately before their appointment, most magistrates (and Local Court 'judges' in the Northern Territory) were senior lawyers working in interesting legal areas. Ninety-five per cent – or more – of what they sit through as magistrates must be repetitive, monoto-nous and vicariously traumatic. High salaries don't protect against cynicism.

I could stand there and debate the judge's ideas about First Nations communities. Even if I could get beyond the optics of two white blokes trading views about 'the Aboriginal problem' in an Aboriginal community, though, I'm acutely aware that I need to appear before him this afternoon on behalf of more clients who hope they won't be flown to Darwin in hand-cuffs. Fifteen minutes later, we're back in court. I usher my client inside and direct him to sit next to me. His English isn't spectacular but he assures me he doesn't want an interpreter. He's pleading guilty to an assault charge. He pushed his wife against a wall during an argument. She wasn't injured, but the Territory's mandatory sentencing laws mean he's going to prison for three months unless the judge is convinced there are 'exceptional circum-stances' that justify a less severe penalty. He looks nervous. I glance briefly at the judge before indicating to the court staff I'm ready to go. The judge gives me the briefest hint of a collegial nod, and resumes his poker face. We're the professionals here, the guardians of our law, dispensing justice to the wretched. 'All rise,' the court staff demands, and we all stand up. 'The Local Court has resumed. Please be seated.'

THE DEFENDERS

Why Aboriginal and Torres Strait Islander Legal Services are so important, and how they fail

Building defences

In May 1964, a group of white students from Sydney University held a demonstration in support of African Americans outside the US Consulate in Sydney. Media coverage was international, and much of it pointed to the obvious irony of white Australian students demonstrating against racial discrimination elsewhere while apparently saying nothing about the increasingly notorious White Australia policy or the legal discrimination against Indigenous people. There was some very low-hanging fruit for protesting students looking for problems. Senior Australian politicians – including Arthur Calwell, then opposition leader – had explicitly advocated a clear distinction be maintained in people's minds between South African apartheid and Australian discrimination.[1] So student newspapers went looking for racial discrimination in Australia, and found plenty. Protests were arranged for July 1964. 'Student Action For Aborigines' – SAFA – was established later that year, with soccer star Charles Perkins as its chairperson. SAFA's first political act was a bus tour of western New South Wales in February 1965: it became known as a 'freedom ride', modelled on the equivalent tour that had left Washington DC for southern states nearly four years earlier.[2]

As the SAFA bus wound its way through Walgett and Gulargambone, Tenterfield and Moree, its young settler participants found Australia's own brand of segregation and discrimination. Cafes where Aboriginal and Torres Strait Islander customers couldn't sit down. Pools in which their kids couldn't swim. Staunchly conservative RSL men who were 'doing as they pleased' with Indigenous women and girls after dark. As a consciousness-raising exercise, the Freedom Ride was extraordinarily effective. 'For the first time,' historian Adam Shoemaker later recalled, mainstream media interest was 'marshalled in favour of the Black Australian cause.'[3]

The Ride also sparked the imaginations of young Indigenous people. Gumbaynggir man Gary Foley, expelled from school in Nambucca Heads in the wake of the Ride, came to Sydney and to Redfern in 1967 under a government apprentice scheme. There, he met other similarly minded young people, including Paul Coe (from Cowra, also in Sydney on an apprenticeship scheme), Michael Anderson and Billy Craigie. New legislation following the 1967 referendum abolished the old 'protection' regime and removed many of the formal sources of discrimination from New South Wales law.[4] As a consequence, Indigenous people were freer to meet, to talk and to plan. A strong community cohered in and around Redfern during these years. There was football and boxing, there were dances at the Foundation for Aboriginal Affairs (FAA) and there was pool at the Clifton Hill and Empress hotels. Sam Juparulla Wickman, originally from Alice Springs and later an archaeologist, recalled a 'network of people that you knew' and 'felt safe around' – and that there was 'politics in the air'.[5]

The FAA had set itself up in an old funeral parlour near Central Station, at 810 George Street. Gary Foley recalls that by 1968, the FAA was the main meeting point for 'the increasing number of young arrivals from the bush and more established Koori city-dwellers'. A discussion group emerged, comprising Foley, Paul and Isobel Coe, Gary Williams and Tony Coorey, among others. Energised by a speech delivered by Vincent Lingiari, they talked about and generated support for the Gurindji who had struck and walked off the Wave Hill Cattle Station to what is now Daguragu in August 1966. They discussed the radical American literature of Malcolm X, Stokely Carmichael, Bobby Seale and the Black Panthers, and Angela Davis, which they sourced from Bob Gould's Third World Bookshop at Woollahra. They also drew on the accumulated wisdom of older hands, including Perkins, Faith Bandler, Chicka Dixon and Dulcie Flowers.[6]

Bob Maza and Bruce McGuinness, president and director of the Aborigines Advancement League ('the League') in Thornbury, arranged for Dr Pauulu Kamarakafego (then known as Roosevelt Brown) to visit from the Caribbean. Kamarakafego was in Bermuda's parliament, but his visit caused a stir because he was also chair of the Caribbean and Latin

American Black Power Movement. Following Kamarakafego's Northcote speech, the League released a 'Statement on Black Power':

> To use the words of Jean-Paul Satre [sic.], 'Not so very long ago, the earth numbered two thousand million inhabitants: five hundred million men, and one thousand five hundred million natives.'
>
> That is white power.
>
> Since the end of World War II, many of the coloured peoples who lived under white colonial rule have gained their independence and coloured minorities in multi-racial nations are claiming the right to determine the course of their own affairs in contradiction to the inferior state under which they had lived.
>
> That is black power.[7]

Foley recalled later that Kamarakafego's visit, and their reading, shook the Redfern group out of a temporary malaise that followed the 1967 referendum. More than 90 per cent of the country voted 'Yes', but their reality in Redfern was still nightly confrontations with NSW police and its notoriously brutal 21st Division which, as Shirley 'Mum Shirl' Smith recalled, would regularly 'drive in, load paddy wagons full of Blacks, and charge them with being drunk' – even though 'quite a lot of the people arrested like this were not only not drunk, but they didn't even drink, ever'.[8]

A cousin of Paul Coe's, Pat Wedge, was shot and killed by police at St Peters train station. When Ken Brindle and Mum Shirl, who was Coe's aunty, went to Newtown Police Station to ask about Wedge's death, Brindle was bashed. Foley was arrested on a flimsy charge at Central Station. And Charles Perkins himself was arrested in Alice Springs shortly after he'd complained about a publican. Sam Watson later recalled:

> all those years when I was growing up we were absolutely terrified of coppers. Blue uniforms used to smash the shit out of us, boom, boom, boom, and we'd all cop it. We were so powerless, so vulnerable. We had no legal service, we had no friends, we had no white supporters, nothing. We'd just get smashed on the streets and then left there, and killed in the jails and left there, and raped, our women would be raped constantly by coppers, and we could never do anything about it.[9]

'What the Sydney Aborigines understood intuitively,' Perkins' biographer Peter Read observed, 'was the brutal reality of Aboriginal daily life.'[10]

So, Foley and his group adapted the 'Pig Patrol' – the countersurveillance network set up by Bobby Seale and Huey Newton's Black Panther Party for Self-Defense in Oakland, California, in 1966 – to the streets of Redfern. One Saturday evening in 1969 they began 'observing and collecting information on the regular police raids' on the Empress Hotel. They also shared their ideas with Indigenous activists in other cities, and similar countersurveillance activities began in Melbourne, Brisbane and Adelaide. In response, police increased their numbers, their surveillance, their harassment and their violence. Over coming months, Foley's group collected what he called 'extensive evidence of arbitrary arrests, beatings, wrongful imprisonment' and other illegal activities by police.[11]

The question soon became: what to do with all this evidence? Giving it to journalists had limited value. By now, though, Paul Coe had commenced a law degree at the University of NSW, where Hal Wootten was appointed Foundation Dean in 1969 after a career at the bar.[12] Politics was indeed 'in the air' during the late 1960s, as increasing numbers of young people involved themselves in the growing movements against the war in Vietnam and apartheid in South Africa, and for women's and then gay liberation. Paul Coe recalled later that he and his Redfern group spoke regularly with people involved in these movements. 'We raised these issues and drew the parallel,' he told the ABC's Jon Faine later. 'We made people aware that similar conditions existed in their own country, under our noses.' The Redfern activists convinced white activists they had 'a moral obligation' to do something about the oppression experienced by First Nations people. 'We were then able to build up a system of support,' Coe said.[13]

Coe approached some non-Indigenous law students, including Peter Tobin and Eddie Neumann who were already known as friends to First Nations communities. Tobin and Neumann began spending their Friday and Saturday evenings at hotels in Redfern, where they saw the police harassment first-hand, and then followed arrested Indigenous people to the police station, where they raised bail.[14] Tobin and Neumann approached Wootten, who was initially sceptical of the accounts the students were giving him. Wootten had appeared as John Kerr's junior counsel on behalf of the pastoralists in the mid-1960s Equal Wages case. But he agreed to see for himself, and was shocked:

I visited Redfern and saw that any Aborigine on the streets of Redfern after 10.15 p.m., even if quietly walking home, was bundled into a patrolling paddy wagon. The standard charge was public drunkenness, but naturally such treatment often led to [a] reaction by an indignant Aborigine which escalated both to additional charges of resisting arrest and assault police, and to physical retaliation by police. In addition, police regularly patrolled hotels frequented by Aborigines, particularly the Empress, and their heavy-handed treatment and oppressive scrutiny of Aborigines often led to violent incidents in and outside the hotel bars.[15]

Police were enforcing their own unofficial curfew in response to what they saw as a serious social problem: if they could just get Aboriginal people off the streets at night, they rationalised, they'd prevent most of the more serious offences – assaults, thefts, burglaries – that would invariably take place otherwise. But an undeclared, unlawful curfew that applied to *all* Aboriginal people, regardless of whether they were suspected of criminal activity, was discriminatory and probably illegal, though the *Racial Discrimination Act* was still five years away.

'Well, you're not going to do any good by taking a few cases [to court] to teach the police a lesson,' Wootten told Coe and Tobin. 'The police would be all the harder when the lawyers go home.' Wootten suggested they set up a permanent Aboriginal Legal Service, drawing on existing levels of sympathy and idealism among the Sydney legal profession. An ALS wouldn't just take the odd case. It would represent Aboriginal and Torres Strait Islander defendants continuously in the courts.[16]

On 11 October 1970, in a room at the back of St Luke's Presbyterian Church, a meeting resolved to establish an ALS, to be staffed by volunteer lawyers and overseen by a council, a third of whom were Aboriginal. Wootten became its president. They secured a vacant shop at 142 Regent Street (it's now a massage parlour) and began a walk-in, shop-front legal service. Meanwhile, Wootten wrote submissions requesting government funding. And on 29 December 1970, Bill Wentworth, then Aboriginal affairs minister, announced an initial grant of just over $20,000 to pay for one lawyer, a field officer and an office staff.[17] For the first time, Indigenous people charged with criminal offences could go to their own lawyers.

The Redfern model quickly spread to other cities and towns. It's difficult to understate its significance. In the 'protection' era, for instance, government officers would routinely decide every aspect of cases against First Nations defendants – including whether they needed lawyers, what pleas should be entered and which witnesses should be called.[18] In Melbourne during the 1950s and '60s, Indigenous people charged with criminal offences could hope to be represented pro bono by sympathetic white lawyers, or else by Doug Nicholls, former VFL footballer turned social worker and field officer with the Advancement League. Following Legal Aid reforms in 1969, more private lawyers accepted criminal defence work representing clients who couldn't pay – though their lack of experience working with First Nations people meant that often they struggled to take meaningful instructions from their clients.[19] Jim Berg later recalled that Indigenous people charged with crimes often had a 'very junior' government solicitor represent them. 'And consequently,' Berg told Faine, 'nine times out of ten, the Koori client went to jail.'[20]

Quite aside from the problems inherent in the legal system itself, most First Nations people's access to adequate legal services was inadequate. In May 1972, Elizabeth Eggleston – who two years earlier had completed her groundbreaking thesis, which documented the 'endemic discrimination' experienced by Indigenous people at all points in the justice system[21] (see chapter 9) – invited Wootten to Monash University to talk about the Redfern ALS. The next month, a meeting at Melbourne University – which included Eggleston, future foreign minister Gareth Evans, League directors Bruce McGuinness and Stewart Murray, and Koori leaders from across Victoria, including Jim Berg and Elizabeth Hoffman – resolved to establish a Victorian ALS ('VALS') in Fitzroy's Gertrude Street. Four decades later I briefly worked there, after its premises had shifted to Preston.

Following Labor's election in 1972, the Whitlam government was convinced of the need for ALS practices all over the country, and funded them out of federal coffers. Within a decade of that first grant of just over $20,000, the Aboriginal affairs department was allocating nearly $5 million annually to ALS services.[22] Similar ALS services were started in most places with significant Indigenous populations, replacing existing and clearly inadequate arrangements.[23]

Dream and reality

Aboriginal Legal Services proved to be no panacea. Twenty years after the Redfern ALS began, Paul Coe said their existence had 'proven that the character of racism is so deeply entrenched and engrained in the Australian make-up, and in particular the Australian police forces, that it's going to take generations before that attitude and that facet of racism can be weeded out'.[24] The ALS was briefly able to broker an Aboriginal–police liaison committee, but it had ceased to function by 1975. (Similar agreements have since been made – and broken – in other states and territories.) The harassment continued. Police began arresting the Aboriginal *staff* of the ALS on what Coe and Tobin called trumped-up charges. Clashes between police and First Nations people in Redfern – often described in media as 'riots' – continued throughout the 1980s.[25]

On 27 April 1989, eight officers of the Special Weapons and Operations Squad armed with shotguns and a sledgehammer stormed into a residential house looking for a suspect in the recent murder of a police member. Their suspect wasn't inside, but David Gundy was, in his bedroom. Police shot and killed the twenty-nine-year-old father. Their claim that the shooting was accidental was accepted by the coroner,[26] though not by deaths in custody commissioner Hal Wootten, who found that 'police had no right to be in David Gundy's bedroom much less to point a loaded and cocked shotgun at him'. The similarities to Walker's death in Yuendumu three decades later are uncanny. 'One detects an assumption', Wootten observed of police attitudes following Gundy's death, 'that the law will look after police acting to catch a serious criminal, and inconvenient legal rules can be safely ignored'.[27] As police numbers soared, excessive police violence in Redfern continued throughout the 1990s and into the next century. When Indigenous people 'rioted' following the death of seventeen-year-old T.J. Hickey, who was impaled on a metal fence during a police chase on 14 February 2004, authorities responded by announcing a new $6 million, seven-storey police station in Redfern.[28]

A similar story was repeated across the country. First Nations people were being represented when they were charged, and police were occasionally being sued, but ALS services couldn't reform police–Indigenous relations, or prevent the over-policing of Indigenous people, any more than the United Nations can prevent war crimes. And during the 1980s, Settler Australia began organising a major backlash against First Nations rights. John Howard's Coalition government, elected in 1996, famously rejected self-determination in line with its broader attack on what historian Geoffrey Blainey called the 'black armband' account of Australian history and culture.[29]

In the new era of backlash, Indigenous Legal Services have faced regular threats from governments wanting to slash or freeze funding. Governments have rarely followed through, especially as prison populations have continued to swell with Indigenous inmates. But what governments have done successfully is to persuade existing ALS services to amalgamate, usually under a threat to withdraw funding.[30] Federal governments now clearly prefer to fund a single state or territory ALS, which is presumably cheaper than funding local organisations on the principle of self-determination. They'll even fund services across state borders. There are legitimate questions about whether ALS organisations should be signing contracts that go against the spirit of self-determination. In 2015, VALS controversially took over the contract previously held by the Tasmanian Aboriginal Centre: an organisation based in Melbourne's northern suburbs now provides Aboriginal legal services to Aboriginal people across Tasmania.

Failures of advocacy

Aboriginal Legal Services are now a far cry from the makeshift three-person operation that opened in Regent Street, Redfern, in 1970. Former stockman Graham Campbell was the single field officer in Katherine's Regional Aboriginal Legal Aid Service (KRALAS) during the late 1980s and '90s. He recalls gathering police briefs from police in Katherine, bundling them into his car and then driving out to places like Ngukurr or Kalkaringi, where he'd take whatever instructions he could get from clients. He'd then lay out the briefs on the trestle table inside the makeshift courtroom to await the arrival of KRALAS's single lawyer, who'd fly in with the magistrate the next morning and race through the court list based on Campbell's hastily scribbled notes. With six full-time criminal defence lawyers, NAAJA's office in Katherine now has remarkable capacity compared with those early days. Employing more than 170 full-time staff, NAAJA is now among the Northern Territory's largest non-government entities, a 'justice agency' that provides a formidable check on government and police power.

At least, it should be. What follows is an account that draws from my own experiences working at the North Australian Aboriginal Justice Agency (NAAJA) between 2017 and 2019. It contains criticisms which are shared by many people who worked for NAAJA during this period, and since. I and others raised our concerns with executive management, to little avail. I'm not suggesting for a minute that NAAJA is responsible for problems caused by bad laws, excessive police surveillance and acquiescent courts. But NAAJA does occupy a position with unique advantages within the settler state's justice apparatus, and it has an opportunity to lead public conversations on behalf of its clients, whose powerlessness is very close to total. Ultimately, by including this account I'm fulfilling a promise to a person who is no longer here.

When I arrived in Katherine in mid-2017, the Royal Commission into the Protection and Detention of Children in the Northern Territory had been running for a year. George Brandis's office had given NAAJA $1.1 million to run a legal advisory service to support the commission.[31] For two years, dedicated staff combed the length and breadth of the Territory, talking to children who had been abused and assaulted in custody, and to their families. So it was something of a surprise that NAAJA was staying silent – at least publicly – on some very concerning developments.[32]

1. Use of Force guidelines

In February 2017, a judge threw out charges against a twelve-year-old boy because a police sergeant, Ben Watson, had tasered him in the back. Watson's use of the taser wasn't illegal, incredibly, but it was against the NT police force's own 'Use of Force' guidelines.[33] In response, the National Children's Commissioner, Megan Mitchell, said police and governments should eliminate the use of tasers against children.[34] But her NT equivalent, the head of the police union and the chief minister all publicly endorsed the use of tasers against children, even while a royal commission was hearing evidence about the mistreatment and abuse of children by authorities.[35] NAAJA – the Aboriginal Justice Agency – had an opportunity to publicly defend the rights and welfare of Aboriginal children. But NAAJA said nothing. Even a fortnight later, when he was interviewed for the ABC's *Law Report*, NAAJA's principal legal officer (and the first Aboriginal person to hold that position), David Woodroffe, stopped well short of advocating a taser ban against children.[36]

Guidelines, instructions, restrictions and limitations on what police officers can or should do in particular situations are contained in General Orders, made from time to time by the police commissioner. The 'Use of Force' Order, in place since 2012, contained detailed restrictions and limitations on when officers should consider using tasers, batons, tear gas and guns – and when they shouldn't. In court, General Orders can be very useful to defence lawyers seeking to determine what a police officer was thinking about when he or she deployed a taser, or made an arrest. But on 14 June 2018, the then commissioner of NT Police, Reece Kershaw, replaced the 'Use of Force' General Order. The new order contained none of the restrictions, limitations or instructions which had been in the old one. In fact, it said very little at all. A spokesperson told the ABC that police wanted to do away with 'prescriptive content' as part of 'a project to streamline and rationalise police General Orders'. In other words, Kershaw wanted his officers to be less accountable. Had Watson tasered the twelve-year-old child after June 2018, the child's lawyers would have found it much more difficult to argue that the sergeant's actions were 'improper', because they wouldn't have been able to compare Watson's actions against the operational guidelines. Charges like resisting arrest and assaulting police – commonly laid against Indigenous people – depend on police officers doing the right thing during an arrest: if prosecutors can't prove they did, then the charges fail, which is what happened when the tasered twelve-year-old child's charges were thrown out. But in response to Kershaw's decision, NAAJA said nothing publicly.

In July 2019, Reece Kershaw was appointed commissioner of the Australian Federal Police, the organisation he'd joined as a junior police officer in 1988. On 25 July, NAAJA issued a public statement congratulating him. 'On behalf of my Board and Management we want to pay tribute to Commissioner Kershaw and thank him for all his hard work for Aboriginal people in the Northern Territory,' said NAAJA's CEO, Eastern Arrernte woman Priscilla Atkins, in the release. It had been over a year since NAAJA's previous media release.

2. Armed police in schools

The Royal Commission into the Protection and Detention of Children in the Northern Territory always played differently among the Territory's settler population, beset by a persistent panic about property crime by Indigenous kids. Even as the royal commission was hearing evidence, schools, teachers, principals and parents in Darwin, Katherine and Alice Springs began calling for the return of police officers to schools.[37] Unarmed police had been in the Territory's schools since the mid-1980s, but an outcry following a decision to have them carry guns led to the program's abandonment.[38] In mid-September 2018 the new education minister, Selena Uibo, herself a Nunggubuyu woman and a former teacher, announced the new 'School-Based Police' initiative. Police would return to ten government schools at the beginning of Term 4. They would be armed with guns, sprays and batons.[39]

Many lawyers working at NAAJA, including myself, became concerned. Reinstating armed police in schools had not been recommended in the royal commission's November 2017 report. The ten schools were also among those with the highest proportions of First Nations students enrolled.[40] We assumed that NAAJA would want to do everything it could to prevent the program's rollout. Priscilla Atkins wrote to the child welfare minister in early October 2018. NAAJA 'strongly opposes' police in schools being armed, she said, and asked some of the questions staff had raised.

The government ignored NAAJA's concerns. Publicly, NAAJA said nothing. Other civil sector organisations were alarmed. 'It actually drove a stake of fear through my heart,' said Shahleena Musk, then a senior lawyer with the Human Rights Law Centre in Melbourne. A Larrakia woman, Musk grew up in Darwin and attended schools with police on campus. She was also a senior youth lawyer at NAAJA before moving south. 'I had a number of children [as clients] who were arrested within their classroom, handcuffed by police and marched out of school,' she told the ABC.[41] The research on police in schools is clear: police in schools are only beneficial when their role is limited to improving relations with the school community.[42] 'In principle,' staff were told, 'NAAJA is not opposed to school-based policing.'

In the end, police returned to department schools across the Territory. Some carried their weapons; others didn't. The following May, the education department released the report of its 'evaluation' of the School-Based Police program's first six months. One student told the review that the presence of police outside the school gates had seemingly contributed to truancy.[43] Some Aboriginal-controlled and other civil sector organisations criticised it. But on behalf of NAAJA, Atkins and another manager told the review 'that they had no problems and hadn't received any complaints about the Police in Schools Program', remarking that 'the implementation to date had been "smooth sailing"'.[44]

3. Tear gas

In November 2017, the Royal Commission into the Protection and Detention of Children in the Northern Territory recommended that the use of CS gas – tear gas – in youth detention centres be absolutely banned.[45] About a year later, on 6 November 2018, the police Territory Response Group (TRG) was called into a disturbance at Don Dale Youth Detention Centre. Footage later leaked to the ABC showed officers in full riot gear aiming assault rifles at unarmed teenagers during what police and the government called an eight-hour 'siege' of the centre. It also shows the boys arming themselves with makeshift weapons before police tear gassed them. The last time children had been gassed on national TV was in July 2016, on the *Four Corners* episode that prompted a horrified Malcom Turnbull to appoint a royal commission within just ten hours. But in response to the leaked video of the November 2018 gassing, there was no political outrage, no prime ministerial proclamation and no major public inquiry. Chief Minister Michael Gunner simply said the police had his support. His government moved the teenagers to the police watch house in Darwin.

NAAJA said nothing, at least publicly. The twenty-four children in the watch house – twenty-three of whom were Aboriginal – were kept in permanent lockdown. They had no privacy, no access to sunlight, recreational areas or therapeutic services, and no pillows or sheets. And they were exposed to adult offenders. Lawyers ran bail applications for their clients. CLANT's president, Marty Aust, described the watch house conditions as 'completely deplorable'. Jared Sharp, then a Legal Aid lawyer (who had previously worked for NAAJA), called the watch house 'draconian'. Even the Australian Medical Association's NT president demanded the government release the teenagers into rehabilitation programs instead of continuing to lock them up.[46] But NAAJA remained silent.

4. Talking up

Three days after the Don Dale gassing, NAAJA staff were invited to an extraordinary meeting convened by Woodroffe, Atkins and, weirdly, an employee of Territory Families, the government department now responsible for Don Dale. Clearly it wasn't an internal meeting. 'NAAJA has a history of working with governments,' Atkins told staff.

When we had a Liberal government they did what they wanted. They were not interested in anything. It was all about 'tough on crime'. We were lucky if we could get a meeting with them. But Labor is going out of its way to work with NAAJA. We have direct links with ministers. We can contact ministers directly on their mobiles. So we will not go and criticise anyone. Whingeing and complaining doesn't work. They'll just shut the door and they won't let you in. This government holds us in high respect because we don't just run to media.

I wondered how people like Gary Foley and Paul Coe would respond to NAAJA's 'inside the tent' strategy. *The government holds us in high respect?* 'You see the issues on the ground every day,' Atkins acknowledged to the lawyers in the meeting. 'You see the effects of mandatory sentencing, you see the bad treatment by police. But we lobby government regularly and you don't see that.'

She was right. But we, and more importantly Indigenous communities in Katherine and the surrounding region, could also see the results of that behind-the-scenes lobbying. Police numbers continue to increase; police behaviour doesn't improve; and prisons swell with more and more First Nations men, women and children. Governments are acutely aware of a large and loud settler constituency that demands they get tougher and tougher on crime. In the Territory, NAAJA is potentially the most powerful voice for another constituency, which is otherwise much quieter. But if NAAJA tells government 'we don't agree with what you're doing, but don't worry, we won't embarrass you publicly', what incentive does government have to change its approach?

On 25 January 2019, an executive manager again addressed staff after the ABC had published the footage of the children being tear gassed inside Don Dale. Staff were told that the children's behaviour on 8 November in Don Dale was 'pretty violent', and the deployment of paramilitary police and CS gas was 'standard practice'. NAAJA did *not* oppose the use of gas in youth detention centres if it was lawful, staff were told.

When one of its lawyers asked NAAJA to lodge a complaint about judge Greg Borchers (see chapter 12), it declined. Nor did NAAJA comment on the Northern Territory government's decision to build a new youth detention centre – to replace Don Dale – next door to Darwin's existing adult prison, against the royal commission's recommendations. (On that occasion, it fell to John Lawrence, a barrister who had once worked at NAALAS, to call out the government's failings.[47]) And nor had it gone on the record about the inappropriateness of Robert Whittington's appointment as the sergeant in charge of police prosecutions in Katherine (see chapter 12).

5. Plea-guilty lawyers

NAAJA's lawyers in Katherine were told by a very senior Darwin-based colleague – at a weekend retreat in Adelaide River in late 2018 – that too many of them were contesting too many charges too often. There was certainly a culture among the six criminal defence lawyers in Katherine then. I was among them. We arrived in the office early, barely sat down at court, stayed late, worked weekends and took work home with us. Part of the reason for this was that we didn't advise our clients to plead guilty unless there was a good reason to. If police briefs arrived without enough evidence to sustain the charges as laid, we advised their clients to wait for more evidence and put the police to proof at contested hearings. Pleading guilty is by far the easier road. It's much quicker, so courts and governments prefer them. At bush court, when a lawyer has been sweating in the sun for hours taking instructions from clients, running a hearing is the last thing he or she wants to do. It takes time, energy, an effort of will and a kind of courage to put the state to proof in a courtroom that's applying a law already stacked mightily against your client. But this senior colleague told us that judges were getting annoyed by the number of charges we were contesting. We ignored him.

One of the reasons ALS services were established was in response to the problem of the 'plea-guilty lawyers' who don't help their clients fight charges. It's still quite common for private lawyers to accept Legal Aid briefs, push those charges to a contested hearing and then encourage their clients to enter guilty pleas on the day of the hearing: happily for the lawyer, this means they'll get paid the full hearing rate, which is much higher than what they'd be paid if they'd advised their client to plead guilty earlier. Most of the time it's impossible to know what instructions people give their lawyers: those conversations are protected by legal professional privilege. There can be very good reasons as to why a guilty plea can't be entered before the hearing date. But occasionally it's clear what's going on.

In one recent case in the Northern Territory, a teenage girl had accused two boys of indecently assaulting her. Her complaints and statements were detailed, but each time she gave her version – on the 000 call, to attending police, in two separate statements and in what's called a 'child forensic interview' – the details she gave were vastly different. Sometimes she implicated one boy. Sometimes she implicated the other. Once she implied the sexual encounter was consensual. Prosecutors cherry-picked the worst allegations from her various statements. Both boys entered pleas of 'not guilty'. But a couple of hours after the hearing began, one boy's lawyer told the judge he'd changed his plea to 'guilty'. This created difficulties for the other boy's lawyer, because the first boy would now become a witness for the prosecution. Under cross-examination, however, when the girl was asked by the second boy's lawyer to explain the inconsistencies in her various statements, she admitted she'd made up the complaint in a moment of shame and panic, and then hadn't felt able to withdraw it. The second boy was acquitted, but by then the first boy had already pled guilty to a serious crime he couldn't possibly have committed. His lawyer should have been asked to account for the way in which he'd represented his client.[48]

'Plea-guilty lawyers' undermine the entire criminal justice system, which is based on an adversarial relationship between defendants and prosecutors. Such lawyers exist, but I hadn't expected to find them inside the Northern Territory's 'Aboriginal Justice Agency'.

Another very senior Darwin-based lawyer who'd briefly visited Katherine to help out had opened a file for a client, 'Clarkson'. It landed on my desk. I read through the brief. It was a domestic assault. Clarkson's wife had claimed he'd hit her. I read through the senior lawyer's handwritten notes of the instructions he'd taken. It appeared to be a verbatim transcript of their conversation. The notes very clearly indicated Clarkson's instructions: he wanted to plead guilty, despite the mandatory sentencing laws that said he'd be sentenced to at least three months in prison. I was surprised. I'd represented Clarkson before, and I knew he was very unlikely to have given those instructions. Nevertheless, the lawyer's notes were clear. I booked a call to Holtze Prison, where Clarkson was waiting for his court date. 'Clarkson,' I said, 'I'm reading the other lawyer's notes. Just checking you still want to plead guilty?'

'I never said that,' he replied. He told me he wanted to plead *not* guilty. What's more, he told me he'd definitely communicated that to my senior colleague. He told me his version of what happened. There was a clear self-defence case. There were no witnesses who supported the wife's complaint.

Clarkson said my senior colleague 'didn't want to listen' when he tried to tell him what he was telling me. In the end, Clarkson sat on remand for six weeks before the assault charge was dropped on the day of the hearing (after the prosecuting lawyer spoke to his wife, who apparently gave a version of events much closer to Clarkson's than the one in her original statement to police). I asked the senior lawyer about this episode the next time I spoke with him. 'Every client is entitled to change their plea,' he said simply.

On another day, another client showed up in the cells. 'Jonathan' was also charged with a domestic assault. His record showed that he'd been *charged* very often for assaulting his wife, but very often those charges didn't succeed. Indeed, Jonathan had another two outstanding assault charges, which were going to hearing in a few weeks. No doubt their relationship deserved to be described as 'volatile'. Who apart from them could know what its true nature was? Legally, questions like this don't matter. What does matter is the evidence. This time, Jonathan's wife had alleged a very serious assault. But the photographic evidence didn't seem to support her allegations. Jonathan told me he wanted to contest the new charges, and requested that my senior colleague represent him. I called my colleague. 'I think that's about enough, don't you?' I wasn't sure what he meant. 'He's accrued too many charges,' the other lawyer clarified. 'He'll probably need to plead guilty.' I resisted. 'I don't think so,' I said. 'He's obviously beaten a number of these charges in the past, and I doubt the evidence is there for the new one. I can hold onto Jonathan if you like?' 'No, I'll take him,' my senior colleague replied. He did. Jonathan ended up pleading guilty to all three charges and going to prison for a long time.

Conclusions

Aboriginal Legal Services are now much more powerful than the one Gary Foley and Paul Coe began on Regent Street, Redfern, in 1970. They're much bigger, partly because the federal government has continued to expand their funding (with frequent threats to cut it), and partly because it has encouraged them to amalgamate. There are now six very large ALS agencies – the ALS (covering the whole of NSW and the ACT), ATSILS (covering all of Queensland), ALS (WA), VALS (now covering Victoria *and* Tasmania), the Aboriginal Legal Rights Movement (SA) and of course NAAJA, which turns fifty this year (2022).

But as the power of these organisations has expanded, many of them have paradoxically become much less willing to actually use it. I've focused mainly on NAAJA here, but similar criticisms are occasionally made about some of the other Indigenous legal services. VALS, for instance, decided in June 2022 to close its books to new criminal clients for three months, citing the fact that VALS has received virtually no additional funding, despite the state building the nation's largest police force.[49] But a client freeze is a far cry from the way Frank Vincent dealt with rampant over-policing at CAALAS during the 1970s. 'Why aren't they using their power to just break the system completely?' one lawyer asked me rhetorically about VALS. 'Fine, they don't have enough funding to properly represent each client. So just push everything they possibly can to contested hearing. That would hurt the courts and the police, and ultimately the government. Simply closing their books for three months only hurts their clients, and allows Dan Andrews to get off scot-free.' VALS later confirmed it wasn't even keeping track of the numbers it turned away.[50] (The main exception to this criticism about the modern services is the original ALS in New South Wales, which builds its in-court legal advocacy – including its criminal appeals – into its broader law reform agenda. And it should be said that VALS has been instrumental in generating significant public support for families – and for reform – during high-profile inquests.) This criticism is consistent with a wider trend among publicly funded non-government organisations. In 2017, Melbourne University researcher Sarah Maddison and her colleague Andrea Carson found that NGOs 'are now engaging in various forms of what we have called "self-silencing" – treading vary carefully in their advocacy work to avoid the risk of financial insecurity and political retribution'.[51]

But this broader trend among funded NGOs doesn't account for the 'self-silencing' among Aboriginal legal services like NAAJA. Most of the policy NAAJA has traditionally criticised – mandatory sentencing laws, for instance – is made by the government and parliament of the Northern Territory, whereas most of its funding comes from the *federal* attorney-general's department. NAAJA and other services would no doubt be even more nervous than they are if their funding depended on the whims of state and territory governments, which are also responsible for funding police forces, prosecutors, criminal courts and prisons. But it doesn't.

So if fear about the withdrawal of its federal funding doesn't explain NAAJA's recent silence in public debate, what does? NAAJA has seemed more prepared to criticise *federal* government policy – such as the cashless 'income management' of Aboriginal social security recipients – than Territory Labor's policies.[52] NAAJA's recent strategy prioritised behind-closed-doors advocacy. It points to the long-awaited creation in June 2019 of a Custody Notification Service (CNS), which police are obliged to contact every time they arrest an Indigenous person in the Northern Territory, as a recent successful example of its advocacy. But Western Australia and the Northern Territory were in fact the *last* state and territory to get a CNS, nearly three decades after the deaths in custody royal commission recommended them. The Territory's CNS, which is operated by NAAJA with a three-year federal government grant, has several design flaws.[53]

At least since the Gunner government's election in 2016, NAAJA had been reluctant to subject the Territory government to any real public pressure. To explain that, its leaders said that 'government makes decisions and media doesn't'. This confuses power with influence. NAAJA has also explained its fear that if it criticised the Labor government, it would be kicked out of the tent entirely. This seems to betray a misreading of both NAAJA's own power as a strong, Aboriginal-led organisation committed to justice for its client base, *and* the Labor government's self-identification as an entity committed to progressive reform. Predictably, the 'inside the tent' strategy was exposed when, in May 2021, the government abandoned its Royal Commission into the Protection and Detention of Children-recommended reforms and rushed through new laws designed to lock up more Indigenous children.[54] Atkins finally went public. 'There wasn't any consultation with the community,' she told the *7AM* podcast, 'and it goes totally against the recommendations that the NT government has committed to.'[55]

A NEW BEGINNING

Why Settler Australia needs to acknowledge it created the problem and doesn't have the answers

It's 6.15 on a November morning in Darwin. The sun is just about to rise, and I'm sitting in the tiny terminal lounge of one of the many small airlines that operate commercial services across the Top End. The air con is already blasting. I suspect it's always on, like it is in many buildings in this city. Two court officers are with me, as is a prosecutor and a judge. The pilot is weighing our bags, loaded with paper files, each one of which records allegations and evidence of human misery and violence.

All five of us are white. We're about to pile into a ten-seater plane, which will fly us over spectacular, tropical country and drop us into one of the Top End's Indigenous communities, many of which began as church missions. Together, we're a travelling court, which arrives once every month or two and takes over a local meeting room or community hall to dispense justice across plastic trestle tables. When we arrive, we'll be met by two, perhaps three, police officers stationed there. They're white too. One of them will sit inside the courtroom and prosecute the less legally complicated charges. The judge will hand down sentences ranging from good behaviour bonds to prison. He will deliver brief lectures to dozens of offenders, and punish them for breaking the law. It is likely that every single defendant will be an Aboriginal or Torres Strait Islander person.

'They're very interesting, the people over that way.' The judge is talking not about the community we're about to fly into, but another one, a Warlpiri community called Lajamanu, established on Gurindji Country in 1949 after the fourth time the Northern Territory government forcibly relocated Warlpiri people from Yuendumu. (On the first three occasions, the relocated Warlpiri, in protest at being forced to work for their rations, walked

back to Yuendumu over the Tanami Desert.)[1] 'They insist on having a meeting with me every couple of months, just to remind me that they had Law
before we arrived.' He chuckles. The prosecutor laughs. If there's a joke here,
it's one that can't be repeated inside an Indigenous community, or with any
Indigenous person present. 'As they do at Lajamanu, of course.'

In Lajamanu, the Kurdiji Law and Justice Group – made up of senior
Warlpiri men and women – have advised visiting judges and magistrates
on sentencing decisions since the mid-1990s.[2] It is said that during the
Kurdiji's first fifteen years, crime rates in Lajamanu fell by over half, while
imprisonment rates in the rest of the Northern Territory skyrocketed.[3]
Kurdiji want to meet with visiting judges because they want to advise them
about Warlpiri law. People in Lajamanu refer to themselves as *Yapa* and to
non-Indigenous people as *Kardiya*. 'Kardiya way, and Yapa way, put them
together,' Elder Jerry Patrick told the ABC in 2016.[4] The expectation in
Lajamanu, as elsewhere, is that if Kardiya law expects Yapa to respect it,
then it must also respect Warlpiri law. Yet, as we've seen, settler law doesn't
even recognise First Nations law.

In January 2008, two police cars carrying five non-Indigenous officers,
including one woman, drove onto restricted ceremony ground while undertaking routine traffic duties. In Warlpiri law, women are prohibited from
entering onto that ground. (Women have their own restricted places.) The
offence is serious, and requires immediate sanction. 'The whole community
was very upset because the police just went ahead and did what they liked,'
Martin Japanangka said in a video released on YouTube. Unable to see what
the big deal was, the officers apologised. Senior Warlpiri men and women
tried in vain to have settler authorities take the offence seriously, to no avail.[5]

As a criminal defence lawyer, most conversations I have with people in
First Nations communities are about how they're alleged to have breached
settler law. The pace is fast. Occasionally, though, there's time to listen, and
to learn. The message is consistently the same: there was law here, before,
and it's still here. During a recent visit to Borroloola, a senior man gives me
a fifteen-minute introduction to Country. Landmarks. Names. Histories.
As we drive over a bridge, he says he told the engineers, when it was being
built, that it would flood every few years. 'They didn't listen,' he says. 'They
said they know how to build a bridge. The first year it flooded, it went over
the bridge.' He tells me of a longstanding wish among the Borroloola community. 'We want a local person to sit with the prosecutor and the judge,

to advise on local law.' The notion that settler law has banned Aboriginal law is outrageous, even ridiculous.

Settler law has experimented with limited recognition of First Nations culture. Chris Vass had worked in Papua New Guinea for fifteen years until its independence, when he returned to Adelaide. He became a magistrate, and began travelling out to Pitjantjatjara communities to run circuit courts from the mid-1980s. It was impossible for him to ignore the colonial tone of the project he was engaged in, or the deep distrust among many Aboriginal people as they were being hauled through the settler justice system. In 1996, he began talking to government departments and the Aboriginal Legal Rights Movement, and listening to local First Nations groups. Three years later, with the permission of his chief magistrate, Vass commenced an 'Aboriginal Court Day', fortnightly in Port Adelaide, monthly in Murray Bridge and Port Augusta.[6] Locals began calling it the 'Nunga Court', using the term of self-identification used by many Aboriginal people in southern South Australia. Instead of sitting in his usual place behind the bench, Vass began coming down to sit opposite the defendant at the bar table. A senior Aboriginal person sat next to him to advise him on relevant cultural matters.[7]

Similar models followed in other parts of the country.[8] They all share a common feature. The law that decides a person's penalty is the settler law, and for a defendant to become eligible to be referred into these courts, they must plead guilty. They're sentencing courts, sentencing according to settler law. The role of the Indigenous person who sits with the judge or magistrate is merely advisory. For this reason, Indigenous sentencing courts – if they can usefully be called that – are notoriously open to what UNSW academic Deborah Bird Rose calls 'deep colonising'.[9] Often, though, even these courts' limited acknowledgement of other systems and experiences was deeply unpopular among existing magistrates and senior barristers, at least initially. '[T]here are [already] many instances where the Aborigines are seen to be able to bend the rules a little bit more than others,' claimed David Galbally QC in 2003. He predicted the Koori Court soon to commence in Shepparton 'will create a greater division between Aboriginal people and the rest of the population'.[10] When Diane Fingleton, as Queensland's first female chief magistrate, held reconciliation ceremonies in six magistrates courts and issued a formal apology to Indigenous people for past injustices in August 2000 as a first step toward the creation of Murri Courts, she raised the ire of other magistrates and the Supreme Court's chief justice,

Paul de Jersey. 'It is no part of the role of the courts to venture publicly into contentious policy areas,' he said, perpetuating the settler myth that courts do law, never politics. 'If a person has been wronged then there is an appeals process,' insisted one retired magistrate.[11]

There is perhaps no better demonstration of the 'deep colonising' critique than what happened in the Northern Territory following the Intervention. Aboriginal sentencing courts began there in 2005, called 'Community Courts'.[12] In accordance with strict admissibility rules, they occasionally allowed evidence of Aboriginal law to help magistrates to better understand a defendant's motivations and moral culpability.[13] But new federal laws passed along with the Emergency Response two years later prohibited Aboriginal law from being used for these purposes. Community Courts fell gradually into disuse. Mary Spiers Williams, who was conducting research in the Territory toward her doctoral thesis, tried to learn why. Some magistrates had been suspicious of Community Courts from the outset, she found. They 'had formed opinions about the local Aboriginal cultural practices and beliefs, and believed that holding a Community Court would have unforeseen negative consequences'.[14] It's an extraordinary insight. Magistrates who were prepared to inflict settler law on what could have been self-governing Aboriginal communities were unprepared to have those communities participate – even in a limited way – in sentencing decisions about their own people. In the end, the Community Court model didn't survive the 2012 election of the CLP government,[15] though the present Labor government says it will revive them under a new Aboriginal Justice Agreement.

Back in the terminal lounge, as we're about to board the plane, the judge expresses a personal opinion. 'I don't see why the people out there can't have a local JP sitting in judgement of minor matters,' he says. 'You could remand the serious cases back to Darwin, and largely leave them to run everything else themselves.' Indeed, most cases this judge will hear during the time we're in the community will be small fry. Driving, consensual fights in public, verbal breaches of domestic violence orders, very low-level assaults. All of it will have local explanations, local antecedents, local effects – and local resolutions. People will resent having to sit around all day just to be fined or handed a good behaviour bond – or even worse, to have their case adjourned so they're forced to come back and do it all again in another month.

We board the plane, and land some time later in a remote township. One of my clients has a minor charge: fighting in public with another man. There's video footage, taken with a mobile. It shows what looks for all the world like a bare-knuckle boxing match, albeit conducted on a dirt verge outside someone's front fence. Surrounding the two belligerents is a crowd, many of whom have their phones out and are making their own videos. It's pretty clear what happened: two men had a disagreement and settled it with a ten-second fist-fight. Unedifying and impolite, sure. But there's no evidence that anyone was seriously hurt, or that the fight extended beyond that point in time. It's more likely that the fight between these two men *prevented* violence extending further. My client is resentful that he's at court at all. 'Why can't they just give me a bloody fine and let me get on with things?' That's what he'd wanted from the beginning, but it's not that simple. Nine months before the fight, another judge had given him a suspended prison term for disorderly behaviour after he swore angrily at a police officer who'd banned him from the local shop. Breaking the law by fighting would breach that suspension and reactivate the prison term. His other problem is that police have also charged him with 'engaging in violent conduct such that anyone in the vicinity would have feared for their safety'. The video is clear: nobody was fearing for their safety. But prosecutors don't want to drop the charge. If he doesn't plead guilty, he needs to take both charges to hearing, which means lots of adjournments. This is the fourth time he had come to court and sat around all day waiting for something to happen.

It's not hard to imagine why even a sitting judge thinks it's all a waste of time and money. The circuit courts' defenders say they're about community outreach, bringing justice to the people where they live. It's better to have circuit courts than to make everyone come to Darwin to answer their bail. But visiting circuit courts, and even Community Courts when they were allowed, are variations on the same idea: settler authorities delivering settler justice on settler priorities. Frank Vincent, who became a judge in Victoria, later recalled working for CAALAS during the 1970s, when he developed his own approach to this problem. 'When I arrived at Yuendumu, the place was not like anything I'd previously seen,' he told Jon Faine:

> We'd driven out from Alice Springs. We did not go in the magistrate's plane, because we were ... endeavouring to point out that we were separate and not simply part of a charade which was performed ... I stood up in the courtroom, announced that I appeared on behalf of all the

accused, and today everyone was pleading 'not guilty'. I've never seen a more obvious look of horror on the face of any individual in my life as I observed on the magistrate that day.

Vincent set about cross-examining police officers about why they charged Warlpiri people with crimes. One man had been charged with behaving disorderly when he argued with the shopkeeper. The shopkeeper was a police officer's wife. 'And so when the matter continued it was absolutely amazing,' Vincent recalled. 'Here was a fellow charged with disorderly behaviour and nobody had bothered ... to ask him why he was annoyed.' It turned out that the shopkeeper had given him incorrect change. Ultimately the court was rained out. 'After a month or two of fighting these cases,' Vincent said wryly, 'we discovered that the crime rate in Yuendumu dropped quite dramatically.'[16]

○

Half a century later, in the community I'm working in, another plane arrives. It's carrying an Aboriginal man in his forties and two prison officers, both white. The man has been flown in from Darwin Correctional Centre – where he'd been held on remand – for a contested hearing. He sits for hours outside the courtroom, his wrists in handcuffs, a prison officer either side of him. His primary school-aged children learn of his presence in town and rush in to see him. After a tense few minutes the officers relax, and the kids end up playing on the floor at their dad's feet. By one o'clock, the witnesses haven't arrived. The hearing can't go ahead. His lawyer applies for bail, but the judge says the charges are too serious. The lawyer reminds the judge his client is pleading not guilty, is innocent until proven guilty, and says the evidence can't prove the charges. But the handcuffs stay on. The man is taken back into a police van and back onto the plane, to wait out at least another month on remand.

○

Three years ago, a woman was charged with assault when she (allegedly) used a star picket – an iron fence post – to attack someone in a remote community. She is Aboriginal. She's pleading not guilty, but for one reason or another, her hearing keeps getting adjourned. If she's found guilty, the law will require her to serve a minimum twelve months' prison. She's since given birth to a child. Whatever happened three years ago, the dispute has long since been resolved. But the law requires witnesses to give evidence. It must pursue its own form of justice, regardless of the real-world consequences. If the hearing runs this time, it risks re-inciting the tit-for-tat conflict that led to the original charge. Nobody's interests are served by these proceedings. Yet the wheels of settler justice must roll on.

o

In August 2006, the Kalgoorlie Magistrates Court became the setting for the first contested hearing based on Western Australia's new racial vilification laws. A fifteen-year-old Aboriginal girl had called a nineteen-year-old white woman a 'white slut'. White people, who don't experience the degradation associated with racism, often find it hard to imagine what all the fuss is about when people who aren't white complain about racial abuse. When she gave evidence in the summary trial, the 'victim' said the abuse was 'offensive, but it's not the end of the world'. She hadn't complained about it to police. But legislation is written in racially neutral language, and to a white prosecutor, calling a white person a 'white slut' seems equivalent to calling an Aboriginal person a 'black' something.[17] So the Aboriginal girl was charged. Magistrate Kate Auty dismissed it. 'I reckon she should have gotten in trouble too,' the girl said after the hearing. 'She called me a black cunt.'[18]

o

A client calls me from Darwin's prison. An Aboriginal man, he's been held on remand for nearly four months on a charge of assaulting his wife, she says by cracking her head against a wall. But police observed no injury on her when they arrived, and I know – after summoning various police records – that she has a history of making false complaints about him, especially when she's intoxicated. Police took her statement *while* she was drunk. He's got two assaults on his record, both times for hitting other men. We're speaking now because a judge has just refused him bail, citing his lengthy history of bail breaches, all associated with his chronic alcoholism. Even if he's found guilty at the summary trial, he's unlikely to do more time than he's already done. But the trial is still another three months away. 'I have to get out,' he says. Covid-19 has been rampant in the prison, causing staffing shortages and extensive 'lockdowns'. 'I didn't do anything wrong,' he tells me, 'but I want to plead guilty.' He does, and is sentenced to just under four months' prison: the time he's already served.

○

If Settler Australia's justice system is an institutional expression of the one-sided relationship between settler and Indigenous communities, then its various components – police forces, correctional agencies, prisons, criminal courts – can never be 'neutral'. Reforming them without acknowledging this basic fact, which has been the aim of most governments since at least the early 1990s, is an impossible task.

How should we tell the story of Aboriginal and Torres Strait Islander incarceration in Australia? Only part of it is in the numbers. And we can't get very far by looking at the crimes that see Indigenous offenders punished by courts and sentenced to prison. The carceral three-act narrative – offence, arrest, prison – to the social problem of criminal behaviour no longer feels like just a story. It feels unalterable, like a rock. But even rocks are worn away by constant pressure, and by such apparently gentle forces as wind and rain. To really grapple with the problem of Indigenous incarceration requires us to accept the possibility that there might be another way. That the current state of affairs – where entire families sometimes spend time behind bars – is not inevitable.

Recognition

'Our Aboriginal and Torres Strait Islander tribes were the first sovereign Nations of the Australian continent and its adjacent islands, and possessed it under our own laws and customs.' So commences the Uluru Statement from the Heart, the outcome of an extraordinary four-day convention of more than 250 delegates in May 2017. The sovereignty of the First Nations 'has never been ceded or extinguished, and co-exists with the sovereignty of the Crown. How could it be otherwise?'

This book has been about the stories settlers have told – through their governments and their courts – about Aboriginal and Torres Strait Islander crime. At no time have those stories ever reflected the simple, profound truth of the Uluru Statement. Running to a single page, it's not a lengthy document. Anyone who hasn't read it yet should take the time to do so. 'Proportionally,' the Statement continues, 'we are the most incarcerated people on the planet.' Linking the incarceration crisis to child removals and the more fundamental questions about sovereignty, the Statement observes: 'This is the torment of our powerlessness.'

For the 229 years between Phillip's arrival and the Statement, the First Nations both resisted the illegal invasion and theft of their lands, and urged in vain to have settler authorities recognise their own sovereign rights to make and enforce their own laws. Initially they met the settlers' violence with their own, but it was an unsuccessful strategy. The Tasmanian War – initially called the 'Black War' by journalist Henry Melville, who excoriated George Arthur's prosecution of it[19] – saw nearly a thousand Aboriginal people and more than two hundred settlers killed between the mid-1820s and January 1832, as settlers violently overran the island they called Van Diemen's Land.[20] The war led to perhaps the first written petition by First Nations people addressed to settler authorities. Arthur, George Augustus Robinson and a Paredarerme man called 'Kickerterpoller' or 'Black Tom' had negotiated the removal of Aboriginal survivors to Flinders Island in the Bass Strait.[21] In 1847, they petitioned Queen Victoria, appealing to 'an agreement which we have not lost from our minds since and we have made our part of it good'.[22] Flinders, under its commandant, Henry Jeanneret, was like a penal colony. The petitioners reminded the Queen they were not prisoners. They may have succeeded. The few dozen survivors – including Truganini – were relocated again to Oyster Cove, south of Hobart.

The petitions continued, their authors aware of their powerless status in settler law.[23] Yorta Yorta people, who in the 1870s had been moved onto the Maloga mission near Moama, on the banks of the Murray, created at least two petitions during the 1880s requesting that first the NSW governor and then Queen Victoria issue grants of land. William Cooper was among the signatories.[24] Another prominent activist, the Wurundjeri Elder William Barak, petitioned from the Coranderrk mission for greater freedom in 1886: 'We should be free like the White Population...'[25] The Coranderrk petition was a direct response to Alfred Deakin's 'Aborigines Protection Bill', introduced into Victoria's parliament in June, which promised to expand the 'protection' regime established seventeen years earlier, and to commence the assimilation of younger First Nations people of mixed parentage by ordering them off the reserves and into unskilled work. Despite some support in the press, the petitioners' pleas fell on deaf ears. First Nations people had nobody in Victoria's parliament. The bill passed into law and became known as the 'Half-Caste Act'.[26]

Indigenous people tried to prevent settler governments and parliaments from enacting a policy they would later apologise for: the removal of 'mixed-descent' children from their parents.[27] Not content with massacres and land thefts, settler authorities – in governments and churches – did it anyway, under legislation enacted between 1869 (in Victoria) and 1936 (in WA).[28] An enormous proportion of Indigenous children were forcibly taken from their families and communities between 1910 and 1970.[29] Settler criminal courts – and prisons – are still swollen with the devastating effects of that policy.

During the 1920s, activist Fred Maynard, whose mother was Worimi, was publicising the plight of Aboriginal people whose land had been taken over by white farmers, and who had been forcibly relocated.[30] By the end of that decade, people seeking refuge from NSW's Aboriginal Protection Board began to congregate in camps on the banks of the Salt Pan Creek. Just to the south of what is now Punchbowl, Salt Pan Creek had been a site of Tedbury's resistance over a century earlier. In 1933 one prominent leader, Joe Anderson, also known as King Burraga of the Thirroul tribe, recorded an appeal direct to camera. 'I am calling a corroboree of all the natives of New South Wales,' he said, 'to send a petition to the King.' Burraga continued: 'One hundred and fifty years ago the Aboriginals owned Australia, and today he demands more than the white man's charity. He wants the right to live!'[31] Meanwhile, south of the Murray, William Cooper – now in his seventies – was doing his own agitating. He began a letter-writing campaign, which soon led to the creation of the Australian Aborigines' League. Among its demands, the League wanted Canberra to take over the administration of Aboriginal affairs from the states (which was eventually achieved by referendum in 1967). It also wanted parliamentary representation 'on the New Zealand model', and for settler law to recognise Aboriginal law. Neither has yet occurred. He organised the Day of Mourning protests on 26 January 1938.[32] A generation later, Robert Menzies' decision to grant mining leases on the Gove Peninsula prompted Yolngu people living at the Methodist mission Yirrkala to make the first formal assertion of native title, on a petition written on bark.[33]

The long history of First Nations' resistance to the takeover of land and destruction of life and livelihoods has not quite amounted to nothing. But the only concessions made to Aboriginal and Torres Strait Islander people and communities have been those settlers have been comfortable with. Civil and land rights have been won *within* a system in which settlers continue to deny the sovereignty of the nations which predated – by tens of thousands of years – their arrival.

This is palpably unjust. According to the law the settlers brought with them from Europe, it was also illegal. The historical record in Australia is peppered with countless instances of settlers – pioneers, police, magistrates, judges – trying again and again to explain the English or Australian law of theft or assault to people whose lands had been stolen and whose ancestors, or immediate families, had been massacred. Even today, the institutions of settler law continue to assert that *its* criminal law, and no other, is the only one that applies. How can such an assertion have any moral force? Yet in the thirty years since a royal commission examined its implication in an emerging incarceration crisis, settler law has become more and more punitive. Imprisonment is the apex of that punishment, has done very little to prevent the violence now so prevalent among many communities, and is in many ways implicated in it. The result is an ever-burgeoning Aboriginal and Torres Strait Islander prison population.

Voice

The First Nations have long demanded a 'Voice' in the creation of policy and law that affects them. 'Voice' is one of the three overarching demands of the Uluru Statement from the Heart. It shouldn't be a controversial idea. Elsewhere, phrases like 'no taxation without representation' have underpinned revolution, and the United Nations now recognises a fundamental right of self-determination. New Zealand's parliament has included Māori seats since 1867, with the passage of the *Māori Representation Act* during war between the settler government and North Island tribes. 'To expect men to respect law who don't enjoy it is absurd,' wrote James Fitzgerald, then Native Minister, in 1865. 'To try and govern a folk by our courts and at the same time to say that our courts shall take no cognisance of their property is amazing folly.'[34] There were initially four seats, which could only be filled by Māori people who had at least one 'full-blood' Māori parent. That qualification was removed a hundred years later, but only Māori people could vote for those seats, which now number seven.[35] New Zealand's parliament hasn't imploded. Indeed, the Māori seats were originally a temporary measure aimed at what we would now recognise as assimilation.[36] But Australian settler authorities, wedded to an old delusion in which Indigenous people already enjoy the same rights and opportunities as settlers, have always resolutely opposed the creation of specific First Nations seats.

The 'Voice' proposal associated with the Uluru Statement isn't even as radical as that. It merely proposes a new representative body of Indigenous people, enshrined in the Constitution to protect it from abolition by a future parliament (as ATSIC was in 2005), which would 'advise Parliament on laws and policies with respect to Indigenous affairs.' Parliament would retain the power to override any advice it received from the representative body, though the moral force such a body would command would be significant. The Indigenous Voice to Parliament was rejected by Malcolm Turnbull's government in 2017, but the Victorian government did take up the idea, creating the First Peoples' Assembly of Victoria, a democratically elected representative body for Traditional Owners and Aboriginal people in that state. Time will tell whether it offers more than lip service and 'deep colonising'. Only 7 per cent of eligible voters turned out for the first election in 2019, and many have expressed distrust of the process.[37]

Treaty

Cook's secret instructions of 1769 – to take possession 'with the consent of the natives' – have been studiously ignored ever since. European colonists were making treaties with 'native peoples' all over the world during the eighteenth and nineteenth centuries, yet never on the Australian continent. John Batman's infamous attempt to come to terms with the Kulin people in what is now Melbourne in 1835 – albeit on terms very favourable to John Batman – was proclaimed void by Governor Richard Bourke. In the wake of the Tasmanian War, Arthur lamented the colonists' 'fatal error' of having not negotiated a treaty.

'Treaty' is the second of the Uluru Statement's demands. At the foundation of the Treaty movement is an expectation that settlers must finally honour Cook's instructions and negotiate with the First Nations for the use of their lands. Settlers must first recognise the First Nations' sovereign rights in those lands. That's never happened, though governments have occasionally come close. On Arthur's recommendation, the Letters Patent, which established South Australia, contained a proviso: 'nothing therein contained shall affect or be construed to affect the rights of any Aboriginal Natives of the said Province to the actual occupation or enjoyment in their own persons or ... their descendants of any lands therein now actually occupied or enjoyed by such Natives.'[38] The proviso was quickly overrun and ignored by pioneering settlers desperate to claim as much land as they could. In 1971, in his judgement in the Gove Land Rights case (see chapter 4), Richard Blackburn dismissed that proviso by concluding that it 'was not intended to be more than the affirmation of a principle of benevolence, inserted in the Letters Patent in order to bestow upon it a suitably dignified status'.[39] Even had treaties been signed, the experience in New Zealand – where Captain William Hobson came to terms with Māori chiefs from the North Island in 1840 – suggests settler authorities would most likely have disregarded them.[40] Settler law, it turns out, can be so tricky that its words – even when written in black and white – actually don't mean anything!

All state and territory governments, and the federal Fraser government, agreed in March 1981 to begin discussions with the National Aboriginal Conference – a short-lived representative body established ostensibly so that settler governments could negotiate with Indigenous people – on 'the question of Makarrata'.[41] Makarrata is a Yolngu word which describes the process of resolving a conflict or struggle through the negotiated recognition and acceptance of rights and wrongs. The process lost steam after the Hawke government won power in 1983. Later, after 40,000 people marched in Sydney on the 200th anniversary of settlement, Galarrwuy Yunupingu and Wenten Rubuntja, then chair of the Central Land Council, presented Bob Hawke with the Barunga Statement on a 1.2-metre sheet of wood. 'We, the Indigenous owners and occupiers of Australia, call on the Australian Government people to recognise our rights,' the Statement demanded, echoing two centuries of similar calls. The Statement called for 'self-determination and self-management', 'permanent control' of ancestral lands, compensation, 'respect for and promotion' of Aboriginal identities, an elected Aboriginal and Torres Strait Islander organisation, and 'a police and justice system which recognises our customary laws'. In response, Hawke famously promised a treaty by 1990. Instead, he created the Council for Aboriginal Reconciliation. Its ten-year mission went unfulfilled. 'Reconciliation' is a word which assumes the restoration of once-friendly relations. Governments are happy to use it. But it's yet more 'deep colonising'.[42]

More recently, the Victorian and Northern Territory Labor governments have commenced preparatory work toward treaties. Victoria's parliament legislated a framework for treaty negotiations in 2018,[43] and in the same year the Territory's chief minister, Michael Gunner, signed the

Barunga Agreement, which committed his government to developing a treaty process in negotiation with the four Aboriginal Land Councils.[44] A Treaty Commission is due, at the time of writing, to deliver a report in 2022. Queensland has also commenced Treaty preparations, to be guided by a Treaty Advancement Committee, co-chaired by Jackie Huggins and Mick Gooda.[45] South Australia's Labor government took initial steps toward a treaty with the Ngarrindjeri, Narungga and Adnyamathanha nations, but the process was paused in 2018 following the election of a single-term Liberal government. And Western Australia's former premier, Colin Barnett, claimed to have created Australia's first actual treaty when his government signed off on the enormous South West Native Title Settlement with the Noongar people of the state's south-west. The settlement is really six land-use agreements made under the *Native Title Act* which recognises Noongar traditional ownership,[46] establishes a trust to hold and manage assets for the benefit of Noongar people, authorises access for Noongar licensees to unallocated Crown land for customary activities, and establishes a range of other partnerships aimed at material assistance and heritage protection.

But as revolutionary as the South West Native Title Settlement is in historical terms, it doesn't recognise Aboriginal sovereignty. The danger inherent in the current treaty processes is that the parties begin their negotiations in a relationship of almost total asymmetry. It doesn't cost settler governments much to pass legislation recognising traditional ownership and establishing trusts. Will they ever be persuaded to recognise sovereignty? Early signs are not promising. Despite commencing a treaty process, the Victorian government at the same time wanted to duplicate a section of the Western Highway between Ararat and Buangor, even though doing so would threaten six trees – including traditional birthing trees – and a surrounding area significant to the Djab Wurrung people, who in mid-2018 established a Heritage Protection Embassy and commenced legal action in settler courts to prevent construction work.[47] In October 2021, Victorian police blocked the Djab Wurrung and their supporters from accessing a site where workers felled a large fiddleback tree, known to the Traditional Owners as a 'Directions Tree', and arrested fifty people.[48] And in May 2020, a cave in the Juukan Gorge in the Pilbara was permanently destroyed by mining giant Rio Tinto, despite multiple representations to the company by Puutu Kunti Kurrama and Pinikura heritage managers about its significance: archaeological evidence showed that the cave had been continuously occupied for 46,000 years, making it the oldest known inland site in Australia. Rio Tinto's actions were entirely lawful under the state's Aboriginal Heritage Act, which had created an approvals process which favoured the destruction of sacred and significant sites. In the wake of the Juukan Gorge destruction – reported around the world – the Western Australian parliament replaced the Act entirely, though with a new piece of legislation which was opposed by Traditional Owners on the basis that it did not address the central flaws in the existing law.[49]

Western Australia has not commenced a formal treaty process. Settler parliaments everywhere continue to claim for themselves the only sovereign lawmaking rights on this continent, and they continue to pass laws that disadvantage First Nations peoples and communities when it suits them.

Truth

When Makarrata was being discussed in the early 1980s, there was an accompanying idea: before there can be an agreement, or a treaty, there must first be an acknowledgement of the truth of what happened here. Settler authorities have been notoriously slow to do so. It wasn't until 1992 that the High Court found that the doctrine of *terra nullius* was a legal fiction in the Australian context. Yet settler institutions *still* haven't recognised First Nations' sovereignty. It's now nearly three decades since Paul Keating's speech at Redfern Park, which bears repeating here:

> Isn't it reasonable to say that if we can build a prosperous and remarkably harmonious multicultural society in Australia, surely we can find just solutions to the problems which beset the first Australians – the people to whom the most injustice has been done? And ... the starting point might be to recognise that the problem starts with us non-Aboriginal Australians. It begins, I think, with that act of recognition. Recognition that it was *we* who did the dispossessing. *We* took the traditional lands and smashed the traditional way of life. *We* brought the diseases. The alcohol. *We* committed the murders. *We* took the children from their mothers. *We* practised discrimination and exclusion. It was *our* ignorance and *our* prejudice. And *our* failure to imagine these things being done to us. With some notable exceptions, *we* failed to make the most basic human response and enter into their hearts

and minds. We failed to ask: how would I feel if this were done to me? As a consequence, we failed to see that what we were doing degraded all of us.[50]

But Keating's 'act of recognition' has yet to translate into very much meaningful action. Most of Australia's governments haven't even acknowledged the most basic fact of this continent's history: that settler achievements were built on the dispossession of the First Nations. There is no formal national memorial to the predominantly Indigenous lives that were lost on the colonial frontier. There is barely even agreement about the numbers of Aboriginal and Torres Strait Islander people killed, let alone recognition of the intergenerational effects of dispossession on nations and communities who were systematically deprived of their economic and spiritual resources. Governments have so far avoided the kind of 'truth and reconciliation' commissions held in nearly fifty other countries, including Canada, New Zealand and South Africa.[51] The closest we've come in Australia is an inquiry by the (then very new) Human Rights and Equal Opportunity Commission between 1988 and 1991 into racist violence. 'An overwhelming feature of the evidence by Aboriginal and Islander people in relation to racist violence,' the report of that inquiry observed, 'was complaints against police officers.'[52] But the Commission's findings weren't binding, and recent Coalition governments have launched remarkable *ad hominem* attacks on the Commission and especially its president between 2012 and 2017, Gillian Triggs. There has been nothing like, for instance, the Commission on Systemic Racism in the Ontario Criminal Justice System, which reported in 1995. By contrast, Australia's governments have until very recently tended to deny or downplay what John Howard as prime minister described – citing Blainey – as the 'black armband view of our history.'[53] As late as 2020, then prime minister Scott Morrison claimed (while defending Cook's legacy) that 'there was no slavery in Australia.'[54]

'Truth-telling' has been acknowledged as central to any treaty process in the Northern Territory, Queensland and especially Victoria, where the Yoo-rrook Justice Commission – with the powers of a royal commission – was created in May 2021. It will set about creating, for the first time in Australia, an official record of colonial injustice perpetrated on First Nations people, and determining 'the causes and consequences of systemic injustice' with a view to making systemic change.[55]

All truth about what really happened as the colonial frontier rolled ever outward from Port Jackson is hard. But some truths, as Megan Davis points out, are harder than others. Davis is a Cobble Cobble woman and a law professor at the University of NSW who has been thinking about and working on these matters for decades. To expect that truth will 'automatically' lead to justice is 'fraught', 'illusory' and 'simply not borne out by the evidence', she wrote recently in *The Monthly*.[56] If truth and reconciliation commissions are established by settler governments, as Victoria's is, the danger is that they become little more than a ritualistic performance of Indigenous trauma, at the end of which nothing changes. We've seen the same sort of thing in the more or less rolling royal commissions over the past decade into the aged and disability care systems, child sexual abuse, and even the protection and detention of children in the Northern Territory: people who have endured real-life horror lay down their trauma so that journalists can build stories and headlines, and then authorities just keeping doing more of the same. Documenting the reality of colonial massacres committed by people who are now long-dead is one thing. But how prepared are we to acknowledge the living truths about Australia's criminal justice system?

Acknowledging the *history* of settler injustice to Indigenous people can have perverse outcomes, especially if it allows present-day settlers to reflect on how much 'better' Indigenous people are treated now. In its *Pathways to the Aboriginal Justice Agreement* booklet (2019), the NT's Department of the Attorney-General and Justice presented Albert Namatjira's criminalisation (see chapter 3) as a clear case of discriminatory injustice.[57] Yet in 2019, the same department was intimately involved in the creation of a new *Liquor Act*, which imposes a maximum twelve-month term of imprisonment on Aboriginal people who live in Aboriginal communities and bring alcohol home.[58] Perhaps even more than its application to the past, truth is required in the present.

Mt Theo

By the 1990s, petrol sniffing had reached epidemic levels among young Indigenous people in many communities. In Yuendumu, as many as seventy kids were regularly sniffing. In a total population of under a thousand, that was a lot. 'The worst petrol sniffers lived in [abandoned houses] away from their families,' recalled Johnny Miller, a Traditional Owner at Yuendumu, later. 'They would sniff petrol all day and fall asleep with that petrol under

their nose.' None of the programs set up intermittently by settler governments was doing a thing to stop it. Elders and other senior Warlpiri people
met in February 1994. Peggy Brown, Elder, wanted to bring every chronic
sniffer to her husband's outstation, Puturlu, known to settlers as Mt Theo.
Puturlu's Traditional Owners agreed. Other communities offered food, cars
and fuel. Mt Theo was entirely Aboriginal run. Kids who sniffed petrol
went – with parental consent – for a month. Youth workers, teachers and
health professionals visited from time to time. Repeat sniffers were brought
back to Mt Theo. Eventually there was also a youth activities program in
Yuendumu, which aimed to divert kids from sniffing. A decade on, and petrol sniffing had been practically eliminated from Yuendumu.[59]

Mt Theo endured, and expanded its focus to other substances. It now
offers a practical sentencing alternative to young Warlpiri people who
would otherwise go into detention. 'We want to send our kids to a place like
Mt Theo Station,' one Yuendumu person said during consultations ahead of
the Northern Territory's belated Aboriginal Justice Agreement. 'We should
have more of a say about what happens to kids from this community –
about disciplining them, about teaching them respect for our culture and
our traditions. Too many of our kids are in jail, when it is our responsibility to look after them and grow them up the right way.'[60]

There could be hundreds of Mt Theos, from Broome to Melbourne.
Each would look different, run differently. They don't need to be reserved
only for teenagers. Similar alternatives could be created as well for adults.

Nor is there any need to accept that this model is exclusively for
Indigenous people. Here's the radical idea – radical for Settler Australia,
that is – underpinning this book: Settler Australia can learn from the First
Nations about social problems and how to address them in a way that
encourages the healing of individuals, families, communities and colonial
relations. Since Thomas Mathiesen published *The Politics of Abolition* half
a century ago, Australia's use of prisons – mirroring the trend in the rest of
the English-speaking world – has dramatically increased, along with our
collective knowledge about the harms they cause, and their ineffectiveness
at solving the problems they're designed to solve.

There are alternatives. 'In Norway, the punishment is just to take away
someone's liberty,' Halden Prison's governor Are Hoidal told the BBC in
2019. 'The other rights stay. Prisoners can vote, they can have access to
school, to healthcare; they have the same rights as any Norwegian citizen.'

Halden is a maximum-security prison. It's been twenty years since Norway jettisoned the traditional approach and committed its criminal justice system to rehabilitation, in line with Jeremy Bentham's original concept. Its recidivism rate is now half that of countries such as Britain and Australia.[61] And in Finland, a third of all prisons are designated as 'open', and allow inmates to leave to go to work and school.[62] Its criminal justice system complements its 'housing first' policy, which makes housing a basic right and removes the many barriers other places (including Australia) have created, like requiring people to overcome mental health and addiction problems before they can qualify.

In Australia, growing numbers of people – from RMIT University's Centre for Innovative Justice (which was created by former Victorian attorney-general Rob Hulls) to islands in the Gulf of Carpentaria – are also working for change. 'Apparently there's been no youth offending on Groote Eylandt in seven months,' my colleague tells me after he's spent a day there representing a client in mid-2022. 'It happens to have coincided with two awesome new youth programs,' he adds. As the Royal Commission into the Prevention and Detention of Children in the Northern Territory heard, and found, when young people have things to do which are relevant and interesting to them, when they're afforded the opportunity to invest in their own communities, when they're not treated like ratbag offenders-in-waiting (as they often are by police in Tennant Creek, for instance), offending can actually be prevented. 'Eighty per cent of our youth that attend cultural camps don't re-offend,' NAAJA's CEO, Priscilla Atkins, told the *7AM* podcast in 2021 (after the government abandoned its royal commission commitments and NAAJA revised its 'inside the tent' strategy). 'So we know that these programs work, but locking them up doesn't work.'[63]

A lot of the work being done to re-imagine Australia's justice system, especially as it applies to First Nations communities, is being done by people outside governments. The Paul Ramsay Foundation is channelling investment dollars into various initiatives, including justice reinvestment pilots which aim to take money away from policing and prisons and 'reinvest' it in ways we already know work to prevent criminal offending in the first place: education, housing, trauma therapy. Change the Record is a coalition of Indigenous peak bodies and settler allies which has had extraordinary influence in its short life on the national debate to raise the age of criminal responsibility from ten to the global standard of fourteen. Within many

First Nations communities there are community policing models which aim to replace and subvert the paramilitary-style violence of modern policing in favour of localised authority structures that rely on building and maintaining relationships.[64] Many communities have alternative dispute-resolution models which emphasise truth-telling, restoration and community-building rather than fact-finding and individualised punishment.[65]

There's nothing immutable or permanent about the 'justice' model we've inherited from England and Americanised into mass incarceration. 'We could empty the prisons of half their numbers overnight if we stopped criminalising mental illness and substance abuse,' says Olga Havnen, a woman of Western Arrernte descent who for nine years until recently was CEO of Darwin's Danila Dilba Aboriginal health service. We don't need to accept that imprisoning people necessarily means locking them away in supermax facilities, cutting them off entirely from their sources of support and from genuine opportunities of rehabilitation in the community. We don't even need to accept that the criminal courts are appropriate venues for the vast majority of low-level assaults, thefts, property damage and driving charges which clog the system.

If we were genuinely prepared to address the drivers of criminal behaviour and not simply punish people – expensively, ineffectively and counterproductively – most of the work of the criminal courts would vanish. Or, it would change dramatically. Imagine if the system were geared to solving problems – for victims, offenders and their communities – rather than simply inflicting greater and greater penalties? Imagine if the significant intellectual, political and practical resources of governments were geared toward collaborating with communities instead of finding ways to imprison more people more often? Why shouldn't innovations like drug courts, mental health courts and sentencing courts co-located with wrap-around services be the norm, rather than the exception? Why must police be increasingly militarised and centralised, instead of answerable to the communities they're part of? As things stand, carceral thinking infects even the efforts we're already making – very half-heartedly – to keep people out of prison. Many mandated rehabilitation facilities are cruel detox prisons by another name. Many community corrections and youth diversion programs tend to function as yet more funnels back into prison rather than genuinely supportive routes away from it. Even many schools, with their expulsions and their school-based police and their rigid insistence on prescriptive curriculum

above sincere and supportive student engagement, have become inextricably linked to the carceral project.[66]

There are dozens of real-world alternatives – even within Western
culture – to the simplistic, expensive, ineffective and brutal 'crime and
punishment' model we persist with in Australia. And there are significant
numbers of people, communities and organisations – both First Nations
and settlers – working on them right now. The only thing stopping us from
changing the way we respond to crime is our collective will. I'm not even
sure that's as insurmountable as it seems. If our political leaders faced the
facts about how futile and costly the current model is, and then committed
themselves to explaining that there are less pricey alternatives which will
actually keep the community safer from criminal behaviour, who could
honestly disagree?

Justice

It's not difficult to see the future. Moral panics about crime and violence
generate regular opportunities for unimaginative politicians to promise longer sentences, lower bars to prosecutions, more police and more
jails. Even as they tear down the social safety net and leave those who
need it most to struggle to stay afloat in desolate, bureaucratic quicksand, they find new ways to blame and demonise individuals for their
poverty and their anger. The prisons and the detention centres keep fill-
ing with Aboriginal and Torres Strait Islander men, women and children.
Families and communities are defined by the prison experience. Aunties
and grandfathers die while their young people are locked up hundreds of
kilometres away.

We can occasionally see glimpses of another future, if we know where
to look. Aunties and grandfathers are empowered. *Truly* empowered. True
partnerships are formed. Settlers are educated on First Nations law and
cultural obligations. Social problems are decriminalised and worked on.
Individuals are afforded the tools with which to take responsibility, not
alone, but as part of whole, self-determining communities. Prisons are rehabilitated and even decommissioned. Communities build, strengthen, heal.

For this other future to become real, the first thing that must happen
is that *we* must change. Not others. For me, the author of this book, the
'we' is settlers, Kardiya, Gubbah, migaloo. *We* must recognise the damage

that we've done and the damage that we're continuing to do by our dogged insistence that the settler criminal law is neutral and fair, and that prison is as necessary as we pretend it is. We must recognise that we don't have all the answers. We must recognise that justice is more than a slogan or a government department.

Often, as Megan Davis points out, Canberra hasn't even wanted to use the word 'justice'.[67] The Council for what was supposed to be Aboriginal Reconciliation and Justice dropped the 'J' word – apparently on advice given to Bob Hawke by his staff – before it was legislated in 1991.[68] The term 'Aboriginal reconciliation' itself implied that First Nations people were the ones who needed to reconcile themselves. Five years later, the Council made seventy-eight recommendations to Hawke's successor, Paul Keating. Among them were recommendations for Treaty, dedicated seats in parliament, an Indigenous bill of rights, and a range of social justice measures.[69] Keating got to work on many of them, but he lost the prime ministership the following year to John Howard, who quickly removed the term 'social justice' from his government's language.[70]

Even where governments do embrace the term, they tend to do so in a limited way. Three decades after the deaths in custody royal commission urged state and territory governments to sign 'Aboriginal Justice Agreements', Michael Gunner's NT government finalised negotiations for its first AJA in 2021. Its vision of 'justice' is the one governments have been trotting out for decades: reduce Aboriginal incarceration rates; improve services to Aboriginal people; and support Aboriginal leadership. 'Justice' is to be achieved within the existing structures and institutions created and imposed by settler governments. There's nothing in it about the more substantive notion of justice that would see the recognition of Aboriginal sovereignty and the realities of dispossession.[71]

Jails seem to Australians about as permanent as Uluru because they've been here for so long. They came with the prison ships and iron chains, the legacy of Britain's imperial vision of a prison colony, which expanded inland from Port Jackson. Any honest accounting of historical fact informed by basic notions of justice and legal reason must conclude that prisons are at the apex of a continuing colonial project determined to insist on an exclusive sovereign right that cannot exist. When exactly did the use of the criminal law as a tool of colonisation end? Have the agents of the settler criminal justice system – its judges and magistrates, its police and prison officers, its lawyers – ever engaged much with Indigenous critiques? The High Court may have dispensed with the legal concept of *terra nullius*, but its psychological equivalent remains in much of Settler Australia.[72] Perhaps they could begin, as Murri legal academic Nicole Watson suggests, by simply reading some literature written by Indigenous authors.[73] From time to time, coroners and law reformers recommend some polishing of rough edges: the end to spit hoods, solitary confinement and mandatory imprisonment; the removal of barriers to First Nations' participation in juries; the decriminalisation of public drunkenness; the repeal of the *Summary Offences Acts*. But all this is tinkering.

I don't have the answers. I don't know whether the solution is in greater but limited recognition by the settler justice system of Indigenous law and culture, perhaps through forms of restorative justice which aim to solve problems instead of merely punishing perpetrators. Or whether the solution is in dual systems operating in parallel, or in wholesale reform of the settler system to take account of historical realities and, at long last, the evidence about what works and what doesn't work when responding to crime as a social problem. That's yet to be decided. For us all to decide, hopefully together, through experimentation and failure and reform and work and thinking and talking and watching and listening. This book does not suggest that the solution lies in somehow reverting to pre-contact Indigenous dispute-resolution systems: those systems have changed significantly (as has the settler legal system), or in some cases collapsed entirely, during the last two centuries. What this book *does* suggest is that the status quo offers no solution. Australia has one of the world's highest rates of recidivism, below only the United States (and New Zealand).[74] What is not in doubt is that mass imprisonment, in its current form, is rarely a solution to anything – in Indigenous *or* settler communities.

This book isn't about solutions. It's about the problem, the one big problem that is perpetuating the subjugation of entire communities. For the entire time that Europeans have been 'settling' on these lands, their original owners have been demanding justice. The problem is the immutability of *settler* expectations, *our* insistence that our system, with its prisons and its courts and its increasingly militarised police, works and is the only way. For 230 years we've believed this, and for 230 years we've been shouting this belief so loudly on other people's lands that we haven't even heard that there are other ways.

When Indigenous people talk about justice, I don't hear people saying there's only one way. Invariably, they're demanding to be heard, to be seen, to be recognised as sovereign peoples who have a right to justice on their own unceded country. They're saying black lives matter.

How about we begin again, from that point?

ACKNOWLEDGEMENTS

There is barely any original research in this book, which relies heavily on the archival excavations of outstanding scholars whose efforts have been so fruitful that they have entirely reshaped the way Australia's history – and its present – is understood. Still, much research into the ways settler criminal law has been applied to First Nations peoples and communities remains 'trapped' in academic texts: expensive books and journal articles whose access is limited to university staff and students (though alumni can generally now borrow books from the university they graduated from). Part of my aim in writing *Black Lives, White Law* was to take the results of this research and make it more widely available: this would not have been possible without the remarkable efforts, bold vision and extraordinary patience of Chris Feik, Kate Morgan and the outstanding team at Black Inc.

It's very difficult to come away from the experience of working with Indigenous legal services with much confidence that the settler criminal justice system is fair and just. My own eyes were prised open by my clients and my colleagues at both the Victorian Aboriginal Legal Service (based in Melbourne) and the North Australian Aboriginal Justice Agency's Katherine office, where I was privileged to work alongside the late Natasha Chong, a Wakka Wakka woman who was raised in Katherine and knew it intimately. Her job title was Senior Client Services Officer, but that doesn't begin to describe what Chongy did in Katherine, where frontier attitudes and the tragedies of dispossession smack visitors in the face.

I'm enormously grateful to Senator Patrick Dodson, Olga Havnen (former CEO of Darwin's Danila Dilba Aboriginal health service), Professor Kate Auty (former ALS lawyer and magistrate in Kalgoorlie), Emeritus Professor Robert Manne and others who provided invaluable comments on drafts of this book, and to Clancy Dane, my employer and friend, for his unfailingly generous support. My biggest thanks to my partner, Thy, social worker and astonishingly clear thinker, without whom this book would have been impossible to write.

I wrote this book on what were, are and will always be Larrakia, Kaurareg, Turrbal and Kaurna lands. On whose land are you reading it?

NOTES

INTRODUCTION

1   See, for example, John Kelly et al., 'How Many Recovery Attempts Does It Take to Successfully Resolve an Alcohol or Drug Problem?', *Alcoholism: Clinical & Experimental Research*, vol. 43, no. 7, July 2019, p. 1533.

2   *Munkara v Bencsevich & ors* [2018] NTCA 4. The Melbourne-based Human Rights Law Centre announced that it was supporting a further appeal to the High Court, but Mr Munkara abandoned the appeal before it was lodged.

3   Erwin Chlanda, 'Whenever You Need a Cop ... There Are Three', *Alice Springs News*, 13 May 2019.

4   *Sentencing Act 1995* (NT), ss 43(5) and 43(7).

5   Elizabeth Shulman, Laurence Steinberg and Alex Piquero, 'The Age-Crime Curve in Adolescence and Early Adulthood Is Not Due to Age Differences in Economic Status', *Journal of Youth and Adolescence*, vol. 42, no. 6, June 2013, p. 848.

6   *De novo* appeals are heard essentially as if the charges are being determined by a court for the first time. The right to a *de novo* appeal from the Magistrates Court was abolished in Victoria by the *Justice Legislation Amendment (Criminal Appeals) Act 2019*.

7   This information comes mainly from *Guardian Australia*'s remarkable database – created and maintained in partnership with UTS's Jumbunna Institute for Indigenous Education – which has tracked each death of an Indigenous person in a custodial situation since 1 January 2008: <https://www.theguardian.com/australia-news/ng-interactive/2018/aug/28/deaths-inside-indigenous-australian-deaths-in-custody>. The thirty-one-year-old male's hanging death was reported in Christopher Walsh, 'Aboriginal Prisoner Hanged Himself While in Custody at Darwin's Holtze Prison: Corrections Sources', *NT Independent*, 3 September 2021: https://ntindependent.com.au/aboriginal-prisoner-hanged-himself-while-in-custody-at-darwins-holtze-prison-corrections-sources/.

8   Amy McQuire, 'The Families Fighting for Justice for Indigenous Deaths in Custody', *Marie Claire*, September 2020.

9   Australian Bureau of Statistics, *Prisoners in Australia 2000*, released 12 June 2001.

10 Lorena Allam, 'Legal Experts Call for Investigations into Indigenous Deaths in Custody to Be Reopened', *Guardian Australia*, 10 June 2020.

11 John Walker and Jennifer Hallinan, *Australian Prisoners 1990: Results of the National Prison Census, 30 June 1990*, Australian Institute of Criminology, 1991, p. 22.

12 Compare Australian Bureau of Statistics, *Prisoners in Australia: 2000* (published 12 June 2001), p.11, Table 3, with John Walker and Jennifer Hallinan, *Australian Prisoners 1990: Results of the National Prison Census of 30 June 1990* (Australian Institute of Criminology), p. 23, Table 3(c).

13 ABS, *Prisoners in Australia: 2010*, released 9 December 2010.

14 ABS, *Prisoners in Australia: 2019*, released 5 December 2019.

15 ABS, *Prisoners in Australia: 2020*, released 3 December 2020.

16   Andrew Leigh, 'The Second Convict Age: Explaining the Return of Mass Imprisonment to Australia', CESifo Working Paper No. 8163, March 2020, p. 12: https://papers.ssrn.com/sol3/papers.cfm?abstract_id=3555590.

17   Bill Stanner, 'The Great Australian Silence', Boyer Lecture delivered as the second in the series *After the Dreaming*, 7 November 1968. The text of the lecture is reproduced, with commentary, in Robert Manne, ed., *The Dreaming and Other Essays*, Black Inc., Melbourne, 2009.

18   ABS, *Prisoners in Australia: 2020*, released 3 December 2020.

19   ABS, *Prisoners in Australia: 2019*, released 5 December 2019.

20   Judy Atkinson, *Trauma Trails: Recreating Song Lines: The Transgenerational Effects of Trauma in Indigenous Australia*, Spinifex Press, 2002.

21   See, for instance, the Productivity Commission's ongoing *Overcoming Indigenous Disadvantage* reports, and the annual *Closing the Gap* reports to the Commonwealth Parliament.

22   Keynes, *A Tract on Monetary Reform*, Macmillan & Co., London, 1923, p. 80.

23   Russell Marks, 'The Reporting of the Zachary Rolfe Trial', *The Saturday Paper*, no. 391, 19 March 2022.

24   Shorten, all in *The Australian*: 'Out of Yuendumu: How Violence Seeps Through Generations', 28 May 2022; 'I Didn't Want Dad Jailed, But I Was Scared He Would Kill Me', 30 May 2022; 'I Want to Go Home but I Don't Feel Safe There', 31 May 2022.

25   Aikman, '"Epidemic of Violence" Plagues Women: Judge', *The Australian*, 4 June 2022, p. 1.

26   Paige Taylor, 'Expert Voices Ignored as Lives Plagued by Violence', *The Australian*, 6 June 2022, p. 8.

27   This paragraph was published in an earlier form in *Dead Right: How Neoliberalism Ate Itself and What Comes Next*, Quarterly Essay, vol. 70, 2018.

28   Debbie Bargallie, *Unmasking the Racial Contract: Indigenous Voices on Racism in the Australian Public Service*, Aboriginal Studies Press, Canberra, 2020, p. 82.

CHAPTER 1

1   This date is often given as 29 April, especially in accounts which reference Cook's journals. But Cook used a nautical dating system by which what he described as 29 April in fact commenced at noon on what we would call 28 April. The journals of Banks and Parkinson, who used the civil dating system familiar to us, both record these events as having occurred on 28 April 1770.

2   Parkinson, *A Journal of a Voyage to the South Seas in His Majesty's Ship, The Endeavour*, London, 1778, p. 134.

3   Ray Ingrey, Shane Ingrey and Paul Irish, 'Warrawarrawa: What Was Really Said to Cook?', in Pauline Curby (ed.), *East Coast Encounters 1770: Reflections on a Cultural Clash*, Sutherland Shire Historical Society, 2020; Shane Ingrey, 'Voices Heard but Not Understood', published on the Gujaga Foundation's website on 29 April 2020: https://www.gujaga.org.au/stories/voices-heard-but-not-understood.

4   Banks' *Endeavour* journal, 28 and 29 April 1770 entries; Cook's *Endeavour* journal, 29 April 1770 entry; Sydney Parkinson's *Endeavour* journal, 28 April 1770 entry.

5   Alan Frost's revisionist work *Botany Bay: The Real Story* (Black Inc., 2012) convincingly argues that the problem of the convicts was not the only concern in the minds of those in the Pitt government when they chose Botany Bay as the site for the new colony.

6   *Journals of the House of Commons*, 19 Geo. III, vol. 37, 1 April 1779, p. 311.

7   See, for example, *Copious Remarks on the Discovery of New South Wales* (London, 1787) and *The History of New Holland* (John Stockdale, London, 1787). The latter text is sometimes attributed to William Eden before he became Lord Auckland.

8   Banks, *Endeavour* journal, 'Scarcity of Inhabitants', p. 307.

9   Arthur Phillip's Second Commission, instructions delivered on 25 April 1787, collected in *Historical Records of Australia, Series I: Governors' Despatches to and from England, Vol. I*, The Library Committee of the Commonwealth Parliament 1914–1925, Sydney, pp. 11, 13–14.

10   He may have actually said 'Ngarabanu' or 'Ngarabóoni', the latter having been recorded by William Dawes as meaning 'I don't understand you': Jeremy Steele, *The Aboriginal Language of Sydney: A Partial Reconstruction of the Indigenous Language of Sydney Based on the Notebooks of William Dawes*, MA thesis, Macquarie University, 2005: https://www.williamdawes.org/docs/steele_thesis.pdf.

11   Watkin Tench, *A Complete Account of the Settlement at Port Jackson*, 1793, chapter III.

12   James Willis, 'Going to Hell in a Cradle': The Relationship Between Transportation and Imprisonment in Eighteen- and Nineteenth-Century Britain: Punishment, Liberty and the State, unpublished PhD thesis, Yale University, May 2000.

13   *Calvin's Case* (1608) 77 ER 377 at 398.

14   *Campbell v Hall* (1774) 98 ER 1045.

15   Barbara Arneil, *John Locke and America: The Defence of English Colonialism*, Oxford University Press, Oxford, 1996.

16   Blackstone, *Commentaries on the Laws of England*, vol. 1, 1787 edition, p. 108.

17   Lisa Ford, *Settler Sovereignty: Jurisdiction and Indigenous People in America and Australia, 1788-1836*, Harvard University Press, 2010, chapter 2.

18   John Moore, *The First Fleet Marines*, University of Queensland Press, St Lucia, 1987, pp. 117–18.

19   Sam Keith Vincent, 'Australia's Oldest Murder Mystery', *The Sydney Morning Herald*, 1 November 2003. The following year, 1803, Hacking would face trial for shooting his mistress, the convict Ann Holmes. He was convicted and sentenced to death, but then almost immediately pardoned, before he was again sentenced to death for stealing naval stores. He earned yet another reprieve. See: G.P. Walsh, 'Hacking, Henry (1750–1831)', *Australian Dictionary of Biography*, National Centre of Biography, Australian National University, 1966.

20   Deputy Judge Advocate Richard Atkins, journal, 26 September 1794, held in the National Library, MS 4039; transcribed at Macquarie University's 'Decisions of the Superior Courts of New South Wales, 1788–1899': https://www.law.mq.edu.au/research/colonial_case_law/nsw/other_features/music_letters_poetry/atkins_introduction/atkins_diary_1794/

21   Lieutenant Colonel David Collins (NSW's first deputy judge advocate, and the first lieutenant-governor of South Van Diemen's Land), *An Account of the English Colony in New South Wales*, James Collier (ed.), Whitcombe and Tombs Ltd, 1804, pp, 246–47.

22   *R v Randall*, 7 June 1799, in NSW State Records, 'Bench of Magistrates, 1788–1820' index, item SZ767, reel 655, p. 83.

23   *R v Powell* [1799] NSWKR 7; annexed as 'Trial for Murder of Two Natives' (the record of a trial held in mid-October 1799 before Judge Advocate Captain Waterhouse) to a letter Governor Hunter sent to the Duke of Portland (who was Home Secretary), 2 January 1800; collected in *Historical Records of Australia, Series I: Governors' Despatches to and from England, Vol. II*, The Library Committee of the Commonwealth Parliament 1914–1925, Sydney, pp. 401 at 405 and 409.

24   John Connor, *The Australian Frontier Wars, 1788–1838*, UNSW Press, Sydney, 2002, p. 43.

25   See: 'Sydney', *Sydney Gazette and New South Wales Advertiser*, Sydney, 19 March 1805, pp. 2–3.

26   'Sydney', *Sydney Gazette and New South Wales Advertiser*, 4 August 1805, p. 2. The *Gazette* conveniently left out of its summary the fact that settlers had killed six Aboriginal people in retaliation for the four settlers they had killed, though as King told the secretary of state for war and the colonies in a letter, he'd kindly offered to forego any further retaliation in recognition of this inequity: King to Earl Camden, 20 July 1805, *Historical Records of Australia, Series I, Vol. V*, p. 497.

27   'Sydney', *Sydney Gazette and New South Wales Advertiser*, 11 August 1805, p. 2.

28   Atkins fled England to escape creditors and arrived in New South Wales in 1792. Apparently on the basis of his family connections – he was the fifth son of Sir William Bowyer, and his three older brothers had excellent reputations – Phillip immediately made Atkins a magistrate. He continued to run up credit he never settled – he was an alcoholic – until, in 1796, John Macarthur called him a 'public cheater' and attempted to have him prosecuted for libel. But, by then, Governor John Hunter had instructions from England to appoint Atkins as acting deputy judge advocate. By 1800, Atkins was permanently judge advocate, which meant he was also president of the criminal and civil courts, the committing magistrate, the judge and the public prosecutor. In those roles he was 'ignorant and merciless', and Governor William Bligh complained that Atkins had passed sentences of death while drunk: J.M. Bennett, 'Atkins, Richard (1745–1820)', *Australian Dictionary of Biography*, National Centre of Biography, Australia National University 1966.

29   Judge Advocate Richard Atkins' Opinion on the Treatment of Natives, 8 July 1805, *Historical Records of Australia, Series I, Vol. V*, pp. 502–04.

30   *Sydney Gazette and New South Wales Advertiser*, 3 June 1815, p. 2.
31   *Sydney Gazette and New South Wales Advertiser*, 17 June 1815, p. 2.
32   Macquarie, letter to Shaw, 9 April 1816, quoted in Connor, *Australian Frontier Wars*, p. 51.
33   Diary of James Wallis, 17 April 1816, collected in 'Colonial Secretary's Papers 1788–1825', State Records of NSW, NRS 897 4-1735, pp. 55–57.
34   Connor, *The Australian Frontier Wars*, p. 52.
35   'Government Public Notice and Order', *Sydney Gazette and New South Wales Advertiser*, 3 August 1816, p. 1.
36   Born in the mid 1790s, by which time the settlers had already destroyed most of the yam beds in the greater Sydney region and replaced them with their own crops, Duall grew up amid conditions of escalating conflict over land and resources. From 1814, that conflict intensified in conditions of severe drought. Macquarie, governor since 1810 and the first since the Rum Rebellion, ordered punitive expeditions which, predictably, led to even greater conflict. Within two years of his being conscripted to guide Hamilton Hume's first expedition into the interior, Macquarie had included Duall on his list of 'hostile natives' and dramatically ramped up his punitive strategy. Four days after he displayed Durelle and Kinabygal's bodies (and removed Kinabygal's head), Parker came across Duall and another man, Quayat, who had taken refuge on the property of an Aboriginal sympathiser, Kennedy. Along with a handful of other captured men, Duall was locked in the Liverpool Gaol for three months before Macquarie announced that the warrior would be transported to Van Diemen's Land without trial: 'Government Public Notice and Order', *Sydney Gazette and New South Wales Advertiser*, 3 August 1816, p. 1.
37   Sydney was initially very small, there wasn't much urgency about its expansion, and the Blue Mountains offered a kind of natural border, within which policing was relatively straightforward. But as Britain industrialised, especially during the 1820s, its demand for wool grew and settlers were increasingly willing to venture outside settled areas, to vast areas where policing was practically impossible. See: Lisa Ford, 'Protecting the Peace on the Edge of Empire: Commissioners of Crown Lands in New South Wales', chapter 9 in Bain Attwood, Lauren Benton and Adam Clulow (eds), *Protection and Empire: A Global History*, Cambridge University Press, New York, 2017, pp 175-93.
38   Timeline, Colonial Frontier Massacres in Australia, 1788–1930, Centre for 21st Century Humanities, University of Newcastle: https://c21ch.newcastle.edu.au/colonialmassacres/timeline.php.
39   The text of the Proclamation continued:

> And finally, His Excellency the Governor hereby orders and directs, that on occasions of any natives coming armed, or in a hostile manner without arms, or in unarmed parties exceeding six in number, to any farm belonging to, or occupied by, British subjects in the interior, such natives are first to be desired in a civil manner to depart from the said farm; and if they persist in remaining thereon, or attempt to plunder, rob, or commit any kind of depredation, they are then to be driven away by force of arms by the settlers themselves; and in case they are not able to do so, they are to apply to a Magistrate for aid from the nearest military station; and the troops stationed there, are hereby commanded to render their assistance when so required. The troops are also to afford aid at the towns of Sydney, Parramatta, and Windsor respectively, when called on by the Magistrates or Police Officers at those stations.

> Before 1824, it's unlikely that governor-issued orders which were inconsistent with British law were lawful: Enid Campbell, 'Prerogative Rule in New South Wales, 1788–1823', *Journal of the Royal Australian Historical Society*, vol. 50, no. 3, August 1964, p. 161 at 180; Rae Else-Mitchell, 'The Foundation of New South Wales and the Inheritance of the Common Law', *Journal of the Royal Australian Historical Society*, vol. 49, no. 1, June 1963, p. 1 at 5; Victor Windeyer, *Lectures on Legal History*, 2nd edition, Law Book Co. of Australasia, 1957, p. 306. The opposite view – that governors' powers were plenary – was argued by H.V. Evatt in *Rum Rebellion* (Angus & Robertson, 1938). See: Bruce Kercher, *Debt, Seduction and Other Disasters: The Birth of Civil Law in New South Wales*, Federation Press, Sydney, 1996, pp. 6–9; Kercher, footnote 5 to Macquarie Law School's entry for *R v Johnston et al* on its Colonial Case Law website: http://www.law.mq.edu.au/research/colonial_case_law/nsw/cases/case_index/1824/supreme_court/r_v_johnston_and_others/#n38.

40 Macquarie, 'Proclamation', *Sydney Gazette and New South Wales Advertiser*, 4 May 1816, p. 1.

41 *R v Mow-watty* [1816] NSWSupC 2, 27 September 1816, as reported in the *Sydney Gazette and New South Wales Advertiser*, 28 September 1816.

42 Robert Popper, 'History and Development of the Accused's Right to Testify', *Washington University Law Review*, vol. 1962, no. 4, January 1962, pp. 454–71.

43 *R v Mow-watty* [1816] NSWSupC 2, 27 September 1816, as reported in the *Sydney Gazette and New South Wales Advertiser*, 28 September 1816. See also: Lisa Ford and Brent Salter, 'From Pluralism to Territorial Sovereignty: The 1816 Trial of Mow-watty in the Superior Court of New South Wales', *Indigenous Law Journal*, vol. 7, no. 1, 2008, pp. 67–86.

44 Diary of Lachlan Macquarie, 1 November 1816.

45 *Sydney Gazette and New South Wales Advertiser*, 23 August 1817, p. 3.

46 See: Wylde to Colonial Secretary, 'Re The Trial of Two Aborigines', 28 December 1822, collected in Colonial Secretary Papers 1788–1825, Reel 6054, 4/1758, p. 145; *R v Hatherly and Jackie*, 'Informations', collected in 'Court of Criminal Jurisdiction, Depositions and Related Papers' [SZ800], State Records of NSW, Reel 1798, pp. 1–19.

47 Marianne Constable, *The Law of the Other: The Mixed Jury and Changing Conceptions of Citizenship, Law and Knowledge*, University of Chicago Press, 1994, pp. 96–113.

48 *R v Binge Mhulto* [1828] NSWSupC 82 per Dowling J, 19 September 1828, reported as 'Case of the "Niger"', *The Australian*, Sydney, 26 September 1828, p. 3. In 'consultation with their Honors the Judges', Baxter ultimately withdrew the charge and released Binghi Multi just before Christmas: Baxter to the Supreme Court, 19 December 1928, SRNSW, 28/10171 4/2005, reproduced at http://www.law.mq.edu.au/research/colonial_case_law/nsw/cases/case_index/1828/r_v_binge_mhulto/#footnote2m.

49 *R v Lowe* [1827] NSWSupC 32 per Forbes CJ and Stephen J, 18 May 1827; reported in *The Australian*, 23 May 1827, p. 3. Unsurprisingly, *The Australian* carried a lengthy summary of the trial, and particular of Wentworth's and Wardell's (its publishers) submissions.

50 Confusingly, Justice James Dowling mistakenly reversed the names of the accused and the deceased when he produced his notes of the trial: Dowling, 'Proceedings of the Supreme Court', vol. 22, Archives Office of NSW, 2/3205.

51 *R v Ballard or Barrett* [1829] NSWSupC 26, Supreme Court of NSW, 13 June 1829 per Forbes CJ, as reported in Dowling, 'Proceedings of the Supreme Court', vol. 22, Archives Office of NSW, 2/3205, pp. 98–103.

52 Lancelot Threlkeld was a former circus and theatre performer who had joined the London Missionary Society and first arrived in Sydney in 1817. In 1832 he was a year into his role as government-appointed missionary to the Awabakal people north of Lake Macquarie, and would go on to publish the seminal study of their language, *An Australian Grammar: Comprehending the Principles and Natural Rules of the Language, as Spoken by the Aborigines in the Vicinity of Hunter's River, Lake Macquarie &c New South Wales*, Stephens and Stokes, 1834. The Awabakal language is no longer spoken.

53 *R v Tommy* [1827] NSWSupC 70 per Forbes CJ, 24 November 1827, as reported in *The Monitor* (Sydney), 26 November 1827.

54 *R v Jackey* [1834] NSWSupC 94 per Forbes CJ, 8 August 1834, as reported in the *Sydney Gazette and New South Wales Advertiser*, 12 August 1834.

55 *R v Wombarty*, 18 November 1837 per Dowling CJ, reported in the *Sydney Gazette*, 23 November 1837.

56 Threlkeld, *Report of the Mission to the Aborigines at Lake Macquarie, New South Wales*, 30 December 1837, pp. 3–4; digitised and transcribed by Gionni Di Gravio, University of Newcastle, March 2005, https://downloads.newcastle.edu.au/library/cultural%20collections/pdf/threlkeld1837.pdf.

57 This insight is Jeannine Purdy's, from 'Royal Commissions and Omissions: What Was Left Out of the Report on the Death of John Pat', *Australian Journal of Law and Society*, vol. 10, 1994, p. 37 at 46.

58 See: 'Trial for Murder of Two Natives', enclosure 1 with Governor Hunter's letter to the Duke of Portland, 2 January 1800, despatch 48, collected in *Historical Records of Australia, Series I: Governors' Despatches to and from England, Vol. II*, The Library Committee of the Commonwealth Parliament 1914–1925, Sydney, pp. 403–22.

59 Governor Hunter to the Duke of Portland, 2 January 1800, despatch 48, collected in *Historical Records of Australia, Series I: Governors' Despatches to and from England, Vol. II*,

The Library Committee of the Commonwealth Parliament 1914–1925, Sydney, p. 401.

60   Lord Hobart to Acting-Governor King, 30 January 1802, *Historical Records of Australia, Series I: Governors' Despatches to and from England, Vol. III*, The Library Committee of the Commonwealth Parliament (1914–1925), Sydney, p. 366 at 366–67.

61   *R v Hawker* [1822] NSWSupC 4 per Wylde DJA on 10 June 1822, as reported in the *Sydney Gazette and New South Wales Advertiser*, 14 June 1822, p. 2.

62   *R v Johnston, Clarke, Nicholson, Castles and Crear* [1824] NSWSupC per Forbes CJ, 6 August 1824, reported in the *Sydney Gazette*, 12 August 1824.

63   *R v Jamieson* [1827] NSWSupC 31 per Stephen J, 16 May 1827, reported in the *Sydney Gazette and New South Wales Advertiser*, 18 May 1827, pp. 2–3.

64   *Queensland Police Gazette*, vol. 27, 1890, p. 141; in Jonathan Richards, *The Secret War: A True History of Queensland's Native Police*, UQP, St Lucia, 2008, p. 32.

65   Lockier Burges, born 1841, was the nephew of another Lockier Burges, who had been born in about 1814 and migrated to Western Australia in 1830. Burges Snr served briefly on WA's Legislative Council between 1879 and 1884.

66   In 1865, Burges joined an expedition led by Maitland Brown which went looking for three missing explorers on the north-west coast. They hunted the truth with a single-minded determination, repeatedly capturing, torturing and questioning Aboriginal people they came across, chaining them to trees or locking them in the hold of Brown's boat. Eventually two of their prisoners led them to the explorers' final campsite. They were dead, apparently at the hands of local Aboriginal people. The two prisoners tried to escape (Brown said) and were themselves shot dead. In his report of the expedition, Brown began the myth that they'd been murdered cruelly in their sleep. The four bullets fired from one of their guns told a different story: 'Inquest on the bodies of Messrs P.K. Panter, J.E. Harding and W.H. Goldwyer', *The Inquirer and Commercial News*, Perth, 24 May 1865, p. 2. But the myth was eternalised on the plaque of a statue built to commemorate the heroic explorers in 1913: Bruce Scates, 'A Monument to Murder: Celebrating the Conquest of Aboriginal Australia', *Studies in Western Australian History*, vol. 10, April 1989, p. 21. Two days later, Brown said, they were ambushed by twenty-five warriors armed with spears. Brown and his party shot as many as twenty of them dead, and miraculously escaped unharmed: Maitland Brown, 'Journal of an Expedition under the Command of Maitland Brown, esquire, in search of Messrs Fred K. Panter, James R. Harding and William H. Goldwyer', published in *The Perth Gazette and West Australian Times*, 19 May 1865, pp. 3–4 and 26 May 1865, pp. 2–4.

67   Sidney Harring, 'The Killing Time: A Legal History of Aboriginal Resistance in Colonial Australia', *Ottawa Law Review/Revue de droit d'Ottawa*, vol. 26, no. 2, 1994, p. 385 at 415–21.

68   Kirby escaped into the bush and was then recaptured by Aboriginal people, one of whom – Burragong – he stabbed, inflicting a wound from which Burragong later died: *R v Kirby and Thompson* [1820] NSWKR 11, 14 December 1820, reported in the *Sydney Gazette*, 16 December 1820.

69   On the Waterloo Creek massacre, see: Bruce Elder, *Blood on the Wattle*, 3rd edition, New Holland Publishers, 2003, chapter 6; Roger Milliss, *Waterloo Creek: The Australia Day Massacre of 1838*, UNSW Press, 1994; Lyndall Ryan, 'Waterloo Creek, Northern New South Wales, 1838' in Bain Atwood and S.G. Foster (eds), *Frontier Conflict: The Australian Experience*, National Museum of Australia, pp. 33–43.

70   See Stan Grant's *Australia Day* (Harper Collins, Sydney, 2019) for the most cogent of the arguments for its retention.

71   Elder, *Blood on the Wattle*, p. 94.

72   Ford, 'Protecting the Peace on the Edge of Empire'; S.J. Gale and R.J. Haworth, 'Beyond the Limits of Location: Human Environmental Disturbance Prior to Official European Contact in Early Colonial Australia', *Archaeology in Oceania*, vol. 37, no. 3, October 2002, pp. 123–36; Enid Campbell, 'Promises of Land from the Crown: Some Questions of Equity in Colonial Australia', *University of Tasmania Law Review*, vol. 13, no. 1, 1994, pp. 1–42. Darling's declarations were made on 5 September 1826 and then on 14 October 1829.

73   Amanda Porter and Chris Cunneen, 'Policing Settler Colonial Societies', chapter 24 in Philip Birch, Michael Kennedy and Erin Kruger (eds), *Australian Policing: Critical Issues in 21st Century Police Practice*, Routledge, London and New York, 2021.

74   M.H. Fels, *Good Men and True: The Aboriginal Police of the Port Phillip District, 1837–1853*, Melbourne University Press, Carlton, 1988.

75 Richards, *The Secret War.*
76 Johnstone, lecture at Centennial Hall, Brisbane, 25 June 1904, reported in *The Queenslander*, 2 July 1904, p. 27.
77 See: Thalia Anthony, *Indigenous People, Crime and Punishment.*
78 *The Australian*, 3 February 1834, p. 2.
79 Wenar to the Superintendent of Public Works, reported in the *Western Australian Government Gazette*, 11 February 1842, p. 1.
80 Jonathan Richards, *The Secret War*, pp. 58–60.
81 W.L.G. Drew, A.C. Gregory and Charles Coxen, *Aborigines Protection Commission: Second Report*, 6 May 1875, printed in *The Telegraph* (Brisbane), 8 April 1876, p. 5.

CHAPTER 2

1 Penelope Gibbs, 'Defendants on Video: Conveyer Belt Justice or a Revolution in Access?', report for Transform Justice, October 2017; Carolyn McKay, 'Video Links from Prison: Permeability and the Carceral World', International Journal for Crime, Justice and Social Democracy, vol. 5, no. 1, 2016, p. 21.
2 The *Royal Style and Titles Act 1953* (Cth) took effect from 7 May 1953, from which date Elizabeth II was known in Australia as 'Elizabeth the Second, by the Grace of God of the United Kingdom, Australia and her other Realms and Territories Queen, Head of the Commonwealth, Defender of the Faith'. One hundred and sixty-five years after 'settlement', Australia finally had its own Crown, albeit one it shared with many other countries. Since 1973, her title has been the slightly more nationalist 'Elizabeth the Second, by the Grace of God Queen of Australia and Her Other Realms and Territories, Head of the Commonwealth': *Royal Styles and Titles Act 1973* (Cth).
3 James Forman Jr, *Locking Up Our Own: Crime and Punishment in Black America*, Farrar, Straus and Giroux, 2017, pp. 8–9.
4 Felicity James, 'Local Lawyer David Woodroffe to be Sworn in as the Northern Territory's First Aboriginal Judge', *ABC News*, 6 July 2022.
5 Kate Galloway, Melissa Castan and Dani Larkin, 'Legal Fictions as the Law's Original "Post-Truth" State', paper presented to 'Real' Laws in a Post-Truth World', Australasian Law Academics Annual Conference, Southern Cross University, Gold Coast, 5 July 2019.
6 Elisabeth Armitage, 'Supreme Court Sittings in Yarralin', *Balance*, May 2005, p. 10.
7 Threlkeld to John Kinchela, February 1836, https://www.law.mq.edu.au/research/colonial_case_law/nsw/other_features/correspondence/documents/document_41/. In *Indigenous Crime and Settler Law: White Sovereignty After Empire* (Palgrave Macmillan, 2012), Heather Douglas and Mark Finnane suggest that Bungaree 'was already well absorbed into settler society, moving between his own people and the settler community with some ease', and came from a 'well-regarded Aboriginal family which had long been recognised as trustworthy by the settler elite' (p. 38).
8 Sidney Stephen's father, John, had been a successful barrister on the island of St Kitts in the Caribbean, as had John's brother James (snr). John returned to England, invested badly and lost his money. By this time his nephew (and Sidney's cousin), James Stephen, was the Colonial Office's in-house lawyer. James used his influence to have his uncle posted to a top job in New South Wales: C.H. Currey, 'Stephen, John (1771–1833)', *Australian Dictionary of Biography*, vol. 2, Melbourne University Press, 1967.
9 'Law Intelligence: Supreme Court, Criminal Side', *Sydney Herald*, Sydney, 8 February 1836, p. 3.
10 'Law Intelligence: Supreme Court, Criminal Side', *The Australian*, Sydney, 9 February 1836, p. 2.
11 The direct quote from Blackstone's *Commentaries on the Laws of England* is 'desart and uncultivated', but I've updated his eighteenth-century spelling in this paragraph.
12 'Supreme Court', *Sydney Gazette and New South Wales Advertiser*, 23 February 1836, p. 3.
13 Karen Fox has contributed an essay, 'Australian Legal Dynasties: The Stephens and the Streets' (17 February 2015), to the National Centre of Biography's *Obituaries Australia* website, http://oa.anu.edu.au/essay/10; and OA also carries Stephen's obituary as originally published in the *Tasmanian Weekly News* on 6 March 1858: http://oa.anu.edu.au/obituary/stephen-sidney-28378. There is also an entry for Sidney Stephens by Ronald Jones in A.H. McLintock's edited *An Encyclopaedia of New Zealand*, 1966. None of these entries carries any reference to his plea in *R v Murrell*.

14   'Supreme Court', *Sydney Gazette and New South Wales Advertiser*, 23 February 1836, p. 3.
15   Judgement of Burton J in the case of Jack Congo Murrell, 11 April 1836, in Miscellaneous Correspondence relating to Aborigines, State Records of NSW, 5/1161, pp. 210–16.
16   Forbes CJ's judgement in *R v Murrell*, as reported in 'Supreme Court', *Sydney Gazette and New South Wales Advertiser*, Sydney, 12 April 1836, p. 3.
17   A correspondent, 'Jack Congo Murrel – The Black Native', letter to the *Sydney Herald*, 5 May 1836, p. 2.
18   Burton J, 'Notes for Judgment', Supreme Court, Miscellaneous Correspondence Relating to Aborigines, State Records of NSW, 5/1161, p. 239, www.law.mq.edu.au/research/colonial_case_law/nsw/cases/case_index/1836/r_v_murrell_and_bummaree/, note [4] (accessed 22 March 2020).
19   Mitchell's official report to Alexander McLeay, now contained in 'Extracts from Proceedings … Relating to Thomas Mitchell's Attack on Aborigines, 1836', State Records of NSW, Colonial Secretary's Office, 4/118, and reproduced in Robert Macklin, *Hamilton Hume*.
20   'Expedition of Discovery', *The Australian*, 8 November 1836, p. 2.
21   *Sydney Gazette*, 14 January 1837, p. 2. As part of a dispatch dated 25 January 1837, Bourke sent a copy of the Executive Council proceedings to Glenelg in the Colonial Office.
22   Glenelg was deeply concerned about Mitchell's actions, and struggled to reconcile them with Mitchell's reputation and his great past deeds. He promised to forward to Bourke the House of Commons select committee's report of its recently concluded inquiry, and reiterated the basic facts: Britain had asserted sovereignty over the continent; therefore, the 'Natives' were subjects of the Queen, entitled to the highest protection of British law. 'I am well aware that legal maxims of this kind will not serve for the solution of practical difficulties such as those in which Major Mitchell was involved,' Glenelg acknowledged. He suggested a formal inquest to determine exactly how Mitchell's victims died, if only to remind the colonists of the importance of the life of each subject. Still, he wasn't prepared to condemn Mitchell. 'It would be difficult to exaggerate the reluctance with which I should adopt any measure apparently at variance with the gratitude, which Her Majesty's Government feel for Major Mitchell's services, and the respect which they entertain for his character': Glenelg to Bourke, 26 July 1837, *HRA* series I, vol. XIX, pp. 48–50.
23   In his doctoral thesis, Eugene Schofield-Georgeson suggests that it was the 1837 case, *R v Wombarty*, in which the Supreme Court extended its jurisdiction to Aboriginal people. Wombarty was brought before the new Supreme Court on multiple murder charges after he'd allegedly killed four white men 'while asleep in their huts'. But Wombarty, from Port Macquarie, was eventually discharged after the court spent months trying and failing to find someone who could interpret. In 1837, New England was 'a district so remote, and where the dialect is so different from that ordinarily spoken by the natives, that no European could be found who understood it': *Sydney Gazette*, 23 November 1837. The case doesn't appear to have had any particular significance in the developing application of British criminal law to Aboriginal people, nor do the materials Schofield-Georgeson refers to (a *Sydney Gazette* entry dated 19 August 1837, which simply reports an adjournment of the case while efforts to find an interpreter continued; and a letter from Lord Glenelg to Governor Bourke dated 26 July 1837, which doesn't mention the case at all) establish any such significance: Schofield-Georgeson, *By What Authority? Criminal Law in Colonial New South Wales, 1788–1861*, Australian Scholarly Publishing, 2018, pp. 32 and 167, notes 86–88. Most other authorities attach much more significance to *R v Murrell and Bummaree* (1836), discussed above. Schofield-Georgeson does mention *Murrell*, though only to suggest that the ordinary rule preventing Aboriginal people from being tried before British law was 'relaxed' in that particular case.
24   Hugo Grotius, *De jure belli ac pacis* (Paris, 1625), as translated by Jean Barbeyrac as *The Rights of War and Peace* (London, 1738), Book II, chapter XXII.
25   James Douglas, 14th Earl of Morton, 'Hints Offered to the Consideration of Captain Cooke, Mr Bankes, Doctor Solander and Other Gentlemen Who Go Upon the Expedition On Board the *Chiswick*', 10 August 1768, in *Papers of Sir Joseph Banks, 1745–1923*, Series I: Correspondence and papers of Joseph Banks, MS 9, item 113; digitised at https://nla.gov.au/nla.obj-222963290/findingaid?digitised=y#nla-obj-222969577.

26 See: N. Bruce Duthu, *Shadow Nations: Tribal Sovereignty and the Limits of Legal Pluralism*, Oxford University Press, 2015.

27 *Wacando v The Commonwealth of Australia and the State of Queensland* [1981] HCA 60 per Murphy J.

28 M.F. Lindley, *The Acquisition and Government of Backward Territory in International Law*, Longmans, 1926, p. 29; quoted in Henry Reynolds, *Truth-Telling* (2021), NewSouth Publishing, Sydney, p. 17 [my emphasis].

29 Cook, *The Voyage of the Resolution and Discovery, 1776-1780* (the third volume of J.C. Beaglehole's edited *Journals of Captain Cook on His Voyages of Discovery*, 1967), p. ccxxiii; Committee on Transportation, 28 July 1785; both referred to in Reynolds, *Truth-Telling*, pp. 18–19.

30 Darling to George Arthur, 4 April 1832, in the George Arthur Papers; quoted in Reynolds, *Truth-Telling*, p. 34.

31 *Slavery Abolition Act 1833* (3 & 4 Will. IV c. 73).

32 Charles Napier, *Colonization, Particularly in Southern Australia; with some Remarks on Small Farms and Over Population*, T. & W. Boone, London, 1835, p. 213.

33 James Stephen to Lord Glenelg, 10 December 1835; quoted in Reynolds, *Truth-Telling*, pp. 42–43.

34 Edith Ophelia Browne and John Richard Burton (eds), *Short Biographies of the Worthies of Worcestershire*, Harvard University, 1916, p. 177.

35 House of Commons, *Report of the Parliamentary Select Committee on Aboriginal Tribes (British Settlements)*, 1837, p. 4; quoted by Willis J in his report of his decision in *R v Bonjon*, NSW Supreme Court, 16 September 1841, in the *Port Phillip Patriot*, 20 September 1841.

36 Susanne Davies, 'Aborigines, Murder and the Criminal Law in Early Port Phillip, 1841–1851', *Historical Studies*, vol. 22, no. 88, pp. 313–35.

37 Clare Land, *Tunnerminnerwait and Maulboyheenner: The Involvement of Aboriginal People from Tasmania in Key Events of Early Melbourne*, City of Melbourne, 2014, p. 23. On the massacre, see: Bruce Pascoe, *Convincing Ground*, Aboriginal Studies Press, 2007.

38 See 'The Van Diemen's Land Blacks', *Port Phillip Gazette*, 22 December 1841, pp. 2–3.

39 *Port Phillip Herald*, Melbourne, 24 December 1841; quoted in full in Ian McFarlane, 'Aboriginal Society in North West Tasmania', unpublished PhD thesis, University of Tasmania, October 2002, p. 240.

40 Willis, quoted in Thomas McCombie, *The History of the Colony of Victoria: From Its Settlement to the Death of Sir Charles Hotham*, Sands and Kenny, 1858, p. 90.

41 Leonie Stevens, 'The Phenomenal Coolness of Tunnerminnerwait', *Victorian Historical Journal* vol. 81, no. 1, June 2010, pp. 18–40; Lynette Russell and Kate Auty, *Hunt Them, Hang Them: The Tasmanians in Port Phillip, 1841–1842*, Justice Press, Melbourne, 2016.

42 *R v Sweet* [2021] QDC 216 per Cash DCJ at note [10].

43 Evatt, 'The Acquisition of Territory in Australia and New Zealand', *Grotian Society Papers 1968: Studies in the History of the Law of Nations*, C.H. Alexandrowicz (ed.), The Hague, 1970.

44 See for instance: Christian Wolff, *The Law of Nations* (1750); G.F. von Martens, *The Law of Nations* (1788); Frederick Carl von Savigny, *Treatise on Possession* (1803).

45 *Worcester v Georgia* (1832) 31 US 515; *Johnson v McIntosh* (1832) 31 US 543; *Mitchel v US* (1835) 34 US 711; *R v Symonds* (1847) NZPCC 388; *Calder v British Columbia (AG)* [1973] SCR 313.

46 *Milirrpum v Nabalco* (1971) 17 FLR 141.

47 *Mabo v Queensland (No. 2)* (1992) 175 CLR 1.

48 An 1819 opinion by the British attorney-general and solicitor-general confirmed that New South Wales had been 'taken possession ... as desert and uninhabited': Shepherd and Gifford, opinion to Earl Bathurst, 15 February 1819, in *HRA*, series 4, vol. 1, p. 330. When the Colonial Office declared – in repudiating John Batman's 'treaty' with Wurundjeri Elders – that 'all people found occupying land without the authority of the government will be considered illegal trespassers', colonial authorities consistently misapplied that to Aboriginal people (most likely, it was directed at settlers): see Reynolds, *The Law of the Land*, Penguin, Camberwell, 1987, ch. 6; the 'all people found' document, dated 10 October 1835, has been lost from Bourke's papers but is in the British Archives.

49   Select Committee on Aboriginal Tribes, *Report of the Parliamentary Select Committee on Aboriginal Tribes (British Settlements)*, 1837, pp. 4, 80 and 84.

50   Richard Wolfe, *Battlers, Bluffers and Bully-Boys*, Random House New Zealand, Auckland, 2005, p. 71.

51   Paul Edwin Le Roy, 'Hutchinson, William (1772–1846)', *Australian Dictionary of Biography*, National Centre of Biography, ANU, 1966.

52   Known as 'the rule against perpetuities', the rule was first articulated by the House of Lords in 1682, after the Earl of Arundel tried to make a will directing how his estate would pass between his sons long after he died: *Duke of Norfolk's Case* (1682) 22 ER 931.

53   *William Cooper v The Honourable Alexander Stuart (Colonial Secretary)* (1889) LR 14 App Cas 286, 3 April 1889, per Lord Watson.

54   Maloga Petition, 1887; reproduced in Bain Attwood and Andrew Markus (eds), *The Struggle for Aboriginal Rights: A Documentary History*, Allen & Unwin, St Leonards, NSW, 1999, p. 52.

55   Andrew Markus, *Blood from a Stone: William Cooper and the Australian Aborigines' League*, Allen & Unwin, Sydney, 1988.

56   *Entick v Carrington* (1765) 19 St Tr 1029 per Lord Camden LCJ at 1066.

57   William Pitt, speech in opposition to the Cider Bill of 1763.

58   Journals of Cook and Banks, entries for 8, 9, 10 and 19 July 1770.

59   *R v Boatman or Jackass and Bulleye* [1832] NSWSupC 4 per Dowling J, 23 February 1832, as recorded in *Proceedings of the Supreme Court of New South Wales*, vol. 64, Archives Office of NSW, 2/3247, pp. 11–12. Boatman was found guilty after what appears to be a cursory examination of the evidence. But at Billy Bulli's trial immediately afterwards, John Palmer himself suggested that the accused men may have believed the sheep had been of no value to him (Palmer), due to the fact that one of his neighbours had recently turned 120 diseased sheep loose into the bush. On that basis the jury found Billy Bulli not guilty, and because he thought the jury would have reached the same verdict for Boatman had they heard Palmer's testimony, Dowling discharged him as well: as reported in the *Sydney Gazette and New South Wales Advertiser*, 25 February 1832.

60   *R v Lego'me* [1835] NSWSupC 4, per Forbes CJ, 12 February 1835; as reported in the *Sydney Herald*, 16 February 1835.

61   *Cooper v Stuart* [1889] UKPC 16 at para 13 per Lord Watson (my emphasis).

CHAPTER 3

1   Mark Finnane and John McGuire, 'The Uses of Punishment and Exile: Aborigines in Colonial Australia', *Punishment and Society*, vol. 3, no. 2, 2001, p. 279 at 287; Don Weatherburn, *Arresting Incarceration*, p. 13.

2   For one of countless examples of this schism, see: Mary Durack, *Kings in Grass Castles*, chapter 32: 'Prosperity, at a Price', 1959.

3   A.P. Elkin, 'Aboriginal Evidence and Justice', *Oceania*, vol. 17, no. 3, March 1947, p. 173 at 199, citing the *Daily Telegraph*, Sydney, 13 April 1933.

4   Credit for this novel approach – examining the NT Supreme Court's jurisprudential history since the 1930s – must go to Thalia Anthony, who did it first in her book *Indigenous People, Crime and Punishment*, Routledge, New York, 2013, pp. 87–5, and to Heather Douglas, who contrasted the sentencing approaches taken by Justices Wells and Kriewaldt in her book *Aboriginal Australians and the Criminal Law: History, Policy, Culture*, VDM Verlag Dr Müller, Saarbrücken, Germany, 2009.

5   The slain victims were referred to in contemporary reports simply as 'Malay', which at the time was a racial category that was applied to people from the Malay Peninsula down to Timor. It is roughly equivalent to today's ethnic category of the same name. Tingha de Hans, who had arrived in Palmerston from Kupang in West Timor during the early 1870s, was also referred to as 'Malay' (see 'The Malay Bay Massacre', *Northern Territory Times and Gazette*, Palmerston, 28 Oct 1892, p. 3; Paul Thomas, 'Interpreting the Macassans: Language Exchange in Historical Encounters', chapter 5 in Marshall Clark and Sally K. May (eds), *Macassan History and Heritage: Journeys, Encounters and Influences*, ANU E Press, 2013). The 'Macassan' trepangers who began visiting the northern coast of Australia during the eighteenth century came from at least as far afield as Sulawesi, though given its

proximity to Arnhem Land, Timor was the most obvious point of origin of the proa that the Iwaidja found on their beach in 1892.

6   'Law Courts: Circuit Court – Palmerston, Tuesday, Feb. 14th, 1893', *Northern Territory Times and Gazette*, 17 February 1893, p. 3. A detailed (and gruesome) account of witnesses' versions was given in 'Law Courts: Police Court, Monday, Nov. 13, 1892', *Northern Territory Times and Gazette*, 18 November 1892, p. 3.

7   'Law Courts: Circuit Court – Palmerston, Tuesday, Feb. 14th, 1893', *Northern Territory Times and Gazette*, 17 February 1893, p. 3.

8   Telegram from Adelaide, dated 19 July 1893, reported in *Northern Territory Times and Gazette*, 21 July 1893, p. 3.

9   Dean Mildren, 'Sketches on Territory Legal History', *Balance: Journal of the Northern Territory Law Society*, February–March 1999, p. 12 at 12. An account of Flannagan's trial can be found in 'Law Courts: Circuit Court – Palmerston, Thursday, Feb. 16', *Northern Territory Times and Gazette*, 17 February 1893, p. 3.

10 Quoted in Mildren, *Big Boss Fella, All Same Judge*, p. 25.

11 See, for instance: *R v Charley*, 11 Sept 1896, reported in the *Northern Territory Times and Gazette*, 18 September 1896, p. 3; *R v Jaydeadda, Wallagoola and Cadininie*, 4 December 1896, reported in the *Northern Territory Times and Gazette*, 11 December 1896, p. 3; *R v Cammerfor and Munkgum*, reported in 'The Daly River Outrage', *Northern Territory Times and Gazette*, 10 August 1900, p. 3.

12 Mildren, 'Sketches on Territory Legal history', *Balance: Journal of the Northern Territory Law Society*, February–March 1999, p. 12 at 13. The era of formal 'protection' ultimately commenced in South Australia in 1910 with the passage of the *Northern Territory Aboriginals Act*.

13 'Circuit Court: Monday, September 24, 1900', *Northern Territory Times and Gazette*, Palmerston, 28 September 1900, p. 3.

14 Michael Bradley, *Coniston*, UWA Press, Crawley, WA, 2019.

15 The exchange is reproduced in full in *Elder, Blood on the Wattle*, 3rd ed (2003), p. 213.

16 AH O'Kelly, *Finding of Board of Enquiry Concerning the Killing of Natives in Central Australia by Police Parties and Others and Concerning Other Matters*, 1929, NLA MS 744. O'Kelly's conclusions are reproduced in Bruce Elder's book, *Blood on the Wattle*, 3rd ed (2003), pp. 213–14. O'Kelly, a police magistrate, produced a confidential report which contradicted the official findings, and later regretted his appointment: John Cribbin, *The Killing Times: The Coniston Massacre 1928*, Fontana/Collins, 1984, pp. 157–58.

17 'Rides Alone, and Gets His Man Always: Policeman Hero of Central Australia', *The Register News-Pictorial* (Adelaide), 6 February 1929, p. 7.

18 'Criminal Sessions at Alice Springs', *Northern Standard* (Darwin), 6 September 1938, p. 4. He was acquitted.

19 See Henry Reynolds and Marilyn Lake, *Drawing the Global Colour Line: White Men's Countries and the Question of Racial Equality*, Melbourne University Press, Carlton, 2008.

20 *Criminal Law Amendment Ordinance 1939–1960* (SA), s 7(a), which amended s 6 of the *Criminal Law Consolidation Act 1876* (SA) as it applied to the Northern Territory.

21 Recounted in *Tuckiar v R* [1934] HCA 49 (8 November 1934) per Gava Duffy CJ and Dixon, Evatt and McTiernan JJ.

22 For an extended discussion of the case, see: Charles Rowley, *Aboriginal Policy and Practice, Vol. 1: The Destruction of Aboriginal Society*, ANU Press, Canberra, 1970, pp. 290–304.

23 Read, 'Murder, Revenge and Reconciliation on the North Eastern Frontier', *History Australia*, vol. 4, no. 1, 2007, pp. 9.1–9.15. Much of the account of the trial and its aftermath reproduced here relies on Read's essay.

24 Heather Douglas, 'Assimilation, Lutheranism and the 1950s justice of Kriewaldt', *Australian Journal of Legal History*, vol. 12, 2004, citing personal communications with Kriewaldt's son. It's also possible that the paintings were by Namatjira's son. As Kriewaldt himself explained when deciding Namatjira's appeal against his conviction and sentence for supplying alcohol to Henoch Raberaba: 'even before I came to the Territory I was an admirer of the art of the appellant. Two pictures by one of his sons have graced the walls of my living room for some years': *Albert Namatjira v Gordon Edgar Raabe*, Northern Territory Judgements No. 100, 11 December 1958, pp. 608–32 at 614. This and all of Kriewaldt's judgements referred to in this book are available to be read at Douglas's (discontinued) *Justice Martin Kriewaldt* website, archived at Pandora/Trove: https://webarchive.nla.gov.au/awa/20160711033004/

http://pandora.nla.gov.au/pan/159527/20160711-1315/www.law.uq.edu.au/jmk-judgements.
html (accessed 28 August 2020). Most of them are also available on AustLII, at http://classic.
austlii.edu.au/au/cases/nt/NTJud/.

25   *Albert Namatjira v Gordon Edgar Raabe*, NTJ No. 100, pp. 608–32. The story of Namatjira's
     trial, sentence and appeals amid public outcry and activism by the Federal Council for
     Aboriginal Advancement (as it was then known) can be found in Sue Taffe, *Black and
     White Together*, University of Queensland Press, 2005, pp. 56–58.

26   *Albert Namatjira v Gordon Edgar Raabe*, NTJ No. 100, p. 614.

27   Geoffrey Sawer, 'Judge Martin Kriewaldt: Nine Years of the Northern Territory Supreme
     Court', *Adelaide Law Review*, vol. 1, no. 2, 1960, p. 148 at 151.

28   Unnamed former Darwin magistrate quoted in Colin Tatz, '*Aboriginal Administration in
     the Northern Territory of Australia*', unpublished PhD thesis, ANU, 1964, p. 260.

29   *R v Aboriginal Charlie Mulparinga* (No. 2), NTJ 31, p. 219 at 223: 'I have considered one
     further aspect, namely, whether any punishment on this prisoner is likely to hasten or
     retard the assimilation of the native population … I have come to the conclusion that,
     unless the legislature prescribes that this factor shall be taken into account, it would be
     wrong to increase or decrease an otherwise just sentence in order to give effect to the
     official policy of accelerating the assimilation of the native population of the Territory.'

30   *R v Aboriginal Patipatu* (1951), NTJ No. 4, pp. 18–20.

31   Thalia Anthony, *Indigenous People, Crime and Punishment*, Routledge, 2011, p. 89.

32   *R v Anderson* (1954), NTJ 36, pp. 240–49.

33   Kriewaldt, 'The Application of the Criminal Law to the Aborigines of the Northern
     Territory of Australia', paper delivered after Kriewaldt's death by Geoffrey Sawer to the 15th
     Annual Conference of the Australian Universities Law Schools Association, Perth, August
     1960; published in the *University of Western Australia Law Review*, vol. 5, no. 1, 1960,
     pp. 1–50 at 15 and 23.

34   *R v Tiger and Captain* (1953), NTJ 29, pp. 211–16.

35   *R v Aboriginal Charlie Mulparinga* (sentencing remarks, 1954), NTJ 28 and 31, pp. 205–10
     and 219–23.

36   Kriewaldt, 'The Application of the Criminal Law to the Aborigines of the Northern
     Territory of Australia', p. 7. Kriewaldt found, for instance, only a handful of cases between
     1910 and 1946 where white men had been tried for allegedly murdering Aboriginal people;
     all of them resulted in acquittals (p. 11).

37   *R v Anderson* (1954), NTJ 36, pp. 240–49.

38   *Albert Namatjira v Gordon Edgar Raabe*, NTJ No. 100, p. 629.

39   Heather Douglas, *Aboriginal Australians and the Criminal Law*.

40   *R v Aboriginal Roy Panaka* (1957), NTJ 72, pp. 453–54.

41   Berndt and Berndt, 'Suggested Recommendations in Regard to Aboriginal Labour on
     Pastoral Stations Under the Control of the Northern Agency', 21 July 1945, p. 52; cited
     in Geoffrey Gray, '"We Know the Aborigines are Dying Out": Aboriginal People and
     the Quest to Ensure their Survival, Wave Hill Station, 1944', *Health and History*, vol. 16,
     no. 1, 2014, p. 1 at 11. The Berndts had been sent by A.P. Elkin to report on the Wave
     Hill workers' conditions and 'contentment' in 1944. 'Their activities are controlled and
     supervised by white people,' the Berndts continued. 'Their language, their social structure,
     and indeed their whole approach to life, must be modified to conform to introduced ideas
     and demands, while the persistent familiarity and sexual intercourse of white men with
     native women, and the steady shifting of authority from the old men to the young workers,
     disrupts the whole pattern of aboriginal life': Berndt and Berndt, 'Some Recent Articles
     on Culture Contact: A Review', *Oceania*, vol. 16, no. 1, 1945, p. 84; also cited in Gray,
     '"We Know the Aborigines are Dying Out"', p. 11.

42   *Licensing Ordinance 1939* (NT), s 142: 'A person who is a ward within the meaning of the
     Welfare Ordinance 1953–1955 and who is found drinking liquor or to have been drinking
     liquor or in possession of liquor is guilty of an offence.' The penalty was ten pounds or seven
     days' imprisonment for a first offence, and four weeks' imprisonment for a subsequent
     offence. *Licensing Ordinance 1939* (NT), s 141: 'A person shall not sell, give or supply, or
     permit to be sold, given or supplied liquor to a person who is a ward within the meaning of
     the *Welfare Ordinance*.' The penalty was imprisonment for between six and twelve months
     for a first offence, and for between one and two years for a subsequent offence.

43 When the law changed in 1953, Namatjira had originally been made a ward. Two years later he was charged with consuming alcohol. The secretary of the Australian and New Zealand Civil Liberties Society wrote to Hasluck. How could Namatjira, of all people, be regarded as a 'primitive native'? 'If there is a clear path to citizenship,' the secretary observed, 'then we are at a loss to understand why Mr Namatjira is not a citizen.' ('Letters Exchanged over Namatjira', *Centralian Advocate*, Alice Springs, 27 May 1955, p. 8.) Hasluck and his department agreed, and removed his name from the list of declared wards when the *Welfare Ordinance* came into effect from May 1957. It was a controversial decision among Alice Springs' white community. Namatjira was already drinking heavily, and was living at one of the town camps where alcohol was regularly implicated in violence. He attracted significant notoriety. When a woman died in the camp, Namatjira played a main role at the inquest. He was alleged to be the town's main alcohol supplier: Heather Douglas, *Aboriginal Australians and the Criminal Law*, pp. 219–22.

44 Tatz, 'Aboriginal Administration in the Northern Territory of Australia', unpublished PhD thesis, ANU, 1964.

45 The *Northern Territory (Administration) Act 1947* (Cth) inserted a new s 4U into the *Northern Territory (Administration) Act 1910* (Cth), authorising the Territory's new Legislative Council (established by the new s 4B) to 'make Ordinances for the peace, order and good government of the Territory'. The consequences of being declared a 'ward' meant that a person was at the whim of the Director of Welfare, who had the power to 'take the ward into his custody' (s 17), move a ward from one reserve or district to anywhere else in the Northern Territory, deport a ward from the Territory entirely (s 21), and sell or dispose of any property owned by the ward (s 25). No ward could marry without the Director's permission (s 67). The *Ordinance* explicitly stated that the Director is the 'guardian' of each ward and each ward's estate 'as if that ward were an infant' (s 24).

46 *Albert Namatjira v Gordon Edgar Raabe*, NTJ no. 194 of 1958, p. 608 at 610, 11 December 1958 per Kriewaldt J; Douglas, *Aboriginal Australians and the Criminal Law*, pp. 222–23.

47 *Namatjira v Raabe*, NTJ no. 194 of 1958, pp. 617–32.

48 *Namatjira v Raabe* [1959] HCA 13 per Dixon CJ on behalf of McTiernan, Fullagar, Kitto and Windeyer JJ.

49 Douglas, *Aboriginal Australians and the Criminal Law*, p. 227.

CHAPTER 4

1 See generally: Jennifer Clark, *Aborigines & Activism: Race, Aborigines and the Coming of the Sixties to Australia*, UWA Press, Crawley, 2008.

2 See chapter 13 and also Clark, *Aborigines and Activism*.

3 The 1967 Constitutional Referendum caused the repeal of section 127 (which had stated that 'aboriginal natives shall not be counted' in population counts) and the amendment of section 51(xxvi) (which had allowed the federal parliament to make laws with respect to 'the people of any race other than the aboriginal race in any state') by removing the words 'other than the aboriginal race in any state'.

4 This history is told in John Chesterman, *Civil Rights: How Indigenous Australians Won Formal Equality*, UQP, 2005.

5 Ronald M. Berndt and Catherine H. Berndt, *End of an Era: Aboriginal Labour in the Northern Territory*, Australian Institute of Aboriginal Studies, Canberra, 1986.

6 Hardy's book of the strike is *The Unlucky Australians*, Nelson, Melbourne, 1968.

7 The *Aboriginal Land Rights (Northern Territory) Act 1976* (Cth) provided for Aboriginal people in the Northern Territory to claim certain rights, based on Aboriginal systems of land ownership, to parcels of unalienated Crown land which would then be owned by new Aboriginal Land Trusts.

8 John Maynard, 'Tracking Back: Parallels Between the 1920s Aboriginal Political Movements and the 1972 Tent Embassy', ch. 6 in Gary Foley, Andrew Schaap and Edwina Howell (eds), *The Aboriginal Tent Embassy: Sovereignty, Black Power, Land Rights and the State*, Routledge, Abingdon and New York, 2014.

9 Miranda Johnson, *The Land is Our History: Indigeneity, Law and the Settler State*, Oxford University Press, 2016, chapter 1.

10 The principle of self-determination was applied specifically to 'colonial peoples' in 1960

by General Assembly Resolution 1514, the *Declaration of the Granting of Independence to Colonial Territories and Peoples:* UN GOAR, 15th session, 947th plenary meeting, UN Doc A/Res/1514 (1960). The right to self-determination was then included in the International Covenants in 1966, and had become a rule of customary international law by the 1970s: *Western Sahara (Advisory Opinion)* [1975] ICJ Rep 12 at para 56; *Barcelona Traction (Belgium v Spain) (Judgment)* [1970] ICJ Rep 5 at 32, confirmed in *Case Concerning East Timor (Portugal v Australia) (Judgment)* [1995] ICJ Rep 90 at 102.

11   For a relatively recent articulation of this principle, see: Mark Lindley, *The Acquisition and Government of Backward Territory in International Law – Being a Treatise on the Law and Practice Relating to Colonial Expansion*, Longmans, Green and Company, 1926.

12   House of Representatives Select Committee on Grievances of the Yirrkala Aborigines, Arnhem Land Reserve, Report and Minutes of Proceedings, 29 October 1963, available: https://nla.gov.au/nla.obj-2796527017/view?partId=nla.obj-2796927868#page/n0/ mode/1up (accessed 3 February 2021).

13   *In re Southern Rhodesia* [1919] AC 211 at 233–34, quoted by Blackburn J in *Milirrpum & ors v Nabalco and the Commonwealth of Australia* (1971) 17 FLR 141 at 263–64.

14   *Amodu Tijani v The Secretary Southern Provinces (Nigeria)* [1921] UKPC 80, p. 3, quoted by Blackburn J in *Milirrpum v Nabalco* at 264–65.

15   Blackburn was paraphrasing from James Harrington's distinction in his *Oceania* (1656), itself drawn from Aristotle's *Politics*, between a civilised 'Empire of Laws, and not of Men' and an uncivilised 'Empire of Men, and not of Laws'.

16   *Mabo v Queensland (No. 2)* (1992) 175 CLR 1.

17   Williams, *Northern Territory Aborigines under Australian Law*, PhD thesis, University of California Berkeley, 1973, chapter 2.

18   *R v Grant and Lovett* [1972] VR 423.

19   *R v Wedge* [1976] 1 NSWLR 581 per Rath J.

20   *Koowarta v Bjelke-Petersen* [1982] HCA 27. In 1974, the Aboriginal Land Fund Commission had provided funds to Wik man John Koowarta and a number of other stockmen to purchase the Archer River cattle station, which was on Wik land. Bjelke-Petersen's Queensland government blocked the sale. Koowarta made a complaint under the *Racial Discrimination Act 1975* (Cth), alleging that Queensland's action was racially discriminatory. Queensland challenged the validity of the *Racial Discrimination Act* in the High Court.

21   Anthony Mason had initially refused Coe's application to amend his original statement of claim: *Coe v The Commonwealth of Australia and the Government of the United Kingdom of Great Britain and Northern Ireland* (1978) 18 ALR 592. Coe appealed that decision to four of Mason's High Court colleagues. Significantly, two of them – Kenneth Jacobs and Lionel Murphy – would have allowed Coe to amend his statement of claim and to continue his proceeding: *Coe v Commonwealth* [1979] HCA 68. With the court split down the middle, Mason's original decision stood (as per section 23(2)(a) of the *Judiciary Act 1903* (Cth)).

22   *Wacando v Australia and Queensland* [1981] HCA 60.

23   This account is in Reynolds, *Why Weren't We Told?*, Viking, Ringwood, 1999, p. 188.

24   *Queensland Coast Islands Declaratory Act 1985* (Qld).

25   *Mabo v Queensland (No. 1)* (1988) 166 CLR 186.

26   *Mabo v Queensland (No. 2)* (1992) 175 CLR 1.

27   Ian Henderson, 'Outrage at desecration', *The Canberra Times*, 5 June 1995, p. 1. Mabo's body and headstone were later relocated to Mer, where they remain.

28   See: Kerry Goettlich, 'The Rise of Linear Borders in World Politics', *European Journal of International Relations*, vol. 25, no 1, 2019.

29   *Coe v Commonwealth* [1993] HCA 42.

30   Gary Foley, 'Black Power in Redfern, 1968–1972', unpublished BA Hons thesis, Department of History, University of Melbourne, available: www.kooriweb.org/foley/essays/pdf_essays/ black%20power%20in%20redfern%201968.pdf; Alyssa Trometter, 'The Fire in the Belly': Aboriginal Black Power and the Rise of the Australian Black Panther Party, 1967–1972', unpublished PhD thesis, School of Historical and Philosophical Studies, University of Melbourne, 2013.

31   *R v Walker* (1988) 38 A Crim R 150.

32   Malbon, 'The Walker Case: The Applicability of Non-Aboriginal Law to Aborigines', *Aboriginal Law Bulletin*, vol. 1, no. 37, 1989, p. 14.

33 Sharon Gray, 'In a Hell on Earth, Aborigines Win Hands Down', *The Age*, Melbourne, 22 February 1995.

34 *Walker v New South Wales* (1994) 126 ALR 321 at 322–23 (per Mason CJ).

35 Tanya Mitchell and Amanda Porter, '*Walker v New South Wales [1994] HCA 64*', ch. 4 in Nicole Watson and Heather Douglas (eds), *Indigenous Legal Judgments: Bringing Indigenous Voices into Judicial Decision Making*, Routledge, Abingdon and New York, 2021.

36 *Commonwealth of Australia Constitution Act* 1900, s 74. The circumstances under which such a certificate could conceivably be given were restricted twice – first by the *Privy Council (Limitation of Appeals) Act 1968* (Cth), and then by the *Privy Council (Appeals from the High Court) Act 1975* (Cth) – but have never been entirely extinguished, because that would require a constitutional amendment by referendum.

37 *Kirmani v Captain Cook Cruises Pty Ltd (No. 2)* (1985) 159 CLR 461.

38 *Mabo v Queensland (No. 2)* (1992) 175 CLR 1 at 43 per Brennan J. See also p. 29.

39 Rod Campbell, 'Aboriginal Law Claim Rejected by High Court', *Canberra Times* and *The Age*, 17 December 1994.

CHAPTER 5

1 Generally, juries weren't (and aren't) entitled to know about a defendant's past convictions, on the basis that while evidence of past convictions is not evidence of guilt in relation to current charges, juries tend to believe it is. An exception in the 1950s arose when a defendant impugned the good character of a prosecution witness: in such cases, prosecutors were entitled to cross-examine defendants on their own records, including their past convictions.

2 Max Stuart's unsworn statement, read to the jury by Reed J during summing up, reproduced as Appendix V in Justices Mellis Napier, Geoffrey Reed and Bruce Ross, *Report of the Royal Commission in Regard to Rupert Max Stuart*, 3 December 1959, pp. 38–40.

3 *Stuart v R* [1959] HCA 27. Formally, the Privy Council rejected Stuart's application for leave to appeal. Its reasons were not published, but a brief account is given in Ken Inglis, *The Stuart Case*, Black Inc., Melbourne, 2002 [1961], pp. 74–77.

4 Playford's appointments of Reed and Napier drew international condemnations of bias, including from senior British politicians.

5 Napier, Reed and Ross, *Report of the Royal Commission in Regard to Rupert Max Stuart*, 3 December 1959, p. 30.

6 Stuart's sentence was commuted on 5 October 1959; see: 'Threat after Reprieve of Aborigine', *Daily Telegraph*, London, 6 October 1959, p. 15.

7 *Statues Amendment (Appeals) Act 2013* (SA) inserted a new s 353A into the *Criminal Law Consolidation Act 1935* (SA); this section subsequently moved into the *Criminal Procedure Act 1921* (SA) as s 159.

8 Jane Perlez, 'Australia Revisits a "Black and White" Murder Case', *The New York Times*, 16 December 2002, p. 4; Ken Inglis, interviewed by Terry Lane for *The National Interest*, ABC Radio National, broadcast 1 September 2002, transcript archived at https://web. archive.org/web/20041130090103/http://www.abc.net.au/rn/talks/natint/stories/s662208. htm. The other surviving officers continued to deny this.

9 Kirby, 'Black and White Lessons for the Australian Judiciary', *Adelaide Law Review*, vol. 23, 2002, p. 195 at 212.

10 'The Daly River Outrage: Arrest of the Alleged Principals in the Affair: The Launch Recovered', *Northern Territory Times and Gazette*, 3 August 1900, p. 3.

11 *R v Padygar and Arkirkra*, stenographer's report of Mallam J's reasons for declining to admit confessional evidence, in *Northern Territory Times* (Darwin), 13 November 1928, p. 4.

12 Pauling, 'Revisiting Anunga', paper delivered at the 12th Biennial Conference of the Criminal Lawyers' Association of the Northern Territory (CLANT), Bali, July 2009, p. 6.

13 Kerry O'Brien, 'We Will Not Be Complete', *The Monthly*, 9 October 2019.

14 Pauling, 'Revisiting Anunga', pp. 3–4 and 10–11.

15 *R v Anunga and ors; R v Wheeler and anor* (1976) 11 ALR 412 at 413–14, per Forster J.

16 *R v Michael Lim*, unreported, NT Supreme Court, SCC Nos. 7–9 of 1975, 21 February 1975 per Muirhead J. Quotes are from the transcript, cited in J.R. Crawford and P.K. Hennessy, 'Appendix: Cases on Traditional Punishments and Sentencing', ALRC Reference on Aboriginal Customary Law Research Paper 6A, September 1982, pp. 5–6.

17   *R v Bobby Iginiwuni*, unreported, NT Supreme Court, SCC No. 6 of 1975, 12 March 1975 per Muirhead J. Quotes are from the transcript, cited in Crawford and Hennessy, pp. 7–8.

18   *Police v Eric Jackson*, unreported, NT Court of Summary Jurisdiction, Nos. 267–68, 352 of 1977, 22 November 1977 per Towers SM. Quotes are from the transcript, cited in Crawford and Hennessy, p. 11.

19   *R v Desmond Gorey*, unreported, NT Supreme Court, SCC No. 107 of 1978, 20 June 1978 per Gallop J. Quotes are from the transcript, cited in Crawford and Hennessy, pp. 13 and 15.

20   *R v Banto Banto, Leo Morris and George King*, unreported, NT Supreme Court, SCC Nos. 45–49 of 1979, 18 April 1979 per Forster CJ, transcript of proceedings, quoted in Crawford and Hennessy, p. 18.

21   *R v Banto Banto, Leo Morris and George King*, unreported, NT Supreme Court, SCC Nos. 45–49 of 1979, 18 April 1979 per Forster CJ. Quotes are from the transcript, cited in Crawford and Hennessy, p. 18.

22   *R v Geoffrey Yumarra Gunambarr*, unreported, NT Supreme Court Nos. 258–59 of 1980, 5 August 1980 per Gallop J.

23   *Aborigines and Islanders (Admissibility of Confessions) Bill 1976* (Cth).

24   Senator Bonner, Notice of Motion, 11 July 1974, p. 71; Senator Bonner, Motion for Compensation, 19 September 1974, p. 1267.

25   Senator Bonner, *Aborigines and Islanders (Admissibility of Confessions) Bill 1976*, second reading speech, 15 September 1976, Senate *Hansard*, pp. 695–700; Senator Bonner, *Aborigines and Islanders (Admissibility of Confessions) Bill 1978*, second reading speech, 26 October 1978, Senate *Hansard*, p. 1658; Senator Bonner, *Aborigines and Islanders (Admissibility of Confessions) Bill 1981*, second reading speech, 5 March 1981, p. 369.

26   Gordon J. Hawkins and Robert L. Misner, 'Restructuring the Criminal Justice System in the Northern Territory', submission to the Minister for the Northern Territory, presented 25 September 1973; Hawkins and Misner, 'Framework for Change: Second Report on the Criminal Justice System in the Northern Territory', tabled August 1974; Hawkins and Misner, 'Some Specific Proposals: Third Report on the Criminal Justice System in the Northern Territory', also tabled August 1974.

27   Hawkins and Misner, 'Restructuring the Criminal Justice System in the Northern Territory', p. 2.

28   Council for Aboriginal Affairs, 'Report on Arnhem Land', 1975, pp. 17–20. The Council for Aboriginal Affairs was, in reality, the economist Dr H.C. 'Nugget' Coombs (who would go on to launch the Aboriginal Treaty Committee in 1979), the anthropologist Professor Bill Stanner (who had delivered the *After the Dreaming* Boyer lectures in 1968) and former diplomat Barrie Dexter (who would become the inaugural secretary of the newly formed Department of Aboriginal Affairs in 1972).

29   See, for instance: Viner, address to the National Press Club, 7 July 1977; published in *Australian Journal of Indigenous Education*, vol. 5, no. 4, August 1977, pp. 5–13; Viner, ministerial report, Department of Aboriginal Affairs Report, 24 November 1978, House *Hansard*, p. 3442.

30   On 10 July 1976, Viner urged Ellicott to raise the question of recognising what he called Aboriginal 'customary laws' with the Standing Committee of Attorneys-General. Ellicott did just that at meetings of the Standing Committee in both October 1976 and March 1977. There was no political will for change, so instead he referred the questions to the ALRC: Ellicott, terms of reference, ALRC inquiry into Aboriginal customary law, 9 February 1977.

31   Max Griffiths, *Aboriginal Affairs: A Short History, 1788–1995*, Kangaroo Press, 1995, p. 111.

32   Law Reform Commission, *The Recognition of Aboriginal Customary Laws*, Report No. 31, 11 June 1986.

33   *Re R v William Davey* [1980] FCA 134.

34   *R v Charlie Limbiari Jagamara*, unreported, Northern Territory Supreme Court, Alice Springs, 28 May 1984, per Muirhead J.

35   *Jadurin v R* (1982) 44 ALR 424.

36   *Mamarika v R* (1982) 42 ALR 94.

37   Anthony, *Indigenous People, Crime and Punishment*.

38   Andrew Ligertwood, 'The Trial of Sydney Williams', *Legal Services Bulletin*, vol. 2, 1976, pp. 136–40.

39   Editorial, *The Australian*, 18 May 1976. Legal Aid Commission lawyer John Bennett was
      secretary of the Victorian Council of Civil Liberties between its inception in 1966 and
      1980, by which time his activities as a high-profile Holocaust denier led to his expulsion.
      He subsequently founded a new rival organisation, the Australian Civil Liberties
      Union (not to be confused with the much more widely accepted Australian Council for
      Civil Liberties), which quickly emerged as one of Australia's main Holocaust-denying
      organisations. He died in 2013.

40   Ward, 'The Wholesome Precedent of Sydney Williams', *Legal Services Bulletin*, vol. 2,
      1976, pp. 141–43. Among Ward's most influential works were *A Show of Justice: Racial
      'Amalgamation' in Nineteenth Century New Zealand* (Auckland University Press, 1974) and
      An Unsettled History: Treaty Claims in New Zealand Today (Bridget Williams, 1999). Ward
      was a historian at La Trobe University between 1967 and 1987, when he was appointed
      professor of history at the University of Newcastle. He died in 2014.

41   Ligertwood, 'The Trial of Sydney Williams', *Legal Services Bulletin*, vol. 2, 1976, pp. 136–40.
      Ligertwood would become one of Australia's foremost experts on the law of evidence.

42   See: *Herald*, 19 May 1976.

43   *R v Miyatatawuy* (1996) 87 A Crim R 574.

44   Anthony, *Indigenous People, Crime and Punishment*, pp. 91–93.

CHAPTER 6

1   See: Dominic Kelly, *Political Troglodytes and Economic Lunatics: The Hard Right in
      Australia*, La Trobe University Press in association with Black Inc., Melbourne, 2019.

2   See: Aileen Moreton-Robinson, 'Writing Off Indigenous Sovereignty: The Discourse of
      Security and Patriarchal White Sovereignty', in Moreton-Robinson, ed, *Sovereign Subjects*,
      Allen & Unwin, Crows Nest, 2007.

3   Gary Johns, *Aboriginal Self-Determination: The Whiteman's Dream*, Connor Court
      Publishing, Ballan, Vic, 2011.

4   Australian Institute of Health and Welfare, 'Aboriginal and Torres Strait Islander Health
      Performance Framework: 2020 Summary Report', 2020, p. 53.

5   *R v Don Gibson*, unreported, NT Supreme Court No. 262 of 1974, 19 November 1974 per
      Forster J. Quotes are from the transcript, cited in Crawford and Hennessy, pp. 4–5.

6   *R v Benny Lee*, unreported, NT Supreme Court No. 221 of 1974, 19 November 1974 per
      Forster J. Quotes are from the transcript, cited in Crawford and Hennessy, p. 5.

7   *Police v Bernard Wurramurra*, unreported, NT Court of Summary Jurisdiction (GE439 of
      1977), Groote Eylandt, 27 July 1977 per Pauling SM.

8   *R v Andrew Spencer Jabaltjara*, unreported, NT Supreme Court No. A24 of 1981, 25 August
      1981 per Muirhead J. The quote is from the transcript, cited in Crawford and Hennessy,
      pp. 37–38.

9   *R v Pat Edwards*, unreported, NT Supreme Court Nos. 155–56 of 1981, 16 October 1981
      per Muirhead J.

10   *R v Morris Alsop*, unreported, SA Supreme Court No. 66/1981, 14 July 1984 per Mathieson J.

11   Barry Lindner, submission no. 213 to the ALRC's inquiry into Aboriginal customary laws,
      10 February 1981.

12   *R v Gus Forbes*, unreported, NT Supreme Court Nos. 22–23 of 1980, 29 August 1980 per
      Gallop J. Quotes are from the transcript, cited in Crawford and Hennessy, pp. 27–28.

13   Wallace, quoted in Joan Kimm, *A Fatal Conjunction: Two Laws, Two Cultures*, Federation
      Press, 2004, p. 78.

14   Catherine Wohlan, 'Aboriginal Women's Interests in Customary Law Recognition',
      Background Paper 13, Law Reform Commission of Western Australia, Project 94:
      Aboriginal Customary Laws, 2005, included in the LRCWA's compendium of background
      papers published in January 2006, available online at https://www.lrc.justice.wa.gov.au/_
      files/P94_Background_Papers.pdf, p. 507 at 508.

15   Bell wasn't the first Australian researcher to take an interest in Aboriginal women's
      experiences: Phyllis Kaberry is usually credited as having published the first major study,
      Aboriginal Woman, Sacred and Profane (from her doctoral thesis), in 1939, and her student
      Catherine Berndt subsequently conducted many others. Berndt's first book, *Women's
      Changing Ceremonies in Northern Australia* (Hermann, Paris, 1950), detailed women's

ceremonies and social participation in communities in the north-western Northern Territory, including among Gurindji women at Wave Hill. As she and her husband, Ronald, would suggest again and again, she observed even in the 1940s that the impact of the 'European type culture which various travellers and settlers brought to Australia within the [previous] two centuries' was having effects on women's ceremonial culture that 'are proving to be on the whole discouraging and deleterious'. But Bell was among the first to emerge from the renewed women's movements of the late 1960s and 1970s, and her aims were, in part, born of the experiences and insights of those movements. Bell's thesis, completed at ANU in 1980, was published to substantial acclaim in 1984 – and, later, controversy – as *Daughters of the Dreaming*.

16 Kimm, *A Fatal Conjunction*, chapter 8.

17 In a two-part essay on 'Violence in Aboriginal Australia', published in the *Aboriginal and Islander Health Worker Journal* in 1990 across issues 2 and 3 of volume 14, Judy Atkinson wrote (issue 3, p. 7): 'in one town in the Northern Territory five women have died because of violent assault over the last five years, while the custody deaths for the Territory are less than that. In Queensland in one community more women have died than all the deaths in custody in that state.' This statistic made its way, in generalised form, into an article Cath Duff published in the journal *Polemic* (vol. 5, no. 1, pp. 36–40) in January 1994, and then – no doubt because Duff was working in the Aboriginal and Torres Strait Islander Social Justice Commission at the time – into Mick Dodson's second Social Justice Report (published by the Human Rights and Equal Opportunity Commission) in the same year. Unfortunately, Atkinson didn't cite her source. She did, however, cite (issue 3, p.8) the recently completed (1990) final report of the National Committee on Violence – tasked to investigate the 'causes and ways of dealing with the apparent rising tide of violence' in Australia – which reported that among women killed as a result of chargeable offences in the NT in 1987, 79 per cent were Aboriginal.

18 Cited in Judy Atkinson, 'Violence in Aboriginal Australia: Part One', *Aboriginal and Islander Health Worker Journal*, vol. 14, issue 2, 1990, p. 5 at 20.

19 Paul Wilson, *Black Death, White Hands*, George Allen & Unwin, North Sydney, 1982. Wilson ultimately implicated Settler Australia in this violence, by creating the conditions for it through colonisation. He was later convicted of historical child sex offences, and did not appeal the verdict.

20 In Kenneth Maddock, 'Aboriginal Customary Law', chapter 9 in Peter Hanks and Bryan Keon-Cohen (eds), *Aborigines and the Law: Essays in Memory of Elizabeth Eggleston*, George Allen & Unwin, 1984, p. 235 [FN 41].

21 See, for instance: Paul Wilson, *Black Death, White Hands*, George Allen & Unwin, Sydney, 198222, Langton et al, 'Too Much Sorry Business': Report of the NT Aboriginal Issues Unit of the Royal Commission into Aboriginal Deaths in Custody to Commissioner Elliott Johnston, July 1990, RCIADIC Report, Vol. 5, appendix D(i). Langton cited Judy Atkinson's 1990 report and video, *Beyond Violence: Finding the Dream*.

23 Judy Atkinson, *Beyond Violence: Finding the Dream*, Office of the Status of Women, Commonwealth Government, 1990, p. 13; Langton et al., 'Too Much Sorry Business'; Audrey Bolger, *Aboriginal Women and Violence*, North Australian Research Unit, ANU, 1991; Jane Lloyd and Nanette Rogers, 'Crossing the Last Frontier: Aboriginal Women Victims of Rape in Central Australia', in Easteal (ed.), *Without Consent: Confronting Adult Sexual Violence*, Australian Institute of Criminology, 1993; Anna Ferrante et al., *Measuring the Extent of Domestic Violence*, Hawkins Press, 1996, pp. 36–37; Jenny Mouzos, *Femicide: The Killing of Women in Australia, 1989–1998*, Australian Institute of Criminology, 1999, pp. 19–22; Paul Memmott, Rachael Stacy, Catherine Chambers and Catherine Keys in association with the Aboriginal Environments Research Centre at the University of Queensland, *Violence in Indigenous Communities: Full Report to the Crime Prevention Branch of the Attorney-General's Department*, 2001.

24 Bell and Nelson, 'Speaking about Rape is Everyone's Business', *Women's Studies International Forum*, vol. 12, no. 4, 1989, pp. 403–16.

25 Moreton-Robinson, *Talkin' Up to the White Woman: Indigenous Women and Feminisms*, UQP, St Lucia, 2000, mainly chapter 4. Huggins, then a young researcher who'd just completed a women's studies honours degree, objected to Bell's right to speak on behalf of all Indigenous women on the issue of rape.

26   Moreton-Robinson, 'Patriarchal Whiteness, Self-Determination and Indigenous Women: The Invisibility of Structural Privilege and the Visibility of Oppression', ch. 4 in Barbara Ann Hocking (ed.), *Unfinished Constitutional Business: Rethinking Indigenous Self-Determination*, Aboriginal Studies Press, Canberra, 2005; Megan Davis, 'Deploying and Disputing Aboriginal Feminism in Australia', in Joyce Green (ed.), *Making Space for Indigenous Feminism*, 2nd ed., Fernwood Publishing, Black Point, Nova Scotia, 2017.

27   Langton et al., 'Too Much Sorry Business', pp. 307, 373.

28   Judy Atkinson, 'Violence Against Aboriginal Women: Reconstitution of Community Law – the Way Forward', *Aboriginal Law Bulletin*, vol. 2, no. 46, October 1990, pp. 6–9.

29   Kimm, *A Fatal Conjunction*, pp. 29–31.

30   Boni Robertson (chair), Report of the Aboriginal and Torres Strait Islander Women's Task Force on Violence, 1999.

31   Langton et al., 'Too Much Sorry Business', p. 287.

32   O'Donoghue, Hyllus Maris lecture, La Trobe University, extract published as 'Indigenous violence: It's everyone's business', *The Age*, Melbourne, 22 October 2001.

33   Kimm, *A Fatal Conjunction*, chapter 5: 'Violence to Women in Traditional Society'.

34   Sutton, 'The Politics of Suffering: Indigenous Policy in Australia since the 1970s', *Anthropological Forum*, vol. 11, no. 2, 2001, pp. 125–73.

35   Sutton relied on the published work of a paleopathologist, Stephen Webb, who had studied thousands of bone samples, including cranial samples, and found an abundance of healed cranial fractures in women as well as a common injury on upper limbs that indicated the kind of 'parry fracture' seen among people who have attempted to defend themselves from attackers' weapons: Webb, *Paleopathology of Aboriginal Australians: Health and Disease across a Hunter-Gatherer Continent*, Cambridge University Press, 1995. But Webb's work was criticised in his field for its methodology – he'd extrapolated from small data sets to explain wide-ranging theories (Graham Knuckey, review of Webb's *Paleopathology of Aboriginal Australians*, in *Australian Archaeology*, no. 43, 1996, pp. 53–56) – and its analysis. 'While Webb interprets this in terms of violent behaviour', wrote one academic reviewer of his discussion of cranial and parry fractures, 'it is clear from ethnographic reports that skeletal evidence of trauma may develop from other sources': Jane Buikstra, review of Webb's *Paleopathology of Aboriginal Australians*, in *Journal of Anthropological Research*, vol. 52, no. 2, 1996, pp. 237–40.

36   Liz Conor, *Skin Deep: Settler Impressions of Aboriginal Women*, University of WA Press, 2016.

37   John Nicol, *The Life and Adventures of John Nicol, Mariner*, William Blackwood and T. Caddell, 1822. Lashing and flogging wasn't outlawed for women under British law until 1817: Joy Damousi, *Depraved and Disorderly: Female Convicts, Sexuality and Gender in Colonial Australia*, Cambridge University Press, 1997.

38   In the course of proceedings, the woman – Deborah Ellam Herbert – conceded that she had also struck her husband, and 'would strike him again were he as big as the Side of a House if he struck [me]'. In response, Collins ordered that she receive twenty-five lashes and return to her 'lawful rib': Arthur Chapman, *First Fleeters John Herbert and Deborah Ellam: Their Lives and the Descent of the Bamford, Bates and Kay Families*, self-published, 1987, pp. 3–4.

39   Chelsea Watego (as Chelsea Bond), 'The Abuse of Aboriginal Women via Racialized and Gendered Discourses', *Black Nations Rising*, no. 4, 25 January 2016, pp. 8–9.

40   Langton, 'Medicine Square', chapter 11 in Ian Keen (ed.), *Being Black: Aboriginal Cultures in 'Settled' Australia*, Aboriginal Studies Press, Canberra, 1988, p. 201 at 202–05, citing W.L. Warner, *A Black Civilization: A Study of an Australian Aboriginal Tribe*, Harper, New York, 1958.

41   Langton, 'Ending the Violence in Indigenous Communities', address to the National Press Club, 17 November 2016.

42   At a teach-in on Aboriginal land rights in Sydney in March 1979, participants demanded that the prime minister, Malcolm Fraser, create an Aboriginal women's 'task force'. The National Aboriginal Conference – a short-lived representative body established ostensibly so that federal governments could consult with Aboriginal people – endorsed the Task Force in June, and after lengthy conversations and bureaucratic delays the Aboriginal Women's Task Force – then housed within the Department of the Prime Minister and Cabinet's Office of the Status of Women – commenced work on its terms of reference in August 1983: Phyllis Daylight and Mary Johnstone, 'History of the Aboriginal Women's Task Force', appendix 2 in *Women's Business: Report of the Aboriginal Women's Task Force*, Canberra, 1986, pp. 85–88.

43 Daylight and Johnstone, *Women's Business*, pp. 54–57.

44 Daylight and Johnstone, *Women's Business*, pp. 61–69; Heather Goodall, quoted in Gwen Baldini, 'Rape and Sexual Abuse within the Aboriginal Communities', paper delivered to *Balancing the Scales: The Second National Conference on Sexual Assault*, Perth, 20 June 1996.

45 Atkinson, 'Violence Against Aboriginal Women', pp. 6–9. Also: Sharon Payne, 'Aboriginal Women and the Criminal Justice System', *Aboriginal Law Bulletin*, vol. 2, no. 46, October 1990, pp. 9–11.

46 Langton et al., 'Too Much Sorry Business'. Also: Judy Atkinson, 'Stinkin' Thinkin' Alcohol Violence and Government Responses', *Aboriginal Law Bulletin*, vol. 2, no. 51, August 1991, p. 4.

47 Atkinson, 'Violence Against Aboriginal Women', pp. 6–9.

48 Langton et al., 'Too Much Sorry Business'.

49 See, for example: Kimm, *A Fatal Conjunction*, chapter 3.

50 M.J. Callaghan, general secretary, Queensland Police Union of Employees, letter to Prime Minister Malcolm Fraser, 28 January 1977; read onto the record by Neville Bonner, *Aborigines and Islanders (Admissibility of Confessions) Bill 1978*, second reading speech, 26 October 1978, Senate *Hansard*, p. 1658.

51 Clyde Holding, Minister for Aboriginal Affairs, response to the ALRC's report, reproduced in the *Aboriginal Law Bulletin*, vol. 23, 1986, p. 5.

52 James Crawford, now a judge of the International Court of Justice, had been the commissioner in charge at the ALRC during the final years of its inquiry. In 1992, Crawford identified a handful of reasons why nothing had been done to implement its recommendations, including strong opposition from the states and territories, a 'slippery slope' argument which worried about opening the door to demands from immigrant communities, and what he described as the 'incompetence' of the Department of Aboriginal Affairs. 'Occam's razor, in its application to Australian politics,' an obviously frustrated Crawford observed, 'suggests that there is no reason to search for complicated reasons for something not happening when sheer bureaucratic incompetence is available as an explanation.' James Crawford, 'The Recognition of Aboriginal Customary Laws: An Overview', chapter 8 in Chris Cunneen (ed.), *Aboriginal Perspectives on Criminal Justice*, Sydney Institute of Criminology Monograph Series No. 1, Institute of Criminology, Sydney University Law School, 1992, pp. 53–75.

53 After four decades working as an anthropologist studying Aboriginal communities, Peter Sutton was 'driven' to enter the debate over Aboriginal violence in 2001 with a paper titled 'The Politics of Suffering'. The paper achieved infamy. The 'raw evidence' was depressingly and urgently clear, Sutton declared. He documented a 'downward spiral' since the 1970s, and reflected Tim Rowse's view that what was being venerated and revered as Aboriginal 'culture' now 'coexist[ed] with indigenous social forms that are recently developed and consciously contrived': Rowse, *Obliged to Be Difficult: Nugget Coombs' Legacy in Indigenous Affairs*, Cambridge University Press, 2000, pp. 132–33.

54 Memmott, Stacy, Chambers and Keys, *Violence in Indigenous Communities*, p. 6.

55 Sue Gordon, *Putting the Picture Together: Inquiry into Response by Government Agencies to Complaints of Family Violence and Child Abuse in Aboriginal Communities*, Department of Premier and Cabinet, Western Australia, 31 July 2002.

56 *R v Yougie* (1987) 33 A Crim R 301 at 304, per Derrington J.

57 *R v Berida* [1990] NTSC 10.

58 *R v Fernando* (1992) A Crim R 58 (13 March 1992), per Wood J. The eventual sentence was four years' imprisonment, to be eligible for parole after nine months.

59 *Amagula v White* [1998] NTSC 60, per Kearney J.

60 Anthony, *Indigenous People, Crime and Punishment*, p. 160.

61 *R v Wurramurra* [1999] NTCCA 45, per Mildren, Thomas and Riley JJ.

62 ABC Radio National, 'Old Law, New Ways', *Background Briefing*, 21 November 2010, https://www.abc.net.au/radionational/programs/backgroundbriefing/old-law-new-ways/2963368.

63 Memmott, Stacy, Chambers and Keys, *Violence in Indigenous Communities*.

64 *R v Ceissman* [2001] NSWCCA 73 per Wood CJ, paras 33 and 48.

65 *R v Morgan* [2003] NSWCCA 230 per Wood CJ. In his judgement, Wood CJ appears to have erroneously believed Darren, and not the Crown, had brought the appeal, because he consistently referred to Darren as 'the appellant'.

66   *Andrews v R* [2007] NSWCCA 68 per McClennan CJ. An Aboriginal man, Ashley, appealed
      against a sentence of two years and three months for brutally assaulting and injuring his
      partner with two glass bottles while he was drunk. Ashley had been born in Broken Hill,
      and saw his father often hit his mother. His parents separated when he was ten, and he
      moved to Ivanhoe to live with his grandmother. But then, when he was thirteen, the welfare
      department placed him with a white family on the Gold Coast. He left that family three
      years later and went to work on the railways. He began drinking, and soon spent most of
      his income on alcohol and other drugs. A psychologist determined that his experience of
      foster care left him feeling displaced and abandoned. Ashley's lawyers argued the original
      sentencing judge should have discounted his sentence because, they said, the *Fernando*
      principles clearly applied to him: he was Aboriginal; he had a deprived childhood in a
      remote place; he was alcohol-dependent. McClennan disagreed.

CHAPTER 7

1   Lloyd and Rogers, 'Crossing the Last Frontier: Problems Facing Aboriginal Women Victims
      of Rape in Central Australia', paper presented to *Without Consent: Confronting Adult Sexual
      Violence*, Australian Institute of Criminology conference, Melbourne, 27–29 October 1992,
      online: https://aic.gov.au/sites/default/files/publications/proceedings/downloads/20-lloyd.pdf.
2   Nanette Rogers, 'Aboriginal Law and Sentencing in the Northern Territory Supreme
      Court at Alice Springs, 1986–1995', unpublished PhD thesis, Faculty of Law, University of
      Sydney, 1998. Her supervisor was the historian Tim Rowse, who later said: 'Nanette finds
      her work distressing and she thinks that people should be more aware of what it is that's
      so distressing ... She is handicapped by the reluctance of Aboriginal people to testify to
      in court what they had been able to produce to police': Munro, '"I Ended up Getting Sick
      of Acting for Violent Aboriginal Men and Putting Up Old Excuses"', *The Sydney Morning
      Herald*, 21 May 2006.
3   Michael Gordon, 'Caught in Apathy's Vicious Cycle', *The Age*, 24 June 2006; AAP, 'PM "told
      how to act on indigenous abuse"', *The Sydney Morning Herald*, 31 May 2006.
4   *R v Lazarus Mangukala*, unreported, NT Supreme Court No. 313 of 1974, 18 April 1975 per
      Forster J. Quotes are from the transcript, cited in Crawford and Hennessy, p. 8.
5   Ronald M. Berndt, *Love Songs of Arnhem Land*, Nelson, 1976. Berndt had conducted his
      fieldwork in and around Yirrkala in 1946–1947, but had delayed publishing it for three
      decades: 'I was not sure that its frankness and its erotic content would be appreciated by
      non-Aboriginal readers.'
6   In many parts of the West, seven remained a rather elastic age of consent through the
      seventeenth century (and until 1895 in Delaware), and the state rarely involved itself in what
      were considered matters of family honour until the latter part of the nineteenth century.
      Britain's *Offences Against the Persons Act* of 1875 raised the age of consent from about ten to
      thirteen. Ten years later, journalist William Stead sensationally exposed the extent of child
      sex slavery in London; the resulting furore led parliament to raise the age of consent to
      sixteen: Stead, *The Maiden Tribute of Modern Babylon*, originally published as four articles
      in *The Pall Mall Gazette* in July 1885, available online at the W.T. Stead Resource Site: https://
      attackingthedevil.co.uk/pmg/tribute/index.php See: Gretchen Soderlund, *Sex Trafficking,
      Scandal and the Transformation of Journalism, 1885–1917*, University of Chicago Press,
      2013. Victorian England's attitudes to childhood sexuality changed rapidly in response to
      the Industrial Revolution and the development of capital; the concurrent emergence of a
      women's movement; and the subsequent expansion of liberal 'rights' and the concept of
      childhood 'innocence'.
7   The case against him proceeded on the basis that she'd consented, but was unable to
      because of her age.
8   *Jamilmira v Hayes* [2003] NTCA 9 (15 April 2003). See also: Anthony, *Indigenous
      Indigenous People, Crime and Punishment*, pp. 98–100.
9   The *Law Reform (Gender, Sexuality and De Facto Relationships) Act 2003* (NT), s 5, made
      all sex with children under sixteen criminal – regardless if the child was married according
      to an Aboriginal cultural tradition – from 17 March 2004 onward.
10   Toohey, 'Payback Victim on New Kill Charge', *The Australian*, 21 October 2002, p. 8.
11   Co-chairing the Committee were Austin Asche (the Supreme Court's chief justice) and

Yananymul Mununggurr, a Djapu woman and regular board member of Aboriginal organisations in Arnhem Land. Non-Aboriginal members were lawyers Peter Boyce, Richard Bruxner, Stephen Gray, Alison Hanley, Max Horton, John Hughes, Anna McGill and Alison Worsnop. Aboriginal members were Gwen Brown, Marjorie Limbiari, Roy Hammer, Agnes Palmer, Robert Hoosan, Warren Williams, Mary Yarmirr and Galarrwuy Yunupingu.

12   Northern Territory Law Reform Committee, *Report of the Committee of Inquiry into Aboriginal Customary Law*, 2003: https://justice.nt.gov.au/__data/assets/pdf_file/0011/238619/ntlrc_final_report.pdf.

13   *The Queen v GJ* [2005] NTSC 48; Anthony, *Indigenous People, Crime and Punishment*, pp. 100–04. In December, the Court of Criminal Appeal increased the total sentence to three years and eleven months, with the defendant to be released after serving eighteen months' imprisonment, and be subject to a suspended sentence for the balance for a period of two years and five months: *The Queen v GJ* [2005] NTCCA 20. The High Court again refused leave to hear the defendant's subsequent appeal, with Kirby J concerned that it was not an 'appropriate case' through which to examine the question of the extent to which Aboriginal law should be considered when sentencing Aboriginal defendants because 'if you remove the Aboriginality issue', even the longer sentence that was imposed by the Court of Criminal Appeal was 'a very light sentence': *GJ v The Queen* [2006] HCATrans 252 (19 May 2006). Michael Kirby had, of course, been the commissioner-in-charge of the Australian Law Reform Commission when it began its inquiry into Aboriginal 'customary law' in 1977. It's worth noting that GJ would probably not have had a defence under the draft laws eventually proposed by the Commission in 1986, because GJ's victim had not consented.

14   Rogers, 'Child Sexual Assault and Some Cultural Issues in the Northern Territory', paper presented at the Police Commissioners' Conference, Sydney, October 2005. See: AAP, 'Babies as Young as 7 Months Raped on Community: Prosecutor', AAP General News, 15 May 2006.

15   NT Law Reform Committee, '*Two Justice Systems Working Together*': Report on the Recognition of Local Aboriginal Laws in Sentencing and Bail, Report No. 46, November 2020, para 21.

16   Caroline Overington and Ashleigh Wilson, 'Desperation that Forced a Hand', *The Australian*, 20 May 2006.

17   Nanette Rogers interviewed by Tony Jones, *Lateline*, ABC TV, 15 May 2006. Rogers' claims went even further when they were reported in *The Australian* the following day. Simon Kearney and Ashleigh Wilson's report ('Child Rape Part of "Men's Business"', 16 May 2006) quoted Rogers as having said the following:

> Men's business is a predominant aspect of life in remote communities, and young men who are initiated are given a certain status in the community and feel they are not responsible for their actions. In other words, they can do whatever they like. Young women are not accorded the same status. Males are given a higher status.

But in the *Lateline* segments that actually aired ('Paper Reveals Sexual Abuse, Violence in NT Indigenous Communities' and 'Crown Prosecutor Speaks Out about Abuse in Central Australia', transcripts of both segments available at https://web.archive.org/web/20070703195445/http://www.abc.net.au/lateline/includes/lateline_20060501.htm), Rogers did not say these words, and no other journalist reported them.

18   Kemarre, interviewed by Suzanne Smith, Hidden Valley camp, broadcast on *Lateline*, ABC TV, 15 May 2006.

19   Betty Pearce, interviewed by Jean Kennedy, ABC News, 16 May 2006; Wesley Aird, 'Culture is No Excuse for Crime', *The Australian*, 18 May 2006.

20   Larissa Behrendt, interviewed by Tony Jones, *Lateline*, ABC TV, 18 May 2006.

21   Betty Pearce, interviewed by Tom Iggulden, ABC News, 16 May 2006.

22   Kerrie Arabena, 'Quick-fix Solutions to Violence Won't Work', *The Age*, 20 May 2006; Ashleigh Wilson, 'Levels of Violence "Surprisingly Low"', *The Australian*, 26 May 2006 (quoting Northern Land Council chief executive Norman Fry).

23   CLP leader Jodeen Carney, a white former lawyer who had been born, raised and educated in Victoria, declared that Aboriginal law was a 'shield' behind which violent men hid: AAP, 'Customary Law "Shield" for Violent Aboriginal Men: Leader', AAP News, 16 May 2006. Nanette Rogers' friend Jane Lloyd, at that time the manager of the Anangu NPY Women's Council, made similar remarks (Lloyd, interviewed by Lindy Kerin, ABC News, 16 May 2006). Lloyd told reporter Ashleigh Wilson that she and Rogers had 'been talking and

thinking about these issues for the past 15 years': Wilson, 'Crusader's Battle from City to Bush', *The Australian*, 17 May 2006. ALP Indigenous affairs spokesperson Chris Evans – also white – said it was 'wrong' for Aboriginal men to 'hide' behind Aboriginal law: Nassim Khadem and Russell Skelton, 'More Police, Less Booze: Brough's Abuse Solution', *The Age*, 17 May 2006.

24   Fraser, 'End the Denial of Wrongs', *The Age*, 24 May 2006.

25   Miranda Devine, 'A Culture of Violence that Must Change', *The Sydney Morning Herald*, 18 May 2006; Rosemary Neill, 'Aboriginal Violence Has a Lengthy History', *The Australian*, 19 May 2006; Andrew Bolt, 'Save These Children', *Herald Sun*, 19 May 2006; Editorial, 'Centre's Dark Side Shocks a Nation', *Centralian Advocate*, 19 May 2006; Geoff Roach, 'We Can't Neglect Indigenous Problems', *The Advertiser* (Adelaide), 20 May 2006; Christopher Pearson, 'Depravity in Dependency', *The Australian*, 20 May 2006; Michael Duffy, 'No More Empty Rhetoric, Please,' *The Sydney Morning Herald*, 20 May 2006; Tory Maguire, 'Are We Brave Enough to Face This Horror Story?', *The Daily Telegraph*, 20 May 2006; John Pasquarelli, 'Shame of Politically Correct Zealots', *The Australian*, 29 May 2006 (in which the former Papua New Guinea parliamentarian and One Nation adviser Pasquarelli declared that the policy of self-determination had resulted in 'apartheid'); Errol Simper, 'Aborigines Must Accept Scrutiny', *The Australian*, 1 June 2006; Tony Abbott, 'Misplaced Tact Stands in the Way of Help', *The Sydney Morning Herald*, 21 June 2006.

26   AAP, 'Treasurer, Indigenous Leaders Back Child Removal', AAP News, 19 May 2006; AAP, 'Call for Exit Grants for Aborigines', AAP News, 19 May 2006.

27   Stanley Cohen, *Folk Devils and Moral Panics: The Creation of the Mods and Rockers*, Paladin, London, 1973.

28   Brough, interviewed by Tony Jones, *Lateline*, ABC TV, 16 May 2006. Within twenty-four hours, Brough had retreated from the specific use of the term 'paedophile rings', but stood by his claim that there was a 'pattern' of violent rape and other sexual abuse of very young children.

29   Howard, quoted in Paul Osborne, 'Leaders Snub Indigenous Summit Called by Brough', AAP News, 18 May 2006.

30   AAP, 'Houses Won't Be Fixed Up Till Law and Order Is: Brough', AAP News, 25 May 2006.

31   Suzanne Smith, 'Sexual Abuse Reported in Indigenous Community', *Lateline*, ABC TV, 21 June 2006, transcript online: https://web.archive.org/web/20071215171030/http://www.abc.net.au/lateline/content/2006/s1668773.htm.

32   AAP, 'NT Govt Launched Aboriginal Child Sex Abuse Inquiry', AAP News, 22 June 2006.

33   Langton, Gordon and Chaney, interviewed by Tony Jones, *Lateline*, ABC TV, 26 June 2006.

34   AAP, 'Former NT DPP Criticises ACC Forced Testimony Plan', AAP News, 11 July 2006.

35   Nassim Khadem, 'Making Courts Culture Free', *The Age*, 14 July 2006.

36   Quoted in Khadem, 'Making Courts Culture Free'.

37   Carney, 'Men Prey on Customary Law', *The Australian*, 21 July 2006; *Sentencing Amendment Bill (No. 2) 2003* (NT private member's bill, introduced 13 August 2003); *Sentencing Amendment (Aboriginal Customary Law) Bill 2005* (NT private member's bill, introduced 30 November 2005). Carney would go on to introduce a similar bill a third time: *Sentencing Amendment (Cultural Practice and Customary Law) Bill 2006* (NT private member's bill, introduced 23 August 2006). In 2021, Carney was appointed South Australia's Commissioner for Equal Opportunity by that state's Liberal government.

38   *Inquest into the deaths of Kumanjay Presley, Kunmanara Coulthard and Kunmanara Brumby* [2005] NTMC 086 at [33].

39   Gregory Andrews, testimony to the Senate's Community Affairs References Committee's inquiry into Petrol Sniffing in Remote Aboriginal Communities, 27 April 2006.

40   Chris, Graham, 'ABC Lateline's "Fake Youth Worker" Wins Plum Abbott Govt Job', NewMatilda.com, 2 July 2014.

41   Martin, *Hansard*, House of Representatives (Northern Territory), 11 October 2006, p. 772. Martin's explanation came after that 2004 memo was reported in *The Australian* that same morning, together with a claim that her office 'knew' about the child abuse and prostitution in Mutitjulu yet 'did nothing'.

42   Martin, *Hansard*, House of Representatives (Northern Territory), 11 October 2006, p. 772.

43   *Crimes Amendment (Bail and Sentencing) Bill 2006 (Cth)*, introduced into the House of Representatives on 14 September 2006.

44   Law Reform Commission of Western Australia, *Aboriginal Customary Laws: The Interaction*

of Western Australian Law with Aboriginal Law and Culture – Final Report, LRCWA Project 94, September 2006: https://www.lrc.justice.wa.gov.au/_files/P94_FR.pdf.

45   Jim McGinty (attorney-general), 'Aboriginal Customary Law to Gain Recognition', media release, 27 October 2006: https://www.mediastatements.wa.gov.au/Pages/Carpenter/2006/10/Aboriginal-customary-law-to-gain-recognition.aspx.

46   Labor's representatives on the Legal and Constitutional Affairs Committee described the bill in a dissenting report as 'completely misguided approach to addressing, in any meaningful way, the endemic problems of violence and child abuse in Indigenous communities'. The Committee's Coalition members agreed that there had been a lack of consultation about a bill whose effects would be discriminatory and against the findings and recommendations of each inquiry dating back to 1986. But with four members on an eight-member Committee – a consequence of the Coalition's control of the Senate – the Coalition used the casting vote of its chairperson, Marise Payne, to endorse the bill with minor changes: they had to, because it represented government policy.

47   Nowra, *Bad Dreaming: Aboriginal Men's Violence Against Women and Children*, Pluto Press, North Melbourne, 2007; Nowra, 'Culture of Denial', *The Australian Literary Review*, vol. 2, no. 2, 7 March 2007. Nowra was no expert on Aboriginal cultures, family violence or child protection. He was born and raised in Melbourne as Mark Doyle, and was subjected to frequent abuse at the hands of his mother, who herself had endured years of alcohol-fuelled violence perpetrated by her own father: Nowra, *The Twelfth of Never*, Picador, Sydney, 1999. It was perhaps this terrifying background which 'moved' him to write about Aboriginal violence after reading (presumably in media accounts) of the 'anal rape' of the teenage girl by the Ngarinyman Elder in 2005, and after hearing stories of similar abuse when he was in Alice Springs' hospital for 'several days' shortly afterwards. In response to Nowra, Aboriginal lawyers Larissa Behrendt and Nicole Watson, both of the Jumbunna Indigenous House of Learning at the University of Technology Sydney and both having long argued for the need to better address family violence in Aboriginal communities, pointed to Nowra's one-eyed reading of the texts he consulted. They wondered whether he had reported the admissions he'd apparently been privy to in the Alice Springs hospital to police: Behrendt and Watson, 'A Response to Louis Nowra', *Alternative Law Journal*, vol. 33, no. 1, March 2008, pp. 45–47.

48   Anderson and Wild, *Ampe Akelyernemane Meke Mekarle*, pp. 68–72.

49   Toohey, 'Last Drinks', p. 49.

50   Tony Barrass, 'Aboriginal "Child Sex Ring" Exposed', *The Australian*, 17 April 2007.

51   Nicolas Perpitch, 'Magistrate Hits Out at Aboriginal Child Abuse', AAP News, 12 July 2007.

52   Annabel Stafford, 'Child Sex Abuse Rife, Says Brough', *The Age*, 1 June 2007.

53   Brough's maternal grandmother, Violet, believes her missing father was an Aboriginal man. Brough's sister, Carol Stubbs, identifies as Aboriginal, and sat for years on Kalgoorlie's Bega Garnbirringu Health Service board, where her husband, Greg Stubbs, was chief executive for sixteen years until he resigned in protest in 2006 when an administrator was appointed at the behest of the federal Department of Health. Greg Stubbs is now a pastor at Yiwarra Palya Ministries at Morapoi Station, where he and Carol run a tourism business: 'Brough's Heritage Is a Family Mystery: Sister', *Crikey*, 30 January 2006: https://www.crikey.com.au/2006/01/30/broughs-heritage-is-a-family-mystery-sister/; 'Govt Frustrates Brough's Brother-In-Law', *The Sydney Morning Herald*, 1 May 2006; Morapoi Station Stay, 'About Us', http://morapoi.com.au/about/.

54   See: Jon Altman and Melinda Hinkson (eds), *Coercive Reconciliation: Stabilise, Normalise, Exit Aboriginal Australia*, Arena Publications, 2007; Central Land Council, *Reviewing the Northern Territory Emergency Response: Perspectives from Six Communities*, CLC, 2008; Claire Smith and Gary Jackson, *A Community-Based Review of the Northern Territory Emergency Response*, Institute of Advanced Study for Humanity, University of Newcastle, August 2008; Kathryn Roediger, 'Northern Territory Emergency Response: Evaluation Report', Department of Families, Housing, Community Services and Indigenous Affairs, 2011.

55   See for instance: Langton, 'Trapped in the Aboriginal Reality Show', *Griffith Review*, no. 19, 2007, p. 143; Langton, 'The End of "Big Men" Politics', *Griffith Review*, no. 22, 2008, p. 13; Katherine Curchin, 'Noel Pearson's Role in the Northern Territory Intervention: Radical Centrist or Polarising Partisan?', *Australian Journal of Politics and History*, vol. 61, no. 4, 2015, pp. 576–90.

56   Murri academic lawyer Nicole Watson explains how the Intervention 'perpetuates the binary of invisibility and control': 'Aboriginal women's ability to exercise an array of rights becomes invisible under such interventions', while 'the state's control over their lives is almost always strengthened': Watson, 'The Northern Territory Emergency Response: Has It Really Improved the Lives of Aboriginal Women and Children?', *Australian Feminist Law Journal*, vol. 35, no. 1, 2011, p. 147 at 156.

57   'Community Furious with NT Government after Alleged Rape of Indigenous Toddler', SBS News, 21 February 2018.

58   Thalia Anthony and Harry Blagg, 'STOP in the Name of Who's [*sic.*] Law? Driving and the Regulation of Contested Space in Central Australia', *Social & Legal Studies*, vol. 22, no. 1, 2013, p. 43 at 55.

59   Australian Human Rights Commission, *2012 Indigenous Social Justice Report*.

60   Leanne Liddle, Central Arrernte woman, South Australia's first Aboriginal policewoman and now director of the Aboriginal justice unit in the NT's attorney-general's department, quoted in Livia Albeck-Ripka, '"Like a Cattle Yard": How Justice Is Delivered in Australia's Bush Courts', *The New York Times*, 6 December 2020.

61   Idriess, *Nemarluk*, Angus & Robertson, 1941.

62   Apart from in Idriess's book and his *Man Tracks* (Sydney, 1935), parts of Nemarluk's story can be found in John Pye's brief *The Port Keats Story*, 1973; in Bill Parry, *The Story of Nimalak*, Batchelor, NT, 1983: https://ngangi.net/system/files/atoms/file/NimalakStoryEnglish.pdf; and in Bruce Shaw, 'Nemarluk (1911–1940)', *Australian Dictionary of Biography*, National Centre of Biography, ANU, 2000: https://adb.anu.edu.au/biography/nemarluk-11222.

63   See: Amanda Carlin, 'The Courtroom as White Space: Racial Performance as Noncredibility', *UCLA Law Review*, vol. 63, 2016, p. 450.

64   Pedersen, 'Preface', in *Jandamarra and the Bunuba Resistance*, Magabala Books, 3rd ed, 2016 (first published 1995).

65   John Ramsland and Christopher Mooney's book, *Remembering Aboriginal Heroes* (Brolga Publishing, 2012), profiles eight Aboriginal men and one woman who achieved greatness within settlers' cultural world.

66   John Taylor, *Social Indicators for Aboriginal Governance: Insights from the Thamarrurr Region, Northern Territory*, Centre for Aboriginal Economic Policy Research Monograph No. 24, ANU, Canberra, 2004; Taylor and Owen Stanley, *The Opportunity Costs of the Status Quo in the Thamarrurr Region*, CAEPR Working Paper No.28/2005, ANU, Canberra, 2005.

67   See: Robert Manne, *Bad News: Murdoch's Australian and the Shaping of the Nation*, Quarterly Essay, no. 43, September 2011. Full disclosure: I was Manne's research assistant on this one.

68   Balan, unpublished letter to *The Australian*, 7 May 2022 (in my possession). It wasn't the first time he'd proposed this kind of 'solution'. In an earlier letter to *The Australian*, published on 15 December 2019, he wrote: 'Remote community dwellers are free to settle anywhere in the country, so they do not have to stay in squalid conditions.'

69   Comparing 'Median unit rental price' of $330 per week on 20 May 2022 according to realestate.com.au with the fortnightly Jobseeker payment to singles from 20 March 2022 ($642.70).

70   Larissa Behrendt, *Indigenous Australia for Dummies*, 2nd ed., John Wiley, Milton, Queensland, 2021.

CHAPTER 8

1   Roebourne was named after John Roe, explorer and Western Australia's first surveyor-general. Local Aboriginal people call the town Ieramugadu.

2   The officer told this to the Royal Commission into Aboriginal Deaths in Custody's inquiry into John Pat's death, and it is recorded in the transcript (at p. 4934; quoted in Jeannine Purdy, 'Royal Commissions and Omissions: What Was Left Out of the Report on the Death of John Pat', *Australian Journal of Law and Society*, vol. 10, 1994, p. 37 at 40). It was left out of Elliott Johnston's 149-page report of the inquiry.

3   Commissioner Elliott Johnston, *Report of the Inquiry into the Death of John Peter Pat*, Royal Commission into Aboriginal Deaths in Custody, 30 March 1991, available online: http://www.austlii.edu.au/au/other/IndigLRes/rciadic/individual/brm_jpp/index.html; Purdy, 'Royal Commissions and Omissions', pp. 37–66.

4   'On the Road for Black Justice', *The Age*, 11 September 1986.
5   Greg Roberts and Simon Kent, 'Holding Orders Inquiry on Cell Deaths', *The Sydney Morning Herald*, 14 April 1987.
6   'Row over Aboriginal Inquiry', *The Sydney Morning Herald*, 15 April 1987.
7   Frank Walker and Bruce Jones, 'Aborigines' Deaths in Police Custody "Tip of Iceberg"', *Sun Herald*, 14 June 1987; 'Inquiry into Black Deaths in Custody', *The Sydney Morning Herald*, 18 June 1987.
8   J.H. Muirhead, *Report of the Inquiry into the Death of Kingsley Richard Dixon*, Royal Commission into Aboriginal Deaths in Custody, 25 January 1989.
9   Tony Hewett, 'Mother says no 14 was murder', *The Sydney Morning Herald*, 22 July 1987.
10   J.H. Wootten, *Report of the Inquiry into the Death of Lloyd James Boney*, Royal Commission into Aboriginal Deaths in Custody, 24 January 1991; Graham Williams and Michael Cordell, 'No Way He Would Kill Himself, Says Aboriginal's Family', *The Sydney Morning Herald*, 8 August 1987.
11   Chris Sherwell, 'Rash of Aboriginal Jail Deaths to Be Investigated', *Financial Times* (London), 12 August 1987. Hand replaced Holding as minister on 24 July and announced the royal commission less than three weeks later. But he frequently clashed with Perkins, who resigned the following year after being accused of poor administration.
12   Quoted in Frost, *Botany Bay*, p. 85.
13   See, for instance: John Howard (the High Sheriff of Bedfordshire), *The State of the Prisons*, 1777.
14   Maconochie, *Report on the State of Prison Discipline in Van Diemen's Land &c*, London and Hobart Town, 1838.
15   Maconochie, *Crime and Punishment: The Mark System, Framed to Mix Persuasion with Punishment, and Make their Effect Improving, Yet their Operation Severe*, London, 1846.
16   John V. Barry, 'Childs, Joseph (1787–1870)', *Australian Dictionary of Biography*, National Centre of Biography, ANU, 1966.
17   All Australian states abolished the death penalty for all crimes between 1922 (when Queensland did so) and 1985 (New South Wales). Commonwealth legislation ended the death penalty for all federal crimes, and all crimes in the Northern Territory and the ACT, in 1973. In 2010, further Commonwealth legislation aimed to prevent any state or territory from re-establishing the death penalty in the future (*Crimes Legislation Amendment (Torture Prohibition and Death Penalty Abolition) Act 2010* (No. 37 of 2010) (Cth), schedule 2), though it is unclear whether this legislation would stand up if challenged.
18   Mathiesen, *The Politics of Abolition*, 1971 (English translation 1974).
19   See, for instance, the work of Bri Lee arguing for amendments to what is meant by 'consent' in sexual offences: her first memoir, *Eggshell Skull*, Allen & Unwin, Crows Nest, NSW, 2018; her paper with Jonathan Crowe, 'The Mistake of Fact Excuse in Queensland Rape Law: Some Problems and Proposals for Reform', *University of Queensland Law Journal*, vol. 39, no. 1, 2020; and a range of opinion journalism in *Guardian Australia*, *The Saturday Paper*, *The Monthly* and *Crikey*.
20   Mathiesen, 'The Politics of Abolition', *Contemporary Crises*, no. 10, 1986, pp. 81–94.
21   Manzie, *Misuse of Drugs Bill 1989* (NT), second reading speech, in Legislative Assembly *Hansard*, 25 May 1989, pp. 6530 and 6534.
22   *Domestic Violence Act 1992* (no. 67 of 1992) (NT), s 10(1).
23   Fred Finch, *Sentencing Bill 1995*, second reading speech, in Legislative Assembly *Hansard*, 18 May 1995, p. 3386.
24   Chris Cunneen and David McDonald, 'Imprisonment as a Last Resort', chapter 10 in *Keeping Aboriginal and Torres Strait Islander People Out of Custody: An Evaluation of the Implementation of the Recommendations of the Royal Commission*, Office of Public Affairs, ATSIC, 1997.
25   Roderic Broadhurst and Nini Loh, 'The Phantom of Deterrence: The *Crime (Serious and Repeat Offenders) Sentencing Act*', *Australian & NZ Journal of Criminology*, vol. 26, December 1993, pp. 251–57.
26   Neil Morgan, 'Capturing Crims or Capturing Votes? The Aims and Effects of Mandatories', *UNSW Law Journal*, vol. 22, no. 1, 1999, p. 267 at 269.
27   It commenced on 9 March 1992 and expired on 8 March 1994: *Crime (Serious and Repeat Offenders) Sentencing Act 1992* (WA), ss 2 and 12.

28 *Criminal Code Amendment Act (No. 2) 1996* (WA), s 5, inserting a new s 401 into the *Criminal Code* (WA).

29 Department of Justice (WA), *Review of Section 401 of the Criminal Code*, 2001, pp. 24–25.

30 Department of Corrective Services (WA), Submission No. 31 to the WA Law Reform Commission's inquiry into Aboriginal customary laws, 4 May 2006.

31 *Sentencing Amendment Act (No. 2) 1996* (No. 65 of 1996) (NT), s 8.

32 *Trenerry v Bradley* (1997) 6 NTLR 175 per Martin CJ, Angel and Mildren JJ.

33 NT Government, *Royal Commission into Aboriginal Deaths in Custody: Northern Territory Government Implementation Report 1996–1997*, tabled in the Legislative Assembly July 1999, p. 131: Section 2.1, 'Northern Territory Average Prisoner Population'.

34 Bernard Lagan, 'Mandatory Madness', *The Sydney Morning Herald*, 12 June 1999, p. 34. Ian Gray resigned as chief magistrate in 1998 and returned to the Victorian Bar before being appointed chief magistrate in that state; he is currently (at the time of writing) Victoria's state coroner.

35 Tippett, 'Throwing in the Towel', *Balance: Journal of the Law Society Northern Territory*, May 1999, p. 11.

36 Mike Seccombe, 'A 15-year-old Hangs in Jail and the System Shrugs Its Shoulders,' *The Sydney Morning Herald*, 27 January 2001; *Findings in the Death of Johnno Johnson Wurramarba* [2001] NTMC 84, 19 December 2001.

37 *Sentencing Amendment Act (No. 3) 2001* (NT), s 6.

38 *Sentencing (Crime of Murder) and Parole Reform Act 2003 (No. 3 of 2004)* (NT).

39 See: Steven Schubert, *Mandatory Murder*, ABC Books, 2019. Following a (continuing) campaign, largely driven by his mother, Grieve's sentence was later partly remitted by the Administrator under the 'mercy' provisions in Part 10 of the *Sentencing Act 1995* (NT).

40 *Sentencing Amendment (Violent Offences) Act 2008* (NT), s 5.

41 For example: Hamburger et al., *A Safer Northern Territory through Correctional Interventions: Report of the Review of the Northern Territory Department of Correctional Services*, BDO and Knowledge Consulting, 31 July 2016; Australian Law Reform Commission, *Pathways to Justice: An Inquiry into the Incarceration Rate of Aboriginal and Torres Strait Islander Peoples: Final Report*, ALRC Report 133, December 2017, chapter 8.

42 *Criminal Code* (NT), s 188(2).

43 The *Criminal Code Amendment Act 2009 (No. 21 of 2009)* (WA), s 4, created a mandatory minimum prison sentence of twelve months (maximum fourteen years) for anyone who assaults a police officer.

44 *Bayley v The Queen* [2013] VSCA 295.

45 Nino Bucci and Rania Spooner, 'Adrian Bayley: How the Justice System Left Him Free to Stalk Melbourne's Streets', *The Age*, 25 March 2015.

46 *Justice Legislation Amendment (Cancellation of Parole and Other Matters) Act 2013* (Vic) (No. 15 of 2013), introduced into Victoria's parliament on 5 February 2013, passed both houses just sixteen days later.

47 McMahon, 'The Changing Function of Bail', published on Deakin Law School's Newsroom website, 9 September 2019: https://lawnewsroom.deakin.edu.au/articles/the-changing-function-of-bail.

48 Eggleston, 'Bail', chapter 4 in *Fear, Favour or Affection*.

49 See for instance: Marilyn McMahon, 'No Bail, More Jail? Breaking the Nexus Between Community Protection and Escalating Pre-Trial Detention', Victorian Parliamentary Library Fellowship Research Paper No. 3, August 2019: https://www.parliament.vic.gov.au/publications/research-papers/send/36-research-papers/13893-no-bail-more-jail-breaking-the-nexus-between-community-protection-and-escalating-pre-trial-detention.

50 Robert Clark MLA, second reading speech on the *Serious Offenders Bill 2018*, Victorian Assembly *Hansard*, 23 May 2018, p. 1523 at 1524.

51 Gordon Rich-Phillips MLC, second reading speech on the *Justice Legislation Miscellaneous Amendment Bill 2018*, Victorian Legislative Council *Hansard*, 18 September 2018, p. 5008 at 5009.

52 McMahon, 'No Bail, More Jail?', p. 18. (She refers to the '*Willie* Horton effect', though Horton said later that he was never known as 'Willie' and that the name was racially demeaning: Jeffrey Elliot, 'The 'Willie' Horton Nobody Knows', *The Nation*, 23 August 1993, pp. 201–06.)

53 'Lynette Daley Death: Adrian Attwater and Paul Maris Jailed for Brutal Attack', ABC News, 8 December 2017.

54　Corrections Victoria, 'Monthly Time Series Prisoner and Offender Data', published September 2021 (comparing February 2020 figure with June 2006 figure): https://www.corrections.vic.gov.au/monthly-time-series-prisoner-and-offender-data.

55　Australian Bureau of Statistics, 'Prisoners in Australia' annual statistical series: https://www.abs.gov.au/statistics/people/crime-and-justice/prisoners-australia.

56　Eggleston, *Fear, Favour or Affection*, pp. 76–77.

57　Lee, *Eggshell Skull*, p. 32.

58　Calla Wahlquist, Nick Evershed and Lorena Allam, 'More than half of 147 Indigenous People Who Died in Custody Had Not Been Found Guilty', *Guardian Australia*, 30 August 2018: https://www.theguardian.com/australia-news/2018/aug/30/more-than-half-of-147-indigenous-people-who-died-in-custody-had-not-been-found-guilty.

59　Quoted in the *Sun-Herald*, Sydney, 31 May 1992.

60　Wai-Yin Wan, Steve Moffatt, Craig Jones and Don Weatherburn, 'The Effect of Arrest and Imprisonment on Crime', NSW Bureau of Crime Statistics and Research *Crime and Justice Bulletin*, no. 158, February 2012.

61　Don Weatherburn, Juizhao Hua and Steve Moffatt, 'How Much Crime Does Prison Stop? The Incapacitation Effect on Burglary', BOCSAR *Crime and Justice Bulletin*, no. 93, January 2006.

62　Patrice Villetaz, Gwladys Gillieron and Martin Killias, 'The Effects on Re-Offending of Custodial vs (?) Non-Custodial Sanctions: An Updated Systematic Review of the State of Knowledge', *Campbell Systematic Reviews*, vol. 11, no. 1, 2015, p. 1.

63　International imprisonment rates as reported by the Victorian Sentencing Advisory Council: https://www.sentencingcouncil.vic.gov.au/statistics/sentencing-trends/international-imprisonment-rates (retrieved 19 March 2021).

64　*R v LAL* [2018] QCA 179.

65　Centre for Innovative Justice, *Innovative Justice Responses to Sexual Offending: Pathways to Better Outcomes for Victims, Offenders and the Community*, report, RMIT, May 2014.

66　Jane Goodman-Delahunty and Kate O'Brien, 'Parental Sexual Offending: Managing Risk Through Diversion' (2014), *AIC Trends & Issues in Criminal Justice*, no. 482; Sarah Dingle, 'The Family Trap', *Background Briefing*, ABC Radio National, broadcast 11 August 2013.

67　Leigh, 'The Second Convict Age: Explaining the Return of Mass Imprisonment in Australia', CESifo Working Paper No. 8163, March 2020: https://papers.ssrn.com/sol3/papers.cfm?abstract_id=3555590.

68　Weatherburn, 'Slash Repeat Offending: The Best Way to Cut Crime', *The Sydney Morning Herald*, 21 October 2010.

69　ABS data, cited as Table 8.4 in Weatherburn and Rahman, *The Vanishing Criminal*.

70　Weatherburn, 'The Effect of Prison on Adult Re-offending', BOCSAR *Crime and Justice Bulletin* no. 143, August 2010: https://www.bocsar.nsw.gov.au/Publications/CJB/cjb143.pdf; Paul Heaton, Sandra Mayson and Megan Stevenson, 'The Downstream Consequences of Misdemeanour Pretrial Detention', *Stanford Law Review*, vol. 69, 2017, p. 711: https://papers.ssrn.com/sol3/papers.cfm?abstract_id=2809840.

71　Samantha Dick, 'Prisoner Advocates Say a Lack of Programs at Darwin Correctional Centre is Contributing to the NT's High Reoffending Rates', *ABC News*, 11 July 2022.

72　Richard Moule, Scott Decker and David Pyrooz, 'Social Capital, the Life-Course and Gangs', in Chris Gibson and Marvin Krohn (eds), *Handbook of Life-Course Criminology: Emerging Trends and Directions for Future Research*, Springer, 2013, pp. 143–58.

73　Australian Institute of Health and Welfare, *The Health of Australia's Prisoners 2018*, Canberra; Joseph Murray, Ivana Sekol and Rikke Olsen, 'Effects of Parental Imprisonment on Child Antisocial Behaviour and Mental Health: A Systematic Review', *Campbell Systematic Reviews*, vol. 4, no. 1, January 2009; Christopher Wildeman and Bruce Western, 'Incarceration in Fragile Families', *Future Child*, vol. 20, no. 2, Fall 2010, pp. 157–77; Tyson Whitten et al., 'Parenting Offending and Child Physical Health, Mental Health and Drug Use Outcomes: A Systematic Literature Review', *Journal of Child and Family Studies*, vol. 28, 2019, pp. 1155–68; Will Dobbie, Jacob Goldin and Crystal Yang, 'The Effects of Pre-Trial Detention on Conviction, Future Crime and Employment: Evidence From Randomly Assigned Judges', *American Economic Review*, vol. 108, no. 2, 2018, pp. 201–40.

74 Western and Sirois, 'Social Environments of Pervasive Incarceration: Lessons from Australia's Top End', in Nicola Lacey et al. (eds), *Tracing the Relationship Between Inequality, Crime and Punishment: Space, Time and Politics*, Oxford University Press, 2020.

75 ABS, *National Aboriginal and Torres Strait Islander Social Survey, 2014–2015*, Cat No. 4714.0, 2016.

CHAPTER 9

1 Langford Ginibi, interviewed by Robin Hughes, *Australian Biography*, 15 November 1995, transcript available: https://www.nfsa.gov.au/collection/curated/australian-biography-ruby-langford-ginibi-0.

2 Louis Waller, 'Elizabeth Eggleston, Aborigines and the Law', chapter 11 in Peter Hanks and Bryan Keon-Cohen (eds), *Aborigines and the Law*, p. 304 at 305.

3 Dickinson, 'The Testimony of Aborigines in Law Courts in the Northern Territory', *South Pacific*, September–October 1958; reprinted in *Balance: Journal of the NT Law Society*, vol. 44, 1991.

4 A.P. Elkin, 'Aboriginal Evidence and Justice in North Australia', *Oceania*, vol. 17, no. 3, March 1947; Martin Kriewaldt, 'The Application of the Criminal Law to the Aborigines of the Northern Territory of Australia', *University of Western Australia Law Review*, vol. 5, no. 1, 1960; Tatz, 'Aboriginal Administration in the Northern Territory of Australia', especially chapter 4.

5 Tatz, 'Queensland's Aborigines: Natural Justice and the Rule of Law', *The Australian Quarterly*, September 1963, vol. 35, no. 3, pp. 33–49. Queensland's 'protection' regime operated until full civil rights were granted to Aboriginal and Torres Strait Islander people. Under it, Queensland's parliament, through its *Aboriginals' Preservation and Protection Act 1939* (Qld), gave extraordinary powers to authorities to control Aboriginal people on missions and reserves: see the various *Aboriginals' Preservation and Protection Regulations* (Qld).

6 Tobin, *Fringe Dwelling Rural Aborigines and the Law in New South Wales: Preliminary Investigation and Report*, Aboriginal Scholarships Society, 1969.

7 Eggleston, *Fear, Favour or Affection*, pp. 173–74.

8 Eggleston, *Fear, Favour or Affection*, p. 22.

9 Section 150 of the *Licensing Act 1911* (WA), as amended by the *Licensing Act Amendment Act (No. 4) 1963* (WA), made it illegal to sell, supply or give any alcohol 'in any quantity whatever' to 'any native', on pain of six months' imprisonment or a fine of £100. The same section made it illegal for 'any native' to receive or possess alcohol, on pain of one month imprisonment or a fine of £5.

10 Eggleston, *Fear, Favour or Affection*, pp. 24–25.

11 Eggleston, *Fear, Favour or Affection*, pp. 55–56.

12 Eggleston, *Fear, Favour or Affection*, p. 63.

13 Eggleston, *Fear, Favour or Affection*, pp. 82–83.

14 Eggleston, *Fear, Favour or Affection*, pp. 134–39 and Appendix 2.28.

15 *The Herald*, Melbourne, 17 May 1967; *The Age*, Melbourne, 8 May 1967; both cited in Eggleston, *Fear, Favour or Affection*, p. 140.

16 *R v Justices of Rankine River; Ex parte Sydney; Ex parte Pluto* (1962) 3 FLR 215 at 218.

17 Eggleston, *Fear, Favour or Affection*, p. 124. See also: Tatz, 'Queensland's Aborigines', pp. 33–49.

18 Eggleston, *Fear, Favour or Affection*, pp. 177–78.

19 Eggleston, *Fear, Favour or Affection*, pp. 179–80.

20 Weatherburn, Arresting Incarceration, p. 22.

21 Weatherburn, Arresting Incarceration, pp. 23–24.

22 Johnson et al., para 1.7.1.

23 The draft was first submitted in 1993 and became the basis of the final Declaration that was adopted by the General Assembly in 2007 following a remarkable vote: 143 nations in favour and 4 against (with 11 abstentions and 34 absentees). The four 'no' votes were cast by the former British settler states with significant but minority Indigenous populations: the United States, Canada, New Zealand and Australia. The vote was cast in the dying weeks of John Howard's Coalition government, and Australia's recalcitrance – primarily due to the Declaration's inclusion of the right to self-determination – became yet another

reason for Labor to bash Howard's record on Indigenous rights. His successor, Rudd, reversed Australia's position two years later, though in a way that didn't require any changes: Australia doesn't consider the Declaration to be legally binding. (Canada, on the other hand, has since committed to amending its federal and provincial laws to bring them into line with the Declaration.)

24　Weatherburn, Arresting Incarceration, p. 128.

25　Chris Cunneen and Tom Robb, 'Criminal Justice in North-west New South Wales', BOCSAR, 1987, p. 220.

26　See, for instance: Samantha Jeffries and Christine Bond, 'Does Indigeneity Matter? Sentencing Indigenous Offenders in South Australia's Higher Courts', Australian and New Zealand Journal of Criminology, vol. 42, no. 1, 2009, pp. 47–71; Jeffries and Bond, 'Indigenous Disparity in Lower Court Imprisonment Decisions: A Study of Two Australian Jurisdictions, 1998 to 2008', Trends and Issues in Crime and Criminal Justice, no. 447, December 2012.

27　Harry Blagg, Chris Cunneen, Anna Ferrante and Neil Morgan, 'Systemic Racism as a Factor in the Over-representation of Aboriginal People in the Criminal Justice System', report to the Equal Opportunity Commission (as it then was) and the Aboriginal Justice Forum, Melbourne, 2005.

28　Jeffries and Bond, 'Indigenous Disparity in Lower Court Imprisonment Decisions'.

29　Cunneen, 'Racism, Discrimination and the Over-representation of Indigenous People in the Criminal Justice System: Some Conceptual and Explanatory Issues', Current Issues in Criminal Justice, vol. 17, no. 3, 2006, p. 329 at 333–35.

30　Weatherburn and Fitzgerald, 'Reducing Aboriginal Over-representation in Prison: A Rejoinder to Chris Cunneen', Current Issues in Criminal Justice, vol. 18, no. 2, 2006, pp. 366–70.

31　While the term 'postcolonial' is often used among historians to refer to a historical period immediately following the end of a colonial period, in social studies and the history of ideas, the term 'postcolonial' refers to a set of ideas and critical approaches to the legacy of colonialism and imperialism. At least, that's how I'm using the term here: in no way should this term imply that Australia's colonial period has somehow ended. Self-evidently, it has not.

32　Frantz Fanon, Black Skin, White Masks (originally published as Peau noire, masques blancs in 1952), trans. Charles Markmann, 1967.

33　Sartre notoriously slammed France's continuing presence in Algeria in Colonialism and Neocolonialism (originally published in French in 1964), trans. 2001. In his famous Orientalism (Pantheon Books, 1978), Said argued that European thought and administration had divided the world into a Western, privileged 'Occident' and an othered, excluded and suppressed 'Orient'. Spivak revived Antonio Gramsci's concept of the 'subaltern' – a subjugated colonial population which is socially and politically excluded from hierarchies of power which produced and reproduced discursive hegemonies in which standards are kept implicitly or explicitly 'white' or 'Western': Spivak, 'Can the Subaltern Speak?' in Cary Nelson and Lawrence Grossberg (eds), Marxism and the Interpretation of Culture, Macmillan, 1988.

34　See, for instance: Derrick Bell, Race, Racism and American Law, 6th ed., Aspen, New York, 2008.

35　Margaret Weir, 'Indigenous Australians and Universities: A Study of Postgraduate Students' Experiences in Learning Research', PhD thesis, University of New England, 2001, p. 6. Weir, a descendant of the Bundjalung people, had in fact been the very first Aboriginal person to attend an Australian university when she enrolled in an arts degree at the University of Queensland.

36　Thalia Anthony and Harry Blagg, Decolonising Criminology: Imagining Justice in a Postcolonial World, Palgrave Macmillan, 2019.

37　The Scottish merchant and magistrate Patrick Colquhoun was among the most curious: he collected enormous amounts of economic statistics, and concluded that the causation of criminality lay in 'indigence' as distinct from 'poverty', as long as 'work is to be had by all who seek it'. His solution to the problem of stolen cargo on the Thames was to create a preventative police force, initially funded by businessmen: Colquhoun, A Treatise on the Police of the Metropolis, London, 1796.

38　Walter, 'Data Politics and Indigenous Representation in Australian Statistics', chapter 5 in Kukutai and Taylor (eds), Indigenous Data Sovereignty: Towards an Agenda, ANU Press, pp. 79–98.

39 See for instance: 'Abolition on Indigenous Land', panel discussion as part of the John Barry Memorial Lecture, hosted by the University of Melbourne, broadcast on ABC Radio, *Speaking Out*, 11 April 2021.

40 *Statutes Amendment (Spit Hood Prohibition) Act* (No. 47 of 2021). South Australia was the first state to ban spit hoods.

41 Porter, 'Aboriginal Sovereignty, "Crime" and Criminology', *Current Issues in Criminal Justice*, vol. 31, no. 1, pp. 122–42.

42 Chelsea Watego (as Bond), David Singh and Helena Kajlich, 'Not a One-way Street: Understanding the Over representation of Aboriginal and Torres Strait Islander Peoples on Charges of Assault Against Public Officers', expert report to the Queensland Sentencing Advisory Council, July 2020: https://www.sentencingcouncil.qld.gov.au/__data/assets/pdf_file/0009/657648/not-a-one-way-street-report.pdf; QSAC, 'Penalties for Assaults on Public Officers: Final Report: Recommendations', August 2020, recommendation 4-2.

43 Watego, 'Who Are the Real Criminals? Making the Case for Abolishing Criminology', John Barry Memorial Lecture, University of Melbourne, 29 November 2021, lecture available on YouTube.

44 Watego, 'Who Are the Real Criminals?' See further: Karl Quinn, 'Academic Sorry Over Calling African Crime Study "Racist"', *The Age*, 14 April 2021.

45 Amanda Porter, 'Decolonizing Policing: Indigenous Patrols, Counter-policing and Safety', *Theoretical Criminology*, vol. 20, no. 4, 2016, pp. 548–65 (from her unpublished PhD thesis, completed at the University of Sydney in 2014).

46 Walter, 'Indigenous Peoples, Research and Ethics', chapter 5 in Adorjan and Ricciardelli (eds), *Engaging with Ethics in International Criminological Research*, Routledge, 2016.

47 Noel Dyck, *Indigenous Peoples and the Nation State: 'Fourth World' Politics in Canada, Australia and Norway*, Institute of Social and Economic Research, Memorial University of Newfoundland, 1985.

48 Walter, 'Indigenous Peoples, Research and Ethics'.

49 The poet Oodgeroo Noonuccal predicted in the mid-1960s the stratification of Indigenous people, families and communities into various socioeconomic classes: Noonuccal (then as Kath Walker), 'Discussion of Papers by Bishop O'Loughlin and Rev. Albrecht' in I.G. Sharp and Colin Tatz (eds), *Aborigines in the Economy: Employment, Wages and Training*, papers from a 1964 seminar on 'The Problems of Aboriginal Employment, Wages and Training', published by Jacaranda Press in association with the Centre for Research into Aboriginal Affairs, Monash University, 1966. See also: Maggie Walter, 'The Vexed Link Between Social Capital and Social Mobility for Aboriginal and Torres Strait Islander People', Australian Journal of Social Issues, vol. 50, no. 1, 2015, p. 69; Stan Grant, *On Identity*, Melbourne University Press, 2019.

50 Tatz, 'Aboriginal Violence: A Return to Pessimism', *Australian Journal of Social Issues*, vol. 25, no. 4, November 1990, pp. 245–60.

51 Sackett, 'Aboriginal Violence: Responding to the Tatz View', *Australian Journal of Social Issues*, vol. 26, no. 1, February 1991, pp. 68–70.

52 See the Australian epidemiologist Michael Marmot's work on the social determinants of health and inequality: for example, Marmot, *Status Syndrome*, Bloomsbury, 2004; Marmot, 'Social Determinants of Health Inequalities', *Lancet*, vol. 365, 2005, pp. 1099–104. See also: Edward Deci and Richard Ryan, 'Self-determination Theory' in Van Lange, Kruglanski and Higgins (eds), *Handbook of Theories of Social Psychology: Volume 1*, Sage, 2012.

53 Michael Chandler and Christopher Lalonde, 'Cultural Continuity as a Hedge Against Suicide in Canada's First Nations', *Transcultural Psychiatry*, vol. 35, no. 2, June 1998, pp. 191–219.

54 Larissa Behrendt, Amanda Porter and Alison Vivian, 'Factors Affecting Crime Rates in Six Rural Indigenous Communities', chapter 4 in Joseph F. Donnermeyer (ed.), *The Routledge International Handbook of Rural Criminology*, Routledge, Abingdon and New York, 2016, pp. 33–43.

55 See, for example: Bessel van der Kolk, *The Body Keeps the Score: Brain, Mind and Body in the Healing of Trauma*, Viking, 2014.

56 This approach is also taken by the criminologist Russell Hogg. See: 'Penality and Modes of Regulating Indigenous Peoples in Australia', *Punishment and Society*, vol. 3, no. 3, 2001, pp. 355–79.

CHAPTER 10

1   The case of 'Lucy' is an amalgamation of three of my actual clients. I've changed names and particulars to protect their identities and confidences.

2   Our Watch, *Changing the Picture: A National Resource to Support the Prevention of Violence against Aboriginal and Torres Strait Islander Women and their Children*, 2018.

3   Anna Clark, 'Domestic Violence, Past and Present', *Journal of Women's History*, vol. 23, no. 3, Fall 2011, p. 193.

4   Anne Summers, *Damned Whores and God's Police: The Colonisation of Women in Australia*, Penguin, 1975, pp. 165–95.

5   Queensland Domestic Violence Task Force, *Beyond These Walls*, 1988, p. 13; quoted in Heather Nancarrow, 'Legal Responses to Intimate Partner Violence: Gendered Aspirations and Racialised Realities', unpublished PhD thesis, School of Criminology and Criminal Justice, Griffith University, 2016, p. 98.

6   *Domestic and Family Violence Protection Act 2012* (Qld), s 177.

7   *Domestic Violence Act 1992* (NT), s 10(1); *Domestic and Family Violence Act 2007* (NT), s 121.

8   See, for instance: (Victorian) Royal Commission into Family Violence, *Report and Recommendations: Volume I*, March 2016, chapter 3: 'Key Family Violence Data'.

9   Tracy Cussen and Willow Bryant, 'Domestic/Family Homicide in Australia', Research in Practice No. 38, Australian Institute of Criminology, May 2015: https://www.aic.gov.au/publications/rip/rip38.

10 In *See What You Made Me Do*, Hill cites two studies in particular: C.L. Yodanis, 'Gender Inequality, Violence Against Women and Fear: A Cross-National Test of the Feminist Theory of Violence Against Women', *Journal of Interpersonal Violence*, vol. 19, no. 6, 2004, pp. 655–75; Lori Heise and Andreas Kotsadam, 'Cross-national and Multilevel Correlates of Partner Violence: An Analysis of Data from Population-based Surveys', *Lancet Global Health*, vol. 3, no. 6, June 2015, pp. 332–40.

11 Claire Grealy et al., 'Literature Review on Domestic Violence Perpetrators', Urbis, 2013, p. 8: https://www.dss.gov.au/sites/default/files/documents/09_2013/literature_review_on_domestic_violence_perpetrators.pdf.

12 See: Anna Terwiel, 'What is Carceral Feminism?', *Political Theory*, vol. 48, no. 4, 2020.

13 See, for instance: Davis, *Are Prisons Obsolete?*, Seven Stories Press, 2003.

14 Moreton-Robinson, *Talkin' Up to the White Woman*; Davis, 'Deploying and Disputing Aboriginal Feminism in Australia'; Watego et al, 'Carceral Feminism and Coercive Control: When Indigenous Women Aren't Seen as Ideal Victims, Witnesses or Women', *The Conversation*, 25 May 2021; Watego, *Another Day in the Colony*.

15 Nadine Miles, PLO of the Aboriginal Legal Service (NSW/ACT), 'Coercive Control In Domestic Relationships', submission 148 to the Joint Select Committee on Coercive Control, Parliament of NSW, 1 March 2021, pp. 2–3, citing Sandra Walklate and Kate Fitz-Gibbon, 'The Criminalisation of Coercive Control: The Power of Law?', *International Journal for Crime, Justice and Social Democracy*, vol. 8, no. 4, January 2019, pp. 94–108. See also: Heather Douglas, submission 21 to the Joint Select Committee on Coercive Control, 26 January 2021.

16 Joint Select Committee on Coercive Control, 'Coercive Control in Domestic Relationships: Final Report', Report 1/57, Parliament of NSW, June 2021. The Committee's membership included three Liberal Party members, two Labor Party members, one Green, one National and one member of One Nation. On 18 December 2021, the government announced it would be introducing new laws in line with the Committee's recommendations.

17 *Criminal Law Consolidation (Coercive Control) Amendment Bill 2020* (SA), sponsored by Katrine Hildyard MP, first read in the House of Assembly on 2 December 2020.

18 Watego et al., 'Carceral Feminism and Coercive Control'.

19 Ben Smee, 'Coercive Control Laws Could Harm Vulnerable Women, Advocates in Queensland Warn', *Guardian Australia*, 7 May 2021.

20 Calla Wahlquist, 'Man Convicted of Murdering 10-month-old Stepson Found Dead in Prison Cell', *Guardian Australia*, 9 September 2015.

21 Michael Gliddon, Inquest into the Deaths of Mervyn Bell, Bevan Cameron, Brian Honeywood, JS (Subject to Suppression Order) and Aubrey Wallam, Coroners Court of Western Australia, 22 May 2019.

22   Corruption and Crime Commission, *Report on the Response of WA Police to a Particular Incident of Domestic Violence on 19–20 March 2013*, 21 April 2016.

23   A description of the assault she'd endured can be found in *Mullaley v State Coroner of Western Australia* [2020] WASC 264 at [12].

24   For more details on this case, see: *WA v Bell [No. 3]* [2014] WASC 341; Jess Hill, *See What You Made Me Do: Power, Control and Domestic Abuse*, pp. 306–15; Hannah McGlade and Stella Tarrant, '"Say Her Name": Naming Aboriginal Women in the Justice System', chapter 5 in Suvendrini Perera and Joseph Pugliese (eds), *Mapping Deathscapes: Digital Geographies of Racial and Border Violence*, Routledge, Abingdon and New York, 2022, p. 106 at 115–19.

25   Lorena Allam, 'WA Government Apologises for Police Treatment of Murdered Baby's Family', *Guardian Australia*, 22 June 2022.

26   Jess Hill, 'Criminalising Coercive Control Will Replace the Broken Lens We Have on Domestic Abuse', speech delivered at the launch of the Criminalise Coercive Control Campaign, published at *Women's Agenda*, 14 October 2020: https://womensagenda.com.au/latest/criminalising-coercive-control-will-replace-the-broken-lens-we-have-on-domestic-abuse/.

27   Heather Douglas and Robin Fitzgerald, 'The Domestic Violence Protection Order System as Entry to the Criminal Justice System for Aboriginal and Torres Strait Islander People', *International Journal for Crime, Justice and Social Democracy*, vol. 7, no. 3, 2018, p. 41 at 45–46.

28   See: Lucy Snowball and Don Weatherburn, 'Theories of Indigenous Violence: A Preliminary Empirical Assessment', *Australian & New Zealand Journal of Criminology*, vol. 41, no. 2, 2008, pp. 216–35; Judicial Council on Cultural Diversity, *The Path to Justice: Aboriginal and Torres Strait Islander Women's Experience of the Courts*, 2016, p. 6; Australian Institute of Health and Welfare, *The Health and Welfare of Australia's Aboriginal and Torres Strait Islander People*, 2015, pp. 44–46.

29   Douglas and Fitzgerald, 'The Domestic Violence Protection Order System as Entry to the Criminal Justice System for Aboriginal and Torres Strait Islander People', p. 42.

30   Nancarrow, *Legal Responses to Intimate Partner Violence*, pp. 112–13.

31   Douglas And Fitzgerald, 'The Domestic Violence Protection Order System as Entry to the Criminal justice system for Aboriginal and Torres Strait Islander People', p. 52.

32   *Midjumbani v Moore* [2009] NTSC 27. The reasoning in this judgement has since been endorsed in *R v Anzac* [2020] NTSC 58 and *Arnott v Blitner* [2020] NTSC 63.

33   Watego et al., 'Carceral Feminism and Coercive Control'.

34   See for instance: Kate Auty and Sandy Toussant (eds), *A Jury of Whose Peers? The Cultural Politics of Juries in Australia*, UWA Press, 2004.

35   Full disclosure: I worked with Jill and Ellie at VALS, and later volunteered briefly at LACW before it received public funding.

36   Harry Blagg et al., 'Understanding the Role of Law and Culture in Aboriginal and Torres Strait Islander Communities in Responding to and Preventing Family Violence', ANROWS Research Report 19, June 2020.

37   Nancarrow, *Legal Responses to Intimate Partner Violence*, pp. 112–13.

38   Police, Fire and Emergency Services, 'Operation Haven Launched in Alice Springs', media release, 15 February 2018: https://pfes.nt.gov.au/newsroom/2018/operation-haven-launched-alice-springs.

39   My argument, with which Judge Woodcock ultimately agreed, was that parliament had not expressly authorised police to use their powers in this way, and that the common law rights of privacy in one's own home must prevail. Because police had acted outside their powers and had therefore obtained their evidence of Aileen's breach improperly or in contravention of the law, Woodcock used his discretion under section 138 of the *Evidence (National Uniform Legislation) Act 2011* (NT) to exclude the officers' evidence. In the absence of any other evidence of Aileen's breach, Woodcock found her not guilty.

40   *O'Neill v Roy* [2019] NTSC 23 per Mildren AJ. I'd left NAAJA by then, and my former colleagues Julian Murphy and Roisin McCarthy represented Aileen in the Supreme Court.

41   All three judges of the Court of Appeal – Stephen Southwood, Judith Kelly and Trevor Riley – upheld the Crown's further appeal, finding that police relied on an 'implied license' to knock on Aileen's door for a 'dual purpose', one of which was to 'check on the wellbeing of the protected person under the Order', which was entirely lawful: *O'Neill v Roy* [2019] NTCA 8.

42   *Roy v O'Neill* [2020] HCA 45 per Kiefel CJ, Bell, Gageler, Keane and Edelman JJ. The two
      judges in the minority – Bell and Gageler – held that the Court of Appeal had conceived of
      the officers' implied licence too broadly, and that their 'coercive purpose' took them beyond
      the scope of any implied license and 'made them trespassers'. But their view did not prevail.
      For an extended discussion, see: Julian Murphy, 'Police Doorknocking in Comparative and
      Constitutional Perspective: *O'Neill v Roy*', *Sydney Law Review*, vol. 42, no. 3, 2020, p. 343.
      Aileen herself suffered no actual consequence: the Director of Public Prosecutions had
      agreed that whatever the appeals' outcome, he would not request a sentencing order.

43   Joshua Robertson, 'Time Served: How Debbie Kilroy Went from Jail to Advising the
      Government on Sentencing', *Guardian Australia*, 4 January 2017.

44   Sisters Inside, submission to the Australian Human Rights Commission's *Wiyi Yani U
      Thangani (Women's Voices) Project*, November 2018. The Project's report is available here:
      https://humanrights.gov.au/our-work/aboriginal-and-torres-strait-islander-social-justice/
      publications/wiyi-yani-u-thangani.

CHAPTER 11

1   Voller's experiences in this chapter were first given by him publicly to the Royal
      Commission into the Protection and Detention of Children in the Northern Territory.

2   Don Dale had recently died when Darwin's new Youth Justice Centre was completed in
      1990, so the chief minister gave him the dubious honour of giving it his name: Marshall
      Perron, *Hansard*, House of Assembly, 20 February 1990, p. 8569–70: https://www.
      territorystories.nt.gov.au/jspui/bitstream/10070/220280/1/D_1990_02_20.pdf

3   Statement of Dylan Voller to the Royal Commission into the Detention and Protection of
      Children in the Northern Territory, 25 November 2016, tendered as Exhibit 051.001, at
      paras [220–28].

4   *Police v Morgan*, 9 August 2012, transcript tendered as Exhibit 330.002 to the Royal
      Commission into the Protection and Detention of Children in the Northern Territory. At
      the time, section 215(4) of the *Youth Justice Act 2005* (NT) required that any charge against
      any youth justice officer had to be laid within six months of the incident.

5   *Police v Tasker* at [39].

6   The footage was aired on *Four Corners* as part of 'Australia's Shame' (25 July 2016), https://
      www.abc.net.au/4corners/australias-shame-promo/7649462.

7   *Edwards v Tasker* [2014] NTSC 56 per Barr J at [13].

8   *NT News*, 21 May 2008.

9   *Police v Tasker* at [70–77].

10   *Edwards v Tasker* [2014] NTSC 56.

11   Children's Commissioner Confidential Report relating to Youth Detention Practices,
      12 February 2015, tendered confidentially to the Royal Commission as Exhibit 053.027,
      and quoted from in its *Report*, volume 2A, p. 203.

12   Statement of Dylan Voller to the Royal Commission into the Detention and Protection
      of Children in the Northern Territory, 25 November 2016, tendered as Exhibit 051.001,
      at paras [259–76]. Footage of the assault was broadcast on the *Four Corners* episode,
      'Australia's Shame', on 25 July 2016.

13   Statement of Howard Bath to the Royal Commission, 5 October 2016, tendered as Exhibit
      011.001, at paras [77–80].

14   Statement of Dylan Voller to the Royal Commission into the Detention and Protection
      of Children in the Northern Territory, 25 November 2016, tendered as Exhibit 051.001,
      at para [12]. Families SA was then embroiled in a major inquiry by Ted Mullighan into
      Children in State Care: Allegations of Sexual Abuse and Death from Criminal Conduct,
      which reported on 31 March 2008. 'I was not prepared for the horror of the sexual cruelty
      and exploitation of little children and vulnerable young people in State care by people
      in positions of trust and responsibility,' Mullighan famously wrote, 'or the use of them at
      paedophile parties for sexual gratification, facilitated by the supply of drugs and alcohol.'
      Families SA has since de-branded back to the Department for Child Protection, but its
      record of massive system failure has never improved. A former Families SA employee who
      contributed to – and eventually administered – an online paedophile website sparked the
      Child Protection Systems Royal Commission, which reported in August 2016. Just months

earlier, the department had failed to act on numerous reports and notifications before an Aboriginal woman, Adeline Wilson-Rigney, and two of her children were killed by her partner: the inquest continues at the time of writing. And after a number of teenagers in state 'care' became pregnant – two to older men who were sentenced to prison terms in 2021 – an independent review by Paul Rice found multiple continuing departmental failures: Rice, *Department for Child Protection Review 2020-21: Report of Independent Inquiry*, 9 February 2021, tabled in redacted form 16 February 2021.

15   Statement of Dylan Voller to the Royal Commission into the Detention and Protection of Children in the Northern Territory, 25 November 2016, tendered as Exhibit 051.001, at paras [44–45].

16   Much of this paragraph was first published in an earlier form in *The Monthly*, March 2017.

17   Statement of Dylan Voller to the Royal Commission into the Detention and Protection of Children in the Northern Territory, 25 November 2016, tendered as Exhibit 051.001, at paras [291–96].

18   Statement of Jared Sharpe to the Royal Commission into the Detention and Protection of Children in the Northern Territory, 24 April 2017, tendered as Exhibit 355.000, at para [178].

19   Peter Scharff Smith, 'The Effects of Solitary Confinement on Prison Inmates: A Brief History and Review of the Literature', *Crime and Justice*, vol. 34, 2006, p. 441; Sharon Shalev, *A Sourcebook on Solitary Confinement*, Mannheim Centre for Criminology, 2008, pp. 15–17.

20   Statement of Dylan Voller to the Royal Commission into the Detention and Protection of Children in the Northern Territory, 25 November 2016, tendered as Exhibit 051.001, at paras [297–99].

21   Michael Vita, *Review of the Northern Territory Youth Detention System: Report*, January 2015; Children's Commissioner, *Own Initiative Investigation Report [into] Services Provided by the Department of Correctional Services at the Don Dale Youth Detention Centre*, August 2015.

22   Statement of Dylan Voller to the Royal Commission into the Detention and Protection of Children in the Northern Territory, 25 November 2016, tendered as Exhibit 051.001, at paras [312–25].

23   It wasn't until 26 April that year that Ken Middlebrook was asked to approve the restraint chair for use at Don Dale, which he did immediately: Email correspondence between Amanda Hobbs-Carcuro and Middlebrook, 29 April 2015, tendered as Exhibit 283.104 to the Royal Commission; NT Department of Correctional Services, NTDCS Directive: Use of Restraints, 6 May 2015, tendered as Exhibit 741.037 to the Royal Commission. But he wasn't 100 per cent sure he had the legal power to approve it, so, to be 'absolutely clear', he and the Corrections department got to work on legislative amendments: Middlebrook, testimony to the Royal Commission, 26 April 2017, transcript pp. 3027–28; *Youth Justice Amendment Bill 2016* (NT), introduced 26 April 2016.

24   Quoted in Bob Gosford, 'Brian Ross Martin is Wrong: Supreme Court Has Dealt with Dylan Voller's Abuse Before', *Crikey*, 29 July 2016.

25   *LO & ors v Northern Territory of Australia* [2017] NTSC 22 per Kelly J at [95].

26   The transcript of the conversation between Jake Roper (referred to as 'E') and Youth Justice Officers is reproduced in the Children's Commissioner's *Own Initiative Investigation Report [into] Services Provided by the Department of Correctional Services at the Don Dale Youth Detention Centre*, August 2015, p. 18.

27   *LO & ors v Northern Territory of Australia* [2017] NTSC 22 per Kelly J.

28   *JB & ors v Northern Territory of Australia* [2019] NTCA 1 per Southwood J and Riley and Graham AJJ.

29   *Binsaris & ors v Northern Territory* [2020] HCA 22.

30   Blagg, *Crime, Aboriginality and the Decolonisation of Justice*, Hawkins Press, Annandale, NSW, 2008, p. 58.

31   Dr Jureidini's oral evidence to the Royal Commission into the Protection and Detention of Children in the Northern Territory, 29 June 2017, transcript p. 5337.

32   Statement of Dylan Voller to the Royal Commission into the Detention and Protection of Children in the Northern Territory, 25 November 2016, tendered as Exhibit 051.001, at para [158].

33   Royal Commission transcript, 29 June 2017, p. 5342.

34 This section was published in an earlier form in *The Monthly*, March 2017, Melbourne.

35 *Wilson v Francis*, paras [36–40]; Office of the Inspector of Custodial Services, *Directed Review into an Incident at Banksia Hill Detention Centre on 20 January 2013*, report date July 2013.

36 *Wilson v Francis* [2013] WASC 157 at paras [28–33] and [77–78].

37 Office of the Inspector of Custodial Services, *Directed Review into an Incident at Banksia Hill Detention Centre on 20 January 2013*, report date July 2013 (my emphasis).

38 *Wilson v Francis*.

39 *Certain Children by their Litigation Guardian Sister Marie Brigid Arthur v Minister for Families and Children* [2016] VSC 796 per Garde J; *Minister for Families and Children v Certain Children by their Litigation Guardian Sister Marie Brigid Arthur* [2016] VSCA 343 per Warren CJ, Maxwell P and Weinberg JA; *Certain Children v Minister for Families and Children & ors* [2017] VSC 251 per John Dixon J.

40 Figure taken from Victorian Youth Parole Board annual reports.

41 Dale Wakefield, 'Northern Territory Government Keeps Election Promise to Ban Restraint Chair', media release, 25 October 2016.

42 *Youth Justice Legislation Amendment Act* 2016 (NT), Part 2. The bill was introduced on 25 October 2016 and passed on 1 December 2016.

43 Royal Commission report, Part 2A, chapter 13, p. 215.

44 *Wilson v Francis* [2013] WASC 157; *Certain Children by their Litigation Guardian Sister Marie Brigid Arthur v Minister for Families and Children* [2016] VSC 796; *Minister for Families and Children v Certain Children by their Litigation Guardian Sister Marie Brigid Arthur* [2016] VSCA 343; *Certain Children v Minister for Families and Children & ors* [2017] VSC 251.

45 *Youth Justice Legislation Amendment Act* 2018 (NT). The bill was introduced on 21 March 2018 and passed on 10 May 2018.

46 An earlier version of much of the following paragraphs was previously published as 'Tear Gas Returns to Don Dale' in *The Monthly*, July 2019.

47 *NT News*, 8 November 2018.

48 *Youth Justice Amendment Act* (No. 7 of 2019) (NT).

49 Jacqui Breen and Jano Gibson, 'Physical Restraints "Used in Youth Detention Centres" After Changes Rushed by NT Government', ABC News, 27 March 2019: https://www.abc.net.au/news/2019-03-27/physical-restraints-back-in-nt-youth-detention,-lawyers-say/10942110.

50 Samantha Johnscher and Jesse Thompson, 'What It's Like on the Frontline of the Northern Territory's Soaring Youth Detention Numbers', ABC News, 7 October 2021: https://www.abc.net.au/news/2021-10-07/nt-youth-detention-centres-stretched-bail-laws/100518998.

51 *R v ALH* (2003) 6 VR 276; *RP v The Queen* [2016] HCA 53; *Criminal Code* (NT) s 38(2).

52 Zizi Averill, 'School Slap to Shape NT Law', *NT News*, 10 April 2022.

CHAPTER 12

1 Was it 22 August 1770, when James Cook stuck a flagpole in the sand on Bedanug – he called it 'Possession Island' – and claimed the entire eastern coastline of Australia for Britain? Was it 25 April 1787, when Phillip was given his instructions to settle 'Our Territory of New South Wales'? Was it 26 January 1788, when Phillip formally proclaimed British sovereignty at Sydney Cove? Or 7 February 1788, when judge advocate David Collins formally read King George III's commission 'with all due solemnity'? (See: C.H. Currey, 'An Argument for the Observance of Australia Day on the Seventh Day of February and an Account of the Ceremony at Sydney Cove, February 7, 1788', *Royal Australian Historical Society: Journal & Proceedings*, vol. 43, no. 4, 1957, pp. 153–74. The phrase 'with all due solemnity' is from the instructions provided to Phillip along with his commission: it's collected in Fred Watson's *Historical Records of Australia*, series I, vol. I, 1914, p. 9.

2 Constitutionally, judges aren't subject to the kind of discipline the rest of us are accustomed to in workplaces. For a judge in the Northern Territory to be removed from office, the chief judge first needed to investigate and conclude that there'd been serious misconduct. The complaint was then referred to the Legislative Assembly, which also needed to recommend the judge's removal on the grounds of 'incapacity or misbehaviour'. Only then, if the

Administrator agreed, could the judge's appointment be terminated: *Local Court Act* (NT), s 57. (This procedure will change now that the Territory belatedly introduced a Judicial Complaints Commission process in DATE.)

3   *Police v [name redacted]*, NT Children's Court, 6 June 2017, transcript.

4   Tom Maddocks, 'NT Lawyers Push for Judge to Be Removed from Youth Court over 'Grossly Insensitive' Comments', ABC News, 21 June 2017.

5   Melissa Coade, 'Controversy over Judicial Bullying Claims "Now Finalised", NT Lawyer Says', *Lawyers Weekly*, 28 January 2018.

6   The transcript unfortunately records that Borchers said 'cage', when in fact he said 'cave'.

7   Knaus, 'Lawyers to Lodge Complaint about NT Judge after "Indigenous Child Abandoning" Comments', *Guardian Australia*, 25 July 2019.

8   NT Remuneration Tribunal, 'Report and Determination No. 1 of 2020 on the Entitlements of Local Court Judges', 15 June 2020, schedule, part 2, 'Salary and Allowances': https://dcm. nt.gov.au/__data/assets/pdf_file/0006/900834/remuneration-tribunal-report-determination-no1-2020-entitlements-local-court-judges.pdf; Department of Human Services, 'How Much You Can Get', archived from the original on 22 December 2019: https://web.archive.org/web/20191222100534/https://www.humanservices.gov.au/individuals/services/centrelink/newstart-allowance/how-much-you-can-get. The Department of Human Services is now known as Services Australia, and NewStart has been rebranded 'JobSeeker'.

9   Editorial, *Legal Service Bulletin*, vol. 4, no. 5, Oct 1979, p. 171.

10   After being rejected by multiple publishers, McLennan entered her manuscript into the Queensland Literary Awards, where three (white) judges gave it an award whose prize included publication by the University of Queensland Press. The same Awards later voted *Saltwater* the 'Best Non-Fiction Book' of 2017. Chelsea Watego's critical review of *Saltwater* was refused publication by the *Australian Feminist Law Journal*, in part on the grounds that she implied McLennan was racist: Watego, 'Talkin' Down to the Black Woman', *Australian Feminist Law Journal*, vol. 49, no. 2, 2019, pp. 185–89. Watego's review appears in her book, *Another Day in the Colony*, UQP, St Lucia, 2021. See also: Russell Marks, 'Crocodile Tears', *Overland*, no. 237, Summer 2019.

11   *Alcohol Mandatory Treatment Act 2013* (NT), ss 7 and 72.

12   *Munkara v Bencsevich & ors* [2015] NTSC 78 at [17–18].

13   Southwood dismissed the appeal in February 2015: *Munkara v Bencsevich & ors* [2015] NTSC 78.

14   *Munkara v Bencsevich & ors* [2018] NTCA 4 at [102] per Blokland J.

15   *Liquor Act 1978* (NT), Part VIIIBA and s 101ZK as amended by the *Liquor Amendment Act 2019*. Both additions were retained in the new *Liquor Act 2019*, as ss 262 (undercover operations) and 250 (expanded Point-of-Sale Intervention powers).

16   Files, second reading speech, Legislative Assembly, 28 November 2018.

17   Despite their trenchant opposition to antisocial behaviour, and despite guzzling more booze per capita than any other state or territory, settler Territorians apparently weren't getting enough alcohol. In late 2016, Woolworths confirmed long-rumoured plans to open a 'superstore' outlet of its cut-price grog warehouse, Dan Murphy's, in Darwin, within walking distance of three dry Aboriginal communities. The Gunner government initially blocked those plans by limiting the maximum floor size, but following a spirited campaign by settler business interests – especially the *NT News* – Gunner backflipped. After being re-elected in 2020, his government rushed through laws which allowed Woolworths to sidestep the regulators by removing their requirement to consider the superstore's negative community impacts: see the *Liquor Further Amendment Act 2020* (NT). Aboriginal organisations and social services maintained their opposition, and Gunner's government *cut* funding to a residential alcohol rehab program designed to reduce imprisonment by providing beds for parolees: Oliver Gordon and Jacqueline Breen, 'Health Minister Among Those Concerned as NT Government Cuts Funding to Parole Rehab Program', ABC News, 3 December 2020. In April 2021, Woolworths announced it had voluntarily decided to abandon its plans to build the store at its preferred site, but didn't rule out building one at a different site in the future: Breen, 'Woolworths Cancels Dan Murphy's Store Plans for Darwin Near Three Dry Indigenous Communities', ABC News, 29 April 2021.

18   J.H. Wootten, 'Report of the Inquiry into the Death of Harrison Day', Royal Commission into Aboriginal Deaths in Custody, 9 August 1990.

19   George Newhouse, Daniel Ghezelbash and Alison Whittaker, 'The Experience of Aboriginal and Torres Strait Islander Participants in Australia's Coronial Inquest System: Reflections from the Front Line', *International Journal for Crime, Justice and Social Democracy*, vol. 9, no. 4, 2020.]

20   Michael Jenkin, Inquest into the deaths of Mervyn Bell, Bevan Cameron, Brian Honeywood, JS (Subject to Suppression Order) and Aubrey Wallam, Coroner's Court of Western Australia, 22 May 2019.

21   Coroners Court of Victoria, *Finding of Inquest into the Death of Tanya Louise Day*, COR 2017 6424, 9 April 2020.

22   Luke McNamara and Julia Quilter, 'Public Intoxication in NSW: The Contours of Criminalisation', *Sydney Law Review*, vol. 37, no. 1, 2015, p. 1 at 4.

23   The *Summary Offences Amendment (Decriminalisation of Public Drunkenness) Bill 2020* (Vic) will come into effect in November 2022.

24   *Liquor Control Act 1988* (WA) s 119 establishes a $2000 fine for drinking alcohol in public. *Summary Offences Act 2005* (Qld) s 10 establishes a fine of two penalty units (just over $300) for being intoxicated in a public place. *Liquor Act 2010* (ACT) s 199 establishes a fine of 5 penalty units (about $1000) for drinking alcohol in particular public places like bus stops. *Summary Offences Act 1988* (NSW) s 11 establishes a fine of $20 for children (under eighteen years) found in possession of alcohol in public. Most Sydney councils have passed by-laws prohibiting drinking in public. Adults possessing alcohol in those councils aren't subject to fines, but police do have the power to dispose of their alcohol.

25   'Edith' is an amalgamation of three clients I've represented.

26   Lauren Monds and Celine van Golde, 'Doctors and Nurses Can't Always Tell If Someone's Drunk or on Drugs, and Misdiagnosis Can Be Dangerous', *The Conversation*, 5 July 2017: https://theconversation.com/doctors-and-nurses-cant-always-tell-if-someones-drunk-or-on-drugs-and-misdiagnosis-can-be-dangerous-69879.

27   Larry Gentilello et al., 'Detection of Acute Alcohol Intoxication and Chronic Alcohol Dependence by Trauma Centre Staff', *Journal of Trauma and Acute Care Surgery*, vol. 47, no. 6, December 1999, p. 1131.

28   *Police Administration Act 1978* (NT), s 128A.

29   *Daniels v Nichol*, unreported, Supreme Court of the Northern Territory, Forster J, 13 August 1976. John Daniels was imprisoned by a magistrate for three months for driving while his license had been disqualified by a court. He'd also had a blood alcohol reading of .255. For that, Daniels 'only' went to prison for one month. He appealed, hoping a Supreme Court judge would see the absurdity of punishing an administrative offence (disqualified driving) more harshly than an objectively dangerous offence (drink-driving), and would lower his total sentence. But Senior Judge William Forster – later the Territory's first Chief Justice – not only failed to see the absurdity. He added a dash of his own.

30   For SA, see: *Police (SA) v Cadd* (1997) 94 A Crim R 466. This was an appeal brought by prosecutors against decisions by five magistrates to not impose immediate sentences of imprisonment on five disqualified drivers. The majority of the five judges who sat on this appeal concluded that imprisonment was the appropriate penalty for disqualified drivers. South Australian courts have continued to apply this rule. For WA, see: *Krakouer v Durka*, unreported, Supreme Court of Western Australia, 14 October 1998. For Tasmania, see: *Brown v Stone* [1995] TASSC 23, in which the Tasmanian Supreme Court sent an eighteen-year-old disqualified driver to prison for three months after prosecutors appealed against the magistrate's original sentence, which had required the offender to complete 126 hours of community service. The 'prison as starting-point' principle was even in Victorian *legislation* until 2010, as one of only three offences which carried a legislated mandatory prison sentence (the others being trafficking a commercial quantity of drugs, or trafficking to a child): *Road Safety Act* (Vic), s 30(2); *Drugs, Poisons and Controlled Substances Act 1981* (Vic), s 71(2). The mandatory sentence of one month for repeat disqualified driving in s 30(2) of the *Traffic Act* was repealed by the *Sentencing Amendment Act 2010* (Vic) s 28. In March 2017 the Victorian parliament legislated for a range of other serious crimes to carry mandatory prison sentences.

31   Legislative Assembly of the Northern Territory, 5 March 2011 per Gerry McCarthy MLA at 7975: https://www.territorystories.nt.gov.au/jspui/bitstream/10070/277652/1/Debates%20 Day%203%20-%20Thursday%205%20May%202011.PDF.

32   Stotz, "'Kurdungurlu Got to Drive Toyota": Differential Colonising Process among the Warlpiri', unpublished PhD thesis, Deakin University Faculty of Arts, May 1993.
33   *Smith v Torney* (1984) 29 NTR 31 at 36 per Muirhead J.
34   See, for instance, the Home Detention Orders introduced by NT corrections minister Don Dale in 1987. He wasn't dismissing the value of prison: 'We can, however, try to avoid imprisoning offenders who pose no apparent threat to the community,' he said (Legislative Assembly of the Northern Territory, 24 September 1987 per Don Dale MLA at 1578–79). A magistrate experimented in 1988, imposing 160 hours' community service on Raymond Sawtell after the nineteen-year-old was caught driving his Honda motorbike at 99 kilometres per hour in a 60 zone while he was disqualified. Considering the Supreme Court's attitude for the previous decade, Sawtell was lucky: he'd been convicted once before of driving while disqualified, and was on a suspended prison sentence when his Honda was clocked. We can't know whether the fact Sawtell was *not* Indigenous was a factor in the magistrate's 'leniency' – his parents were business owners in Darwin, and Sawtell was a modelling student at the time. Prosecutors appealed, decrying the latest punishment as 'manifestly inadequate'. Judge Phillip Rice agreed, and said he should have served six weeks in prison. But in the meantime, Sawtell had completed his 160 hours' community service, so Rice reluctantly allowed him to avoid prison (*Pryce v Sawtell* (1988) 32 A Crim R 111).
35   *Oldfield v Chute* (1992) 107 FLR 413 per Mildren J (though he reduced Joey's prison sentence from six months down to four).
36   Anthony and Blagg, 'STOP in the Name of Who's [*sic.*] Law?', p. 43 at 55.
37   Thalia Anthony and Kieran Tranter, 'Travelling Our Way or No Way! The Collision of Automobiles in Australian Northern Territory Judicial Narratives', *Griffith Law Review*, vol. 27, no. 3, 2019, p. 281.
38   Details come from an actual case in the Katherine Local Court in 2019.
39   *Dungay v R; R v Dungay* [2010] NSWCCA 82.
40   NSW Department of Justice and Corrective Services, Custodial Operations Policy and Procedures, Ch 16.13: 'Immediate Action Teams', online: https://cpsunsw.org.au/wp-content/uploads/2017/09/Policy-16.13-Immediate-Action-Teams.pdf.
41   Video footage accompanying Helen Davidson's article, 'David Dungay Inquest: Shocking Video Shows Prison Officers Restraining Inmate Before Death', *Guardian Australia*, 16 July 2018, online: https://www.theguardian.com/australia-news/2018/jul/16/david-dungay-inquest-told-inadequate-resuscitation-may-have-contributed-to-death.
42   Magistrate Derek Lee, *Inquest into the Death of David Dungay*, Coroner's Court of New South Wales (2015/381722), findings, 22 November 2019, 24.20.
43   Each name is inspired by death and heavy metal music culture: Judas Priest is an English band; 'Evil Warriors' is a 1985 song by the American band Possessed.
44   *Inquest into the Death of Robert Jongmin* [2007] NTMC 80 at paras 45–55, per Cavanagh SM.
45   NT Police Internal Memorandum, Gregory Hansen to OIC, Operational Training Unit, 4 October 2001; in *Coronial Inquest into the Death of Robert Jongmin* D200/2002, Folder 8, Exhibit 31.
46   Whittington, interviewed 23 October 2002, D200/2002, Folder 6, Exhibit 27.19, transcript, pp. 30–32.
47   *Inquest into the Death of Robert Jongmin* [2007] NTMC 80 at paras 45–55, per Cavanagh SM.
48   Dr Ted Owen, stat dec, 30 October 2002, D200/2002, Folder 5, Exhibit 26.27.
49   *Inquest into the Death of Robert Jongmin* [2007] NTMC 80 at para 66.
50   Julie Stitfold, *Report on the Examination of Items in the Case of an Alleged Police Shooting*, 1 May 2003, p. 2.
51   Allan Cala, 'Autopsy Report for the Coroner', C292/02, 25 October 2002.
52   Northern Territory Coroner's Court, *An Inquest into the Death of Robert Jongmin on 23 October 2002 at Wadeye*, 8 October 2007, transcript, pp. 344–45 (examination-in-chief of Allan David Cala by Phillip Strickland SC).
53   *Inquest into the Death of Robert Jongmin* [2007] NTMC 80 at para 63, per Cavanagh SM.
54   That was, in part, because of an old 1937 High Court decision which made it clear that what mattered at the time Whittington fired his four bullets was his *subjective* belief about the need to do so – not the objective facts: *Hamilton v Halesworth* [1937] HCA 69. In that case, a park ranger, Halesworth, had arrested Hamilton for having plucked a number of

pansies from Centennial Park in Sydney. Halesworth had no power to do so, so Hamilton was discharged. Hamilton then commenced his own action against Halesworth, charging him wrongful arrest, assault and malicious prosecution. That prosecution failed, and Hamilton appealed all the way to the High Court. Judges Starke, Dixon and McTiernan all agreed that Halesworth had acted outside the law – but, they said, he'd *believed* he was acting lawfully at the time. And that was all that mattered.

55 *R v Whittington* [2006] NTSC 64, per Mildren J.

56 Acting Commander Kendrick to Deputy Commissioner Wernham, internal NTPOL memo, 10 March 2007. In the Northern Territory Coroner's Court, *An Inquest into the Death of Robert Jongmin on 23 October 2002 at Wadeye Northern Territory*, D200/2002, Box 3 of 6, Envelope 1, Exhibit 20.

57 Hooper, *The Tall Man: Death and Life on Palm Island*, Hamish Hamilton, Melbourne, 2008.

58 Michael McGowan and Lorena Allam, 'WA Police Officer Escaped Sanction for "Shocking" Force Against Indigenous Boy', *Guardian Australia*, 23 June 2020. The footage, which shows the officer dragging the boy to the ground, was captured by a civilian passer-by who was herself arrested, handcuffed and charged with obstructing police. Three of the officers created statements falsely claiming she'd refused repeated requests to move away. That wasn't borne out on the footage she'd captured, and the charges against her were dropped.

59 Hannah Barry, 'Officers Weren't Wearing Body Cameras, Ballistic Vests in Geraldton Shooting: Commissioner', *WAtoday.com.au*, 19 September 2019.

60 Paige Taylor, 'Cop's Shot Killed "Distressed" Mum', *The Australian*, 5 October 2021.

61 Hannah McGlade, 'Death in Geraldton: How Joyce Clarke Became Another Indigenous Statistic', Crikey.com.au, 25 October 2021.

62 *Police Administration Amendment (Powers and Liability) Act 2005* (No 11 of 2005) (NT), inserting a new s 148B into the *Police Administration Act 1978* (NT). The two-month time limit now applied only to police officers charged with offences specifically against the *Police Administration Act*, and not – for instance – murder, manslaughter, rape, assault, theft, fraud and other crimes listed in the *Criminal Code* and the *Summary Offences Act*.

63 Michael Gunner, second reading speech re the Police Administration Amendment Bill (Serial 177), Assembly *Hansard*, 27 June 2016, pp. 8532–34.

64 *Police Administration Amendment Act 2016* (No. 30 of 2016) (NT), replacing the existing s 148B. The new s 148B read: 'A [police officer] is not civilly or criminally liable for an act done ... in good faith in the exercise of a power or performance of a function under this Act.'

65 Mildren, *Big Boss Fella, All Same Judge*, pp. 178–79; Russell Goldflam, 'The White Elephant in the Room: Juries, Jury Arrays and Race', *Indigenous Law Bulletin*, vol. 7, no. 26, September–October 2011, pp. 35–38. In 2013, the Northern Territory Law Reform Committee recommended a number of amendments to the *Juries Act* to encourage greater Aboriginal representation; these recommendations were never taken up.

66 Phillip Strickland SC, Sophie Callan SC and Joanne Poole, 'The Queen v Zachary Rolfe: Prosecution application to adduce tendency evidence: Outline of submissions', 3 December 2021; Claudia Campagnaro, statements dated 19 August 2020 and 10 September 2021.

67 Transcript of proceedings, *Police v Ryder*, file number 21801980, Alice Springs Local Court, 9 May 2019 per Borchers J.

68 Electronic record of police interview with Cleveland Walker, 2 April 2019; Statement of Cleveland Walker, 29 October 2021.

69 Strickland et al., 'Outline of Submissions', 3 December 2021, p. 18.

70 Statement of Detective Senior Sergeant Andrew Barram, 16 November 2021, [34–35], [44–46], [49–51]; Strickland et al., 'Outline of submissions', pp. 18–23.

71 Campagnaro, transcript of recorded interview with Detective Senior Sergeant Kirk Pennuto, Christies Beach Police Station, 19 August 2020, pp. 24–26.

72 'Publican Not Guilty on Death Charge', *Canberra Times*, 15 May 1986, p. 10.

73 Greg McIntyre, 'R v Wicks (wilful murder charge – Manslaughter verdict – Sentence of 13 years and 6 months)', *Aboriginal Law Bulletin*, vol. 1, no. 37, 1989, p. 14. The graphic description is taken from *The West Australian*, 15 April 1989, p. 1. Peter Wicks, who was convicted of manslaughter, later appealed against the severity of his sentence, notwithstanding that he'd committed what was described as 'one of the most violent' homicides in the state's criminal history. His appeal was dismissed: *Wicks v R* [1989] WASC 394.

74 Paige Taylor, 'Elijah Doughty Lost and Kalgoorlie Simmers', *The Australian*, 21 July 2017.

75 Calla Wahlquist, 'Man Who Killed Indigenous Teenager Elijah Doughty Given Parole', *The Guardian*, 27 March 2018. See: Kate Wild, *Waiting for Elijah*, Scribe, Melbourne, 2018.

76 McGlade, 'All-White Juries Are a Symptom of Structural Racism', NITV / SBS, 14 March 2022: https://www.sbs.com.au/nitv/article/2022/03/14/opinion-all-white-juries-are-symptom-structural-racism.

77 See, for example: Michael Chandler and Christopher Lalonde, 'Cultural Continuity as a Moderator Of Suicide Risk Among Canada's First Nations', in Laurence Kirmayer and Gail Guthrie Valaskakis (eds), *Healing Traditions: The Mental Health of Aboriginal Peoples in Canada*, UBC Press, 2009.

CHAPTER 13

1 See: Arthur Calwell, Opposition Leader, Commonwealth of Australia Parliamentary Debates (*Hansard*), House of Representatives, 31 March 1960, p. 779.

2 Anderson, *The Movement and the Sixties*, pp. 51–54; Curthoys, *Freedom Ride*, pp. 1–8.

3 Shoemaker, *Black Words, White Page: Aboriginal Literature, 1929–1988*, University of Queensland Press, 1989, p. 107.

4 See, for example, the *Aborigines Act 1969* (NSW), which, among other things, abolished the Aborigines Welfare Board and brought Aboriginal children under the mainstream child welfare legislation.

5 Sam Wickman, interviewed by Scott Robinson, 28 July 1991, quoted in Robinson, 'The Aboriginal Embassy, 1972', unpublished MA thesis, ANU, p. 27.

6 Robinson, 'The Aboriginal Embassy, 1972', p. 28; Foley, 'Black Power in Redfern 1968–1972', 2001, online at KooriWeb.org: http://www.kooriweb.org/foley/essays/pdf_essays/black%20power%20in%20redfern%201968.pdf.

7 AAL, 'Statement on Black Power', 1969, reproduced in Attwood and Markus (eds), *The Struggle for Aboriginal Rights*, pp. 243–44.

8 Mum Shirl to Angela Pitts, as quoted at 'NSW Police 21st Division', *A History of Aboriginal Sydney*, online: https://www.historyofaboriginalsydney.edu.au/central/nsw-police-21st-division.

9 Watson, 'I Say This to You', *Meanjin*, vol. 53, no. 4, Summer 1994, p. 589 at 592.

10 Peter Read, *Charles Perkins: A Biography*, pp. 132–33.

11 Foley, 'Black Power in Redfern 1968–1972'; Foley, 'Teaching Whites a Lesson', in Verity Burgmann and Jenny Lee (eds), *Staining the Wattle: A People's History of Australia Since 1788*, McPhee Gribble, 1988, p. 203. See generally: Johanna Perheentupa, '"To Be Part of an Aboriginal Dream of Self-Determination": Aboriginal Activism in Redfern in the 1970s', PhD thesis, School of Humanities and Languages, Faculty of Arts and Social Sciences, UNSW, August 2013, pp. 69–70.

12 Wootten, 'Living in the Law', speech, reproduced in *UNSW Law Journal*, vol. 32, no. 1, 2009, pp. 198–212; Wootten, interviewed by Peter Thompson, ABC Radio National Wisdom Interviews, *Big Ideas*, broadcast 1 May 2005, transcript available online: https://www.abc.net.au/radionational/programs/bigideas/wisdom-interviews-hal-wootten-qc/3446536.

13 Paul Coe, interviewed by Jon Faine, ABC Radio National, *Law Report*, 1991–1992; transcript published as chapter 3 of Faine's book *Lawyers in the Alice: Aboriginals and Whitefellas' Law*, Federation Press, 1993, pp. 14–15.

14 Anne Summers and David Marr, 'One White Man Who Won the Trust of Aborigines', *The National Times*, 6–11 June 1977.

15 Wootten, 'Aborigines and Police', *UNSW Law Journal*, vol. 16, no. 1, 1993, p. 265 at 268.

16 Wootten, interviewed by Peter Thompson, ABC Radio National Wisdom Interviews, *Big Ideas*, broadcast 1 May 2005.

17 '$20,000 for Aboriginal Legal Service', *The Australian*, 29 December 1970, p. 1. See also: Peter Howson, Minister for Environment, Aborigines and the Arts, *State Grants (Aboriginal Advancement) Bill 1971*, second reading speech, reproduced in *Hansard*, House of Representatives, 30 September 1971, p. 1738 at 1747: 'Grants to Aboriginal Welfare Organisations, 1970–1971, New South Wales'.

18 See, for instance: Kate Auty, 'Silence(s) and Resistant (Dis)quiet in the Shadow of the Legal System: Race-ing Jurisprudence in Western Australia by Reference to the Courts of Native

Affairs, 1936–1954', unpublished PhD thesis, School of Law and Legal Studies, La Trobe University, 1999.

19   Gregory Lyons, 'A Study of the Victorian Aboriginal Legal Service', unpublished PhD thesis, Monash University, June 1984, pp. 67–68.

20   Jim Berg, interviewed by Jon Faine, ABC Radio National, *Law Report*, 1991–1992; transcript published as chapter 4 of Faine's book, *Lawyers in the Alice: Aboriginals and Whitefellas' Law*, Federation Press, 1993, p 23.

21   Eggleston, 'Aborigines and the Administration of Justice: A Critical Analysis of the Application of the Criminal Law to Aborigines', PhD thesis, Faculty of Law, Monash University, 1970; later published as *Fear, Favour or Affection: Aborigines and the Criminal Law in Victoria, South Australia and Western Australia*, ANU Press, 1976.

22   House of Representatives Standing Committee on Aboriginal Affairs, *Aboriginal Legal Aid: Report*, July 1980, Parliamentary Paper 149/1980, p 163.

23   Neil Hargrave, interviewed by Jon Faine, ABC Radio National, *Law Report*, 1991–92; transcript published as chapter 1 of Faine's book, *Lawyers in the Alice*, pp. 2–3.

24   Paul Coe, interviewed by Jon Faine, p. 17.

25   Chris Cunneen, 'Aboriginal–Police Relations in Redfern: With Special Reference to the "Police Raid" of 8 February 1990', report commissioned by the National Inquiry into Racist Violence, Human Rights and Equal Opportunity Commission, May 1990, pp. 5–8.

26   Hal Wootten, 'Report of the Inquiry into the Death of David John Gundy', Royal Commission into Aboriginal Deaths in Custody, 27 February 1991. Gundy's death is discussed in chapter 13.

27   J.H. Wootten, 'Report of the Inquiry into the Death of David John Gundy', Royal Commission into Aboriginal Deaths in Custody, 27 February 1991.

28   Chris Cunneen, 'Riot, Resistance and Moral Panic: Demonising the Colonial Other', chapter 2 in Scott Poynting and George Morgan (eds), *Outrageous! Moral Panics in Australia*, ACYS Publishing, 2007, pp. 24–25.

29   Blainey, Sir John Latham Memorial Lecture, April 1993, published as 'Drawing Up a Balance Sheet of Our History', *Quadrant*, vol. 37, nos. 7–8, July–August 1993, pp. 10–15. Blainey's lecture has since been quoted often.

30   The Aboriginal and Torres Strait Islander Legal Service (ATSILS), based in Brisbane, is now Queensland's only ALS, covering everyone from Brisbane to Thursday Island to Mt Isa. The Katherine Regional Aboriginal Legal Aid Service, which commenced in 1985, and Nhulunbuy's MIWATJ Aboriginal Legal Service (1996–) were both merged with the Darwin-based North Australian Aboriginal Legal Aid Service to form NAAJA in 2006, in line with a Howard government requirement: 'Legal Services Merge', *Sunday Territorian*, 31 July 2005, p. 6. Then in late 2017, CAALAS in Alice Springs was told that its funding was also being diverted to NAAJA, which from January 2018 became the Territory's only ALS: Andrea Johnston, 'CAALAS Funding Ceases', *Centralian Advocate*, 7 November 2017. NAAJA itself had tried to reverse the decision – on the grounds that ALS services should be run by their local communities – until the attorney-general's department made it clear it would fund an Alice Springs service jointly run in Perth and Brisbane rather than reinstate CAALAS's funding. Locals and lawyers in Katherine, Nhulunbuy, Tennant Creek and Alice Springs now regularly complain that they feel well-down the list of priorities for a Darwin-based organisation that's now forced to stretch itself across the Territory.

31   Brandis, 'Legal Advisory Service for the Royal Commission into the Protection and Detention of Children in the Northern Territory', media release, 10 October 2016.

32   See: Jacqueline Breen, 'Aboriginal Organisations Split over NT Government Royal Commission Response', ABC News, 5 September 2018.

33   *Police v KL and DP* [2017] NTLC 6 per Judge Fong Lim (9 February 2017), relying on *Evidence (National Uniform Legislation) Act 2011* (NT), s 138(1).

34   Jill Poulsen, 'Chief Won't Outlaw Use of Tasers on Kids', *NT News*, 12 February 2017.

35   Lucy Marks, 'Taser Use on Kids Can Be Acceptable, NT Children's Commissioner Says,' ABC News, 13 February 2017; Jill Poulsen, 'Chief Won't Outlaw Use of Tasers on Kids', *NT News*, 12 February 2017.

36   Woodroffe interviewed by Damien Carrick, *Law Report*, ABC Radio National, 28 February 2017.

37   Judith Aisthorpe, 'Schools Calling for Cop Program', *NT News*, 17 March 2018; Gary

Shipway, 'Parents Backing Police in Schools', *NT News*, 16 September 2018, p. 3; Department of Education (NT), *Report: School-based Police Program Review*, May 2019, p. 5, online: https://education.nt.gov.au/__data/assets/pdf_file/0011/707573/2019-School-Based-Police-Program-Report.pdf.

38 Marty McCarthy, 'Armed Officers at Schools: NT Police Commissioner Defends Decision as "Operational"', ABC News, 11 December 2013.

39 Selena Uibo and Nicole Manison, 'Safer Communities: Territory Labor Government Brings Back School-based Policing', media release, 17 September 2018: https://newsroom.nt.gov.au/mediaRelease/27122.

40 Using MySchool data, the most recent (as at August 2018) proportions of Aboriginal and Torres Strait Islander students enrolled at the ten schools chosen for the reinstated School-based Police Program were as follows: Sanderson Middle School (37 per cent); Dripstone Middle School (18 per cent); Darwin Middle and High Schools (7 per cent and 5 per cent respectively); Nightcliff Middle School (21 per cent); Palmerston College (34 per cent); Taminmin College (19 per cent); Casuarina Senior College (24 per cent); Katherine High School (55 per cent); Tennant Creek High School (82 per cent); Centralian Middle School (62 per cent). By contrast, the proportions of Indigenous students enrolled at the schools that weren't selected are as follows: Essington School (2 per cent); St Philip's College (13 per cent); St Joseph's Catholic College (31 per cent); O'Loughlin Catholic College (15 per cent); Palmerston Christian School (8 per cent); Sattler Christian College (9 per cent); Good Shepherd Lutheran College (7 per cent).

41 Alexia Attwood, 'School-based Policing Faces Fierce Opposition as NT Government Prepares to Revive Program', ABC News, 11 October 2018.

42 Katherine McLachlan, 'Police in Schools: Helpful or Harmful? It Depends on the Model', *The Conversation*, 15 February 2018: https://theconversation.com/police-in-schools-helpful-or-harmful-it-depends-on-the-model-91836; Anne Wilkin, Emily Lamont, Shona McLeod, *Police Officers in Schools: A Scoping Study*, National Foundation for Educational Research, October 2011; Carolyn Black et al., *Evaluation of Campus Police Officers in Scottish Schools*, Scottish Government, 16 March 2010.

43 Department of Education, *School-based Police Program Review: Report*, NT Government, May 2019, p. 15: https://education.nt.gov.au/__data/assets/pdf_file/0011/707573/2019-School-Based-Police-Program-Report.pdf

44 Department of Education, *School-based Police Program Review: Report*, NT Government, May 2019, pp. 15–16.

45 Recommendation #13.3.

46 Phillippa Butt, 'Children "Shouldn't Be Jailed"', *NT News*, 11 November 2018, p. 5

49 'New Client Freeze at VALS Due to Lack of Funding and Increasing Demand', Victorian Aboriginal Legal Service media release, 23 June 2022; Chris Vedelagho and Royce Millar, 'Thick Blue Line: Victoria Builds the Country's Biggest Police Force', *The Age*, 13 November 2021.

50 Nino Bucci, 'Community Legal Services Turn Clients Away Amid Funding Shortfall as Family Violence Spikes', *Guardian Australia*, 11 July 2022.

51 Maddison and Carson, *Civil Voices: Researching Not-for-Profit Advocacy*, Pro Bono Australia and the Human Rights Law Centre, October 2017, online: https://civilvoices.com.au/wp-content/themes/probono_theme/download/CivilVoices_reportfornonforprofitadvocacy_Web.pdf.

52 Tom Stayner, 'Indigenous Groups Condemn Cashless Cards as Labor Pushes for Voluntary Scheme', SBS News, 24 September 2019.

53 Russell Marks, 'Custody Battle', *Inside Story*, 14 June 2019.

54 Russell Marks, 'Backsliding', *The Monthly*, May 2021; *Youth Justice Legislation Amendment Act 2021* (NT), which became law within a fortnight of the bill being introduced into Parliament.

55 'The Plan to Lock Up More Indigenous Children', *7AM* podcast, 7 April 2021, transcript available: https://www.themonthly.com.au/7am/plan-lock-more-indigenous-children.

CHAPTER 14

1 Jeannie Nungarrayi Herbert, 'Community Languages at Lajamanu', *Batchelor Journal of Aboriginal Education*, September 1990, pp. 1–3.

2 Thalia Anthony and Will Crawford, 'Northern Territory Indigenous Community

Sentencing Mechanisms: An Order for Substantive Equality', *Australian Indigenous Law Review*, January 2013, vol. 17, no. 2, p. 79.

3   Court listings data, discussed by Will Crawford in his paper 'Participatory Action Research: A Tool for Community Legal Education, Crime Prevention, Activism and Capacity Building', delivered to the National Community Legal Centres Conference in Adelaide in August 2012. Slides available: https://clcs.org.au/sites/default/files/resources/2020-07/Session%2044%20Will%20Crawford_0.pdf.

4   Stephanie Zillman, 'Indigenous Warlpiri Elders Helping Locals in Court System with Reference Letters,' ABC News, 21 October 2016.

5   Thalia Anthony and Robert Chapman, 'Unresolved Tensions: Warlpiri Law, Police Powers and Land Rights', *Indigenous Law Bulletin*, vol. 7, no. 5, 2008: http://classic.austlii.edu.au/au/journals/IndigLawB/2008/21.html.

6   Elena Marchetti and Kathleen Daly, 'Indigenous Courts and Justice Practices in Australia', *Trends and Issues in Crime and Criminal Justice*, Australian Institute of Criminology, no. 277, May 2004; John Tomaino, 'Aboriginal (Nunga) Courts', *Information Bulletin*, Office of Crime Statistics and Research (SA), no date: https://www.indigenousjustice.gov.au/wp-content/uploads/mp/files/resources/files/aboriginal-nunga-courts-office-of-crime-statistics-and-research.v1.pdf.

7   Colleen Welch, 'South Australian Courts Administration Authority: Aboriginal Court Day and Aboriginal Justice Officers', *Indigenous Law Bulletin*, vol. 5, no. 14, 2002, p. 5.

8   The Wiluna Aboriginal Community Court, in WA's mid-west, commenced in 2001; Murri Courts commenced in Brisbane in August 2002 and then regionally; Koori Courts began in Shepparton in October 2002 and then in other parts of Victoria. Variations on the model, called 'Circle Courts', commenced in Nowra in February 2002 and in the ACT in May 2004.

9   Deborah Bird Rose, 'Land Rights and Deep Colonising: The Erasure of Women', *Aboriginal Law Bulletin*, vol. 3, no. 85, 1996, p. 6.

10   Galbally, 'Koori Court Tips Scales', *Herald Sun*, 13 March 2003, p. 18.

11   Byron Vale and Margaret Wenham, 'Magistrate Apology Draws Flak from Peers', *Courier-Mail*, 10 August 2000, p. 3. As if to confirm the mythic status of the settler myth that courts don't do politics, Fingleton was later prosecuted for interfering with a witness after she'd sent an email (in her capacity as chief magistrate) to a coordinating magistrate asking why he'd supplied an affidavit in support of another magistrate's review of Fingleton's decision to transfer her. Fingleton told the coordinating magistrate she didn't believe she had his confidence, and asked him to show cause as to why he should remain in a coordinating position. A jury found her guilty of interfering with a witness without reasonable cause, the trial judge sentenced her to imprisonment for one year, and her appeal to the Court of Appeal failed unanimously: *R v Fingleton* [2003] QCA 266. All seven High Court justices later allowed her further appeal, and quashed her conviction: *Fingleton v R* [2005] HCA 34.

12   Chief Magistrate Hugh Bradley, 'Community Court Darwin: Guidelines', 27 May 2005, archived at: https://web.archive.org/web/20060813173807/http://www.nt.gov.au/justice/ntmc/docs/community_court_guidelines_27.05.pdf.

13   Judges were entirely ignorant of Aboriginal law, which wasn't written down. Defence lawyers were accused of fabricating it. As we've seen, when Aboriginal law was seen to excuse child sexual abuse or violence against women, settler opinion erupted in outrage. The Territory's response was to legislate a strict procedure: advance notice was to be given to the other side, and any evidence of Aboriginal law had to be given under oath: *Sentencing Amendment (Aboriginal Customary Law) Act 2004* (NT) (no. 1 of 2005).

14   Williams, 'Why Are There No Adult Community Courts Operating in the Northern Territory of Australia?' *Indigenous Law Bulletin*, vol. 8, no. 4, January–February 2013, p. 7.

15   John Elferink, 'Focus on Providing Core Services', media release, 4 December 2012.

16   Frank Vincent, interviewed by Jon Faine, in *Lawyers in the Alice*.

17   On the phenomenon of 'legal liberalism', see: Andrew Altman, *Critical Legal Studies: A Liberal Critique*, Princeton University Press, 1989; Carol Aylward, *Canadian Critical Race Theory: Racism and the Law*, Fernwood Publications; Mari Matsuda, *Where Is Your Body? And Other Essays on Race, Gender and the Law*, Beacon Press, 1996.

18   Kym Daly, 'WA's First Racial Vilification Case Thrown Out of Court', AAP, 14 September 2006.

19   See: Melville, *The History of the Island of Van Diemen's Land, from the Year 1824 to 1835*, London, 1835; reprinted by Cambridge University Press in 2012.

20 Nicholas Clements, *The Black War*, University of Queensland Press, 2014. Lyndall Ryan argues that we should refer instead to 'the Tasmanian War': Ryan, *Tasmanian Aborigines*, Allen & Unwin, 2012, pp. 145–46.

21 Henry Reynolds, *The Fate of a Free People*, Ringwood, 1995.

22 Walter G. Arthur et al., 'Petition to Her Majesty Queen Victoria', 17 February 1846; reproduced in Attwood and Markus (eds), *The Struggle for Aboriginal Rights*, pp. 38–39.

23 See generally: Chiara Gamboz, 'Australian Indigenous Petitions: Emergence and Negotiations of Indigenous Authorship and Writings', unpublished PhD thesis, UNSW Faculty of Arts and Social Sciences, October 2012.

24 Maloga petition, 1887; reproduced in Attwood and Markus (eds), *The Struggle for Aboriginal Rights*, p. 52. See: Attwood and Markus, *Thinking Black: William Cooper and the Australian Aborigines' League*, Aboriginal Studies Press, 2004.

25 The Coranderrk petition, 1886; reproduced in 'The Protection Bill and the Coranderrk Blacks', *The Herald*, Melbourne, 21 September 1886, p. 3; and in Attwood and Markus (eds), *The Struggle for Aboriginal Rights*, pp. 50–51. See: Diane Barwick, *Rebellion at Coranderrk*, Aboriginal History Inc., 1998.

26 *Aborigines Protection Act 1886* (Vic).

27 See: Matthew Kropinyeri, addendum evidence, 6 May 1913, in *Progress Report of the Royal Commission on the Aborigines*, Adelaide, 1913, p. 37. At that stage in South Australia, the proposal was that the state would remove fourteen-year-old Aboriginal teenagers in order to train them in skills useful for work: it wasn't until the 1930s that the state seriously commenced the widespread removal of young children.

28 The *Aboriginal Protection Act 1869* (Vic) allowed the government to make regulations for the 'care, custody and education of the children of aborigines': s 2(v). The *Northern Territory Aboriginals Act 1910* (SA) made the Chief Protector of Aborigines the 'legal guardian of every Aboriginal and every half-caste child up to the age of 18 years'.

29 Human Rights and Equal Opportunity Commission, *Bringing Them Home: Report of the National Inquiry into the Separation of Aboriginal and Torres Strait Islander Children from their Families*, May 1997.

30 John Maynard, *Fight for Liberty and Freedom: The Origins of Australian Aboriginal Activism*, Aboriginal Studies Press, 2007.

31 *Cinesound Review* No. 100, 29 September 1933; text reproduced in Attwood and Markus (eds), *The Struggle for Aboriginal Rights*, p. 73. Segments of the *Review* footage has been posted in various places on the internet.

32 Andrew Markus, 'William Cooper and the 1937 Petition to the King', *Aboriginal History*, vol. 7, no. 1, 1983, pp. 46–60.

33 Wells, *Reward and Punishment in Arnhem Land, 1962–1963*, Australian Institute of Aboriginal Studies, 1982, p. 70; Yirrkala petition, August 1963; text reproduced in Attwood and Markus (eds), *The Struggle for Aboriginal Rights*, p. 202.

34 Fitzgerald to Richmond, cited in Claudia Orange, *The Treaty of Waitangi*, George Allen & Unwin, 1987, p. 176.

35 Parliamentary Library (NZ), 'The origins of the Māori seats', 2nd edition, Parliamentary Library Research Paper, May 2009: https://www.parliament.nz/en/pb/research-papers/document/00PLLawRP03141/origins-of-the-m%C4%81ori-seats.

36 Ranginui Walker, 'The Māori People: The Political Development', in Hyam Gold (ed.), *New Zealand Politics in Perspective*, 3rd edition, 1992.

37 Noel Towell, 'Historic Vote, But Only 7 Per Cent Turned Out for Aboriginal Poll', *The Age*, Melbourne, 10 November 2019.

38 Order-in-Council Establishing Government [of South Australia], 23 February 1836 (UK).

39 *Milirrpum v Nabalco* (1971) 17 FLR 141 per Blackburn J, p 281.

40 See: Miranda Johnson, *The Land Is Our History: Indigeneity, Law and the Settler State*, Oxford University Press, 2016, pp. 121–23, citing R.M. Ross, 'Te Tiriti O Waitangi: Texts and translations', *New Zealand Journal of History*, vol. 6, no. 2, October 1972, p. 129.

41 Northern Territory Cabinet Decision No. 1863, 11 August 1981: https://tfhc.nt.gov.au/__data/assets/pdf_file/0003/266376/Decision-1863.pdf.

42 Damien Short, *Reconciliation and Colonial Power: Indigenous Rights in Australia*, Ashgate, Aldershot, 2007.

43 *Advancing the Treaty Process with Aboriginal Victorians Act 2018* (Vic).

44   NT Government, Central Land Council, Tiwi Land Council, Northern Land Council and
        Anindilyakwa Land Council, 'Barunga Agreement: Joint Land Councils and Northern
        Territory Government Statement', 8 June 2018: https://nt.gov.au/news/2018/june-2018/
        barunga-agreement.

45   Department of Seniors, Disability Services and Aboriginal and Torres Strait Islander
        Partnerships (Qld), 'Treaty Advancement Committee' (reviewed 22 June 2021): https://
        www.dsdsatsip.qld.gov.au/our-work/aboriginal-torres-strait-islander-partnerships/
        reconciliation-tracks-treaty/tracks-treaty/path-treaty/treaty-advancement-committee.

46   *Noongar (Koorah, Nitja, Boordahwan) (Past, Present, Future) Recognition Act 2016* (WA).

47   Courts have three times told federal environment ministers they haven't made adequate
        decisions under Commonwealth legislation (*Clark v Minister for the Environment* [2019]
        FCA 2027; *Onus v Minister for the Environment* [2020] FCA 1807), and had granted
        injunctions preventing construction: *Thorpe v Head, Transport for Victoria*, S ECI 2020
        04091, 29 October 2020; *Thorpe v Head, Transport for Victoria & ors* [2020] VSC 804.

48   The Victorian government only belatedly agreed to abandon its reliance on a cultural
        heritage management plan – which had been approved in 2013 by a now-defunct
        Aboriginal corporation in exchange for land – and, at the time of writing, has commenced
        a new heritage assessment process: Daniel Miles, 'Supreme Court Dismisses Djab Wurrung
        Fight to Protect "Culturally Significant" Trees', ABC News, 23 November 2021.

49   Greg McIntyre, 'The Demolition of Juukan Gorge', *Precedent*, no. 165, August 2021, pp. 21–25.

50   Keating, speech to mark the Year for the World's Indigenous People, Redfern Park, Sydney,
        10 December 1992.

51   New Zealand established the Waitangi Tribunal in 1975 to investigate Māori claims of
        breaches of the Waitangi Treaty. One of Nelson Mandela's first acts as South Africa's president
        in 1994 was to create a Truth and Reconciliation Commission as a way of attempting to heal
        the nation from the wounds caused by Apartheid. And Canada's Truth and Reconciliation
        Commission investigated the abuses in the Indian residential school system.

52   HREOC, *Racist Violence: Report of National Inquiry into Racist Violence in Australia*,
        Australian Government Publishing Service, Canberra, 1991.

53   Howard, 'The Liberal Tradition: The Beliefs and Values Which Guide the Federal
        Government', Sir Robert Menzies Lecture, 18 November 1996.

54   Morrison, interviewed on Radio 2GB, Sydney, 11 June 2020. The following day he clarified
        those comments at a press conference, explaining that he'd been referring only to 'how
        the New South Wales settlement was first established'. As well as the Pacific and South Sea
        Islanders who were 'blackbirded' to work in parts of New South Wales and Queensland
        between 1847 and 1908, large numbers of Aboriginal people were indentured to white
        pastoralists – and prohibited from leaving – throughout the twentieth century.

55   Eleanor Bourke et al., 'From Dispossession to Massacres, the Yoo-rrook Justice
        Commission Sets a New Standard for Truth-telling', *The Conversation*, 5 November 2021.

56   Davis, 'The Truth About Truth-telling', *The Monthly*, December 2021.

57   *Pathways to the Northern Territory Aboriginal Justice Agreement*, NT Department of the
        Attorney-General and Justice, 2019, p. 3: https://justice.nt.gov.au/__data/assets/pdf_
        file/0009/728163/Pathways-to-the-northern-territory-aboriginal-justice-agreement.pdf.

58   *Liquor Act 2019* (NT), s 173. The precise offence is 'bring liquor into', or 'possesses liquor
        in', or 'consumes liquor in', or 'sells, supplies or serves liquor in' a 'general restricted area'.
        Most Aboriginal communities are 'general restricted areas'.

59   Quoted in Karissa Preuss and Jean Napanangka Brown, 'Stopping Petrol Sniffing in Remote
        Aboriginal Australia: Key Elements of the Mt Theo program', *Drug and Alcohol Review*,
        vol. 25, May 2006, p. 189 at 190.

60   Quoted in *Pathways to the Northern Territory Aboriginal Justice Agreement*, NT Department
        of the Attorney-General and Justice, 2019, p. 36.

61   Emma Jane Kirby, 'How Norway Turns Criminals into Good Neighbours', BBC News,
        7 July 2019.

62   Daniel Allen and Mark Abadi, 'At Prisons in Finland, Inmates Are Learning AI and Taking
        Online Tech Courses as a Bridge to Life on the Outside', *Business Insider*, 11 August 2020.

63   'The Plan to Lock Up More Indigenous Children', *7AM* podcast, 7 April 2021.]

64   Porter, 'Decolonising Policing', Marcia Langton, 'Aborigines and Policing: Aboriginal
        Solutions from Northern Territory Communities', Wentworth Lecture, published in

Australian Aboriginal Studies, no.2, 1992, pp. 2–13; Perun Bonser (dir.), *Our Law*, six-part documentary series, Pink Pepper, 2022 (screening on SBS TV).

65 Loretta Kelly, 'Mediation in Aboriginal Communities: Familiar Dilemmas, Fresh Developments', *Indigenous Law Bulletin*, vol. 5, no. 14, 2002, p. 7.

66 See for instance: Erica Meiners, 'Schooling the Carceral State: Challenging the School-to-Prison Pipeline', ch. 13 in David Scott, ed, *Why Prison?* Cambridge University Press, Cambridge, 2013.

67 Davis, 'The Truth about Truth-telling', *The Monthly*, December 2021.

68 Robert Tickner, *Taking a Stand: Land Rights to Reconciliation*, Allen & Unwin, 2001, p. 34.

69 *Going Forward: Social Justice for the First Australians*, Council for Aboriginal Reconciliation, 1995. The recommendations were published in the *Australian Indigenous Law Reporter*, vol. 1, no. 1, 1996, p. 67.

70 See: John Gardiner-Garden, 'From Dispossession to Reconciliation', Parliamentary Research Paper 27, Department of the Parliamentary Library, Canberra, 1998–1999.

71 *Northern Territory Aboriginal Justice Agreement, 2021–2027*, NT Department of the Attorney-General and Justice, 2021: https://justice.nt.gov.au/__data/assets/pdf_file/0005/1034546/northern-territory-aboriginal-justice-agreement-2021-2027.pdf.

72 Larissa Behrendt, 'White Picket Fences: Recognizing Aboriginal Property Rights in Australia's Psychological *Terra Nullius*', *Constitutional Forum*, vol. 10, no. 2, 1999, p. 50; Behrendt, 'Mabo Ten Years On: A Psychological *Terra Nullius* Remains', edited extract of a paper presented to an ANU seminar, *Impact*, vol. 1, July 2002, pp. 1, 8–9; Megan Davis, 'Chained to the Past: The Psychological *Terra Nullius* of Australia's Public Institutions', chapter 7 in Tom Campbell, Jeffrey Goldsworthy and Adrienne Stone (eds), *Protecting Rights Without a Bill of Rights: Institutional Performance and Reform in Australia*, Ashgate, Aldershot, 2006.

73 Nicole Watson, 'Justice in Whose Eyes? Why Lawyers Should Read Black Australian Literature', *Griffith Law Review*, vol. 23, no. 1, 2014, pp. 44–60.

74 Denis Yukhnenko et al., 'A Systematic Review of Criminal Recidivism Rates Worldwide: 3-year Update', *Wellcome Open Research*, vol. 4, no. 28, 2020.

INDEX

www.ingramcontent.com/pod-product-compliance
Lightning Source LLC
Chambersburg PA
CBHW022101210326
41518CB00039B/352